W9-CTY-518

enigma books

SANTI CORVAJA

Hitler and Mussolini

The Secret Meetings

Translated by R. L. Miller

enigma books

Printed in Canada

Hitler and Mussolini
The Secret Meetings

Table of Contents

Foreword

More than a half-century has passed since the deaths of Adolf Hitler and Benito Mussolini, but the grim reminder of the living hell their Axis alliance represented for the people of Europe and the world remains. The fact that they did not succeed is our good fortune.

The mystery surrounding the Axis alliance and its leaders remains as deep today as it was during its lifetime.

Few political associations have had as disastrous an outcome as that between Hitler and Mussolini. The Axis alliance ultimately destroyed its founders and their regimes, as well as millions of people in Europe, Africa, and Asia. The motivations behind the alliance between Germany and Italy, as well as the political and personal relationship between Hitler and Mussolini, still remain unclear.

Veteran Italian journalist Santi Corvaja has written a book that fills an important gap in recording the events that brought about the fateful bonding of the two dictators. It is the only complete chronicle of all the meetings between Hitler and Mussolini, placed in context, as well as the history of their broader political and personal relationship. Many studies of the Axis concentrate on specific periods, such as the books by Elizabeth Wiskemann, *The Rome-Berlin Axis 1934-1945*, and F. W. Deakin, *The Brutal Friendship*, limited to the years from 1942 to 1945, to cite two of the most remarkable early works on the subject. These books, however, do not integrate the 1933-1945 period with the first exchanges between Hitler and Mussolini, which took place between 1922 and 1934. These early contacts, revealing many of the key aspects of the relationship between the two dictators, are traced in detail in this book.

In presenting *Hitler and Mussolini: The Secret Meetings*, some important issues which characterized the relations between Fascist Italy and Nazi Germany must be considered. For example: the relationship between their respective ideologies, Fascism and National Socialism; the significance of racism and anti-Semitism and their consequences; the crisis leading to the war and ultimate defeat of the Axis; and, finally, the personal and political relationship between the two dictators.

From the beginning, both regimes repeatedly referred to their "ideological affinities" through official propaganda and communications. Hitler frequently paid homage to Fascism and Mussolini, in whom he recognized his model as leader of the Nazi party. However, Italian Fascism, during its early years, appears rather weak on doctrine when compared to the Nazi program developed by Hitler, long before his ascent to power. The initial Fascist program had a left-wing flavor, stemming from Mussolini's recent socialist past. The 1919 manifesto of the Fascist movement demanded the end of the monarchy, the distribution of land to the peasants, the representation of workers in management, the right of women to vote, and a minimum wage. Many initial supporters of Fascism soon turned away from Mussolini once his authoritarian nature began to surface. According to Denis Mack Smith in his *Mussolini, A Biography*: "Fascism is not a system of immutable beliefs but a path to power." Mussolini unmistakably wanted to seize political power and hold on to it, come what may.

As the Fascist party turned to the far right after its electoral defeat of 1919, it adopted many of the positions of the predominantly middle-class Nationalist movement. Most Nationalist writers, such as Enrico Corradini, Alfredo Oriani, and the poet, Gabriele D'Annunzio, articulated the main political themes and attitudes that became the dogma of Italian Fascism. Territorial claims against all of Italy's neighbors were justified by the presence of significant Italian-speaking minorities: in Nice, Corsica, Tunisia, and along the Dalmatian coast. The Nationalists also provided a powerful rhetoric, filled with lyrical references to the past glory of the Roman Empire—a strong Italy must rightfully inherit through imperial and colonial expansion within the Mediterranean and Africa. Fascism relied on the secret police and the OVRA as it established strict law and order within Italy through a bitter struggle against socialism, communism, and all other "foreign" influences, occasionally taking on an anti-Semitic flavor even before the racial laws of 1938. The conservative Nationalist movement and the Fascist party would formally merge in 1923, to form the *Partito Nazionale Fascista*, best known by its initials, PNF.

The famous article in the *Enciclopedia Italiana*, under the heading "Fascism," intended as a doctrinal explanation of Fascism, and to a large extent written by the neo-Hegelian philosopher, Giovanni Gentile, was published in 1932. It took Fascism over ten years to produce a rather limited philosophical definition of its own political ideology.

* * *

The State was the cornerstone of political power, the center from which Fascism operated. Fascism had to conquer and place members of the Fascist elite within all the vital organs of the State in order to create the "gerarchia," or hierarchy, that would effectively run the country. Mussolini, the "Duce," was the epicenter of the State and of the Fascist hierarchy. By the late 1930s, the Fascist one-party system had progressively extended its membership to include the entire adult population of Italy, according to the figures published by Salvatore Lupo in his recent book, *Il Fascismo*, party membership by 1939-1943 reached the amazing figure of over 20 million members, once all Fascist youth and professional associations are factored in, almost half of the entire population. Once Achille Starace became secretary of the Fascist party in 1932, a position he would hold until 1939, the party became progressively more intrusive in the daily life of most Italians. Starace was credited with the creation of a Fascist "style," heavily colored by propaganda and the Mussolini cult of personality. Most major opponents of the regime emigrated to France and elsewhere and continued their struggle against Fascism as political émigrés.

The Nazi party, by contrast, did not seek universal membership of the entire German youth and adult population; it preferred to remain a political "elite" within the country. However, party membership was required in Germany for many jobs in and out of government, though strangely not for the officer corps of the Wehrmacht, at least not until the putsch of July 20, 1944, and the attempt on Hitler's life.

Some very specific characteristics were to make Fascism and Mussolini even more attractive to Nazi Germany. Hitler, despite his claim that Nazism was the result of a purely German experience, repeatedly acknowledged his debt to Fascism. Germany adopted many of Fascism's trademarks before and during the Nazi consolidation of power in 1933-1934. In particular, as shown by George L. Mosse in his book, *The Fascist Revolution*, the external aspects of Fascist propaganda, the uniforms, mass meetings, flags, marches, and songs, that were essential to create an atmosphere and excite the imagination of the participants, were carefully studied, modified, and imported by the Nazis from Italy. Hitler and Mussolini were both essentially propagandists and derived much of their power from the enthusiasm they were able to instill in the masses. Hitler, the failed artist, as Mosse points out, relied upon a visual aesthetic combined with his powerful sense of oratory to convey his message. Mussolini, the print journalist, was more comfortable with banner headlines, simple slogans, and journalistic polemics, which easily spilled over into his speeches.

As Hannah Arendt noted in *The Origins of Totalitarianism,* the Nazis operated as a parallel structure to the official government apparatus, and many decisions made by Hitler were not intended to be formally recorded or even announced to the people but issued only as verbal orders to a trusted group of politically reliable party officials—the same dual structure of Party and State was operating in the USSR under Stalin. In Italian Fascism, however, the Party structure would overlap with that of the State. By 1937, Mussolini's aim was to radically "fascistize" the entire Italian state bureaucracy. Severe political repression through a well-organized secret police, the OVRA in Italy and the Gestapo in Germany, and visceral anticommunism were fundamental characteristics of both Fascist and Nazi regimes. The Nazis inaugurated the concentration camps as early as February 1933 with Dachau, located just outside Munich, to isolate Communist and other opposition politicians, as well as the first Jews to be openly persecuted. Fascist Italy used political confinement, either in prison or through internal exile to desolate islands off Sicily and Sardinia, where the victims were cut off from all contact with the outside world for indefinite periods of time.

The main doctrinal difference between Fascism and National Socialism was clearly the Nazi emphasis on race and anti-Semitism. Italian Fascism would introduce the racial issue and anti-Semitic policies in the summer of 1938 to the amazement of most Italians, who had never shown much interest in anti-Semitism. There had even been a small number of Jews among the founding members of the early Fascist party in 1919 and many Italian Jews were Fascist party members in 1938. This was certainly not the case of the Nazi party. In *Mein Kampf* and innumerable speeches, Hitler made anti-Semitism the cornerstone of his political message. Hitler was to give anti-Semitism a new and more aggressive slant when he added racist "biological" justifications to his message, as well as his own brand of fanatical propaganda, perfectly suited to arouse a large segment of the German public. His early rhetoric lumped together the "November criminals," who had signed the "shameful 'diktat' of Versailles," the "Jewish Bolsheviks," inspired by the example of the Russian Revolution, and the "Jewish bankers," who in some obscure way supported Bolshevism out of a purported racial solidarity.

All these elements were "exposed" as part of a vast anti-German conspiracy to defeat "Aryan" Western culture as a first step before taking over the world according to the *Protocols of the Elders of Zion*, a forgery the Nazis would republish and disseminate all over Europe in many different translations. In addition, the exploding German population justified the need to acquire new land, the Nazi quest for *lebensraum* requiring expansion to the east at the expense of Russia. The Slav populations were to be pushed back further toward Asia, or else be exterminated in a vast depopulation plan aimed at killing some thirty million people. This second genocide was to follow the successful implementation of the Final Solution, which would result in the extermination of eleven million Jews, according to the Wannsee Conference documents of early 1942. These policies were explained quite clearly in the unpublished *Second Book*, which Hitler dictated in 1928. How such violent fanaticism could be enthusiastically accepted or even tolerated by large segments of the German people has been thoroughly examined by Ian Kershaw in his 1999 biography, *Hitler 1889-1936 Hubris*.

Hitler and Mussolini often discussed anti-Semitism, either directly or through their diplomats and party officials. At first, from 1933 to 1935, the essentially nonracist Mussolini, through the Italian ambassador to Berlin and other private channels, cautioned Hitler that his anti-Semitic policies could harm Germany's image in the world in many ways. It should be noted that Mussolini was careful not to reject Hitler's anti-Semitic ideology, for fear of turning the German dictator against him, since it was obvious to anyone who had approached the Führer that the fanatical streak was an essential component of his personality and program, as well as a key negative element to his charismatic hold on the German public.

* * *

Only a handful of Jewish intellectuals in the 1930s, such as Revisionist Zionist leader Vladimir Jabotinski, were convinced that Hitler's policies would lead to the physical elimination of the Jews. Italian Fascism had based its 1938 racial policy on obviously cynical political decisions rather than the fanatical Nazi racial-biological doctrine. The intellectual origins of Hitler's own brand of anti-Semitic ideology are well documented: from the racist Austrian publications circulating in pre-1914 Vienna to the various editions of the *Protocols of the Elders of Zion*, and the writings H. S. Chamberlain, Nazism had innumerable sources to follow. More importantly, as Kershaw observes, anti-Semitism gave Hitler a "world view," a mental grid that could be easily applied to every situation. Hitler tested this appeal on his early audiences in Bavaria: when he needed to whip up the flagging enthusiasm of a crowd he would resort to brutal, racially inspired harangues, in which the Jews were inevitably cast as the arch villains.

Italian racial policies, thoroughly analyzed by Renzo De Felice in his *The Jews in Fascist Italy, A History*, were spread through propaganda, although they found only reluctant acceptance even within the Fascist party. The racist enthusiasts were for the most part political careerists and naïve younger generation Fascists, who hoped that this issue would revive the party which, by 1938-1939, was already perceived as an ailing institution. Mussolini, in private, repeated that he was neither a racist nor an anti-Semite, and criticized Hitler and the Nazis for their fanatical excesses. Mussolini even made the following statement to his German doctor, Georg Zachariae, in February 1944:

"I am not an anti-Semite, and I admit that Jewish scientists and technicians have given the world some exceptionally talented individuals . . . I cannot approve of the way the Jewish problem has been resolved in Germany, because the methods used are unacceptable to the free life of the civilized world and dishonor Germany."*

While Mussolini was making this statement in private, the Fascist Republican Party in northern Italy had declared that the Jews were both foreigners and enemies of the state and was actively sending thousands of victims to concentration camps both in Italy and to the Third Reich—all in the name of the Duce. The anti-Semitic issue illustrates the profound contradictions at the center of the ideological differences between Fascist Italy and Nazi Germany. Clearly, Mussolini and many Italian Fascist leaders knew what was happening to Jews and others who were being "resettled in the east," not to mention the Vatican and the Pope himself. The ultimate consequences of the racial policies, while not immediately apparent at their inception in either Germany or Italy, were progressively radicalized until the Final Solution was implemented from 1941 to 1945. Ideology alone was an important but insufficient factor in bringing about the Axis alliance. The political events of the 1930s, especially after Hitler became chancellor in 1933, were the true markings of the Axis alliance and the war. These events are recounted in chronological order throughout this book. Renzo De Felice, in his controversial eight-volume biography of Mussolini, has shown how Mussolini achieved the unlikely goal of creating a new Italian empire in East Africa that captured the imagination of most Italians, despite the opposition and economic sanctions by most democratic countries critical of Fascist policies. Nazi Germany automatically became Italy's only potential ally of any consequence. De Felice and other historians argue that Italy would have converged toward Germany in any case, because Mussolini was essentially an adventurer in foreign policy and in search of the extreme radical approach Hitler offered.

The Spanish Civil War, which broke out in July 1936, was the first opportunity for Germany and Italy to collaborate militarily. In

---

* N. Cospito and H. W. Neulen, *Salò-Berlino: L'Alleanza Difficile*, p. 174.

October 1936, Mussolini coined the expression that an "Axis" between Rome and Berlin existed, around which the balance of power in Europe was being redistributed. The convergence of the two countries on the path to conflict with the democracies is examined in detail in *Hitler and Mussolini: The Secret Meetings.*

The military defeat of the Axis in North Africa in 1943 sealed the fate of Mussolini and Fascism and effectively turned Italy into a vassal of Nazi Germany. The final act for Italian Fascism, the Quisling-type regime of the Italian Social Republic, was a desperate attempt by a minority to hang onto the threads of power just as the war was irretrievably lost.

Finally, there remains the most nebulous of all the aspects of this strange story: the personal relationship between the Führer and the Duce. The evidence overwhelmingly indicates that it was not an intimate relationship in the sense that neither man appears to have been capable of genuine feelings of kinship with the other, even on political and ideological levels. Certainly nothing like the real personal friendship that existed between FDR and Churchill. According to eyewitness accounts, Mussolini, alone in his giant office at the Palazzo Venezia, where he spent most of his time, maintained only formal relations with his subordinates and visitors. There was a coarseness to Mussolini, a lack of worldly sophistication in spite of his travels to Switzerland and France as a young man, that struck many of his visitors at the Palazzo Venezia, US Ambassador and Boston Brahmin William Phillips among them: "At the height of his popularity he was constantly out among the people, and in his own way he believed he was governing Italy for their benefit. They in turn regarded him more as a father of the family than as a dictator, for in spite of his many talents he remained a simple man. While in fascist uniform which he ordinarily wore, he had a commanding stature, but when occasionally I saw him in civilian dress he looked not only the sturdy peasant, but a very rough customer."*

During his twenty-one-year rule, and in sharp contrast to Hitler, Mussolini would periodically revamp the entire leadership of the

---

* William Phillips, *Ventures in Diplomacy,* p. 191, Beacon Press 1952.

government and of many layers of the Fascist Party. Two bloodless purges took place, in 1939 and 1943, when key personalities were dismissed and laterally shifted to other positions as new faces appeared within the upper echelon of Fascist political leadership. The Mussolini "method" was more civilized than Stalin's, but nevertheless it shocked Hitler and the Nazi inner circle so much that Martin Bormann commented that every time the Duce arrived for a conference, there were different people surrounding him. Hitler wondered how Mussolini could count on anyone's loyalty and ensure the continuity of his policies.

Hitler was far more predictable regarding personnel and surrounded himself with deputies who readily followed his orders, interpreting and carrying out his policies, no matter how criminal. The core Nazi team never really changed, and Hitler proved extremely adept at selecting the type of person he needed: Göring, Himmler, Heydrich, Ribbentrop, Bormann, Keitel, Jodl, Goebbels, Speer, Frank, Funk, Ley. Only a few would be liquidated, like Röhm, or disappear unexpectedly, like Hess, or plot his overthrow, like Canaris and Rommel.

Pure opportunism clearly appears to have been the strongest motivation drawing the two dictators together, despite the many expressions of admiration and emotional attachment that Hitler, on his part, lavished on Mussolini. The language of communication they used offers revealing insight into their relationship. Hitler spoke and understood only German. Mussolini had been a French high school teacher and claimed to speak German fluently, along with some English. The interpreters at the Hitler-Mussolini meetings, such as Paul Schmidt and Eugen Dollmann, both indicate that Mussolini was certainly not fluent enough to understand the rapid and endless flow of German that Hitler subjected him to. In more than one meeting, Mussolini is described as silent and unable (or unwilling) to interrupt the Führer's oratory, which he probably largely misunderstood. The Duce almost never appears to have made laudatory statements about Hitler, whom he always professed either to despise or fear. Mussolini often repeated that had Italy been cool to Germany or joined the British and French, Germany would no doubt have invaded Italy sooner or later. Mussolini had no evidence to support this conclusion, and perhaps a victorious Germany would have eventually turned on a neutral Italy.

The experience of the First World War remained on everyone's mind. In 1914 Italy abandoned the Triple Alliance with the German and Austro-Hungarian Empires by remaining neutral at first and then joining the Allies in 1915. Also in 1914 Mussolini broke with the pacifist Socialist party to become an ardent pro-Allied "interventionist" in the war against Austria-Hungary and Germany. While Hitler repeatedly expressed his loathing of the multinational and tolerant Austria of the Hapsburgs, with its mix of cultures and nationalities, he occasionally lent an ear to those who warned him not to rely on Italy as an ally. The German officer corps, representing the Prussian military caste, and Rommel in particular, who typified this attitude, had very little faith in the capabilities of the Italian army. It was Hitler's essentially revolutionary nature, his own anti-establishment prejudices and the foreign policy plans he outlined in his *Second Book*, that included an alliance between Germany and Italy, that also made the Axis a reality. Nazi Germany's need to find allies within Europe to avoid isolation was a powerful motivation drawing Hitler into a closer relationship with the Italian dictator. But deeper within the German-Italian alliance lingered the German suspicion that Italy could not be trusted as an ally in 1939 just as in 1914, a suspicion that surfaced periodically within German military and diplomatic circles. The notable exceptions were a few high-ranking Nazis, such as Göring, and even fewer military professionals, like Kesselring, who were both pro-Italian and maintained their optimism about the Axis alliance until the overthrow of the Duce in 1943.

Mussolini was well aware of these doubts in the minds of his ally and was determined to improve Italy's image as a worthy partner within the Axis. However, Italy would be severely hampered by a string of military defeats, accusations of disloyalty by German military leaders, and, finally, by an enraged Hitler in June and July 1943, when the fighting had reached Sicily and the Italian army collapsed in the face of the overwhelming Allied invasion.

The Axis which caused such cataclysmic death and destruction and ultimately met its own violent end may have been doomed from the beginning. This book will show how and why the Axis alliance was formed and evolved as it did, ultimately failing both internally and externally to achieve its goals.

—*Robert L. Miller*

Author's Introduction

The meetings and discussions between Adolf Hitler and Benito Mussolini reveal many of the root causes and secret events of the Second World War. They are an important, if not fundamental, part of the history of the twentieth century.

Over a ten-year period, from June 14, 1934, to July 20, 1944, the two dictators met seventeen times for brief exchanges of ideas lasting only a few hours, or for state visits covering several days. For ten years prior to their initial meeting, Hitler attempted on various occasions to have an official conference with the founder of Italian Fascism. Mussolini was suspicious and used several excuses to delay as long as possible the initial meeting that was to trigger a fateful chain of events. After Hitler became chancellor of Germany on January 30, 1933, however, Mussolini could no longer procrastinate, due to the many pressing requests from Berlin reaching his desk.

These summit talks followed the crescendo of the European political crises of the late 1930s: four meetings took place in peacetime, from 1934 to 1938, and thirteen during the war, from 1940 to 1944. It is significant to note that after the first contacts, the roles played by the protagonists changed: Mussolini traveled to Germany ten times, and met the Führer halfway at the Brenner Pass three times; Hitler came to Italy only four times.

I have attempted to simplify the vast material available by treating each conference as a separate report. Each chapter corresponds to a meeting, with the exception of the first chapter, which serves as prologue.

In this work, I used original German and Italian documents, many eyewitness accounts written or recorded by major and minor participants, and historical works by various scholars that are quoted in these pages. I extend my sincere thanks to all.

—Santi Corvaja

I

A Ten-Year Quest

1924-1933

History has not recorded the exact moment when Adolf Hitler learned of Benito Mussolini's existence. We must assume that this discovery took place during the troubled years immediately following the end of the First World War. The case of the Italian revolutionary socialist, who had begun his swing toward the right in 1914 and emerged as the founder on March 23, 1919 of the extreme rightist Fascist party, was well known at that time. Mussolini's dramatic political switch had been highly publicized in the international socialist press, still dizzy from the unexpected success, at the other end of the political spectrum, of the Bolshevik revolution in Russia under the leadership of the former Democratic Socialist, Lenin, in Petrograd on November 7, 1917.

Hitler, in 1941, insisted upon the "home-grown" characteristics of Nazism—National Socialism—when he said, "Our program was worked out in 1919, and at that time I knew nothing about [Mussolini]. Our doctrines are based on the foundations proper to each of them, but every man's way of thinking is a result. Don't suppose that events in Italy had no influence on us. The brown shirt would probably not have existed without the black shirt. The March on Rome, in 1922, was one of the turning points of history. The mere fact anything of the sort could be attempted, and could succeed, gave us an impetus." *

Mussolini, likewise, was unaware of the Führer of the NSDAP, at least until the eve of the "March on Rome" on October 28, 1922. The very first Nazi "ambassador" the Duce was to meet was Kurt G. W. Ludecke, a trusted aide to Hitler at that time and who would later leave Germany to escape the Nazi regime. The meeting took place in Milan in September 1922. Mussolini was interested in learning more about the confusing politics of Weimar Germany. Ludecke, following Mussolini's request, read him the twenty-five points of Hitler's program as the Führer had presented them to his comrades of the NSDAP during the evening of February 24, 1920, at a rally at the Hofbräuhaus in Munich. It was a curious mixture of conservatism, liberalism, militarism, and radicalism all wrapped in the most fanatical pan-Germanism, which included a call to rid the fatherland of all foreigners and, first and foremost, the Jews.

Puzzled by the details of this confused program, Mussolini was not satisfied by these explanations and requested more information regarding this Herr Heidler, Hidler, or Hitler. The man's last name was unclear to him. Ludecke then gave Mussolini an enthusiastic summary of Hitler's life.

Several points in Hitler's curriculum appeared obscure and, at first, Mussolini was unable to ascertain if Hitler was in fact Austrian, Bavarian, Bohemian, or some other nationality. Furthermore, Mussolini could not fathom why the very popular and conservative Field Marshall Erich Ludendorff had decided to honor with his immense prestige the evening beer hall meetings organized by the former infantry corporal from the 16th Bavarian "List" regiment. Ludecke was unable to answer any of Mussolini's questions to his

---

* *Hitler's Table Talk 1941-1944*, Hugh Trevor-Roper, Enigma Books 2000, pp. 9-10.

satisfaction. Just one month later, Mussolini, now both prime minister and foreign minister, repeated the same questions to the Italian consul general in Munich, Giovanni Cesare Majoni, with the following note: "Rome, November 4, 1922, 10:30 p.m. Kindly report urgently and in detail on current political situation in Bavaria and possible actions by extreme rightist elements."

Majoni answered the note two days later with a telegram full of generalities. The consul general's excessive caution went unnoticed because it was immediately overshadowed by an unsolicited and very detailed report from Bad Ems, submitted by the Italian delegate to the Interallied Office for the Rhineland Commission, Adolfo Tedaldi, addressed to the Italian foreign minister. Tedaldi was obviously intent on making a good impression on his new minister in Rome, who also happened to be the head of the government. The Tedaldi document is surprising, however, by its detail and insights into the future and deserves to be quoted almost entirely:

"Bad Ems, November 17, 1922. All these groups are very clearly separatists, but even though they have the majority of the country behind them, they do not wish to take any action until certain expected events unfold. These groups do not wish to be seen as traitors to the 'German' idea. They do, however, seek to be recognized as the saviors of Germany facing the growing disorder attributed to the communists in north and central Germany.

"Here are some details regarding the interviews I have had:

"Government circles: I have met, in Count Leyden's house, Minister Herr Wutzelhofer, a petty bourgeois who actually doesn't even speak high German but the dialect of his village; on the other hand he is a practical person, very knowledgeable about the inner workings of his department. Due to his position as minister, he did not volunteer any information at all. Our conversation, which lasted about three hours, was concentrated on economic matters for the most part; . . . however, the political situation kept on surfacing as we spoke, and Herr W., even though voicing skepticism regarding any immediate confrontations, recognizes the extreme gravity of the situation that would certainly favor a separatist move should a Communist regime take over in north and central Germany.

Regarding Italy, Herr W. recognizes the vital need for Bavaria to draw closer to Italy, to use the ports of Venice and Trieste rather than Bremen and Hamburg, and dreams of a common border with Italy to ensure faster, safer, and more cost-effective trade relations. Herr W. had some harsh words for the bad administration in Berlin, with its centralized methods that are ruining Bavaria... In practical terms, Herr W. requested better trade tariffs and better port concessions to improve Bavaria's import capabilities, and the creation in Italy and Bavaria of consortiums for the exchange of merchandise.

"The leadership of the Bavarian People's Party: I was able to meet Herr Buchner, director of the *Müncher Zeitung*, and some of his friends at the offices of the newspaper. . . . I felt some kind of odd contradiction in these people. On the one hand, they are definitely all pan-Germanists, but, on the other hand, they are also the most rabid separatists. . . . I would need to have more frequent contact with them to fully understand their thinking. I feel I can explain their basic attitude by emphasizing that they are essentially monarchists and anti-Semites, while the current government of the Reich is pro-Semite and in favor of centralization. With respect to Italy, this is the most dangerous group, because some of its members, while not stating their thoughts openly, are actually thinking of the Alto Adige and would be ready to place the question on the agenda, for no other reason than to use it as a bargaining chip.*

"They openly desire the separation of Bavaria from the Reich and the restoration of the monarchy; but they also dream of an enlarged Bavaria that would include the Austrian Tyrol, Carinzia, Salzburg, and the Vorarlberg. But should this annexation program be unrealistic, they would support a Tyrolean state that would include these regions, linked to Italy and Bavaria through an economic agreement and guaranteed military neutrality. In any case they all want a common border with Italy.

---

* The region, formerly part of Austria-Hungary, known as Süd Tyrol was awarded to Italy in 1919 and renamed Alto Adige.

"Cardinal Faulhaber: Along with his friends, the Cardinal states that he doesn't wish to separate Bavaria from the Reich, but that, at the same time, this could become necessary on rather short notice... They also wish for a common border with Italy and for the creation of an autonomous Tyrolean state as a means to achieve this goal... Regarding Alto Adige, they declare that it is an Italian internal problem, and they are confident in Italy's liberal traditions to allow the German language heritage to remain unhampered.

"Hittler [sic], the head of the Fascists: He is the youngest of these leaders. By temperament and through his voice and gestures, he seems more of a Latin than a German. He speaks well, more like a soapbox orator, and one understands how he could get the crowds excited. His program and its very name are for the most part a copy of the Italian Fascist program. Return authority to the State; put an end to strikes, corruption, waste; reduce the bureaucracy—in short, restore order—that's the basic program. As for the means: use the most active propaganda to conquer the State through ideals and moral example if it is sufficient; but be ready, when necessary, to take over. Hittler wishes to have direct contact with the Italian Fascists to gain insights in directions and methods to follow.

"In foreign policy, his ideas are clear and to the point. With respect to Italy, he has made simple and direct statements, not in private, but at an open meeting attended by the entire leadership of the *Müncher Zeitung* group.

"Hittler said in substance: 'Germany must accept that, having lost the war, it must pay the price as its current strength allows. To achieve this, it must work harder than it is working now. We must do away with the eight-hour workday, and we must return to the prewar shifts; strikes have to be stopped, with draconian methods if necessary. If we are to regain the consideration and the confidence of the outside world, Germans must be asked to make enormous sacrifices. But only a government made up of new men, untouched by the responsibilities of having declared war or of having signed the peace treaty at Versailles with all its horrible consequences, can demand such sacrifices from the German people.'

"Hittler does not believe that Bavaria can remain part of the Reich; like the others, he thinks separation is inevitable. But he also says: 'We can only emerge from the current situation with help of a great power, and, among all the nations, the best one would be Italy. We must welcome today and in the future an Italy ready to help us. We must not [because of a feeling of brotherhood towards 200,000 Germans who are being well treated] forget that there are millions of Germans who are being completely oppressed elsewhere and that the very existence of Bavaria is in the balance. We must tell Italy openly and sincerely that for us there is no Alto Adige problem and that it will never be brought up again and that we intend to back up the seriousness of these words with actions and facts.'"

Tedaldi's long document goes on to describe the economic situation in Bavaria and the first reactions to the spectacular triumph of the Italian Fascist movement. He concludes with a request to be called to Rome for a more detailed presentation.

Mussolini found the details of this report alarming. On the one hand, Herr "Hittler," according to Tedaldi, had created good will in making a clear renunciation to the Alto Adige when he declared that for the Nazis this was a "nonexistent problem," while, on the other hand, he requested "insights and directions" from the Italian Fascists, a request that sounded like a euphemism for money. Had Mussolini accepted such a request at that time, he would have damaged the relationship between Italy and Weimar Germany. The Duce's intuitions were quickly confirmed through the same efficient go-between, Herr Ludecke, who in August 1923 returned to request funding from the Fascist comrades so that "the Führer can do in Munich and Berlin what the Duce was able to do in Milan and Rome in October 1922." Mussolini, immersed in his new position as the head of the government, remained unimpressed; the offer decidedly was not worth following up. But Mussolini did make a concession to Hitler by offering political asylum to Hermann Göring, Hans Frank, and a few other Nazi leaders after the failed beer hall putsch of the Bürgerbräukeller of November 9, 1923, that appeared to him to be a very badly scripted copy of the March on Rome.

Göring, who was seriously wounded and on the run from the German police, was happy to come to Italy to get medical treatment after the clash with the Munich gendarmerie. He promptly requested a meeting with Mussolini, whom he professed to admire, and the two met in the spring of 1924. The Duce was careful to let it be known that he was meeting with the German air force ace from the famous Richthofen Escadrille, Hermann Göring. No mention was made of the fact that Göring was a follower of Adolf Hitler, whose name was now spelled correctly in the Italian press, due to the notoriety he achieved during his arrest and trial, which ended in a comfortable cell in Landsberg Castle with a view of the River Lech. Some forty other Nazis, including his deputy, Rudolf Hess, shared the fortress as prisoners with their Führer. On December 20, 1924, Hitler was pardoned, and the thirteen months in prison were the real stepping stone on his way to becoming chancellor of the Reich.

According to Hitler, the period spent in Landsberg prison enabled him not only to improve his own philosophical pursuits "at the taxpayer's expense," but also to dictate the manuscript of *Mein Kampf*, the book that would enhance his fame and fortune, helped greatly by the commercial flair of his administrative secretary, Max Amann. Hitler's long absence from the political fray led to a weakening of purpose within the party under the temporary leadership of the theoretician Alfred Rosenberg. Upon his release, the Führer had to shoulder the task of revitalizing his movement on new foundations. The economic recovery of Germany had hastened the demise of the NSDAP. German industrial performance had begun to improve, creating the basis for political stability the young Weimar Republic desperately needed in order to defeat the extremism of both the left and right. During this period, Hitler, now referred to as the founder of German Fascism, did not contact Mussolini until 1927, when he requested an autographed picture of the Duce. The Duce's office replied: "The Duce regrets being unable to fulfill his (Hitler's) request but thanks him for the expressions of support. . ."

This negative answer did not discourage Hitler, who was preparing for the elections of May 20, 1928, which he could not even participate in, since he was not a German citizen. Hitler needed Mussolini's open support to legitimize the Nazi party in the eyes of international opinion and help him improve his chances at the polls. Mussolini, however, did not want to show any kind of support until after the vote. Filippo Anfuso, then Italian vice consul in Munich, remembers:

"Even the very first electoral success of the National Socialists at the elections for the Reichstag with 12 seats out of a total of 489 with 810,000 votes did not encourage Mussolini to meet with a 'clandestine' Hitler. In truth, the man sitting in the Palazzo Venezia did not believe such a meeting was worth the risk of creating problems with the government of the Reich."

The Hitler file was on hold as far as Mussolini was concerned. During the summer of 1928, Mussolini told journalist Nino D'Aroma, who was about to vacation in Bavaria:

"You should personally undertake for me a confidential fact-finding mission regarding this character who is appearing on the horizon in Germany and who the world press already calls the German Fascist, Adolf Hitler. Can you bring me some in-depth information? Go to Vienna and to his hometown as well if necessary, because I want to know clearly and in detail who this man is and what he represents. In Vienna you should contact these useful friends"—and Mussolini wrote with a red pencil the names of the "useful friends"—"I need this information, and you have two weeks' time, because Major Giuseppe Renzetti, from the embassy in Berlin, is requesting that we do something very important for the German Nazis. Now, before I jump on board, I need much more information."

All the reports produced by Anfuso, Renzetti, D'Aroma, and other professional and amateur "informers" had not succeeded in convincing Mussolini that he should indeed meet with the Führer. In *Mein Kampf*, Hitler had attempted to allay the Duce's fears by declaring that the only possible allies for Germany were Great Britain and Italy. Furthermore, as for Italy, Hitler recognized its claim to be the dominant power in the Mediterranean. He also stated clearly that the question of South Tyrol (Alto Adige), which the

Austrian government was always ready to use, would never inter-fere in the future friendly relations between Fascist Rome and a Nazi Berlin. Hitler volunteered his position of indifference regarding the Alto Adige question when he had occasion to meet the Italian Fascist leader Luigi Federzoni on July 24, 1930, during the course of an evening of opera at Bayreuth, where Arturo Toscanini conducted *Tannhäuser* and *Tristan*.

Federzoni wrote: "On that day, after we were introduced, Hitler began speaking and did not stop for an hour. . . He said many things, and reiterated that there would be no antagonism between Germany and Italy. He used a little story to make his point. We know, he said, a poor man who had been amputated of both arms and legs. They also had to amputate ein Ohrläppchen, an earlobe. Naturally this Läppchen doesn't count that much compared to the greater loss of arms and legs. Our arms and legs are Upper Silesia, Poznan, Saar, and Danzig, and the earlobe is Alto Adige. Italy has its sphere of interest in the Mediterranean, where we do not intend to go. As for Germany, it will be able to forget its lost colonies once it can colonize the territories in the East through political and economic expansion that Italy will have no reason to oppose."

Meanwhile, after the first electoral success of the Nazi party with 107 seats in the Reichstag on September 14, 1930, Major Renzetti, Italian consul general in Germany, was again trying to get Mussolini to approve an official visit of Hitler to Rome.

Renzetti wrote to the Duce in October 1931: "Hitler was very pleased with his meeting with Hindenburg, who was very friendly and willing to listen and also promised that, should the Brüning cabinet be unable to obtain a majority vote, he would call on the National Socialists to form a new government. . . Following this meeting, Hitler's position has gained legitimacy. Hitler told me that he was now able to visit Your Excellency, the head of the Italian government, and asked me to transmit his wish to the Duce. Hitler had spoken to me a few months ago of his request. I replied that I found it difficult to make such a request in view of the problems that would not permit a visit at this time. Hitler added that the heads of the Socialist party made the rounds in London and Paris, and he would like to go to Rome, first, out of friendship for Italy and admiration for the Duce, and second, to reiterate his desire to strengthen Italian-German relations that would then be completed by German-British relations. What should I answer?"

Mussolini finally answered yes, as is apparent from the recorded reply sent to Rome by Renzetti on November 20, 1931: "I have transmitted to Hitler the Duce's opinion on the danger for National Socialism to tie itself to a coalition government. Hitler requested that I tell Your Excellency, the head of the government, that he will take your advice in great account. . . The misunderstandings between Nazis and other right-wing groups continue. In order to smooth things out, I will have a meeting in my house on Friday the 27th with the heads of the movements themselves. . . Hitler is very happy to be able to come to Rome and pay his respects to the Duce and to be welcomed as a guest of the Fascist party. He could leave on the evening of December 11, 1931, from Munich and reach Rome in the afternoon of the twelfth. He would be accompanied by myself and Göring, his secretary Rudolf Hess, and another party functionary. His stay in Rome will be short due to the situation in Germany. . . Hitler's visit will be followed by visits by members of parliament, heads of the SA, heads of youth organizations for study purposes, etc. With Hitler, I planned working trips by groups of the best party members, leaders and ordinary members in Italy, not just to study the inner workings of Fascism but also to foster feelings of comradeship between the National Socialists and the Fascists."

Once all these preparations were well in hand, the German embassy in Rome suddenly communicated very discreetly that President Hindenburg was not really an admirer of the Nazis and their leader and that the meeting Hitler had with the German president that Renzetti reported as being positive, actually had ended disagreeably. After the "confrontation," Hindenburg became very upset and displeased, saying that you wouldn't create anything worthwhile with "that Bohemian corporal" and that Hitler's aptitude would make him at best a postmaster general in a coalition government.

The order canceling the visit reached Renzetti as an unexpected disappointment, since he was proud of the months of preparation he had put into making this visit possible. Nevertheless the major did not give up and wrote to Rome on January 12:

"I spoke to Hitler today about his planned trip to Rome. He told me that he understood perfectly well the obstacles that prevented his wish from becoming reality and that he would not insist. He asked me to say that in the current state of affairs, it would be impossible for him to leave Germany. I repeated to him that the Duce is thinking about Germany and is well acquainted with the situation.

"I would like to advance the idea, just to keep these gentlemen satisfied, of inviting Göring to visit Rome. Obviously his trip would be kept secret and justified by his ill health. Göring, who broke a rib during a trip to Sweden, is also badly in need of rest because of his heavy workload and to overcome his sadness at the death of his wife, whom he passionately loved. A Göring trip would in effect please the National Socialists and not be the cause for any alarm. I have not shared this idea with anyone yet."

On April 10, 1932, Hindenburg was reelected president of the Reich. In the runoff against Hitler, the field marshal received nineteen million votes, but the loser was able to score an impressive thirteen million votes. It was now clear that the "Bohemian corporal" was seen as the new man in Germany's future. Consequently, on June 12, 1932, Renzetti, having secured approval for a visit by Hitler to Italy, wrote enthusiastically to the Duce's secretariat a note that stated, among other things:

"His Excellency, the head of the government, has given his complete approval to the visit. Hitler will come in civilian clothes for two or three days; he will meet with His Excellency, the head of the government, and with His Excellency, the Fascist party secretary, whose guest he would officially be. . . The visit would not be kept secret, to avoid any possible rumors spread by our enemies.

"His Excellency, the head of the government, has asked that I make arrangements with Grand Officer Chiavolini, his private secretary. . . I have naturally not yet communicated any of this to Hitler or any other German official. . . I have not made any promises to Hitler, but I wish to point out that I am very much committed to the success of this trip. Hitler is well aware of the international ramifications of such a visit, as I have explained to him in the past. However, he does not feel that negative aspects are as important, since by now he considers that his party is practically in power. . . "

Three days later, from the Adriatic town of San Benedetto del Tronto, where he was on vacation, Renzetti wrote to the secretary of the Fascist party to reiterate the program of Hitler's visit to Italy as approved by Mussolini. Considering the fact that the Führer would be the guest of the Fascist party, Renzetti pointed out:

"Grand Officer Chiavolini ordered that I arrange with Your Excellency the details surrounding the visit by the head of the German National Socialist party to Italy, scheduled to take place in the very near future. . . Hitler would prefer to come between the first and fifteenth of July, stay two or three days, and go back to Germany in time to organize the campaign for the July 31 elections. Hitler will be accompanied by Göring, a member of parliament, who had the honor of visiting with the Duce last year, and [Hitler's] private secretary, [Rudolf] Hess. . . The group will officially be guests of the Fascist party. Hitler is a vegetarian and does not drink wine. He is a great lover of music and he will also wish to visit, if the weather is not too hot, the major monuments and a few museums in Rome. . . He speaks only German. . . "

Just six days later, there was another last minute cancellation. The visit was stopped by Mussolini himself. Renzetti, once again thwarted and confused, explains in a note dated June 21:

"I have communicated to Hitler the points made by His Excellency the head of the government. He listened to me with great satisfaction and attention, pleased and proud of the interest and friendship for his mission displayed by the Duce. As I have said elsewhere, Hitler worships Mussolini.

"Concerning Austria, Hitler told me that country cannot be trusted: its politicians threaten the Anschluss only to extort money. France pays them, and things keep going in their usual way.

"Hitler then asked about his long-desired trip to Italy. I answered that the Duce would be pleased to welcome him, but that he would need to think whether a visit before July 31 was well advised. The internal situation in Germany, I pointed out, would not appear to allow his absence at this time. . . Hitler was very disappointed (he had made plans for his trip: a day in Florence, two days in Rome, one or two days in Naples). From Munich to Verona or Milan by plane, then by car, he had to accept the points I made and is anxious to meet the Duce in person.

"I don't know if I overstepped my authority . . . but I did not close any doors and assured Hitler, who is a very touchy person, that the postponement of his visit was not our doing . . ."

Mussolini and Renzetti, having succeeded in convincing Hitler that this was not the right time to visit Italy, were shocked to witness the electoral victory of the National Socialist party one month later as it captured the relative majority at the Reichstag with 230 seats out of 608, with a total of 13,745,000 votes. The next elections, on November 6 (induced by the democratic parties hoping to neutralize the Nazi threat), did in fact mark a decline in the seats won by the Nazi party, from 230 to 196. Hitler, nevertheless, was named Chancellor of Germany by President Hindenburg on January 30, 1933.

Renzetti had kept Mussolini closely informed regarding developments in Berlin, including his own discreet maneuvering behind the scenes to facilitate Hitler's takeover. Renzetti also accurately predicted the eventual physical liquidation of Gregor Strasser and Ernst Röhm, who represented the left and right wings of the National Socialist Party, respectively.

Hitler did not forget the promised trip to Italy. He told Renzetti the day after his political triumph:

"I wish to have a meeting with Mussolini, and in the meantime, I ask you to please transmit my personal admiration and my warm regards. I can now go where I wish. I can take a plane to Rome even as a private citizen. I got this far certainly because of Fascism: if it is true that the two movements are different, it is also true that Mussolini created the Weltanschauung that links the parties together;

without his success I may not have reached this position. If it is also true that systems and ideas cannot be exported, it is also true that ideas travel like the rays of the sun or the waves."

Renzetti replied that Italian policy was quite simple: to reach, in Europe, a four-nation peace agreement. To achieve this goal, it was necessary for Italy, Germany, and Great Britain to reach an understanding to persuade France to either remain isolated or to join the four-power pact. With this report, Renzetti had accomplished his mission at the Führer's court. From that day forward, Hitler, as Chancellor of the Third Reich, was officially the responsibility of the Italian ambassador, Vittorio Cerruti.

The first meeting of the new chancellor with foreign diplomats was recorded by the wife of Ambassador Cerruti. She was Elisabeth de Paulay, a former actress, who kept a critical and amused eye on the new regime:

"Eight days after Hitler was named Chancellor, President Hindenburg gave his annual dinner party and it was announced that Hitler would attend . . . Everyone was very excited. No one had ever seen the chancellor socially and we were all very curious to meet him. The phones rang constantly. The ladies asked whether Hitler would wear tails, a brown uniform, or simply a dinner jacket . . . I suspected the dinner would prove to be very interesting. I had just had a phone conversation with Mrs. von Meissner, wife of the head of the presidential chancellery, two days before . . . I was informed that I was chosen to be escorted by the Chancellor into the dining room on the evening of February 7th . . .

"My first reaction was very feminine: what do I wear? I ran to tell my husband. He said: 'It will be very interesting,' and he asked me to observe Hitler carefully and not to forget anything he said, since I would be the first lady of the diplomatic corps to speak with him. My husband would then be able to draft an interesting report based on what I heard . . . The presidential palace, a rather ugly structure, like most Berlin palaces, did have a certain grandeur. The night of the dinner it was all lit up . . . In the entrance, there was a sketch of the seating arrangements which translated perfectly that German habit of giving even the simplest things a militaristic flavor.

"We were waiting for our turn to be announced, and I felt myself blushing, when a deep voice said: 'The Ambassador of Italy and Mrs. Cerruti' . . . Hitler followed Count von Bassewitz, who guided him toward me, as [Hitler] crossed the crowded room with an expressionless face and bowed as he kissed my hand. We exchanged the usual small talk until dinner was announced, and Hitler offered me his arm.

"When I placed my hand on his arm, I was so excited that I felt an electric shock; this strange sensation made me nervous. Despite the fact that I consider myself a skeptic, who does not believe in the supernatural, I became convinced that he had some sort of magnetic power he could display at will. The physical shock was so strong that I turned to look at him in disbelief. He was standing there, pale and calm as usual. It felt strange to be sitting next to the man who was at the center of every conversation, and I made an effort to observe his every word and gesture.

"During that very first evening of his official career, I took a good look at him close up, and even though I saw him quite often in the following years, I never altered my opinion from that first meeting. He struck me as revolting, threatening, and dangerous, even if he did demonstrate a certain poise. His presence made me cringe . . . Physically he was not low class, just ordinary, vulgar . . . He grabbed his knife and fork, making a fist like a peasant, although he had enough manners not to bring the knife to his mouth. He actually never had any reason to use the knife because he never ate any meat. He had large beautiful eyes, but they had a dark look to them; his skin was fair, healthy looking, and his voice was warm and modulated. The ugliest part of his face was the horrible nose. His hands were ordinary, white, and graceless, as if he did not use them except as weapons to make the gestures that punctuated his speeches.

"For the duration of the dinner, he never stopped talking, and I soon realized that it was impossible to engage in normal conversation with him . . . My first question was: 'Your Excellency, are you pleased to have won?' He answered condescendingly: 'The real battle is about to begin.' He then began a long monologue on Mussolini, which he pronounced 'Muzzolini.' He was very enthusiastic about the Duce, whom he considered the spiritual leader of the Nazi movement. Without him, the Nazi party would not have grown to what it is today. He regretted not having been able to meet Mussolini yet, but, he explained, he had too much respect for the man to dare disturb him before having some positive accomplishments to show. Nevertheless, he couldn't wait to meet the Duce. 'That will be the most beautiful day of my life.'"

The message relayed by the wife of the Italian ambassador remained unchanged for the past ten years: Hitler had a burning desire to meet the Duce. The founder of Fascism could no longer delay the meeting. Hitler, after the elections of March 5, 1933, had consolidated his power with a strong majority of 288 seats out of 647 in the Reichstag, along with full political powers for four years. At his age (he wasn't yet 44), Hitler had legally become the dictator of the Third Reich. For Mussolini, the relationship would now evolve from an arms-length exchange of wishes and desires to the disagreeable reality of hard facts.

One of the very first requests coming from Hitler to Mussolini was the training of pilots for the reemerging Luftwaffe. The terms of the agreement were reached in Rome during the first week of April 1933 in a meeting between Göring and Italo Balbo. In July, a large group of German pilots appeared in Friuli and Apulia, wearing Italian air force uniforms and posing as Italian citizens from Alto Adige, to follow training courses in the Italian air force schools. Among them was Adolf Galland, who went on to become an ace fighter pilot in the Second World War. Hitler badly needed this favor from Mussolini because he had just broken the secret Rapallo Agreement with the USSR which had been in force since April 16, 1922. The Rapallo Agreement had allowed the Weimar Republic to secretly train, over the course of ten years (since 1923), its armored divisions in Kazan and its pilots at Lipetzk Air Base, about 370 kilometers southeast of Moscow, without alerting the victorious allies that Germany was not abiding by the clauses of the Versailles Treaty, which drastically limited its armed forces.

Yet the Duce was still not ready to meet Hitler as the "fellow dictator" he had suddenly become. There was another troublesome issue, a dislike of sorts that he could not overcome, in fact it can perhaps be said that Hitler's rise was not welcomed by Mussolini. The two dictators were separated by two issues, anti-Semitism and Austria, with the related problem of Alto Adige.

Regarding the Jewish issue, Renzo De Felice in his *The Jews in Fascist Italy, A History*, writes:

"On March 29, 1933, less than two months after Hitler had become chancellor, the Nazi party published its famous manifesto against the Jews. The world reaction of both horror and indignation was immediate. The Italian ambassador to Berlin, Cerruti, sent a telegram to Mussolini who, on the very same day, as Cerruti was to write later, had 'just harshly condemned the Führer's anti-Semitism.' Illustrating to him what the situation of the German Jews would be, Cerruti was convinced that 'a friendly but tough word from Your Excellency to Hitler' could possibly be the only hope to obtain a suspension of this decision.

"Mussolini answered immediately. [He] ordered Cerruti to transmit his personal message to Hitler, where Mussolini, while reiterating that this reaction was meant to be friendly and helpful to the beginnings of the new regime and stating that anti-Semitism could effectively coalesce against Hitler 'the Christian enemies of Germany as well,' said also 'I believe that the manifesto of the Nazi party for the struggle against the Jews, while it will not strengthen National Socialism inside Germany, will contribute to increase the moral and economic pressure by world Jewry.' Without the new element provided by the manifesto, the campaign would have weakened progressively and eventually would disappear. The Fascist regime has been involved in several similar campaigns and overcame each one by using alternatively the weapon of indifference or the counterattack to reestablish the truth for all to see . . . The German Jews themselves should be encouraged to tell the truth, but following the publication of the manifesto, it is obviously difficult for them to do so . . . "

Cerruti went to the chancellery with this message on March 31. The meeting turned out to be a fiasco for everyone: Hitler did not hide his displeasure regarding the Italian initiative and stated very strongly that he intended to pursue the path he had embarked on two days before. This was no longer the Führer full of blind devotion to Mussolini. It was already the Hitler the world would discover and learn to fear. The Hitler-Cerruti meeting ended in a clash, the first of a long series, between Germans and Italians after the Nazi seizure of power.

After the war, Cerruti related the story in an article in the Turin daily, *La Stampa*, on October 12, 1945, where he wrote, among other things:

"Hitler, after reading the message from Mussolini, was unable to contain his irritation. At first he answered calmly, then began to get progressively excited until he was screaming like a man possessed: 'You know what great admiration I have for Mussolini, whom I consider the spiritual head of my own movement, since, had he not been able to take power in Italy, National Socialism would not have stood a chance of succeeding in Germany. For the past three years, the bust of Mussolini has been placed on the mantelpiece in my office in the Brown House in Munich, facing my own desk. Having said this, allow me to state that MUSSOLINI DOES NOT UNDERSTAND A THING ABOUT THE JEWISH PROBLEM which I know intimately, having studied it for years, from every angle, like no one else has before.

"You, in Italy, have the luck of having very few Jews. I am happy about that, but it is no reason for you to ignore the danger represented by Jewry, since it is intimately tied to worldwide Bolshevism. I have recent and very precise information showing that the United States must stand up to this dangerous problem to free itself from the Marxist menace. In America, they will need much harsher methods than those I have initiated, and I can predict that very soon there will be pogroms on an unprecedented scale. In any case, please inform Mussolini that I appreciate his communication, but that I feel I must continue in the path I have embarked upon, the result of long research and meditation on this subject, and to fulfill the task that I have set for myself . . . '"

The failure of this initiative could not be more complete. Mussolini, brutally dismissed by his former pupil as having understood nothing about anti-Semitism, was trying to understand where Hitler was going with his extremism, because, at the same time, the Nazis had stirred up pan-German demonstrations in Alto Adige.

The relations Mussolini wanted with Austria were clear and unambiguous. In 1925 he had declared to the Italian parliament: "Italy will never tolerate the blatant breach of all the treaties that an annexation of Austria to Germany, the so-called Anschluss, would represent."

This firm statement came six years after the Allies had vetoed a motion, introduced on February 16, 1919, at the Austrian constitutional convention, calling for an immediate union between Austria and Germany into a federation reminiscent of the Kaiser's empire. In 1926, Mussolini had reiterated the same position, but in even stronger terms, when he reacted to the anti-Italian declarations by the Bavarian Premier Heinrich Held and German Chancellor Gustav Stresemann. As political attitudes went, Hitler was certainly a most explosive blend of Prussian and south German. His ideology and his programs were not the fruit of fantasy, of the intuition of the former corporal in the Bavarian army, or the impoverished and shiftless émigré from a decadent Austria. These policies, in effect, represented the will of the German people "to seek revenge from the Allies for the defeat of 1918."

National Socialism was also the expression of the mix of theories of Gobineau, Mendel, J. G. Fichte, and the absolute idealism of Hegel, as well as the ideas of Houston Stewart Chamberlain, the Englishman who became a German national out of love and respect for the Germanic race.

From Mussolini, Lenin, and Trotsky, Hitler learned the techniques of structuring the party along paramilitary lines: using squads, flags, badges, symbols, rank, revolutionary guards, et cetera, even though the Germans had little to learn about this type of choreography. The French and British allies, with their contradictions and the harsh peace that had been imposed at Versailles, actually gave the National Socialists the most effective slogans to mobilize the scorned and humiliated German masses, forced into poverty and unemployment to pay for the mistakes of Kaiser Wilhelm II, who was now living in comfortable retirement in The Netherlands.

The view from Berlin in the 1920s can be found in a letter sent by Chancellor Gustav Stresemann to the crown prince, who continued to hope for a return of the Hohenzollern dynasty to the imperial throne of Germany and save it from the chaos that was then gripping the country. On September 7, 1925, Stresemann wrote:

"I see German foreign policy in the near term as having three main objectives . . . To find a solution to the problem of the Rhineland; to assure protection for 10 to 12 million Germans now living under foreign occupation . . . the modification of our borders, the return of Danzig, of the Polish Corridor, and the redrawing of the borders of Upper Silesia. In the longer term, the union of Germany and Austria. The most urgent question is the first one stated above, the liberation of our territory, the departure of the occupying troops; . . . first of all our oppressors must let go of their prey; German policy should follow Metternich's plan for Austria after 1809: to act quietly and make noise only when it is worthwhile to do so."

During a meeting in Paris on August 26, 1928, with French Premier Raymond Poincaré, who had been complaining "about the rumors coming from Germany regarding an imminent *Anschluss*," Stresemann answered very clearly: "In Germany we know that an *Anschluss* taking place now would have only symbolic value. The German government is convinced that this is not an urgent problem. However, the love the German people harbor toward Austria will never end and can never be denied. Austria is part of our lives."

Hitler, who had only recently been granted German citizenship on February 26, 1932, considered Austria as a family problem, and he quickly named the former Communist Theo Habicht as his representative to Vienna. These nostalgic feelings harbored by Hitler were confirmed by Galeazzo Ciano during his first visit to the Führer at Berchtesgaden, as incoming Italian foreign minister, on October 24, 1936. As they spoke Hitler drew him closer to the picture window that dominated the reception room to show Ciano a city that was visible in the distance. After a few seconds of silence, the Führer said theatrically:

"That is Salzburg. Now I am condemned to look at my Austrian fatherland with a telescope." Filippo Anfuso, who witnessed the meeting, wrote: "We remained silent. How could anyone stop him from looking at Salzburg with a telescope?"

Ciano had to report back to Mussolini: "He showed us Austria." To the Duce's surprised reaction, Ciano had to explain how the view with a telescope worked, and Mussolini commented: "It's difficult to close one's eyes."

Many major events, such as the unexpected death of Stresemann on October 3, 1929, and the Wall Street crash on October 28, to name two, influenced the early string of victories of the NSDAP at the polls, beginning with the elections of September 14, 1930. Mussolini, who was well aware of German plans, decided to take the initiative and styled himself as the protector of Austrian independence.

In 1930, he met with Prince Ernst Rüdiger Starhemberg at the Palazzo Venezia and quickly understood that Austria was close to being manipulated by the Nazis even though they were not yet in power.

Starhemberg, who came from an aristocratic family older even than the Hapsburgs, had organized the Heimwehr, or civil guard, that included the Heimschutz militia, which was intended to counter the "Schutzbund" of the Social Democrats. The prince had gone to war against Italy when he was very young (he was born in 1899), and had demonstrated considerable courage in battle. After the armistice, he joined the Frei Korps that were attempting to win back Upper Silesia, lost by Germany at Versailles. He also was part of Austro-German movements seeking a Greater Reich that would include all Germans. Starhemberg, who fled Austria on the eve of Hitler's Anschluss of 1938 to join the French and British forces, wrote his memoirs, *Between Hitler and Mussolini*, in 1942.

During Starhemberg's first meeting with Mussolini, the Duce became very agitated upon hearing that, while the Heimwehr was set against the annexation of Austria to Germany, it was favorable to some form of political and economic union:

"An Anschluss with Germany should never be allowed. You are correct in assuming that you Austrians are at a higher cultural level than other Germanic peoples . . . but there are always people who will create problems in Europe. I have already told you that Austria must survive as Austrian, not German. You must turn the Heimwehren into an Austrian militant movement. It must have the courage to fight an ill-conceived notion of nationalism. Austria is a political necessity to safeguard Europe. Should the day come when Austria falls and is swallowed by Germany, it will mark the beginning of chaos in Europe. Austria must also preserve its culture because it is the bastion of European civilization. Germany is in the hands of the Prussians, and Prussia means order and efficiency. But it also stands for war and brutality.

"Prussia means a form of barbarism. For this reason you must fight for an Austrian Austria. Perhaps the day will come when you along with other countries on the Danube River will succeed in creating a new Danube regional organization. You must become the undisputed leader of the Austrian Heimwehren. It's a bad idea to split up the command structure. With the Heimwehren you must set the stage for the national rebirth of Austria. You must defend Austria against the Communist danger, yes, but also against any attempted annexation by Germany or any form of Prussian domination. You are young and well known as a fighter; as an activist, it is your mission to assemble the Austrian youth to fight for their country. Come and see me when you need my help."

Eugenio Morreale, press attaché at the Italian embassy in Vienna, was another witness of that troubled period:

"It is debatable whether the Austrian politicians of that period were right in turning to Mussolini to help fight Nazism. The Nazi plan was to wipe Austria off the map of Europe. France and Great Britain did not favor the Nazi-Fascist alliance because it made Mussolini the only guarantor of Austrian independence. As in all the 'ifs' of history, the answer to this and other such questions will be a function of current thinking on the subject and the interpretation of historians.

"To us, in hindsight, it appears that in Austria in the period 1918 to 1933 there were those who by conviction (the pan-Germanists) or because of party discipline (the Social Democrats) or for short-term gain (the Social Christian Party)—all of these, in one way or another, had entered into the game Berlin was playing, whether it was Prussian or Nazi, both of them acting the same way; they spent all their energies talking about the Anschluss, creating outside Austria a lot of uncertainty as to the true wishes of the Austrian people regarding this issue."

By the end of 1932, the Austrian pan-Germanists, during a government crisis, changed their allegiance and went into opposition, combining their votes with those of the Socialists and forcing the government to either resign or accept the support of the pro-Heimwehr forces to form a new parliamentary majority. The Socialists rejected a call by Monsignor Ignaz Seipel, a right-wing priest, to form a coalition with the Social Christian Party. At the same time, on April 24, in the regions of Vienna, Lower Austria, and Salzburg, the local elections, covering two-thirds of the Austrian voters, turned into a victory for the Austrian Nazi party. It was under these circumstances that Engelbert Dollfuss became chancellor of Austria on May 20, 1932, about eight months before Hitler in Berlin.

Dollfuss (sarcastically nicknamed "MilliMetternich" because he was short) at first attempted to strike a balance between the pressures coming from both extremes, right and left. The Nazis, however, did not stop harassing Dollfuss. Starhemberg, returning to Vienna in July after a second visit to Mussolini, was able to reassure the chancellor that the Duce was committed to the defense of Austrian independence, not just with words but also with deeds and, in this case, a first arms shipment and a large amount of money, about two million Austrian shillings. When Mussolini had asked Starhemberg what he intended to do with the weapons, the prince answered:

"We must prepare for the time when the Nazis will take over in Germany. Once they realize that they cannot come to power in Austria through the parliamentary process—because we will not allow elections to take place as they did in Germany in order to play up to Hitler—they will begin to fight, not because they will have any hope of winning, but only to give the Führer a reason to intervene."

On the evening of February 1, 1933, two days after Hitler was named chancellor, a large crowd of Nazis demonstrated through downtown Vienna, chanting the slogan: "Ein Volk! Ein Reich! Ein Führer!" (One people! One state! One leader!). The time had come for Mussolini and Dollfuss to meet on April 11. It was a very friendly dialogue. The Duce confirmed the messages that Starhemberg had relayed previously, namely, that Italy would have defended Austrian independence by force of arms, and the Italian army's high command was asked to prepare the "K Plan." Dollfuss reiterated his firm intention to "govern as a dictator until a new Austrian constitution had been approved." The constitution Dollfuss had in mind had been part of the political program of his Christian Social Party since 1926 and was modeled on the Vatican's Encyclical, *Rerum Novarum*, with corporate principles for trade unions. As for foreign policy, Mussolini pressured Dollfuss into entering an agreement with Hungary and ignoring the threats that came from Berlin.

In an unusual display of personal friendship and willingness to forego his jealously guarded privacy, Mussolini invited Dollfuss, his wife, and their two small children to his house in Riccione, on the Adriatic. From August 19th to the 29th, the two friends went swimming, toured the coast on a boat, and had a grand time as they fine-tuned the main points of an agreement between Rome, Vienna, and Budapest that was signed on March 17, 1934. Mrs. Alwine Dollfuss, as if to compensate for her husband's diminutive physical presence, was a beautiful, shapely, and very pleasant brunette, the kind Mussolini obviously enjoyed.

This was enough to give rise to all kinds of rumors that were even more persistent a year later when the same invitation was repeated and accepted but with a very tragic conclusion. With a deep suntan and recharged energy, Dollfuss returned to Vienna, determined to stop the Nazi party, which had been outlawed since June 19. The Nazi reaction was to prepare for a coup against the Austrian government; it was to unfold on October 15, 1933, the same day as the fall meeting of the cabinet. But the Führer, in Berlin, vetoed the action because "the international situation was not ready for such a move."

On September 9, 1933, Mussolini had written the following letter to Dollfuss:

"Dear Chancellor, I have just met with Prince Starhemberg, and in two long discussions he illustrated the current situation of the Heimwehr, its relationship with the government, with the other parties, and other paramilitary groups in Austria.

"According to the prince—and this information has reached me from other sources—the National Socialist movement is working undercover, since they have been outlawed, but with unabated intensity, as we have seen, since they were preparing a putsch. In the opinion of Starhemberg, the great majority of these so-called Nazis are, in effect, simply dissatisfied citizens who could very well be won over if the government and the parties supporting it would decide to follow the path of Fascism. This would remove the main obstacle to the Nazis' opposition to the government, based on what they see as an unwillingness to reform the structures of the Austrian state."

Hitler's very harsh answer to Mussolini, as transmitted by Ambassador Cerruti on March 30, 1933, caused great alarm at the Palazzo Venezia. The Duce was convinced that Berlin had fallen into the hands of a "monster" who was completely unpredictable. The French and British were satisfied that the Führer's extremism would provide medicine strong enough to inhibit the Fascist virus from spreading in Europe. They were to be proven wrong, as the next ten years would show, at the expense of continental Europe. Hitler's program, plus or minus a few details, was clearly spelled out for everyone to read in *Mein Kampf.*

Beyond the skirmishing they engaged in openly on the Austrian question, Hitler and Mussolini were on opposite sides of the Jewish question. Rome attempted, unsuccessfully, to induce Berlin to reverse its unacceptable policies, now aimed at German Jews. The Italian government then began helping Jewish refugees from Germany by offering them political asylum in Italy or providing a gateway to immigration to Palestine, most notably through the port of Trieste.

Hitler was very annoyed at Mussolini's attitude on this issue, while Mussolini hoped to bring the Führer back to his senses by enlisting his support for the much-trumpeted four-power pact between France, Great Britain, Germany, and Italy, which was signed in Rome on June 7, 1933. The pact, Mussolini's brainchild, would, he hoped, be an instrument of peace in Europe, was defunct before the ink was dry. Only Germany and Italy were to ratify it, while, for different reasons, France and Great Britain were to take no further action. The indifference on the part of the French and British provided a restless Hitler with one more reason to announce in October 1933 that Germany was leaving the League of Nations.

Since July 20, 1932, Mussolini had become his own foreign minister, while Dino Grandi, who had previously held the post, was appointed Italian ambassador to Great Britain. The daily management of the ministry was, in effect, under the direction of Undersecretary Fulvio Suvich, a highly intelligent businessman from Trieste. Suvich, a former citizen of the Austro-Hungarian Empire of the Hapsburgs, was the foremost expert in the Italian government on all Central European issues. He was opposed to the policies of the German government and, most of all, contrary to any agreement between Rome and Berlin that might damage Austria and upset the fragile balance holding the countries along the Danube in harmony. Hitler, in his personal contacts with Mussolini, used the services of Göring, who was quite happy commuting between Berlin and Rome.

Suvich traveled to Berlin in December 1933 on a fact-finding mission. There were many open issues between Berlin and Rome. The Jewish problem now held worldwide attention. The Nazi ordinances no longer appeared as yet another milestone in the long history of periodic discrimination against the Jews; they were seen and understood as a violent pogrom. Suvich returned to Rome empty-handed, with the exception of a vague promise that Germany aimed at keeping an independent Austria in a state of limited sovereignty. The Germans were now demanding the resignation of Dollfuss, the Duce's friend and the Führer's enemy, and the formation of a new government with a phalanx of Nazis in key positions. In the meantime, the Nazis continued to secretly undermine the government in Vienna. Hitler refused any discussion of the Jewish problem and had not the slightest intention of changing his position since his outburst in March in front of Ambassador Cerruti.

Suvich went to Vienna in January 1934 in the hope of finding a way out of the Austrian mess with Chancellor Dollfuss. Immediately after Suvich's trip, Austria was rocked—as Eugenio Morreale recalls—by a riot of the Schutzbund in Linz which spread to Vienna and other cities on February 12, 1934, while most other workers, including railway employees, remained on the job. The street fighting was very useful to the Nazis. Dollfuss ordered the army and the Heimwehren of Prince Starhemberg to fight with the rioters and even approved the use of artillery, provoking a real massacre in working-class neighborhoods in Vienna.

The day ended in tragedy: over 1,000 dead and 3,000 wounded (most of them workers). On February 28, the Nazis, who, so far, had remained on the sidelines, went back to throwing bombs around town. Mussolini described the situation: "In Austria the fire is burning under poor Dollfuss. Hitler is fanning the embers, and the Social Democrats supply the wood."

Shortly thereafter, the pressure cooker exploded. Besides Göring, Hitler also used the skills of a well-known diplomat of the old school: his Vice Chancellor Franz von Papen, who had two meetings with Mussolini between March 30 and April 2, 1934, at the Palazzo Venezia. They agreed that the long-delayed meeting between the two dictators was now overdue. The diplomatic secretaries went to work. From Berlin, there appeared to be scheduling problems: since Hitler was the younger of the two, both in years (born in 1889, to Mussolini's 1883) and in tenure in office, the Führer would naturally be the one to travel to Italy.

The strange objections by the German Foreign Ministry gave no cause for alarm even though the Führer had waited for ten years to meet the "founder of Fascism." The true explanation of the Nazi hesitations would become apparent after the visit. It would be the first signal that, in his mind, Hitler had already cast Mussolini in a secondary role in his coming political and military adventures.

Against this background a visit to meet the Duce was an excellent idea. During those weeks, besides the Austrian problem—where Hitler behaved like a successful emigrant returning triumphantly home to impress the locals—a larger political problem loomed on the horizon: the opposition within the party led by Ernst Röhm.

Having reached the coveted goal of supreme power, Hitler—like all revolutionary leaders, Lenin with his Red Guards, Mussolini with the Blackshirts, Garibaldi with his followers—had the unwelcome surprise of having to subdue the very forces that had brought him to power. These forces included the 400,000 strong SA (Sturmabteilungen, literally "assault squads"), or "storm troopers," who now demanded to be transformed with all the required ranks and salaries into a new "People's Army." The official German army, the Reichswehr, was limited by the treaty of Versailles to just 100,000 men, and it became obvious that the demands of the SA posed a serious threat that could only be resolved by the force of arms. The SA were restless. The promises made to them were being ignored. They were a definite danger to the Prussian military establishment. They openly talked about the second wave that would "free Hitler from the reactionary cliques" so that he could really take over the German State and transform it into a Nazi stronghold.

Hitler had other ideas. His plans went farther and wider, since Hindenburg, by now an ailing old man confined to his sick bed in his vast estate at Neudek, was still president (he was soon to die on August 2, 1934). Hitler was preparing his very own "second wave": to take over the presidency of the Republic and, in a way, to "Americanize" the German state by combining the offices of President and Reich Chancellor. To prepare for this event, Hitler met, on April 11, aboard the cruiser *Deutschland*, with General Werner von

Blomberg, the unofficial representative of the officer corps of the Reichswehr, and reached an agreement. The understanding sealed the fate of the Weimar Republic: Hitler would have the army's support to become president after Hindenburg's now obviously imminent passing, and, in turn, he would cut down the SA once and for all. The stage was set for the massacre of the "The Night of the Long Knives."

The trip to Italy, in this context, was also intended to lull Röhm into thinking he was perfectly secure. Before taking action, Hitler made a last attempt, on June 4, 1934, at reaching an understanding with his old comrade in arms (Röhm was one of the very few Nazi leaders to address the Führer in the familiar "du" form). He asked him to be patient and wait for the solutions that would be offered to his restless legions. The stormy meeting went on for some five hours. Röhm rejected any compromise. He only agreed, since Hitler was on his way to Italy, to take, together with all his top men, a well-deserved one-month vacation.

Upon the Führer's return, the negotiations would resume. It was the lull that Hitler needed and that would allow Heydrich, Himmler, and Göring to lay the groundwork for the fateful night with the participation of the SS (the Schutzstaffen), the party's praetorian guard. Reinhard Heydrich, head of the SD section of the SS and overseer of the Gestapo, the state secret police, had compiled a thick file on purported cash payments of more than twelve million reich marks made by the French ambassador to Berlin, André François-Poncet, to Röhm in order to overthrow Hitler and create a new leadership triumvirate that would include Röhm, Gregor Strasser (the head of the Nazi party's left wing), and former German Chancellor General Kurt von Schleicher. As for the Austrian plan, Hitler told his entourage that there would be new developments upon his return from Italy. Habicht secretly invited the Nazi leaders in Vienna to meet with him in Zurich on June 25.

With both the SA and Austrian agendas in hand, the German foreign ministry told its Italian counterparts that Hitler's visit could take place June 14 to 16, 1934, as agreed, in Venice. Mussolini had insisted on Venice because of its incomparable setting and because it was halfway for both leaders to travel. In Berlin and Rome, there were high expectations about the results of this trip. The German ambassador to Italy, Ulrich von Hassell, was very insistent with his Foreign Minister, Konstantin von Neurath, that Germany confirm very clearly once again that it would respect the independence of Austria, as the Führer had done to Suvich during his visit to Berlin in December 1933.

For Hitler, the context for the first meeting between the two dictators was clearly to answer, on the one hand, an internal need to keep Röhm and the SA quiet until his return and, on the other hand, to avoid upsetting Mussolini regarding the imminent coup that he, Hitler, was preparing in Austria, which would possibly erase any negative effects produced by the struggle against the SA now set for the last days of June. Hitler also hoped that a spectacular foreign policy success would facilitate his aim at replacing Hindenburg, who was now dying, as President of the Reich.

II

The First Encounter

Venice and Stra:
June 14 and 15, 1934

At 10:00 a.m. on Thursday, June 14, 1934, the German JU-52 aircraft bearing a swastika clearly marked on its wing, landed at the airfield of San Nicolò, with the Führer's personal pilot, Hans Baur, at the controls. Adolf Hitler quickly came down the ramp followed by press secretary Otto Dietrich, and interpreter Hans Thomsen. Behind them appeared the tall and stately Minister of Foreign Affairs, Konstantin von Neurath. Two other German planes had just landed ahead of the Führer with about twenty other members of his party. Benito Mussolini stood at the foot of the ramp and welcomed Hitler with a long and strong handshake, sealing the historic moment of the first meeting between the dictators.

It was indeed a warm, sunny day that inaugurated a partnership that was to affect the world and rip the foundations of civilized life and peace throughout all five continents after many crises, wars of aggression, and tragic deaths. In ten short years, France and the British Empire would lose their preeminence to the rising power of the United States and the Soviet Union.

Hitler wore typical diplomat's civilian clothes, black jacket and striped gray trousers with patent leather shoes, and an awful looking yellow coat. He held a gray fedora in his left hand, looking more like a civil servant on his way to a ceremony. His complexion was very pale and somewhat sickly. Mussolini, by contrast, was deeply tanned, having just spent a day at the beach at Riccione with Undersecretary of Foreign Affairs, Fulvio Suvich, Secretary of the Fascist Party, Achille Starace, and his son-in-law, Galeazzo Ciano, then head of the Duce's press office. More significantly, Mussolini was wearing the flashy uniform of corporal of the Fascist militia, with all his decorations, high black boots, and a dagger at his side. The Führer understood that he had been upstaged and bitterly complained to von Neurath, who had insisted on Hitler's strictly following the dictates of protocol rather than wearing his own theatrical uniforms which he had left behind in Berlin.

However, the Führer's Nazi party pin, a solid gold eagle with a swastika, on his lapel did overshadow the copper Fascist party pin that Mussolini had on his uniform. (The only thing the two dictators had in common on that day was the identical age of their respective mistresses, both Eva Braun and Claretta Petacci were 22 years old.) After reviewing the honor guard, Hitler left for the Grand Hotel and Mussolini went to the Villa Pisani in nearby Stra, which was to be the location of their first formal meetings. Among the chronicles of this event, the most interesting is that of Elisabeth Cerruti, who was accompanying her husband, the Italian Ambassador to Berlin:

"The first meeting between Hitler and Mussolini was organized very quickly and had not been properly prepared. My husband was worried that there would be problems with protocol and that an unplanned or foolish decision would further complicate a tense world situation. In view of the nature of the players involved, his fears were not entirely unfounded. The meeting took place in Venice, city of dreams and, if I may add, of twisted diplomacy. Mussolini had probably picked Venice because it was the least 'official' Italian city and thought this would have given the visit less emphasis. However, any location would have conveyed enormous importance to the event.

"Mussolini was at the height of his power and confident that he could secure approval for any initiative from the international community. Hitler's Germany was still a mystery to almost everyone. The great powers, fearing the unknown, were happy to let Mussolini be the first to deal with Hitler and hoped he could exert a certain influence on the German dictator. Mussolini was convinced that Hitler considered him the spiritual head of the Nazi-Fascist movement and, therefore, would look up to the Italian dictator for leadership. So Mussolini considered himself the arbiter of the international situation in charge of dealing with Hitler. This mission had been handed to him by those lacking the courage or the energy to quickly deal with a difficult situation. There was great interest in this meeting. When we reached Venice, we were surprised to see over 400 newsmen on the scene covering the event, including all the American correspondents based in Rome. The atmosphere was very charged, filled with gossip."

Italian journalist, Orio Vergani, in his book, *Ciano: Una lunga confessione*, wrote about a rising star soon to become world famous, his old friend Galeazzo Ciano:

"In Shanghai and Peking," writes Vergani, "Galeazzo, as Italian Consul General, had made an excellent impression during the Japanese and Chinese crisis and had become fluent in English. It was also said that his wife had much influence [Edda Mussolini was the Duce's oldest daughter and had married Ciano on April 24, 1930] and gave Ciano an importance he would never have achieved on his own. Mussolini wanted to have his favorite daughter close to him. And so it was that the Cianos packed their bags and took an ocean liner back to Italy. The young man, who was born in Leghorn on March 18, 1903, spoke several languages, and was as tactful as a diplomat when dealing with people. At the time, Fascist propaganda efforts outside Italy were considered more challenging, and Mussolini thought that his press office was the best place for his son-in-law to show his talent. He would be under his direct supervision as a first step toward a political career. Ciano was to be the Duce's spokesman with Italian and foreign newsmen.

"But Ciano had scant knowledge of people. His life had been an easy one, and now it had just become even easier. He was the first person to believe in Mussolini's capacity to perform miracles and to be convinced that he was the spokesman for an infallible man . . . In a short time the old press office would become a large bureaucracy . . . Ciano's first important mission (after his appointment on August 1, 1933) was to guide and assist newsmen at the first Hitler-Mussolini meeting, in June 1934 in Venice. The evening before the meeting, Ciano assembled the newsmen at the Hotel Danieli. That is where, after eight years, I was reunited with my friend from my youth. He had gained weight, his face was somewhat fuller. He recognized me, ran over, and gave me a bear hug."

Mussolini had decided upon Stra to impress Hitler but was unaware that Villa Pisani was not at all equipped for such an event since Napoleon had spent the night there on November 29, 1807, on the banks of the sleepy river Brenta. Dozens of technicians and government officials came up from Rome to prepare the villa in a few short days. The local hotels provided the service and equipment, and finally the magnificent eighteenth-century ballrooms and sitting rooms, along with a modern kitchen, were given the finishing touches. However, the success of these efforts was overshadowed by the presence of innumerable giant mosquitoes that kept a very nervous Mussolini awake for three nights and forced him to change the program of the meetings. Unaware of the mosquito problem, Hitler boarded a motor boat at 11:30 a.m. and then an automobile at the Piazzale Roma to meet with a smiling Mussolini at Villa Pisani. The two dictators took a short stroll before lunch on the grounds, where Mussolini pointed out that the villa, after having been owned by Napoleon, became the property of the Hapsburgs of Austria.

Mussolini sat at the center of the rectangular table in the magnificent dining room, with Hitler seated directly across from him. To Mussolini's right sat the German ambassador, von Hassell, and to his left, Foreign Minister von Neurath. Starace sat at Hitler's right and Suvich to his left. At the end of the meal, the two dictators went into a meeting alone and without interpreters because the Duce, from that first encounter, insisted that he spoke excellent German, an exaggeration that was to create many problems, because his German "was adequate only for a political conversation without any nuances" according to Eugen Dollmann, and without any complicated discussions. Dollmann, an SS colonel who would witness and interpret at various meetings between Hitler and Mussolini, was to write:

"The Duce was convinced his German was good enough for him to handle the conversation alone, and this fateful mistake must have cost Italy dearly. His German was barely adequate for a simple conversation or to chat with Göring as old veterans using expressions known to any corporal. When dealing with the depths of the Hitlerian mystique, which actually referred to extremely concrete political realities, if the conversation became too technical, then Mussolini played a passive role rather than having to admit his inability to understand what was being said."

Even though Dollmann was not exactly an impartial witness, the problem of Mussolini as a polyglot (he also claimed to be fluent in French, which he had taught in school, and to speak some English) was to cause many misunderstandings and create confusion in Italy's foreign relations.

Before the meeting with Hitler, Mussolini had thoroughly prepared himself on all pending questions. Besides the precise and candid memorandums prepared by Suvich, the Duce had also read an explosive secret file sent to him by Dollfuss, documenting a Nazi coup in the planning stages in Austria. The discussions lasted an hour and a half. Hitler did most of the talking, repeating the objectives of the Nazi party: the revision of the Treaty of Versailles and the bringing together of all the German minorities. He went on to say that this was justified from the racial point of view to maintain the superiority and purity of the Nordic races from being contaminated by the "Negroid characteristics" of the Mediterranean populations. This was the underlying reason Nazism went ahead with its anti-Semitic policies. If Italy adhered to these principles, Germany was ready for an economic and military alliance. During a break, Mussolini went to the window—they were on the second floor—and made a strange gesture to the officials and assistants who were standing around in the garden, talking and smoking. Many witnesses said they thought the gesture was intended to convey that Hitler was crazy.

Ciano told Vergani: "He is a madman. He proposed to Mussolini that he [Hitler] invade France, and assured us that he can succeed in twenty-four hours if we help him and do nothing. It seems he has thousands of motorcycles with machine guns. After passing the bridges over the Rhine, he could be in Paris in less than eight hours. Mussolini was flabbergasted. Hitler has only one thought: revenge and war. For the German people he's something of a Muhammad with the plans of a Genghis Khan!"

After the break, Hitler spoke of the problems created by the SA. He failed to mention, obviously, the plan that was being elaborated in Berlin and Munich by Göring and Himmler to get to the root of the problem. Mussolini naïvely advised him to follow the example of Tarquinius, who, as legend had it, was in the habit of chopping off the heads of the tallest flowers. He also reiterated the calls to caution that he had previously transmitted through Ambassador Cerruti regarding the Jews and the Catholic Church, against whom Hitler was reviving the Lutheran thesis. The Austrian problem was barely touched upon at the first meeting, due mostly to the sightseeing program for the afternoon that took Hitler along the Grand Canal and the smaller islands. In the evening, they attended a concert in the courtyard of the Palace of the Doges, after which Hitler returned to the Grand Hotel and Mussolini to the Villa Pisani with its giant mosquitoes and Napoleon's ghost.

The next morning, Hitler visited the Venice Biennale with Elisabeth Cerruti, who wrote:

"The Führer went through the rooms full of art works in complete silence but with a look of disgust on his face. At the German pavilion his manner changed: he stopped in front of the most ordinary paintings, which looked as if they were painted-over photographs and appeared very pleased. He had no artistic feeling and would become irritated at any hint of human feeling or imagination. . . .when we walked back to the motorboat, he lectured about healthy art works. It reminded me of one of his observations regarding music: that the only masterpiece after Wagner's death was Puccini's *Madama Butterfly*. That is certainly a beautiful opera, but it showed his ignorance of modern composers, including Debussy,

Stravinski, Bartok, Ravel . . . I felt relieved when the boat reached the small landing at the golf club of the Lido."

Mussolini, who had literally fled Villa Pisani because of the mosquitoes, was now back waiting for the visitor for lunch. There was an intense heat wave, and all the participants would have much preferred to refresh themselves bathing than face a meal.

As Elisabeth Cerruti wrote: "It was the first social gathering with the presence of ladies and never had so many older society women been assembled for the occasion. Mussolini and Hitler sat next to each other, the wife of von Hassell was at Mussolini's right, I sat next to the Chancellor. The food was awful and the conversation, as usual with Hitler, was deadly. We all were relieved when coffee was served, not just because it signaled the end of the meal but also because the coffee in Venice was usually excellent. But as soon as we tasted it, all of us instantly stopped drinking. Somehow salt had been served rather than sugar."

It was clearly too much. Hitler and Mussolini stood up and walked on to the golf course and sat on a bench while their entourage stood at a distance. From afar only three persons listened in: von Hassell, von Neurath, and Suvich. It was the moment of truth concerning Austria.

Hitler accompanied his torrent of words with angry, chopping gestures. He appeared to want to choke his country of origin and the Austrian chancellor, Dollfuss. According to a memorandum written by von Neurath, Hitler handled the issue in the following terms: (1) It was useless to discuss the Anschluss because it was unrealistic in view of the attitude of other nations; (2) It was impossible to deal with Dollfuss; (3) Dollfuss must be replaced with someone who will organize new elections; (4) With a Nazi electoral success, a new government with "our" people will be possible; (5) All issues regarding Vienna must be resolved between Berlin and Rome.

Mussolini asked the name of the person Hitler had in mind as a replacement for Dollfuss. Hitler cleverly said he didn't have a candidate and, to quiet Mussolini's pro-Austrian stance, said that he had no confidence in the Austrian regime, given that the Austrians had been "double-crossing everyone for years." Hitler interpreted Mussolini's question about a successor to Dollfuss as an indication that the Duce's attitude was beginning to change and that a pan-German change in Austria would be tolerated. It was perhaps this misunderstanding that prompted Hitler to approve the attempted putsch in Vienna forty days later.

The second and final part of the meeting is captured in a note written by Mussolini himself on June 22, 1934, to Cesare Maria De Vecchi, who was at the time the Italian Ambassador to the Holy See:

"In my second talk with Hitler, I touched upon the relations between Nazism and the Vatican. I transcribe almost word for word what he told me: 'I understand perfectly well the need to avoid a Kulturkampf, but one must not forget that the Catholics represent one-third of the population of the Reich. I am a Catholic. For the pact with the Church, to work it requires: (1) that the Church be the Church and nothing else: no sports, no trade unions, no theater, no social assistance programs; (2) that the heads of the Church not take a negative attitude like the archbishop of Munich; (3) that no useless antagonistic decisions be made, such as the condemnation of Rosenberg's book, *The Myth of the 20th Century*, that no one would have noticed had the Catholics not attacked it, and that was only a reflection of its author and not the Nazi party; (4) that the Catholic Center party, its leadership and style, are not just the mouthpiece of the Church itself.' It is useless to repeat what I told Hitler. He is rather irritated against the Catholic leadership—even for what is happening in Austria—but it may be possible to soften his position somewhat."

The talk lasted two hours, and the dictators were expected in the Piazza San Marco, where the Duce spoke to the crowd while his guest listened from a nearby palace window. Mussolini addressed the crowd about issues regarding Venice and other internal problems and mentioned his meetings with Hitler only in passing to reassure public opinion. He did say that the meeting would not change the map of Europe nor add to the current problems, but would actually clear some of the gathering clouds. That evening Hitler offered Mussolini a dinner at the Grand Hotel. The Duce had little appetite and was clearly bored when he exchanged the usual toasts with his host. The following morning at six Hitler, with Ambassador Cerruti, visited the Basilica of San Marco. As the two men walked across the square, the Führer was pleasantly surprised to see a small crowd greeting him with 'Heil Hitler,' as someone had leaked the planned early morning walk. Hitler then boarded the motorboat back to the airfield and, from there, flew back to Germany.

Back in Riccione, Mussolini told his family, by now very curious, what had happened:

"At first, the Führer is not very likable. He is without a doubt intelligent and a good speaker, although too long-winded for me. He speaks like a biblical prophet. He assured me of his feelings of friendship for Italy and myself on his part and that of the German people. I can perhaps believe in his friendship, but as for that of the Germans . . . there were disagreements. He dreams of creating a greater Reich. So on the question of Austria, we do not agree."

The results of the visit were ambiguous. In fact, Hitler, having shown Mussolini his willingness to encourage the widening of Italy's the sphere of influence in the Mediterranean, assumed he had Mussolini's acceptance for his pan-German plans, beginning with Austria.

Mussolini had limited himself to noting the German Chancellor's requests, which would be answered through the customary diplomatic channels. The following Monday, June 18, the Duce, meeting with Ambassador von Hassell at the Palazzo Venezia, was careful to point out the high opinion, friendship, and mutual respect that Rome held for the head of the Austrian government, Chancellor Dollfuss. He also wished to thank Hitler for visiting Italy at such a difficult time for Germany. It would be three years and three months before Mussolini and Hitler would meet again. During that interval, Rome and Berlin—because of their similar regimes, because of the mistakes of others, and because of the fateful course of events—after staring each other down, were to end in the deadly embrace of the Axis alliance.

Back in Berlin, Hitler went immediately to work on settling the score with Röhm, who was completely unaware of his fate. Röhm, with key members of his staff, was on vacation at the Hanselbaur Pension in Bad Wiessee, a well-known Bavarian resort. The move was set for dawn, on Saturday, June 30. Hitler began moving around

Germany in a frenzy. On June 20, he went to a memorial service for Göring's wife, who had died in 1931. The next day he flew to Neudek, the Prussian residence owned by Hindenburg, to brief the President officially regarding the meeting with Mussolini. Hitler confirmed to the head of state and to General von Blomberg that he was about to keep his promise regarding the taming of the SA. He then went on an inspection tour of the Austrian border. On Thursday, June 28, he telephoned Röhm to confirm that he'd be present two days later at the conference of the staff of the SA to review their relations with the German army.

Röhm was so pleased that the Führer was going to attend that he told his friends: "All misunderstandings and clashes have been resolved." He then called the Vierjahreszeiten Hotel in Münich to make reservations for a grandiose reconciliation dinner with Hitler, who arrived on the morning of June 30 carrying a gun. And so began the "Night of the Long Knives." The exact number of the victims will never be known, but they were certainly in the hundreds. The best known names stand out, Röhm, Gregor Strasser, and General Kurt von Schleicher, the three "traitors," who, as Hitler would declare at the Reichstag on July 13, "had met with a foreign ambassador without informing me, and I gave the order that they be executed, even if it were true that they only spoke of the weather, numismatics, or other similar issues." After the massacre, having wiped out all internal opposition, Hitler was praised by the Reichswher and Hindenburg himself. From abroad, most commentators reacted with amazement and even panic.

Mussolini was very upset and remembered his anecdote about flowers having their heads cut off that he thought gave Hitler the idea for the blood bath. Mussolini was actually thinking about giving Hitler sound advice on how to refresh the Nazi party as he himself did so successfully in Rome through his frequent "changing of the guard," mostly through lateral promotions of the officials involved. To his sister Edvige, who was worried after reading the news from Germany, the Duce said:

"Look at how vicious this man can be! Some terrible names from history come to mind: a new Attila? And he killed some of his closest colleagues . . . It's as if I were to personally execute Balbo, Grandi, Bottai . . . "

Immediately following the Nazi "purge," Mussolini was troubled by disturbing rumors from Vienna. The local Nazis were angry that the meeting in Venice had not advanced the cause of the Anschluss and were ready to take action through a coup. From a secret SS report of October 1938—found in a cement box fished out of the Black Lake in Bohemia after the war—while Hitler was touring the Austrian border on June 25, 1934, a secret meeting took place in Zurich between Habicht and the head of the Austrian Nazis within the army, Fridolin Glass. A plan was approved to arrest the Austrian government ministers during a meeting of the cabinet; the president of the Republic, Wilhelm Miklas, would be forced to name a Nazi cabinet. The radio station would be occupied first. A small contingent of about 150 men from the 89th Standarte, about thirty of them in army uniforms, was to occupy the command of the Vienna military district during the afternoon while the cabinet meeting was in progress. A truck full of weapons would enter the courtyard of the command center. The radio would broadcast a communiqué saying:

"The Dollfuss government has resigned. The [Austrian] Ambassador to Rome, Anton Rintelen, has formed a new government."

Only after this announcement would the coup actually begin. The SS document goes on:

"As ambassador to Rome, Rintelen was well informed regarding Austria's position in Europe. At that time the Austrian attitude on many foreign and internal policy questions followed the same line as Rome."

While Mussolini had declined to join the protest made by France to Germany in 1933 regarding "German involvement in the affairs of Austria," this did not mean that Italy was no longer interested in Austria's independence. Mussolini saw himself as the protector of an independent Austria. Italian foreign policy was strongly influenced by Undersecretary Fulvio Suvich, who was not as negative as the rest of the Italian government regarding Italy's participation in an anti-German front. The statements made by Suvich on the Austrian problem sounded more and more hostile to Germany . . . In

March 1934, Mussolini, Dollfuss, and Romanian Prime Minister Gömbös signed a protocol in Rome whereby the three countries guaranteed each other's independence.

French Foreign Minister Louis Barthou took advantage of this change in Italy's position to influence Italian policy towards Germany. Dollfuss also tried to improve Austria's position by ignoring any pan-German sentiments. The repeated complaints by Austria to the Italian government against the German government tended to increase Germany's political isolation. This was the background of the Venice meeting between Hitler and Mussolini. Dollfuss did everything he could to prevent an agreement between Italy and the Nazi Reich . . . The Austrian complaints to the Italian government prompted growing hostility in the Italian press against the Nazi government.

In May 1934, on orders from the government, the Italian press unleashed a violent anti-German campaign with respect to Austria. This press campaign reached its climax in an article by Virginio Gayda, a mouthpiece of the Duce, reproduced in every Italian newspaper with the headline: "Stop Terrorism in Austria!" One sentence of the article read: "These terrorist actions, directed and prepared by German agitators, are continuing to threaten the relations between Italy and Germany."

The actual position Mussolini took with Hitler on the problem of Austria can be inferred from the articles in the Italian press and the fact that Dollfuss was invited with his family to visit the Duce in Riccione shortly thereafter . . . Dollfuss also began seeking closer relations with Britain and France and attempted to further isolate Germany. The government-sponsored newspaper, Wiener Zeitung, wrote on July 22: "Should German diplomacy reject the British proposals, it will get lost in the desert of isolation; if it accepts, then the last leaves from the tree of Nazi promises will fall . . . " Dr. Rintelen—the Nazi candidate chosen to replace Dollfuss—spoke of the dangers the situation held for Germany and of the consequences the recent talks Dollfuss was having with Mussolini in Riccione, and then with Barthou in Paris that led him to expect possible economic and military help from France to Austria . . .

Rintelen was also anxious to go on vacation in July and announced that he would not return to his posting in Rome.

A meeting in a Viennese restaurant during the evening of July 23, 1934, set the date of the putsch for two days later. Despite all the meticulous preparations, the coup resembled a Viennese operetta, full of delays, unplanned mishaps, misunderstandings, and bad luck. Dollfuss was wounded at 1:02 p.m. on July 25 by one of the terrorists who broke into the palace. He was left to bleed to death. The Austrian loyalists succeeded in reestablishing order and even arrested Dr. Rintelen while he was in his hotel room waiting to become Chancellor! The President of the Republic appointed Dr. Kurt Schuschnigg as the new Chancellor. By 7 p.m. the Palace of the Chancellery was emptied. On July 31, a military court condemned all the major figures of the conspiracy to death by hanging, notably the former officer who had been fired from the Austrian army because of his Nazi leanings and was responsible for murdering Dollfuss.

Most of the conspirators were Nazis, whom the Austrian government had dismissed because of their militant views. Dollfuss had underestimated the sympathy that his persecution of the Nazi party and of pan-German ideas had generated. When, in March 1938, German troops marched triumphantly into Austria, Rudolf Hess honored the "Nazi martyrs" of July 24, 1934. He said in a ceremony: "Here 154 soldiers of the 89th SS Standarte fought for the cause of Germany. Seven lost their lives to the hangman."

Hitler at the time had gone off to Bayreuth to attend a production of Wagner's *Das Rheingold*. From his box, he was following the situation in Vienna as assistants kept bringing in telephone messages on the development of the putsch. Friedelinde Wagner, niece of the composer, relates:

"After the opera, the Führer became very excited. He became even more entranced after hearing how the events took place. At the restaurant, he could barely contain himself, and he ordered every entree with great care as usual. He said, 'I must show myself to the public for one more hour, or else they might think I had something to do with what's happening in Vienna.'"

While overjoyed by the elimination of his personal enemy, Dollfuss, Hitler was also worried about the negative consequences of the aborted coup. He was especially nervous about Mussolini's reaction because, at that moment, the Duce was at the beach with his guests, the Dollfuss family, and they were expecting the Austrian Chancellor to arrive that evening, since he had scheduled his departure from Vienna right after the cabinet meeting. Just before dying, Dollfuss was able to say to one of his ministers: "Please tell Mussolini to protect my family."

Hitler quickly dismissed the German Ambassador to Austria, Rieth, who was clearly implicated in the putsch. He was replaced by the conservative politician and former Prime Minister, Franz von Papen, who, it was said, had barely saved his own skin during the purge of June 30. Hitler wrote von Papen a letter, where he pointedly deplores the "horrible crime" and asks him to go immediately to Vienna as German Minister Plenipotentiary. "It is an alarming situation, and you therefore cannot refuse," wrote Hitler. Von Papen proved to be flexible, true to his reputation, and ready to lend a helping hand to the Nazi regime and to Hitler himself.

At the Nüremberg trials, Göring confirmed that Hitler was fully aware of the preparation of the Vienna putsch but had been misled by Habicht into believing that the coup to overthrow Dollfuss was to be carried out by regular Austrian army troops rather than by a few hundred desperate Nazis recently dismissed from their government jobs and clearly lacking initiative and proper leadership. While Hitler attempted to save face by distancing himself from the Vienna fiasco, Mussolini was drawing his own conclusions on the new situation in Europe.

The Duce learned of the Vienna coup during an automobile trip in the company of his wife while he was still vacationing in his native region of Romagna. They were expected to return in the late evening, but as the Duce's son, Vittorio Mussolini, remembers:

"Instead, we saw them return right after lunch in a hurry, and looking very somber. My father went directly into his study with his private secretary and was on the phone. My mother told us: 'They murdered Dollfuss.' Later as a violent thunderstorm broke out, my father, unable to hide his sadness and his anger, asked that my mother accompany him to the house where Mrs. Dollfuss was staying to announce the sad news. This was the kind of task that my father had difficulty performing, and my mother's presence would be a great help. Deeply embarrassed, he went the house where Mrs. Dollfuss was staying with her children. She immediately took a plane to Vienna at six o'clock in the evening, leaving us all very sad."

In an interview given after the war by Rachele Mussolini, the Duce's widow, on the death of Dollfuss and the meeting with Hitler in Venice, she said:

"Benito told me that Hitler was a violent man, unable to control himself. He was more stubborn than intelligent. For hours during their meeting at Stra he insisted on quoting from his book, *Mein Kampf*, rather than discussing serious problems. Had the French and British been more clever, the alliance with Germany would never have happened. Especially after they murdered Dollfuss. He was a great friend to Benito, and the day he was killed, his wife and children were our guests at Riccione."

After the funeral, Dollfuss' widow came back to Riccione. According to Rachele Mussolini:

"She came back looking older, a changed woman. Nevertheless, she brought back with her, to give to the Duce, the old key to the city of Vienna that Dollfuss had prepared to give to Mussolini as a gift along with other gifts for our children. Shortly after, Mrs. Dollfuss took her children to the United States."

Mussolini took this incident as a personal affront. In the discussions they had in Venice, the Duce was convinced that he had persuaded Hitler to show prudence and realism, especially on the question of Austria. Instead he found himself humiliated and misled internationally and in Italy as well, because his ally's wife, his own guest, had to leave as a widow.

Before returning to Rome, the Duce ordered four Italian army divisions stationed in the Val Gardena, in the Dolomite mountains, to be moved up to the Italian-Austrian border at the Brenner Pass. He also sent a message of solidarity to Vice Chancellor Starhemberg, declaring that Italy would continue to defend Austrian independence. "The memory of Dollfuss will be honored not only in Austria but in all the civilized world which has already morally condemned those responsible, be they directly or indirectly involved." The reference to Hitler could not have been clearer. Finally, Mussolini sent instructions to Italian diplomats in Paris and London to ask the British and French governments: "In the event of a German counterattack, what support could Italy expect to receive." London answered that it needed to consult with Paris; Paris replied that it would give Italy "absolute freedom of action."

King Victor Emanuel III, whose experience with the former allies of the First World War when dealing with Germany was more extensive than Mussolini's, reacted to the troop movements the Duce had ordered by telling him:

"If it is for prestige, go ahead and mobilize all the soldiers you wish, but if you think it could mean war, then I am resolutely opposed to it. We don't go to war to save a concubine [i.e., Austria] that has been courting Berlin since 1918."

On September 6, 1934, in Bari, Mussolini gave a speech to a crowd of local Fascists. He was answering Hitler's assertions in Venice regarding the superiority of the Germanic race compared to the Mediterranean peoples, and did not mince his words:

"Thirty centuries of history allow us Italians to consider the pitiful theories that come from the other side of the Alps, theories concocted by the offspring of men who could not write and could therefore not inform us of their own existence at the time when Rome already had Caesar, Virgil, Augustus. Italy had a centuries' old civilization when Berlin was still a marshland populated by wild boars."

But both Paris and London were content at leaving the entire problem in Mussolini's hands. French Ambassador André François-Poncet wrote in his memoirs: "Had France and Britain made a move, it would have been disastrous for Hitler."

From the Foreign Office and the Quai d'Orsay, the only actions were simple notes protesting in lofty words against German behavior. Only on September 27, 1934, did Rome, London, and Paris issue a common declaration in defense of Austrian independence.

At the beginning of August 1934, Vice Chancellor Starhemberg came to thank Mussolini for his intervention during the tragic days at the end of July and to prepare a meeting between the Duce and

Schuschnigg. He also inspected the "Austria camp" near Ostia where members of the Jung-Vaterland, a right-wing youth movement supported by Italy, were being trained. Starhemberg welcomed Mussolini at the camp and spoke about the gratitude of Austria towards Italy, concluding with a wish to see Mussolini continue to support Vienna until his country was freed from the dangers that threatened its independence.

In a private meeting Mussolini told Starhemberg: "What I did I did for Europe! If this group of criminals and pederasts should take over in Europe, it would mean the end of our civilization." Starhemberg then gave an account of the events that proved beyond a doubt that "the attempted coup in Vienna had been organized by the government of the Reich." They had found various agents infiltrating from the north, new shipments of brand new Mausers, and propaganda material.

Mussolini replied:

"It's a fact that this putsch was organized by the Nazi government. The Reich Chancellor had ordered the murder of Dollfuss." Then, without raising his voice, he repeated three times: "Hitler is the murderer. Hitler is the murderer. Hitler is the murderer." He went on repeating how much he despised the Führer: "A dangerous madman, a revolting individual, a sexual degenerate. Hitler will create an army, will rearm the German people, and go to war, perhaps in two to three years. I can't hold him off by myself. Something must be done immediately."

Two days later, Starhemberg returned to Vienna to tell Schuschnigg that Mussolini was ready to meet with him. The meeting took place in Florence on August 21.

That meeting was to reestablish the principle of Austrian independence. Instead, and incredibly so, it marked the beginning of the Anschluss, just as Hitler had planned. Schuschnigg essentially eluded every effort Mussolini made to have Austria accept a treaty open to the participation of other countries that would guarantee the sovereignty of Austria. In addition, the Chancellor was to surprise the Duce by declaring quite candidly that: "The passage of Italian troops north of the Brenner Pass would not have been politically acceptable."

Italian diplomat Eugenio Morreale commented upon Schuschnigg's sudden declaration:

"Mussolini knew about this attitude in part because of the biographical notes concerning Schuschnigg that clearly showed him not be an admirer of the Italy that had won the First World War at Vittorio Veneto. However, to have declared his open aversion to the passage of Italian soldiers in Austria, especially now that they were talking about alliances, was equivalent to precluding any Italian military assistance, and to handing over the country because Germany was rearming and about to do as it pleased in Europe."

Nine days after this meeting, Mussolini, having understood that the Italian army would not be welcome in Austria even to defend its independence, said to his closest aides (much to their amazement): "We must stop talking about Austrian independence; that is a matter for Vienna to worry about." Schuschnigg was to remember this sudden halt by Mussolini when, on February 12, 1938, Hitler was to bully him at Berchtesgaden, forbidding him to smoke and forcing him to sign a new treaty that practically sealed the fate of Austria as an independent state.

Mussolini also would recall the consequences of the August 21, 1934, meeting in 1938 when he declared to the Italian parliament: "When an event such as the union between Austria and Germany is fated to take place, it is best that it happen with you rather than in spite of you or, even worse, against you . . . "

The meeting in Venice, appearances to the contrary, was clearly the most important meeting between Hitler and Mussolini, not because it was the first meeting or because of what was said, but because of its immediate consequences that in sum gave a clear picture of the kind of person the new German Chancellor was. In less than two months, from June 14 to August 21, 1934, the Duce had about five examples to ponder: the savage purge within the Nazi party; the aborted Vienna putsch; the horrible murder of his friend Dollfuss; the indifference of France and England; and the rejection by Schuschnigg of the pro-Italian policies of his predecessor.

III

The Duce in Germany

Munich-Berlin:
September 25-29, 1937

Hitler's personal invitation to Mussolini to visit Germany was delivered on September 23, 1936 by Hans Frank, Reich minister of justice, who was in Rome for an international legal conference, thus completely bypassing the new Italian Ambassador to Berlin, Count Bernardo Attolico. Frank, whose political career was to end on the gallows at Nuremberg in 1946, was best known as the legal defender of the Nazis during the innumerable trials of the 1930s. Well educated, dynamic, and extremely efficient, Frank was part of the Führer's closest staff. A student of the humanities, and lover of the arts, of good food, and Mediterranean sunshine, he led the pro-Italian faction within the Nazi party that was locked in a struggle with the pro-British group gathered around Goebbels and von Ribbentrop.

Mussolini accepted the invitation with some reservations, since he had many other complicated issues to address. In the course of a pleasant conversation Frank, was careful to demonstrate to the

Duce his unequivocal admiration for the achievements of the "world's foremost statesman," as the Führer had referred to Mussolini. After the meeting, Frank hurried back to the German embassy to phone the news to Berlin that Mussolini would honor Hitler with a return visit after their initial encounter in Venice.

Pleased with his success, Frank invited his entire entourage to dinner to celebrate. At dinner, he told everyone how the Duce had answered his question, "How did Italy reach a compromise with the Catholic Church?" with one of his categorical aphorisms: "The fight against religion is useless; religion is like the fog, you can't grab it with your hands!" Those words were bound to make an impression on the Führer, who was being pressured by many Nazis to increase the struggle against Jews and Catholics.

Months went by and Mussolini was unable to set a date for his trip to Germany. Hitler kept the idea alive by dispatching, almost every week, one of his men to Rome under various pretenses. Among this group of "commuters" the best known was Göring, Hitler's closest aide. In May 1937, Mussolini renewed his promise to go to Germany to General von Blomberg, the German War Minister, who had been invited by the Italian high command to attend the yearly maneuvers. Finally, in August, Mussolini informed the Germans that he could travel during the month of September. The only preconditions were that he would not have to wear the formal black coat and striped pants of the prime minister and would be able to have direct contact with the German masses.

Three years after the June 1934 meeting, which had ended with cold good-byes at the Grand Hotel in Venice, many events had taken place in Europe and in Africa, but most of all, both dictators had increased their power and their prestige. Hitler had won the plebiscite that reunited the Saar to Germany on January 13, 1935, and had reinstated universal conscription on March 16, 1935. On March 7, 1936, he proceeded to remilitarize the Rhineland with Britain's acquiescence, thus overcoming any French objections. Britain had entered into a naval agreement with Germany on June 18, 1935, which—as Sir Ivone Kirkpatrick was to write—amounted to forgiving Germany for having blatantly breached the Versailles treaty and allowed Germany to build a navy that would reach up to thirty-five percent of the strength of the Royal Navy. Britain had in effect rehabilitated the Nazi government without informing France or Italy, with whom it had signed the three-power Stresa Pact on April 11, 1935, which was essentially directed against Germany.

The Führer had successfully drawn every advantage from the many crises that erupted between Rome and its former Anglo-French allies after the assassination of Dollfuss, when Mussolini was left to fend for himself in facing the Nazis. Then came the Ethiopian crisis with the ineffective sanctions against Italy on November 18, 1935—sanctions that had pushed Mussolini, out of necessity, toward Hitler, who was only too happy to sell, at exorbitant prices, all the supplies Italy needed until the conclusion of the war in East Africa on May 5, 1936. It became clear that British policy, especially regarding the war in Ethiopia, was aimed at driving a wedge between the two dictators, in the hope that on any one issue, Austria, Alto Adige Tyrol, or the Balkan and Yugoslav issues, or other rivalries, they would end up quarreling. But as time passed, the two dictatorships found more reasons to converge than to fight, as in the case of the Spanish Civil War, which was still raging while the Duce was preparing for his German visit.

Hitler's opportunism at this time in European politics was confirmed in a secret speech he made to his generals on November 5, 1937: "A one hundred percent victory for Franco is not in our interest, since we will benefit if the Spanish civil war continues and increases tension within the Mediterranean." This is corroborated in a report from the German Ambassador in Rome: "The Spanish conflict could have the same result as the Ethiopian war had in relations between Italy, France, and Britain. This will push Italy even further to Germany's side."

The Duce was not to be outdone by anyone when it came to opportunism. Once Germany recognized Italy's East African Empire on October 24, 1936, Mussolini thanked the Führer for his friendship in a speech in Milan's Piazza del Duomo on November 1, and launched the formula of the "Axis" with the following words:

"The conversations in Berlin—between the Führer and For-eign Minister Ciano—have produced an agreement between our two countries regarding a number of particularly serious problems. But these agreements, which have been set in the appropriate docu-ments and duly signed, this vertical Berlin-Rome line is no dia-phragm; it is, more appropriately, an axis, around which all Euro-pean states can converge in the search for collaboration and peace."

However, as soon as he returned to Rome, and after reflecting on his speech, the Duce summoned the correspondent of the *Daily Mail* for an interview intended to be conciliatory toward Britain. The British were unhappy at the moment about the conclusion of the Ethiopian affair and in a state of panic regarding the events in Spain. In that interview, Mussolini said: "Anglo-Italian interests in the Mediterranean are not antagonistic but complementary." It was a positive move. The declaration succeeded in opening the way to the "Gentlemen's Agreement" of January 2, 1937, signed by Sir Eric Drummond and Galeazzo Ciano, stating that both Italy and Great Britain "would respect the status quo in the Mediterranean," clearly alluding to the inevitable outcome of the Spanish Civil War in Franco's favor. The document would serve as a useful blueprint for all countries engaged in supporting either side of the conflict.

Mussolini was the first—among many others—to understand what Hitler expected to obtain from the visit to Germany of the founder of Italian Fascism and of the Italian East African Empire: mainly Austria, a problem in limbo since the tragic days of 1934. Mussolini's only concession was to propose a friendship and non-aggression agreement between Rome and Vienna on July 11, 1936, with important secret clauses—amnesty for the Austrian Nazis guilty of political crimes, authorization for many to return to Austria, and nominations to government posts of important Nazi party mem-bers. The departure of E. R. Starhemberg—Mussolini's friend and high level informant in Austria—was part of the bargain, and Schuschnigg forced his resignation from the post of vice chancel-lor of the Austrian government.

Mussolini thought that, with this agreement, he had the Aus-trian problem under control once again. But Hitler would not relent: he wanted all of Austria, without any reductions or compromises.

On January 15, 1937, Göring, the "commuter," came to the Palazzo Venezia with a proposal: "since Rome and Berlin are, as you said, an "Axis," we should move very quickly to remove any obstacles that could throw it off balance. Austria is one of those obstacles, and it is a problem very close to the Führer's heart, sentimentally among other reasons." Göring concluded: "We should certainly not waste time on a negative position for the sake of seven million Austrian good-for-nothings!" These silly words to describe such an explosive issue angered Mussolini, bringing him up out of his chair to reply on the top of his voice: "No *Anschluss*! The July agreement gives you a free hand. Try at least to respect appearances!"

On September 13, Mussolini informed King Victor Emanuel III of his trip to Germany: "My trip is more to show the solidarity between the two regimes, rather than having any political-diplomatic significance. It will end with a rally in Berlin with speeches by Goebbels, Hitler, and finally myself." At half past noon on September 24, 1937, Mussolini left Rome by special train carrying about one hundred "pilgrims," Foreign Minister Galeazzo Ciano and his deputy, Filippo Anfuso, Dino Alfieri, head of the press office, and Achille Starace, secretary of the Fascist party.

Mussolini had become extremely impatient during the preparations for the trip. The requests by Fascist leaders to be included in the historic traveling party were much greater than the available space. Those excluded and shunted aside formed a disgruntled group demanding participation in any future travel. The happy few had to buy new uniforms, complete down to the boots, since any civilian clothes were strictly forbidden.

Roberto Farinacci, the pro-German and anti-Semitic loudmouth, best known as the "mother-in-law" of the Fascist regime, having no official reason to be on board Mussolini's train, was sent off separately to attend the Nazi party congress at Nuremberg as the Italian Fascist representative. It was the same for Marshal Pietro Badoglio, who as army chief of staff went privately with General

Pariani and Admiral Cavagnari to Mecklenburg to attend the maneuvers of the German army. Just before leaving, Mussolini took pains to show his entourage that he was going to Germany as a chore more than anything else, given Hitler's insistent invitations: "Let's see what this strange individual has to say to me," he kept on repeating.

Hitler was about to put on the most lavish spectacle the world had seen, intent on demonstrating, in the most brutally visible way, the strength and iron discipline the German people had mastered in every field: technical, industrial, and military. French Ambassador François-Poncet, wrote:

"Everything was designed to flatter the Duce, to excite his pride, and at the same time, to strike his imagination with an organizational display of power that was truly extraordinary. Never before had a ruling monarch been greeted by Germany with such glory. In Munich and Berlin preparations were made on a colossal scale."

Preceded by an advance train, Mussolini's convoy, made up of two locomotives, five sleeping cars, a restaurant car, and a baggage car, picked up speed quickly towards Florence. In Bologna, Rachele Mussolini and their children, Romano and Anna Maria, were on the platform to greet the Duce. In Trento, the train stopped for the night. The next hours were to be very eventful, first with the Austrians, who were always complaining and requesting favors.

Cristano Ridòmi, head of the press office at the Italian embassy in Vienna, remembers Mussolini's passing through: "In August, before going to Vienna, I was received by Galeazzo Ciano, who told me: 'The Austrians are our friends. The Germans are also our friends, but they are uncomfortable friends to have, especially on our borders. So now you know how to view things. Good luck and write to me personally if you have some confidential information.'

"The head of the Italian legation was Senator Francesco Salata, who was originally from Lussimpiccolo in the Adriatic. Salata was one of those traditional Italian patriots who, having been raised under the Austrian Empire and despite ingrained antagonism, retained much respect for the old order it represented and especially for Vienna, its capital. He was a middle European, comfortable in the Mitteleuropa that Italy should have used more judiciously to counterbalance the rise of German power . . . Salata was optimistic about Germany, or at least he pretended to be, following the agreements of July 11, 1936, which had created a sense of equilibrium, despite the vast concessions made by Schuschnigg toward the common German 'race.' Salata had been a smart and clever negotiator. He had been rewarded with the post of Minister to Vienna.

"On the morning of September 24, we took a train to Innsbruck to wait for the passing of Mussolini's train the next day on his way to Berlin; a trip that was to have important consequences. A police officer came to tell us that two terrorists had been identified but not yet apprehended. We dreaded the possibility of harm coming to the head of the Italian government on Austrian territory: he was still the only political figure who had shown any courage after the murder of Dollfuss and had sent four Italian divisions to the Brenner Pass. We waited for news late into the night, then we all went to sleep, hoping for the best. The Italian train stopped for just a few minutes in Innsbruck the next day. It was a beautiful train. The shining cars looked as if they had just been manufactured. High Fascist officials looked out the windows in their well-pressed uniforms, ready to receive the lacquered decorations of the Third Reich. No one got off the train, since it had been agreed that it was only transiting. Only the local authorities were on the platform, and Mussolini saluted them very quickly. He walked on Austrian soil for the first and last time.

"A unit of Alpen-Jaeger with the red faces of mountaineers of about ten men, was reviewed. After the soldiers, it was our turn as representatives of the Italian legation. Mussolini did not look at anyone, and proceeded, almost running, as if he had absolutely no interest either in that stop or in those people. He got quickly back on his train and resumed his journey. Salata had boarded the train with the help of Filippo Anfuso. He was to stay on board until the German border and return a few hours later. Mussolini had not spoken to him."

At the Austro-German border at Kiefersfelden, the Führer's Deputy, Rudolf Hess, came on board. Shortly thereafter, the train arrived at Munich. On the platform of the station, festooned with German and Italián flags, Hitler stood waiting, dressed in a new and well-tailored uniform. The meeting between Hitler and Mussolini looked like a bizarre loving embrace. The Duce was driven to his apartment in the Prinz Karl Palais for his short stay. The walls were covered with old master paintings commandeered from local museums, among them a Rubens and a Lenbach. Hitler then received Mussolini in his luxurious private residence at 16 Prinzregentenstrasse, but he did not show the Duce the mausoleum room where his niece and lover, Geli Raubal, committed suicide on September 18, 1931. Hitler also was careful to avoid having Eva Braun present, and the honors were made by the Führer's beautiful and faithful housekeeper.

Once in his private study, Hitler anxiously expected Mussolini to offer him Austria, the gift he coveted the most. Instead, Mussolini pulled out a long parchment proclaiming Hitler honorary corporal of the Italian Fascist militia, as "Leader of the German people who has given Germany renewed faith in its greatness. Builder of public, political, and social order, he guides with a firm hand the German nation to its highest destiny. He has proclaimed and defended European civilization against any attempted subversion; he has given Italy, in moments of trial, his great solidarity and friendship." Hitler conferred on Mussolini the Iron Cross of greater Germany. The Duce had a precise request on his agenda that Italy not be left with the heavy burden of supplying all aid to Franco in Spain, because it now appeared that the war would last much longer than previously foreseen (it would conclude only in March 1939, when Madrid finally fell to the Nationalists).

According to Mussolini, no promises regarding Austria's fate were made, as he related to King Victor Emanuel III in his report of October 4, 1937:

"My trip to Munich and Berlin, as intended, was essentially a demonstration of friendship. The only political conversation took place in the Führer's private apartment in Munich, where Hitler confirmed that he would continue sending help to Spain in the form of war supplies. Göring, on the other hand, did speak about

Austria to reassure me that no move would take place in that direction without a prior agreement with Italy. My impression is that the Reich has by no means given up on the *Anschluss* but is only waiting for events to take their course."

Between the lines of this report, we can already see a Mussolini who is tired "of being the lonely guardian of the Treaty of Versailles in defense of Austria." The Duce was ready to accept the *Anschluss* as long as he was informed of the Nazi plans in advance. The Italian minister, Alessandro Lessona, wrote in his memoirs:

"Hitler had told the Duce back in 1937 that he was determined to annex Austria to Germany and that this was a precondition to their friendship. Mussolini told me this in confidence in July of that year."

Therefore, Mussolini, upon visiting Munich, was ready to accept the bitter taste of the Austrian pill as long as it allowed him to save face. It appears that following the meeting in Hitler's Munich apartment, there had been a second meeting between the dictators in Berlin. The Führer had no intention of letting the Duce leave, after having spent millions of Reich marks to celebrate his visit, without some kind of approval for his plans for Austria, even those in the more distant future. According to some observers, the agreement was part of a secret pact that established: "If either one of the two parties were to seek a closer relationship with Great Britain, the other party would benefit proportionately. . . " This being clearly intended to thwart any British initiatives to drive a wedge between the Axis partners. And finally, "The interests and opportunities for Italy in Spain and the Mediterranean will not be opposed by Germany, just as special German interests in Austria will not be opposed by Italy."

A lunch with the Alten Kameraden—the old Nazi party members—ended that morning in Munich. In the afternoon, Mussolini paid his respects at the monument dedicated to the Nazis who had died during the failed putsch of 1923, and then he visited the Brown House, of which Hitler was particularly proud, having personally overseen its refurbishing and decoration as "proof" of his artistic capabilities. A long parade on the Königsplatz of Nazi party troops marked the end of that intense day in Munich. That evening, the entire party left Munich for Mecklenburg to see the final moments of the military maneuvers by the Wermacht and the Luftwaffe. The Italian generals under the direction of Marshal Badoglio were already present.

As Filippo Anfuso wrote:

"Mussolini saw the new Messerschmitt fighters and air ace Ernst Udet—who was to commit suicide on November 18, 1941, after many clashes with Göring—who landed his Storch plane almost perpendicularly a few feet away from the tree where the two dictators were watching the event. It was one of the very first Storch planes, and it made a considerable impression. These would be the planes that made the 1943 liberation of Mussolini possible when he was a prisoner of Marshal Badoglio at Campo Imperatore, waiting to be handed over to the advancing allies. Marshal Badoglio had a brief meeting with Mussolini and was able to tell the Duce that he had seen nothing exceptional in the German maneuvers, that both men and equipment had appeared mediocre and that Italy was far ahead in all fields, not to mention the great strides made by the French army.

"Hitler had concentrated, on a long and gray beach, all types of artillery pieces and machine guns that opened an intense fire on moving targets with tracer bullets: green, red, and turquoise. Huge fireworks lit up the entire scene. When we returned, we found the villages of Mecklenburg filled with thousands of school children. There were too many of them to all be from the region; they had probably been brought there from the surrounding areas; their happiness and cheering betrayed the enthusiasm of having the day off more than anything else."

The superficial and biased opinion voiced by Marshal Badoglio on the state of preparedness of the German army would be sufficient to cast doubt over his judgment as well as that of the other Italian general staff officers. Mussolini, a former corporal in World War I, was impressed by what he had seen, especially the armored divisions and the dive-bombing exercises by the Stukas. But when writing his report to the King, Mussolini said: "In Germany, rearmament is proceeding very quickly. As things stand, we have little to learn from it. During the military review in Berlin, there was no lack of incidents and foul-ups." The Mecklenburg visit ended with mutual congratulations between the two dictators. Essen was the third stop of the journey, and both trains were now en route at full speed. At lunch on the train, the Italian high command, Badoglio, Pariani, Cavagnari, and Valle, were guests at the Führer's table, while Mussolini was entertaining his old friend Göring, who kept reminding him about Austria.

Essen was the world capital of the steel industry and the birthplace of the Krupp dynasty. Gustav von Bohlen, the head of the clan, was on hand to welcome the two dictators. He had become "Krupp: in 1906 by decree of Kaiser Wilhelm II after his wedding to the famous Bertha, who was also present on that morning of September 27, 1937. Mussolini was amazed at the gigantic proportions of the iron works and the monstrous steel press that weighed 1,500 tons, a giant cannon and the incredible cleanliness of the factory floors. As Anfuso noted: "Krupp von Bohlen introduced the cannon as if they were children dressed up in Sunday clothes: he was not really a merchant of death; the cannon had come to him through his wife, a dignified and retiring lady who was introduced to Mussolini. Hitler paid his respects very formally. I saw so many guns, enough to give me stomach ache, and exactly at the moment when I could no longer take it, I noticed that we had been taken aside and not all of us were allowed to follow the two dictators past certain steel doors which led to other special rooms where more secret cannons were on display. It was a vision meant only for the faithful ... In front of each one of these doors stood something of a super general who allowed only Hitler, Mussolini, Ciano, and Krupp inside.

"Fortunately Heinrich Hoffmann, Hitler's photographer, whom no one could resist, was able to slip in with the group and left us a picture of the two dictators looking at the barrel of a truly colossal cannon, as Mussolini later described it. We can't fully see the cannon in the photograph for security reasons, but you can see Hitler showing off, as it were, his newborn child. Mussolini walked through the factory and the rest of the steelworks while Hitler explained in detail the political evolution of the workers, their long Communist past and their gradual but complete switch to National Socialism."

The two trains left Essen on parallel tracks as if to symbolize the identity of views of both regimes. As it reached Berlin Hitler's train overtook that of his Italian guest so that the Reich chancellor could be on the platform to welcome the Duce. Mussolini could certainly remember his previous visit as a news reporter to Berlin in March 1922. Back then, he stayed at the Hessler Hotel near the zoo, and he interviewed the leaders of the Weimar Republic, including Walther Rathenau. A left wing Berlin daily attacked Mussolini in harsh terms as "the betrayer of the Italian people," making him welcome to the German right wing of the time. As Anfuso wrote:

"Mussolini saw Berlin from an angle that comprised most of its population. Hitler had the trains stop at the Kaiserdamm station so that he could line up on this interminable avenue and up the chancellery on the Wilhelmstrasse a few square miles of Germans. On the station platform, the entire Nazi leadership was present, two rows deep and in perfect order (apart from Göring, who stood one step ahead of the others): Goebbels, Himmler, Neurath, Schacht, and all the generals stood at rigid attention, waiting for the Duce to walk by. This disciplined review of the most illustrious representatives of the Nazi leadership impressed Mussolini favorably when compared to the picturesque disorder displayed by his own party leaders. Under a steady rain, we boarded the large open cars to take the longest possible route, allowing millions of Berliners to see the Duce and the Führer sitting side by side in the same car."

The heavy rain reinvigorated the visitors who had spent some four days almost uninterruptedly traveling by train. A state dinner was offered that evening at the Reich chancellery for two hundred high officials, including the entire diplomatic corps. Early the next morning, September 28, Mussolini visited the palace of Sans Souci, with its famous orchids, and the tomb of Frederick the Great in Potsdam. He then paid a visit to the Italian embassy and the Fascist house. The high points of the day were to be the lunch offered by Göring and the speech at the Maifeld.

The occasion to engage in what could be referred to as "agritourism" was carefully choreographed by Göring at his manor, Karinhall, about seventy kilometers northeast of Berlin. The 100,000-acre area had been donated to Göring by the Prussian state, and he had built an ostentatious villa made up of various wings around an old farmhouse. Göring had designed everything himself: the entire construction and furnishings, buildings, gardens, decorations, moldings, furniture, tapestries, statues, and even the burial chapel dedicated to his wife Karin, who had died some years before and to whose memory the manor was dedicated.

Anfuso noted: "Göring spared no expense to honor the Duce's visit and prepared a lavish reception. He owned a lake and a forest, and in that forest was a company of soldiers who doubled as guards and groundskeepers. On a hill overlooking a river, Göring had built his royal palace, bursting with paintings, porcelains, miniature watercolors, tapestries, tables, and chairs fit for a lord of the manor, miniature airfields with tiny bomber airplanes . . . Giant-looking servants and plump hausfraus who walked about this encampment dressed in ancient hunter's costumes with a horn at their side."

The lunch Göring had offered was as oversized as the rest of his property and certainly not to the Duce's liking. Mussolini was intrigued to see in one of the living rooms a model train with dozens of cars and locomotives powered by an electric panel. It was obvious that the toy was intended for the childless Göring himself. While the visitors had tea, two young lion cubs came into the living room and proceeded to playfully bite the very frightened guests. The high point of the trip, the speeches at the Maifeld, was approaching. Berlin had been invaded since dawn by millions of Germans from all over the country. That morning, about 800,000 people had been seated in the sports complex, and special clean-up teams had rid the area of the garbage left over by campers.

The appearance of Hitler and Mussolini was welcomed by a huge ovation from the crowd. As Gauleiter of Berlin, Goebbels spoke first, offering the city's welcome to the illustrious visitor. Hitler then began by declaring Mussolini "one of those few men who are not just part of history but who actually make history." The Führer then warmly thanked Italy as a country that "never had a part in the humiliations inflicted upon our people, but that actually had welcomed the demands of a great nation that was only asking for equal treatment and equal rights to fulfill the needs of its material existence and sacred national honor." Hitler then concluded: "The strength of our two countries represents today the best chance to preserve a Europe consistent with its civilizing mission, unwilling to fall and dissolve itself under the threat of destructive forces."

An autumn thunderstorm poured a steady rain over Berlin. The marching bands continued playing military music, and when it was Mussolini's turn to step up to the podium with his prepared speech in hand, the rain turned into a violent storm. The Duce stuck to his program even though he could barely read his speech. What he said was difficult to understand because of the poor acoustics and his very approximate German with its distinctly southern accent.

"My visit to Germany and its Führer and the speech I am about to give are important events for me and in the history of our peoples. Fascism and Nazism are two expressions of the historical parallel positions that draw our two nations closer together, having become united during the same century . . . To the people all over the world questioning what will come out of this Berlin meeting, war or peace, both the Führer and I can answer together in a loud voice: peace."

Mussolini, handling his dates loosely, stated that the Axis between Rome and Berlin was born in the fall of 1935 and that it had worked well up to now "for an increasing understanding between our two countries and an effective policy of peace in Europe."

Well aware that the Italians, after 1914, were considered the champions of switching partners in the middle of the waltz when it came to alliances, Mussolini added pointedly: "Fascism has its code to which it intends to remain faithful, and this is also my own code: speak clearly and openly, and when we are friends, march together until the end." Mussolini's final words were the signal to the crowd to leave the Olympic stadium and return through the streets singing the national anthems of both countries. It was a truly Wagnerian third act to the meetings.

As Filippo Anfuso wrote: "I was still with Schmidt, who kept silent. We returned to the palace on the Wilhelmstrasse—the foreign ministry—where Mussolini was staying in von Hindenburg's former residence. We were brought into the Duce's apartment; he was drenched but pleased. He was at his best in the crowds, and that day, he'd had more than he could hope for . . . He was not so impressed by the choreography of the events, but the order and enthusiasm of the crowds had greatly impressed him." Mussolini returned to his room to change and call his mistress, Claretta Petacci: "It was a triumph. I want to feel you close to me at this special moment."

The next day, Mussolini had a farewell review of the troops at Charlottenburg. Again the sound of goose-stepping jackboots, cannon, and armored vehicles, enough for a lifetime. Finally, at 3:45 p.m. on September 29, the Italian train left Berlin to return to Rome. At the station came a final farewell from Hitler: "What I am for Germany, you, Duce, are for Italy. But what we shall both be for Europe will be judged by future generations."

No official communiqué was issued on the Hitler-Mussolini meetings. The semi-official Italian news agency, Stefani, issued a statement saying that the Duce's trip to Germany "had nothing in common with the usual state visits." The events of September 25 to 29, 1937, were statements in and of themselves. But German precision could not just let the trip pass without comment, and German diplomatic offices throughout the world received the following instructions: "Both parties want a rapid conclusion to the Spanish Civil War and the reconstruction of Spain; priority in this area will go to Italy, which will in no way be hampered by Germany in the Mediterranean, while the special German interests in Austria will not be hampered by Italy. It is however true as stated by Mussolini that the Rome-Berlin Axis is not directed against any other country and nothing has been discussed or decided that could be considered damaging or threatening to the independence of Austria."

The note contained specific references to Austria and Spain, for which the Duce had vague Napoleonic designs, such as offering the Spanish crown to the Italian Duke Amedeo d'Aosta, a cousin of King Victor Emanuel III. The note therefore contained some of the topics of the secret agreement reached in Munich referred to above. The train stopped in Verona—after a night filled with telegrams of congratulations and thanks—because the poet Gabriele D'Annunzio, who had come down from his palace in Gardone to pay his respects to the Duce, was waiting on the platform. It was well known that Mussolini was always on edge whenever he met the poet, mainly because any conversation with D'Annunzio always ended in pleas for money for his household or for the Vittoriale Foundation which had been donated to the Italian state in advance of his death. This, however, was to be the final meeting with D'Annunzio, who died on March 1, 1938, and was thus spared the sight, unacceptable to him, of Nazi troops marching into Vienna.

Italians were to learn on March 12, 1938, that Austria had finally fallen into Hitler's clutches. It is impossible not to make the connection between this event and Mussolini's visit to Germany even though both dictators had given each other as many alibis and congratulatory statements as possible. The final operation regarding Austria began on February 11, 1938, when Chancellor Schuschnigg was suddenly summoned to visit Hitler at Berchtesgaden for a meeting to "clear the air" of any misunderstandings between the two German-speaking countries. Von Papen had prepared the summit just before leaving Vienna to become German ambassador to Ankara. Schuschnigg bravely accepted the invitation to visit the Führer even though he suspected that it could be an ambush. Hitler, through von Papen, had promised to respect the agreement of July 11, 1936. Schuschnigg had naively prepared a surprise offer, should Hitler become more demanding and to close the issue of Nazi demands by offering Germany the birthplace of its Führer, the small village of Braunau.

During the evening of February 11, 1938, Kurt von Schuschnigg and the Austrian foreign minister, Guido Schmidt, who was more or less a Nazi agent by that time, had arrived by car at Salzburg. The next morning, accompanied by von Papen, the two Austrians reached the famed "Eagle's Nest" where Hitler was waiting for them, surrounded by Generals Keitel, Reichenau, and Sperrle, creating an atmosphere that was quite the opposite of a friendly conversation.

Schuschnigg ignored the implied threats and began chatting about the weather and the beautiful snow and how wonderful it was to breathe the mountain air. Hitler reacted brutally, suspecting some kind of trick that the Austrian chancellor may have up his sleeve, and cut off his small talk by saying: "We're not here to comment on the scenery." Hitler went into one of his famous tirades, slamming his fist on the table: "The Austrians are traitors when they consider themselves different from other Germans."

Hitler, the former Austrian, humiliated in his youth in Vienna by the teachers who had flunked him out of the entrance examination to the school of fine arts, the rebel son of the customs official of the Hapsburgs, which all pan-German ideologues held responsible for all the ills of the German-speaking peoples, the man who left Vienna in 1913 because, he was to say later, it was the "nest of every pestilence, moral and ideological . . . "—this was the enraged Hitler facing the Austrian Chancellor.

For two hours, Schuschnigg had the most virulent accusations hurled at him by the relentless Führer, who suddenly came to the heart of the matter:

"I have a historical mission to accomplish, and I shall see it through because Providence has directed this course for me, and those not willing to cooperate with me shall be mercilessly destroyed. Your border defenses are ridiculous, and I can blow them away in one night. But it is my wish to spare the Austrian people a river of blood, because following the regular military units will come the SS and the Austrian legion that have been trained in Bavaria. Then no one will be able to stop the sacred revenge that will follow."

And just as suddenly, Hitler calmed down and looked at his watch and, with a disarming smile, invited his guest to the second-floor dining room for lunch. Schuschnigg remained alone with Braun at the end of the meal while Hitler took a two-hour break with von Papen and the new Nazi foreign minister, von Ribbentrop. It was a long wait.

Finally, the Austrian chancellor was brought into Hitler's study, and lying there on the table was the final act in two thickly typed pages spelling out the future of an Austria integrated to the greater Reich. Schuschnigg was destroyed, while von Ribbentrop kept repeating to him: "Sign it, sign it now, because once Hitler has decided upon a course, he never goes back." Hitler then cut in again: "Schuschnigg, I gave you half a day to think it over. I can wait no longer." Then Hitler called on General Keitel to come in. The Austrian Chancellor thought to himself: this time he will have me arrested. He signed the document in the hope of being allowed to return to Vienna, where he could, if need be, denounce the document and repudiate what he had done under duress.

There was an element of farce in this tragedy, once the Austrian chancellor had departed as fast as he could after refusing an invitation to stay for dinner as Hitler's guest. Keitel was then told he had been brought in to frighten Schuschnigg, not to arrest him. Everyone laughed. Von Papen confessed he had "suggested" to Schuschnigg that he sign the document because "now that Mussolini is deeply involved in Spain, he would no longer be able to help Austria"; neither could he count on the French and British.

On February 24, Schuschnigg spoke in Parliament to reiterate that Austrian independence was sacred and that on March 13, there would be a plebiscite to "affirm that Austria is free, independent, German, and Christian." Mussolini's comment on Schuschnigg's decision was: "It's a mistake." By then the Duce had decided to abandon the Austrian chancellor to his fate. Schuschnigg had failed to understand that only Mussolini could have done anything to save Austrian independence and probably still could have been cajoled into doing so by a more persuasive attitude.

Ciano told Undersecretary of State and Roosevelt advisor, Sumner Welles, during his fact-finding trip to Rome in 1940:

"Before the German occupation of Austria, Schuschnigg came to Rome. He admitted that if Germany marched into Austria, the majority of Austrians would have been in favor of such a move and that if Italy had sent troops into Austria, the Austrians would have supported the Germans against the Italians." Even though Schuschnigg denied having made such a statement after the war, it appears that, in substance, Ciano's perceptions were correct at the time.

Hitler reacted to the Vienna plebiscite announcement: a negative result for him would have been disastrous for his pan-German plans, an unacceptable outcome. He adopted emergency measures. First, he dispatched emissaries to Vienna to hand Schuschnigg an ultimatum: delay the plebiscite to prepare another election in agreement with Hitler. Schuschnigg agreed, but this was obviously no longer sufficient for Hitler, who now demanded all of Austria for himself and had already ordered the borders closed and the army to a state of readiness.

Meanwhile, Schuschnigg was calling on the Italian Embassy for help and advice, and the Italian Minister to Vienna, Pellegrini Ghigi, kept on calling Rome in a vain attempt to reach anyone in the government. Mussolini was not in Rome but at his private estate, the Rocca delle Caminate, near Forlì, and Ciano was nowhere to be found. Even the general secretary of the foreign ministry was not at his desk. Finally, in late afternoon, Filippo Anfuso answered the telephone:

"Rome," he said, "has nothing to say about this crisis. Our advice to the Austrian government in the past, went unheeded. We have no idea when Mussolini and Ciano will be back in their offices. Act as best you can without involving Rome in any way. Good luck."

The predator was now at the door, and at dawn on March 12, Nazi troops crossed the borders into Austria, welcomed by festive crowds chanting "Heil Hitler!" all the way. Flowers were strewn all over the streets, and swastika flags were to be seen everywhere. Hitler, in a radio address that morning, explained his move. Schuschnigg was nothing but a common criminal—he had already been arrested and replaced with the Nazi lawyer, Arthur Seyss-Inquart—and he, Hitler, had been compelled to intervene to prevent a false plebiscite from crushing the generous Austrian people under the yoke of a reactionary regime that was set on preventing its vote for freedom. At noon, Hitler fulfilled his twenty-five-year-old dream; he entered his hometown of Linz in triumph, just like a King, after a brief stop at his birthplace of Braunau-am-Inn. It was "a war of flowers," wrote Marshal von Manstein years later, recalling how the German troops were welcomed by the happy crowds. The new plebiscite engineered by Hitler and the Nazis confirmed the Anschluss by 99.75% yes votes in Austria and 99.08% yes votes in Germany. The secret agreement between Mussolini and Hitler had sealed the fate of Austria according to the prearranged script.

On Thursday, March 10, Hitler sent a letter to the Duce, predated the eleventh and brought by Prince Phillip of Hesse, the husband of King Victor Emanuel III's daughter, Princess Mafalda of Savoy. Ciano accompanied the princely postman to the Palazzo Venezia, where Mussolini carefully read the letter that stated, among other things:

"Your Excellency, at this fateful hour I must inform you of a decision that events have imposed upon me and can no longer be changed . . . In the past few months, I have witnessed with growing anxiety a budding friendship between Austria and Czechoslovakia . . . The Austrian state had begun reinforcing and fortifying its own borders . . . I have resolved to reestablish the rule of law and order in my native country . . . I wish to give Your Excellency as Duce of Fascist Italy the following assurances: I am acting only in self defense; I have set the border line between Germany and France, and now I can also trace the border between Germany and Italy: it is the Brenner Pass. This decision will never be changed nor subject to discussion." After reminding Mussolini how Germany had helped Italy during the sanctions that had been imposed by the League of Nations, Hitler closed his letter expressing regret at not being able to hand the Duce the document himself and speak to him face to face on such a momentous occasion.

As Anfuso was to write:

"The Duce, having read the letter, accepted its contents as best he could, shrugging off this checkmate of his Austrian policy. He then proceeded to study very carefully the manner in which the

Italian press was to present the whole affair and to be sure that it placed Italian policy in the most favorable light."

At 10:30 p.m., the Prince of Hesse telephoned the Führer: "I have just returned from the Palazzo Venezia. The Duce accepted the whole thing in the most friendly way, and he sends you his best regards."

"Tell Mussolini," replied an emotional Hitler, "that whatever happens, I shall never forget his gesture. Even if the entire world were to gang up against him, or if he were in danger, he can always count on my support." From March 12, 1938, Austria was effectively part of the German Reich.

Besides the Anschluss, Mussolini's visit to Germany produced two other events of paramount importance: on November 6, 1937, Italy joined the symbolic anti-Comintern Pact, which had already linked Berlin and Tokyo, and in August 1938, the Italian government enacted the anti-Semitic campaign, placing it under the supervision of the extremist Fascist leader, Roberto Farinacci. Finally, Mussolini made Germany fashionable in every respect: in the arts, film, and even cuisine, Germany was almost imposed upon the Italian public as the best choice in things foreign. Axis cultural centers sprouted up all over Italy and Germany, and cultural exchanges and commissions of all kinds were the order of the day in both countries.

Mussolini most admired the fact that Hitler had soldiers who were "handsome, strong, tall, blond, and fierce-looking," soldiers who knew how to march with their amazing goose step that was, in the Duce's words, "the greatest thing in the world to watch." The Duce was extremely envious, displaying an almost weird inferiority complex towards Nazi Germany. He made one of those decisions that were both silly and funny at the same time: Italian soldiers would also march with a new form of goose step that Mussolini christened the "passo romano," or the "Roman step," which, due to the smaller stature of the average Italian recruit, plus a few morphological characteristics that greatly differed from the tall Germans, became the laughing stock of Italy and the world. The experiment turned into something of a major propaganda disaster and it quickly became painful to watch the Roman Step displayed by certain units of the Italian army. Marshal Emilio De Bono told Mussolini:

"Even if you classify me as insane, I will tell you that with soldiers averaging five feet six, you'll have a ridiculous show of mechanical dwarfs."

The King, who was also very short (just about five feet), but who also had his reasons, tried to stop the decision to introduce this novelty into the Italian army. But nothing could modify Mussolini's decision. He vented his frustrations with Ciano:

"It's not my fault if King Victor Emanuel III is no taller than a bottle. Obviously he can't march with the Roman step without looking ridiculous. They say the goose step is Prussian. That's patently false. The goose is a purely Roman animal that saved the capitol of ancient Rome!"

The "new" forms of Fascist behavior that went far beyond the goose step, were introduced: the handshake was strictly forbidden and replaced with the Fascist salute for everyone; the form of address in the Italian language was changed from "lei" to "voi" in order to sound less "French"; and the multiplicity of new uniforms which looked more and more like their Nazi counterparts with peaked caps.

Despite all these "innovations," the Italian soldier went to war in 1940 with the same old leggings he had worn during the nineteenth century! The implacable executor of the Duce's wishes was Fascist party secretary Achille Starace, who unquestioningly issued directives to all Fascist federations throughout Italy and the world, laying down in minute detail the private and public manners of all party members. After the war in Ethiopia, derogatory political jokes began to circulate once again—the only form of protest against a humorless regime that was completely intolerant of any kind of opposition.

IV

The Führer In Italy

Rome-Naples-Florence:
May 3-9, 1938

O n the evening of September 28, 1937, while he was still stunned by the cheering German crowds at the end of his speech at the Maifeld, Mussolini called Ciano: "Galeazzo, when we get back to Rome, your most important job will be to set up the return match. We've been challenged here. We must win it regardless of the expense." The invitation for Hitler's visit to Italy was extended the very next day by the Duce in Berlin, without even consulting the real host, King Victor Emanuel III.

On February 28, 1938, the first rumors that Hitler was about to come to Italy began circulating. Twelve days later, the *Anschluss* exploded like a bomb. This "problem" delayed the preparations by twenty days, until the official Italian news agency, Stefani, confirmed the trip and even its date: "Rome—March 28, 1938—Hitler will be Italy's guest during the first half of May. He will visit our country for about one week. During his stay in Rome, he will be a guest at the Quirinal Palace. A vast program that will occupy the entire trip, including visits to Naples and Florence, as well as, among other events, an imposing review of the Italian navy, a parade by the armed forces . . . "

Obviously, this bulletin demonstrated better than any other that the Nazi coup in Austria had a liberating effect on Rome, knocking down a cumbersome barrier separating the two dictators. It was true that the issue of Alto Adige was still open, but Berlin was sending reassuring signals: Hitler would keep his promises, publicly and solemnly.

When he had visited Germany, Mussolini explicitly excluded any women from his party, even as secretaries. With a theatrical flourish, the Duce gave a masculine image to his regime. To emphasize the austerity that characterized Fascism, he had limited his delegation to one hundred. And he expected Hitler to do the same out of reciprocity. He was mistaken. The Duce's plans were to be severely altered. He originally wanted a much simpler and less costly welcome for Hitler. No German official would be able to travel, all expenses paid, to the Italian sunshine, alone, without his family, and not risk divorce.

Hitler did not like being far from Berlin for an entire week allowing his minions to run things, especially since those in charge would be unhappy to have been left behind. On the other hand, since Hitler was also Head of State, he had many more duties and administrators around him than Mussolini. The wife of the Italian Ambassador to Berlin, Eleonora Attolico, solved the problem by saying in the Berlin salons, "Everyone should go to Rome." That sounded very good to all those present. The first ladies of the Third Reich got started, and women's seamstresses worked as hard as the tailors to be ready. Hitler wanted to personally approve all the wardrobes to be sure that his "extras" would make him look good.

As Hitler's architect, Albert Speer, wrote:

"With his trip to Italy, Hitler wanted to show his gratitude to Mussolini for letting the German army march into Austria. The Duce had shown himself to be a disinterested and generous statesman because a neutral Austria was, for Italy, a useful buffer and therefore preferable. German troops were now at the Brenner Pass and this was bound to put pressure on Rome soon enough. With this trip to Italy, Hitler was pleased to see the monuments and art treasures of Rome and Florence. Elegant uniforms were prepared and approved of by Hitler for his entourage. He enjoyed luxury, and if he preferred to dress simply, it was part of an image he wished to project on the masses: 'My entourage should make a grand impression so that my own simplicity stands out even more.'"

When the Nazis began packing for their Italian vacation, Eva Braun demanded to be included in the party as her lover's secretary, as she was listed in her travel papers. Hitler was unable to deny his young girlfriend's wish but made sure she was with the guests and not part of the protocol.

Ciano, who had been appointed by Mussolini to direct the Hitler "operation," created a special office within the Foreign Ministry in November 1937. He created a perfect machine which succeeded in coordinating the movements of the various ministries that were to contribute to the visit. All the German-speaking Italian diplomats and employees of the foreign ministry were recalled to Rome for the occasion, and each one had a Nazi leader to handle and accompany as interpreter. Mario Luciolli, a young and promising diplomat who would go on to become Italian Ambassador to Germany in 1964, was assigned to the "terrible women," who, although not part of the official party, were to be present at every phase of the festivities.

Luciolli remembered:

"There were clearly two types: the holdover survivors of pre-Nazi Germany and the new princesses of the Third Reich. The lack of communication and inferiority complexes were visible in both camps, but they had different origins. The survivors despised the new ladies as representatives of a recent and grossly bad-mannered privileged class, while the Nazis despised the others as the remnants of a bourgeois world that the Nazis had not yet completely liquidated . . . The wife of Justice Minister Hans Frank was less impatient with the allure of Baroness von Weiszäcker, wife of the permanent state secretary of the foreign ministry, than by the young and elegant Madame von Bülow-Schwante, wife of the head of protocol. Annelie, wife of Foreign Minister Ribbentrop, looked down on Ilse, wife of party secretary Rudolf Hess and other more provincial ladies, who, in turn, envied her as they mistakenly thought her to be more refined than they themselves were.

"In the end, most of these social differences and antagonisms among wives were just the mirror of their husbands' . . . Right after the Italian visit, the chief of protocol, who had not been judged obsequious enough with the leadership, was 'fired' and sent off as ambassador to Brussels . . . In the days preceding the visit, some of my colleagues made fun of me and spread the rumor that I had been put in charge of the 'harem.' I would respond by showing the identity photos we had received to be used on the identity tags for my flock. The malicious smiles were replaced by funny expressions of sympathy!"

The first German to arrive in Italy was Walter Schellenberg of the SD, the secret police within the SS, who was to organize security for the visit. Dozens of Gestapo agents, dressed as ordinary tourists, were placed on the itinerary Hitler would follow from the border to Naples. The Italian police also arrested and detained about six thousand suspects. On the Italian side, preparations were difficult. Organizers had to write and rewrite the lists of guests to each ceremony. Diplomatic rules of precedence did not apply so easily. The owners of buildings along the railroad tracks from the Brenner Pass to Rome had their houses cleaned even though some walls were full of pro-Nazi graffiti. Even the King came out a winner. Ciano made the poisonous comment when visiting the apartment of the crown prince in the Quirinal Palace (which had been completely refurbished for Hitler): "They renovated their house at our expense. Umberto and Maria Jose had disgusting bathrooms. Now they will have, as they say, 'princely' ones."

The King remained aloof and went hunting at his estate at San Rossore, near Pisa. He had difficulty accepting the Nazi fare Mussolini was heaping upon him at the Quirinal.

The Vatican made no mystery about its unhappiness at seeing the "barbarian" Hitler arrive in the Eternal City, and the *Osservatore*

Romano, the Vatican newspaper, did not even mention the event. In moments of crisis, Pius XI withdrew, as he usually did, to his country residence of Castel Gandolfo and gave orders to close the Vatican museums so that they would not be "desecrated" by the unwelcome tourists. The Pope also had every light inside the Vatican grounds turned off at night, which provided a dark contrast with the rest of the city.

Finally, on May 2, 1938, four special trains left Berlin with over three hundred passengers representing the who's who of Nazidom. Hitler, aware of the low stature of the average Italian and, most of all, the tiny size of the King, picked as his escort the tallest specimens available, all of them well over six feet. He thus repeated the insult made by Kaiser Wilhelm II when he visited the young King Victor Emanuel III back in May 1903. Eva Braun had an entire coach for an independent group that included Mrs. Dreesen, owner of the hotel of the same name in Bad Godesberg, where the Führer had spent the night preceding the Night of the Long Knives. Also in this coach were Mrs. Dreesen's sons, as well as Drs. Theo Morrell and Karl Brandt, their wives, and a few maids.

Just after eight in the evening of May 3, Hitler arrived in Rome. He was welcomed by the King and Mussolini. Hitler was surrounded by his lieutenants: Goebbels, Hess, Himmler, Ribbentrop, Frank, and Sepp Dietrich of the SS. The arrival ceremony took place at the Ostiense Station, given a cardboard facelift for the occasion, rather than Termini Station because it looked too old. Göring stayed behind in Germany as Deputy Führer and second in line as head of state to run things in Hitler's absence.

Mussolini's pride was about to be deeply wounded during this momentous visit. So much so that he would dwell on it in his 1944 book, *Storia di un anno*.* After defining the dual leadership of the King and Duce in Italy (for which he coined the term "diarchy") and recounting some of the anecdotes where the relations between the two dictators were quite tense, he wrote (referring to himself in the third person):

---

* *The Fall of Mussolini. His own Story.*

"The problem became serious and grotesque within the sacred labyrinths of protocol. The worst example was to be on the occasion of the Führer's trip to Rome. The diarchy was on display to the fullest, for an entire week, with moments that surprised, irritated, and amused the public. Mussolini had gone to Germany in 1937. There had been a memorable welcome in Berlin and Munich. Millions of Berliners gathered at the Maifeld to listen to speeches by the Führer and the Duce. The visit resounded the world over. In May 1938, the Führer came to Rome. It was not always easy to plan the formal visit, but it was clear the Führer had expected to visit the Duce's Rome.

"When the train from Germany pulled into the beautiful new station of San Paolo, the Duce was there with the King to greet Hitler. But then the Führer got into the royal carriage next to the King and went to the Quirinal Palace. The crowd standing along the way in the Via dei Trionfi, Via dell'Impero, and the Piazza Venezia looked for the Duce but could not see him; he had gone back to his office by the back alleys of the Testaccio. This appeared to irritate the Führer. During the next few days, there was a sort of rotation of the hospitality chores: in the morning the King, in the afternoon the Duce, or vice versa. Each would accompany the Führer to various events, depending upon whether the event was more or less political or Fascist. In the glacial atmosphere of the Quirinal, due in part to small problems of a mundane nature, the Führer felt uncomfortable.

"At the military parade in the Via dei Trionfi, the Führer's entourage noticed the Queen and her ladies in waiting bowing low in front of the army flags, while they pretended not to notice those of the Fascist militia. In those ceremonies where the King and the Duce appeared together, the Duce would take a step back to allow the King's guards precedence. This was most apparent at the costumed event in Piazza di Siena, one of the most grandiose and picturesque events of the last few years in Rome. The Führer invited the Duce to stand next to him in the front row. Finally, the Roman visit came to an end. Coming out of what one Berliner called 'the air of the royal catacombs' and arriving in Florence, the

Führer's disposition changed. If he had been impressed by the majesty of Rome, the grace of Florence was much more to his liking. He would have liked to stay longer. "It's the city of my dreams," he said."

And not just because of Florence itself, but also because he was finally alone with the Duce, the King having stayed in Rome. In the Quirinal Palace, Hitler was in a remote, silently formal world, in contrast to his swaggering Nazi lieutenants, full of stiff butlers who spoke in hushed tones and were strictly correct in their bearing, with the Savoy family crest on their lapels. Himmler, according to Mussolini's book, exclaimed: *"Man atmet hier eine Katakombenluft."* ("Here you breathe the air of the catacombs.") Anecdotes abound surrounding Hitler's stay in the crown prince's apartment. When he went to his room, Hitler apparently rang for "a woman," giving rise to many salacious rumors (given the Führer's reputation), but it was only to request an additional blanket and to remake his bed.

The next morning, May 4, Hitler made the usual visits: the tomb of the unknown soldier, the Pantheon, the mausoleum of the Fascist martyrs. At the welcoming toast, King Victor Emanuel said:

"Führer, we are particularly pleased to address to you, our most cherished guest, our sincere and cordial welcome. In you, Italy salutes the leader of a great and friendly nation, the warrior who has returned Germany to greatness and to its mission of civilization. Many deep bonds, both spiritual and political, tie the new Italy to Germany and make the friendship of the two peoples an intimate and secure one. This will be in the future an instrument for peace in Europe. That is the goal of both the government of the Reich and our government. From your first crossing of the Italian border down to Rome, you have experienced, in the enthusiasm that welcomed your arrival, the depth of good feelings Italy has for you and your homeland . . . Let us drink to your good health . . . "

While Hitler listened to the King, he was considering Queen Elena, who had bored him moments before with small talk: "Physically she's built like one of the horse guards. But she's empty inside."

The visit went on without any incident. In Rome, Hitler went through a full program of ceremonies and events. In Piazza di Siena he saw an act of Wagner's *Lohengrin*; on the Via dei Trionfi, at Santa Marinella, and Furbara, there were parades and military exercises. The German military attaché in Rome, General von Rintelen, commented that the parade in the Via dei Trionfi, even though excellent, showed that "the artillery and the special troops did not have modern equipment." The high point of the trip was the naval review at Naples on May 5, with the participation of "the fleet that Mussolini has forged in the image of ancient Rome," as reported in the *Corriere della Sera*. In the Gulf of Naples, there were two battleships, eighteen destroyers, eleven frigates, twelve torpedo boats, and twenty-four antisubmarine attack boats.

The final surprise was provided by one hundred submarines which dove and emerged in perfect unison under a blazing sun. Many commentators noted that this was the "naval day" for the Axis, because it convinced Hitler that in the end Italy may have been poor for many things, but it did have a good fleet (the world's fifth largest), and that sat as very useful to his own plans. In Naples, the image projected was one of power and discipline, which surprised not only the German guests but also the Italians themselves, who had not realized how good they were. Eva Braun sent her parents a postcard that read: "We saw the fleet, and it was a beautiful parade."

Filippo Anfuso wrote: "Hitler had no fleet, and those superb ships that he could actually recognize by name (it was one of his hobbies) filled him with the connoisseur's admiration . . . I can see him walking on the deck of the battleship, *Cavour*, while he enthusiastically studied the silhouette of the destroyers, like an adolescent envious of his friend's toys. As the submarines emerged together from the water, Mussolini looked at Hitler, who looked back at him with an envy that made the Duce ecstatic. It was the peak of the whole trip. Right after Naples came the first concrete offer of an alliance from Germany."

However, Mussolini and Ciano agreed to soft pedal the alliance project because of the deadlines of the so-called Easter Agreement of April 16, 1938, between Italy and Great Britain, which promised the recognition of the Italian African Empire, while Italy agreed to withdraw all its troops from Spain as soon as the civil war there ended.

Ribbentrop, following Hitler's orders, immediately pursued Ciano to obtain an agreement regarding the German proposal for a political and military alliance between Italy and Germany. There was almost a clash between the two on the subject, the German insisting more and more and the Italian shaking his head more and more. Hitler's interpreter, Paul Schmidt, wrote: "The argument between Ribbentrop and Ciano was in grotesque contrast with what the public was witnessing officially. Ribbentrop's greatest asset was his persistence. I watched him as he would keep on insisting on a proposal without ever realizing he was being rude. It was a tactic to wear out the opponent until he would agree out of sheer fatigue. He tried this with Ciano but did not succeed." Ciano closed the issue with a smile and said: 'The solidarity of our two regimes was so obvious in these last few days that a formal treaty is not even necessary.'"

Eva Braun, who was staying at the Excelsior Hotel with her group, was very happy and enjoying herself because she was out of Hitler's reach, while he was a virtual prisoner at the Quirinal Palace. In his biography of Eva Braun, Glenn Infield wrote:

"Eva created more excitement in Italy than any other women in the Nazi entourage. She was more beautiful than any of them and much more carefree . . . Hitler found time to visit her occasionally, but she spent much of her time with the handsome, virile SS men and the Italian officers assigned to watch over her while she was in Italy . . . Eva did a lot of shopping during the trip. She loved handbags, shoes, and other articles made from alligator hide, and after one shopping trip in Rome, she returned to her hotel looking as if she had been on a hunting trip to the Congo. She also purchased some expensive jewelry. Between shopping trips, she was squired around the city's night spots . . . Eva loved to dance and on two occasions, she returned to her hotel shortly before daybreak. When Hitler was told about this, he was angry and told Eva that he 'wanted her back at her hotel at a decent hour.' 'I will be back at a decent hour,' she told him, 'when you quit holding hands with the Italian madonnas at the Grand Hotel.'"

The visit to Naples was an exhausting day for the Nazi leadership. They were under extremely heavy protection by the Italian police due to intelligence reports indicating possible assassination attempts against some of the Führer's closest lieutenants. The tension was heightened when there were crowds, but nothing happened. The royal palace of the Bourbon kings at Capodimonte was the setting for an official banquet that included the wives of the Nazi leaders. The ladies, unfamiliar with etiquette, were given a crash course in good manners by Eleonora Attolico, wife of the Italian ambassador to Germany, in the reception rooms of the Grand Hotel. The German ladies wished to be formally introduced to the Queen and be taught how to curtsy. It proved to be a disaster; most of them kept tripping over their evening gowns or bowing too low.

Hitler was to solve the most delicate etiquette problem personally. Frau Ribbentrop was convinced that she was the "first lady of Germany." That title, however, belonged to the wife of the German ambassador to Rome, the young and beautiful Frau Mackensen. The Führer gave his orders and summoned Foreign Minister von Ribbentrop, telling him to control his wife. The Queen was informed of this flap and made sure that at the banquet Frau Mackensen sat on her right and Frau Ribbentrop on her left. The Queen also made it a point to speak only Italian that evening, a language in which Frau Ribbentrop was not conversant. The conclusion of the day in Naples came at the opera house of San Carlo, where the soprano playing Aida had almost been crushed by falling scenery. One can only assume that she was somewhat cheered up later when she received flowers from and the personal congratulations of Hitler himself. The entire party then boarded the trains back to Rome.

Back at his residence, Villa Torlonia, Mussolini told his family the details of that day. His sons, Vittorio and Bruno, had witnessed the naval exercises from the deck of the ocean liner, *Rex*, and Vittorio remembered his father's version of the day's events:

"At the opera, the show was marred by falling scenery that almost crushed the singers. But Hitler enjoyed himself. He told me that mishaps happen even in the very organized country that Germany is. There is always the unplanned problem that appears. The people of Naples said that for a racist like Hitler, *Aida* was the wrong choice. It's about an Egyptian general falling in love with a black woman. But Hitler liked the first ballerina made up in black face, and she was more beautiful than talented. He was enthusiastic about our naval exercises. The bay of Naples on a sunny day is a magnificent sight for us Italians, so it must look even grander to a German. The navy, I must admit, is the most disciplined and best-prepared part of our armed forces. Getting one hundred submarines to emerge in unison is no easy task technically. Today we have the best trained and most powerful underwater fleet in the world."

Hitler failed during this visit to formalize the Axis between Italy and Germany into a military alliance, in spite of Ribbentrop's relentless harassing of Ciano. Hitler's old promise, made when his troops entered Austria, to formally declare the Brenner Pass as the "eternal" border between Italy and Germany remained open. The Führer had to live up to that promise if he was to retain Mussolini's friendship and good will. The formal dinner given by the Duce at the Palazzo Venezia on May 7 provided the Führer with the right setting. He lifted his glass in a toast and said to Mussolini:

"Now that we have become close neighbors, strengthened by two thousand years of history, we intend to recognize the border that History and Providence have both drawn for our peoples. This border separates clearly Italy and Germany and opens the life of both nations, allowing not only a peaceful and lasting collaboration but also a bridge for assistance and cooperation. It is my unbending will and also my political testament to the German people that it must always consider the natural barrier of the Alps as permanent and untouchable. I am certain that for both Rome and Berlin, the result will be a glorious and prosperous future."

Even though Hitler had managed to avoid pronouncing the expected word—Brenner—Ciano, as he wrote in his Diary, was satisfied: "Hitler's speech has altered the situation; the Italians probably liked, more than the statements about the borders, the enthusiastic lyricism with which they were delivered."

The Nazis did not share this view, especially those from Alto Adige-South Tyrol, who longed to be reunited with the greater Nazi Germany. An insistent rumor placated these Tyrolean militants: "The Führer, after the war that is expected to provide living space in the east, sensitive to the overwhelming desire of the German people, has asked his friend, Benito Mussolini, in exchange for significant territorial gain elsewhere, for the reunification of Alto Adige-South Tyrol with Germany." This information was given to the author by Giuseppe Mastromattei, former prefect of Bolzano. On May 8, at Santa Marinella and at Furbara airport, outside Rome, there were more parades, ending with a nighttime event at the Foro Mussolini to honor the Führer.

Finally, on May 9, Mussolini had the personal satisfaction of being alone with Hitler during his official visit to Florence. Hitler was also glad to be rid of the fastidious presence of King Victor Emanuel. The German Chancellor was in his favorite element in Florence, where everything appeared to be a work of art. He was ecstatic as he visited the Pitti Palace and the Uffizi Gallery for over four hours—much to the annoyance of the impatient Mussolini, who disliked antiques and painting in general. The Duce was clearly making a point that it was his very first visit to the famous museum. After attending the first two acts of the opera, *Simon Boccanegra*, Hitler was ready to board his special train back to Germany. On the platform, the two dictators looked into each other's eyes at length. Hitler finally said: "No power in the world can come between us now."

Albert Speer, the Führer's architect and Nazi party rally choreographer, later to become minister of war production, related in his memoirs Hitler's first reactions after his Italian trip:

"I am so relieved that we no longer have the monarchy! I was right not to listen to those who were attempting to make me restore it! All those courtesans! All that etiquette! You can't even begin to imagine! And the Duce always playing second fiddle! At the table, in the reviewing stands, the best seats were for the royal family, while the Duce who is the real representative of the State, was always kept at a distance."

As an expression of gratitude for the Duce's hospitality, Hitler decided to rename the "Adolf Hitler Platz" in Berlin to "Mussolini." But the project never came to pass because the urban restructuring never got underway. Perhaps the most tragic effect of Hitler's visit to Rome was the beginning of the Italian racial and anti-Semitic campaign. One possible reason was that Berlin could not accept that its closest ally not adopt its own ideology in what it considered a vital point, and because in Italy, conformists and worshippers of things foreign have always been numerous and extremely vocal. In spite of the fact that Mussolini, in 1932, had said to the German writer Emil Ludwig, "Anti-Semitism does not exist in Italy," and had had a long and intimate relationship with Margherita Sarfatti, who was Jewish, he welcomed a Nazi delegation of race "experts" to visit the extremist wing of the Fascist party only one month after Hitler's visit.

Clearly, Hitler was, at least in part, the inspiration behind Mussolini's anti-Semitic decisions. As Eucardio Momigliano wrote:

"Mussolini was so far from being a racist that on July 2, 1938, he appointed a military man named Levi, who was obviously Jewish, as general in command of a division; but thirteen days later his 'racism' exploded violently because obviously Hitler had become impatient... On July 15, the Fascist government published a "manifesto" by a group of scientists, who remained anonymous for the moment, declaring that Italians belonged to the Nordic race and are completely Aryan, while the Jews are not of the same race as the Italians."

The infamous manifesto that became the opening shot of the Italian racist laws was published on July 14, 1938. The Manifesto of Racist Scientists stipulated that Italian citizens of the Jewish race, except those who had served the country or Fascism, would henceforth be considered pariahs, with the related moral and economic consequences. There are various interpretations of Mussolini's anti-Semitic stance, which had been brewing since the Nuremberg laws of 1933-1935. Though Hitler never lost an opportunity to pressure

Mussolini on the subject of race, he always remained within the limits of diplomatic acceptability.

There is an eyewitness account partially explaining the reasons behind Mussolini's anti-Semitic policies, which were superficial and amateurish compared to the brutality Hitler was known for. The eyewitness was Nino d'Aroma, who took notes at a meeting between King Victor Emanuel III and Italian Air Marshal Italo Balbo, who was the governor of Libya, while the King was on an official visit to the African colony. Balbo, along with other Fascist leaders such as Giacomo Acerbo, Emilio De Bono, and Luigi Federzoni, had voiced his opposition to the anti-Jewish laws at a session of the Grand Council of Fascism.

Balbo began speaking about Mussolini's dangerous "passion" when it came to Hitler and asked the King: "Are we just imitating the Germans on the Jewish question?"

Victor Emanuel replied: "Listen, Balbo, I am not in the habit of anticipating things to come, but on this matter, I have spoken to Mussolini more than a few times and told him: 'My dear president, the Jews are a hornet's nest, let's not stick our hands in it.' First, Mussolini said I was right, and then he did an about-face: he invited [the Jews] to come to Italy in droves. You can imagine the complaints of our professionals, our businessmen in seeing all these Austrian and German Jews, who are also, I am told, a bit arrogant and aggressive. Mussolini kept silent and let things go on. Now, I know he changed his mind and wants them out because during the war in Ethiopia, and I can't blame him for this, they took sides very harshly against us in America, in England, in France. You know him better than I—Mussolini holds a grudge for that . . . and he's also jealous that German anti-Semitism is so popular in the Arab countries in the eastern Mediterranean."

The sudden violent coups that followed Hitler's visit to Venice in 1934, the "Night of the Long Knives" and the failed putsch in Vienna, had not taught Mussolini much about the strange personality of the man and the ambiguous political games he indulged in. Mussolini would have been well advised to ask himself in Florence when he saw Hitler off, "What new surprise does he have in store for me now?" The answer was soon on the front page of every newspaper in the world: Czechoslovakia. The Austrian scenario was to repeat itself; when leaving for the Venice rendezvous, Hitler informed the Austrian Nazis that there would be news upon his return. About one month before the visit to Rome, he summoned Konrad Henlein, the leader of the Sudetendeutsche Partei, to finalize the "Green Plan," involving the takeover of Czech territory (the Sudetenland), populated by German ethnic minorities.

Czechoslovakia, created by the Treaty of Versailles at the end of World War I, with Prague as its capital, was a country of about ten million people. There was a twenty-five percent German minority and ten percent made up of Magyars and Poles. The Czech state, carved out of the former Austro-Hungarian Empire, had a long, mountainous border with Germany (the western part a spearhead lodged in the side of the Third Reich) and common borders with Hungary and Romania. The first move came on April 24, 1938, in Karlsbad. Henlein, on Hitler's instructions, made public the "reasonable demands" of the German minority to the Prague government. In view of the outrageous nature of the demands, both Hitler and Henlein were convinced this document would trigger a violent political crisis within Czechoslovakia that would serve to justify German military intervention. The crisis actually went in the opposite direction for the Germans.

On May 28, after his return from Italy, Hitler had set October 1, 1938 as the final date for the "Green Plan." Prague announced a partial mobilization of its army and Czech President Beneš, after disarming the Nazis, suddenly accepted the "reasonable demands" made at Karlsbad. Henlein went with the good news to Nuremberg, where the Nazi party congress was about to begin and where the Führer would give a speech addressing the dramatic Sudenten problem.

On September 12, in scathing and insulting language when referring to the Czechs, whom he considered inferior people, Hitler told his generals: "It is my firm decision to crush Czechoslovakia militarily in the near future." However, he did not burn all his bridges toward a peaceful solution, which would allow him to invade the coveted Sudeten regions without firing a shot. British Prime Minister Sir Neville Chamberlain provided Hitler with his opportunity. Chamberlain was prepared to go to great lengths to save peace in Europe, even if it meant paying a high personal cost. On September 15, Chamberlain flew to Germany to meet with Hitler: "It is an effort to avoid a war that appeared imminent," wrote the *Daily Herald* that day, "and as such everyone will support it, regardless of their political views."

After seven tiring hours on the plane, Chamberlain, who was sixty-nine at the time and making his first flight, arrived at Hitler's residence, Berchtesgaden. It was indeed the end of an era: the former Austro-Bavarian corporal was being sought out by the prime minister of the British Empire. Sir John Wheeler-Bennett wrote:

"Hitler, hiding his deep satisfaction of the event, did not even walk down the steps to greet his guest. He waited for him at the top of the stairs, surrounded by General Keitel and a few other members of his entourage . . . That was the first of three historic meetings between Hitler and Chamberlain . . . Hitler said in very clear but polite terms that he had decided that the Germans in the Sudetenland had the right to self-determination and to be reunited with the Reich if they so desired. If they could not do so alone, he would help them even at the risk of a world war."

The Führer complained about "British threats," but Chamberlain cleverly pointed out that threats should not be confused with warnings. Chamberlain asked his younger and excited host: "Why did I come all the way over here to waste my time?" Hitler coldly replied that if he had obtained an immediate guarantee from the British government on self-determination for the Sudeten Germans, he would be ready to discuss the matter. After more than three hours, Chamberlain closed the first round of talks and adjourned to consult his cabinet in London.

Mussolini was following all these events from a distance as he visited cities in the Veneto region. In Trieste on September 18, he warned: "If there are two camps, for and against Prague, let it be known that Italy has chosen its side." In Padua on September 24, he even spoke of imminent deadlines "so that the leaders in Prague take the path of wisdom" by giving up the Sudeten territories peace-fully and without tricks.

The British cabinet met with Chamberlain on September 16 to hear about the results of his mission to Bavaria. Lord Walter Runciman was present at the debate. He had been sent on a previ-ous mission by Chamberlain to Prague in an attempt to mediate an agreement between the Czechs and Germans. While the British were working out a compromise, Beneš and his advisor, Jan Masaryk, were taking a tough position by ordering the arrest of Henlein and outlawing the German Sudeten Nazi party. At this point, the French Premier, Edouard Daladier, and his Foreign Minister, Georges Bonnet, arrived in London adding even more proposals to find a solution; they went from war with Germany to the slicing of Czecho-slovakia in favor of the Third Reich. Finally the Franco-British plan emerged: imposing on Prague to cede to Germany those territories where Germans represented over fifty percent of the Sudeten popu-lation. In exchange the French and British governments would guar-antee and protect the remaining Czechoslovakian state.

This possible solution was rejected both by Prague and the po-litical opponents of Daladier and Chamberlain. Nevertheless, Cham-berlain took to the air once again and flew back to Germany for meetings with Hitler on September 22. Before boarding the plane, Chamberlain told the press: "My objective is peace in Europe, and I trust this trip is the way to that peace." Upon his arrival in Co-logne, the band played "God Save the King," and he was taken to the Hotel Petersburg in Godesberg. The Germans lavished a grand welcome on the British delegation this time; flowers and gifts had been placed in everyone's suite.

According to Chamberlain's thinking, the British and French position of having accepted all of Hitler's demands without any reductions or changes would necessarily force Hitler to accept an immediate agreement. "Does this means," asked the Führer, a bit surprised, "that the Allies have agreed, with Prague's approval, to the transfer of the Sudetenland to Germany?" "Precisely," answered Chamberlain. Hitler shook his head. The Allied offer was insuffi-cient; in brief, he wanted the Czechoslovak state to be wiped off the map of Europe and its spoils distributed to Germany, Poland, and Hungary by October 1. Take it or leave it.

Chamberlain was deeply shaken. Hitler argued heatedly that the Czechs had muddied the waters in the last few days, while he had waited patiently for Chamberlain to reply. To further dramatize the moment, upon a prearranged signal, one of Hitler's aides would enter the room bringing fresh messages of "bloody" events, where "Germans were being killed in Czechoslovakia." Hitler, his face flushed, began screaming: "I will avenge every one of them. The Czechs must be destroyed." After three more hours of questions and answers, Chamberlain returned to his hotel to think things over. The next morning he sent Hitler a letter wherein he reiterated every concession the Allies were prepared to make so long as the Sudeten problem would remain peaceful and not be subjected to useless military solutions. There was no answer from Hitler for most of the day.

In the late afternoon, one of Hitler's "letter carriers" appeared at the Hotel Petersburg carrying a large envelope emblazoned with the Führer's eagle; he made no concessions of any kind. Chamberlain could only fly back to London. But that evening, Hitler, worried about having gone too far, informed Chamberlain that he would be pleased to meet with him at 10:30 that night. During this third round with Chamberlain, Hitler simply demanded that the Czechs begin their evacuation of the German majority areas by eight o'clock on September 26 and be completed by the twenty-eighth. This amounted to an ultimatum that Chamberlain rejected out of hand. In the end Hitler agreed to a delay until October 1, the original date of the Green Plan, the beginning of military operations in the Sudetenland. He said this was the one concession he was willing make out of respect for the British Prime Minister, as a "gift" to his guest for having yielded somewhat in his position.

Hitler, having finally calmed down, assured Chamberlain that with the annexation of Sudetenland, he felt satisfied. Germany had no further claims against Prague, and he was ready to enter into a collective agreement to guarantee the borders of the Third Reich and Czechoslovakia.

Finally, Hitler said that if the negotiations reached a satisfactory conclusion, he would be happy to reopen the talks with Chamberlain to settle the matter of the former German colonies in Africa in a spirit of continued peaceful cooperation. On the morning of September 24, Chamberlain returned to London with a very heavy message: Hitler's latest demands for the annexation by Germany of the Sudeten areas without delay.

In France and Britain, those political groups that wanted to confront Hitler once and for all were gaining momentum, even though it meant war. Masaryk was elated by this development and said: "The nation of Saint Wenceslas will never be a nation of slaves." The disagreements between Paris and London, meanwhile, were growing. Göring's Luftwaffe, which was being heavily publicized at the time, was on everyone's mind like a terrible menace waiting to fall from the sky. Meetings were taking place in rapid succession. The press and radio were keeping the public informed with the pace of events. Numerous other projects and solutions to save the peace, as well as to save face, were being discussed. The lights were rarely off at 10 Downing Street.

On September 26, Chamberlain sent, via his close confidant Sir Horace Wilson, a personal letter to Hitler. The Allies confirmed their intention of resolving the Sudeten problem in a civilized manner. Hitler's reply, delivered that evening in a violent speech at the Sportpalast, was that, henceforward, the deciding factor between Germany and Czechoslovakia would be a force of arms, with a deadline of 2:00 p.m. on September 28. But at 10:00 a.m. that very day, four hours before the deadline, British ambassador to Rome, Lord Perth, called Galeazzo Ciano, the Italian Foreign Minister, to request an urgent meeting. At the Palazzo Chigi, the offices of the Italian Foreign Ministry, the British diplomat told Ciano that, on instructions from Chamberlain, he was requesting Mussolini's intercession with Hitler to delay the ultimatum in order to continue negotiating. Ciano went to see Mussolini at 11:00 a.m. at the Palazzo Venezia.

Mussolini told Ciano that Chamberlain's request could not be ignored, and called Attolico, the Italian ambassador to Berlin. "Go to the Führer at once, and tell him that whatever happens, I will be at his side, but that I request a twenty-four-hour delay before hostilities begin. In the meantime, I will study what can be done to solve the problem." Hitler received the message while he was in a meeting with the French Ambassador. He accepted the delay and told the diplomat: "My great friend, Benito Mussolini, has asked me to delay for twenty-four hours the marching orders of the German army, and I agreed." Lord Perth returned to the Palazzo Chigi at noon, bearing Chamberlain's thanks and with a new request for a four-power conference of Germany, Italy, France, and Great Britain in order to settle the Sudetenland problem. Ciano returned to the Palazzo Venezia and, before 2:00 p.m. with calls to Berlin, London, and Paris, a summit of the four powers was agreed to in Munich on September 29. Hitler's only precondition was that the Duce would also attend the conference.

The Munich conference was announced to the House of Commons at 4:15 p.m., September 28 by Chamberlain:

"Whatever opinions you, my honorable colleagues, may have had in the past about Mussolini, I think each one of you will recognize in his action a desire to contribute with us to peace in Europe. I have just been informed that Hitler has invited me to meet with him at Munich tomorrow morning. Mussolini has accepted, and I don't doubt that Daladier will do the same. I don't have to tell you what my response will be."

The news was greeted with enthusiasm everywhere, except in Prague, which already knew it was being sacrificed to avoid a war in Europe, and in Moscow, which had been deliberately kept out of the entire matter. Mussolini, naturally, was the most satisfied since he was about to live the greatest day of his life.

V

Munich 1938: Mussolini as Mediator of World Peace

Munich: September 29, 1938

A t 5:00 p.m. on September 28, 1938, emergency orders were issued by the Fascist party in Rome for a demonstration at the Termini station to cheer the Duce, who was about to leave for Munich. He went as the mediator for the meeting of the century between the "big four." Chamberlain, Hitler, Daladier, and Mussolini himself. Fascist leader Giuseppe Bottai recorded the scene in his memoirs:

"A crowd of onlookers was kept at bay. Starace, Fascist Party Secretary, was under the awning surrounded by newsmen and cabinet ministers, looking like a film director. Mussolini appears with Ciano. The mood is gray, lifeless. Nothing livens it, certainly not the ritualized cries from the crowd. Only the soul is uplifted after the anxiety of the last few days. But the silence is heavy."

Bottai appeared bitterly disillusioned because he had been reduced to the role of a spectator. The honor of accompanying the leader was reserved for one of the latest arrivals in government: young Galeazzo Ciano, whose critics said his greatest merit was having married the Duce's daughter. Bottai had to earn his living by being the Minister of National Education. It was a lost opportunity for those left behind. Bottai noted in his diary how, after Hitler's visit:

"Nazi Germany is the standard by which we measure ourselves and our loyalty. A trip to Germany was a credit to any Fascist leader high and low looking for advancement, as well as for our home-grown theorists of an ever more totalitarian totalitarianism. It is around things German that the game of factions and counterfactions defines itself . . . They are pro-German as in earlier times they had been pro-French."

Bottai was to wait five more years, until the meeting of the Grand Counsel of July 25, 1943, to settle accounts with Mussolini by voting against him at the meeting, thus contributing to the fall of Italian Fascism.

Meanwhile, the *Corriere della Sera*, Italy's most prestigious daily newspaper, offered the official viewpoint:

"The news of the Duce's departure for Munich reached the newspapers just after 5:00 p.m. and immediately became common knowledge. It brought a large enthusiastic crowd to the railroad station that understood Mussolini's great impending mission in the cause of world peace . . . As we wait for the Duce to arrive, all the discussions are in praise of the towering historical figure of Mussolini.

"By 6:00 p.m., we hear the echo of the immense greeting the public offers the Duce as he arrives by car accompanied by Foreign Minister Count Ciano. The applause, the strong cries of 'Duce! Duce!' follow Mussolini as he jumped out of his car in front of the awning. The ministers and other public figures salute the leader and crowd around him, cheering. The Duce is a portrait of virile seren-ity and answers everyone with the Fascist salute, while the demon-stration grows in enthusiasm and grandiose intensity. Mussolini, in civilian clothes, speaks for a moment very cordially with the Ger-man ambassador . . . he then boards the presidential train. Everyone is crowding on the platform around the saloon car. The Duce looks out the window, and the train pulls out of the station immediately . . . "

The lightning trip to Munich was decided at the Palazzo Venezia between noon and three on the afternoon of September 28. It posed quite a few problems for the Italian Foreign Ministry because Mussolini, despite his many speeches in the Veneto region in the last few days, had been kept at a distance from the Sudeten problem both by the Allies, especially the French, and by Hitler. Chamberlain had been instrumental in inviting the Duce back into the diplomatic crisis because it suited British strategy to widen the participants to a "diktat" that was about to be imposed upon Czechoslovakia, the latest victim to be sacrificed to keep the peace.

Inside the Palazzo Chigi at the time, was a small group of diplomats of high caliber, such as Filippo Anfuso, Blasco Lanza d'Ajeta and Mario Luciolli. They had to prepare the Sudeten briefing book so that Mussolini, now the official mediator of the crisis, would have a comprehensive background of all the problems likely to arise: borders, minorities, majorities, legitimate and illegitimate demands, fine points, and excuses.

Luciolli wrote about that very busy afternoon: "According to the ministry's rotation of cabinet functionaries, it was my turn to be on duty during the night of September 27-28. It felt like the final night of peace. I was reading the cables that kept arriving from the various capitals; there wasn't a glimmer of hope in any one of them . . . At dawn in the code office, I saw a cable from our Paris embassy mentioning an attempt to save the peace. A few French politicians had asked Renato Prunas if he thought a British initiative toward Mussolini had any possibility of succeeding . . . Prunas had encouraged them to pursue the matter . . . During the first hours of the 28th, Alessandro Farnese took over from me . . . When I returned to the Palazzo Chigi, I crossed paths with Lord Perth, the British Ambassador, as he was leaving. I was quickly briefed in the office as to the latest developments: Chamberlain had asked that Mussolini propose to Hitler a four-power conference, which would seek to find a solution that would satisfy German demands. Mussolini had called Attolico and now Attolico was meeting with Hitler . . . The rest of the day was taken up by the rushed preparations for the conference. Mussolini, Ciano, and their entourage, of which I was a part, along with Anfuso and Blasco Lanza d'Ajeta, were to take the special train to Munich at six in the afternoon."

Luciolli reveals how Mussolini received the final agenda containing the German demands: "Just before leaving the office, I received a cable message from Attolico containing the final German demands for the transfer of the Sudetenland to Germany." However, Mussolini had probably already received, possibly from Prince Philip of Hesse, a German plan outlining the transfer of Sudeten territory to Berlin's control by October 10. The document had been secretly prepared by three German "doves" within the Nazi clan—Göring, Neurath, and Weiszäcker—and approved by Hitler before his talks with Chamberlain. According to Nino d'Aroma, the Duce, after having studied each detail at length, had drawn up a synopsis that he would present as the basis of an eventual compromise.

Once in Munich, the Duce immediately sensed that the Germans, and especially the "hawks" (now assured of having bagged the Sudetenland), wanted to play for higher stakes. Attolico had confirmed this feeling, having just arrived from Berlin that morning, nervous and full of foreboding. Luciolli wrote:

"Before leaving Berlin, the Ambassador had heard confidentially from Ernst von Weizäcker, the Secretary of State for Foreign Affairs, his good friend and a man committed to peace, that Hitler, following Ribbentrop's suggestions, wanted to declare that the previous conditions had been rendered obsolete and that they intended to replace them with much harsher demands."

Hearing this, Anfuso asked Luciolli to give him the cable from the day before in Rome and handed it to Mussolini, "who put in it his pocket like someone who just received a promissory note." The day before, in Berlin, Attolico had lived through the most dramatic hours of his brilliant diplomatic career.

Cristano Ridòmi, his press attaché, remembered: "Wednesday, September 28, it was either peace or war . . . We are, each one of us, at our stations inside the embassy. We feel the day will be decisive, the air is full of electricity even in that small street near the green oasis of the Tiergarten . . . An unforgettable day is about to begin . . . The phone rings at eleven. It's very urgent. Attolico calls for his number-two man, Massimo Magistrati, to take notes on the second telephone. Mussolini's voice is calm . . . The call lasted only a few minutes."

In a few seconds, Magistrati had translated the Duce's message for the Führer, and Attolico took it at top speed by taxi to the Reich chancellery. Hitler, at that very moment, was speaking with French Ambassador, François-Poncet. Attolico succeeded in interrupting the conversation and handed the Führer Mussolini's note requesting the ultimatum to Prague be delayed. Hitler accepted the Duce's request, and two hours later the four-power Munich conference was agreed to. The Italian ambassador, up to the time he boarded the overnight train to Munich with Magistrati and Ridòmi, counted a total of eighteen phone calls to Rome that day. Once inside his sleeping car cabin, the ambassador crashed like a knocked-out prizefighter. Mussolini himself, stressed out, high strung, thoughtful, and elated all at once, took advantage of the night trip between Rome and the Brenner Pass to rest and prepare for the next day's tournament. Talking with Ciano, Anfuso, and Osvaldo Sebastiani, his private secretary, there was only one topic: Germany, Hitler, the Sudeten crisis, and Chamberlain.

Mussolini had told Anfuso just before the first meeting between Hitler and Chamberlain: "As soon as Hitler sees that old man, he'll know he's won the game. Chamberlain doesn't know that to face Hitler in the role of the bourgeois British parliamentarian is like giving the taste of blood to a wild animal." He went on to complete his views on the British: "A country where animals are idolized to the point of creating cemeteries, hospitals, and houses for them; when people enter their parrots into their will, it's a sure sign that decadence has set in. Besides all the reasons, it is also the result of the English people themselves. There are four million more women than there are men. Four million sexually frustrated women artificially creating as many problems to excite and then quench their senses. Since they can't embrace a single man, they want to hug all of humanity."

While the special trains from Berlin and Rome raced toward Munich, in London and Paris the planes with the French and British delegations were about to leave for the same destination. Mussolini was up and ready at dawn. Hitler's equerry, Rudolf Hess, met the Italian train at the border, bearing the official greetings and announced that the Führer would meet the Duce halfway between the border and Munich. It was now only five months since they had bid each other farewell at the railroad station in Florence. The meeting took place at 9:30 a.m., as recounted by a Fascist journalist:

"Hitler had been waiting for Mussolini on a bench at the station and now went over to greet him cordially. Minister Hess, who had gone to the Brenner Pass to formally welcome the Duce into Germany, accompanied the guest. This early morning meeting along the old German border, almost directly beneath the Führer's residence with a view of the Bavarian mountains, confirms the friendship uniting the two leaders and the two peoples. Mussolini was wearing the uniform of General Commander of the Fascist militia. He smiled and saluted the crowd . . . After reviewing the honor guard, the Führer accompanied the Italian leader to his own special train, followed by Count Ciano, Minister Hess, and the Italian delegation. At 9:40 a.m. the train was on its way to Munich, and for an hour and a half both leaders discussed the problems which had brought about the conference. Present were Minister Hess, Prince Philip of Hesse, and SS Commander Himmler."

On the train, Hitler's saloon car was spacious, with a large table in the center where maps had already been spread out. Mussolini caught a glimpse of how the Führer, as supreme commander of the armed forces, would be working during the coming war years. The script that Hitler, as theater director, had prepared was the kind of cheap emotional soap opera that matinee audiences love. Lots of histrionics, tearful declarations of one's own kind heart and the meanness of his neighbors. Rather than discussing the four-power summit, Hitler was pleased to have those present listen to General Keitel's presentation of Fall Grün (the "Green Plan") for the invasion of Czechoslovakia, which was to begin within forty-eight hours.

Hitler resumed his presentation in front of a giant map of the western front as recounted by Anfuso:

"I have completed the Siegfried Line and improved it to the point of making it impervious to any attack. But the democracies will never dare attack the German defenses: I will not give them the time! I intend to concentrate the German attack in one specific point and strike a decisive blow even before the democracies can finish mobilizing their armies. The German army is ready and waiting for my plans to unfold. Duce, believe me, I wouldn't sacrifice the life of a single German soldier if I didn't know that to delay this moment would be fateful to the future of my people. The democracies are expecting me to give in! If I were to do so, I would forever mortgage the future of the German people. The only way to avoid allowing them to gain the upper hand is to attack them when they appear disoriented. They want to stop the German people, but they know the moment has not yet arrived. If we do not intervene quickly, we will have accepted and will be surrounded. The time will come when we must fight together against France and Great Britain."

The Führer continued his strategy lesson, proudly concentrating on the newly built bunkers along the Siegfried Line, Germany's great achievement in military engineering. These fortifications were a series of 500 permanent bunkers stretching from Basel to Aachen, facing the Maginot Line just across the border in France. They had been designed and built by master engineer Fritz Todt. Excited by his own harangue against the allies, Hitler pointed at the Maginot Line, clearly drawn on the map, and said, as if it were made of sand: "We shall destroy it."

Filippo Anfuso wrote: "The train was speeding toward Munich, and Hitler kept on speaking as if the war had already broken out and he was directing operations from that train. No one brought up the subject of the conference. Mussolini patiently waited for the moment he could finally place his question: 'What are your demands as to Czechoslovakia?' Hitler looked at him, surprised by an unwelcome interruption of his train of thought. He then produced a sheet of paper with the heavy, last-minute demands Germany was about to make. 'These are the minimum German requirements: if France and Britain can make Beneš accept them, the Reich is not opposed to reaching an agreement.' Hitler gave Ciano a few minutes to read the new demands and continued: 'The democracies hate the German people because they know we have a social organization equaled only by that of Italy, Duce, and this is perhaps the reason the democracies plan to strangle Germany.' The train was now entering Munich."

The paper contained the Führer's demands: the entire Sudeten region would be annexed to Germany regardless of population percentages within the territories, be they a majority of Germans or Czechs. As he got off the train, Mussolini told Ciano, handing back the demands: "We have to gauge the intentions of those gentlemen we are meeting with. If, that is, they come with the intention of reaching an agreement. As to that one [i.e., Hitler], with all that talk on the train, he wants me to let the others know he's ready to go all the way."

The two dictators were welcomed at the station by Göring, Ambassador Attolico with Magistrati, and various German and Italian officials. Mussolini reviewed the honor guard and was offered a bouquet of flowers by a Hitler Youth girl. The automobile convoy took the same route as during the 1937 visit, to the familiar Prinz Karl Palace adorned with the Fascist symbol on the balcony to honor the Duce. Hitler left his guest at the entrance and went directly to the Führerhaus where the conference was to take place. It was 11:30 a.m., and Mussolini had only a few minutes to prepare for the start of the session at 12:30 p.m.

On the train, Hitler had spoken as if war was not just inevitable but as if it had in fact begun. In the past two months, Mussolini had received, directly or indirectly, no less than three German proposals to resolve the Sudeten problem. The Führer had clashed with

Chamberlain at Godesberg because he felt the original Franco-British formula—giving Germany the border areas with over fifty percent German inhabitants—was no longer realistic. That original proposal also stipulated that the four powers, Britain, France, Italy, and Germany, would have guaranteed the new border provided the Czech government abandon any bilateral agreements with France and the USSR. Now the new demands presented on paper were more radical than the preceding ones and implied a threat that Germany would increase its demands.

Italy also had its old allies along the Danube, especially Hungary, which, like Poland, had minority populations within Czechoslovakia. Both countries wanted to share in the spoils. Ambassador Attolico warned Mussolini on the steps of the Prinz Karl Palace, regarding the confidential information he had been given by Weiszäcker regarding the German intent, to increase the "price." Mussolini took all the documents to his room and prepared his strategy. He was, in that confusing moment, the only participant with a clear view of the crisis and had the advantage of being able to speak in French, English, and German. The Duce then waited for the call to the Führerhaus, where Chamberlain and Daladier had already arrived. Mussolini was the last one to reach the conference along with Hess, Ciano, Attolico, and the Italian foreign office officials who had come with him from Rome. Along the route the German crowds cheered the Duce's car. Hitler was waiting for him at the front door. Anfuso, at Ciano's side, intercepted an attempt at small talk by Chamberlain with Mussolini: "Do you like fishing?" asked the Prime Minister. Mussolini's reaction was to look puzzled and then he formally shook hands with Daladier.

The meeting began at 12:30 p.m. in Hitler's study, where some large armchairs had been added. In addition to the big four were Sir Horace Wilson, assistant to the British Prime Minister; Ribbentrop; Alexis Léger, General Secretary of the Quai d'Orsay; and Ciano. Paul Schmidt was there as Hitler's interpreter. The Russians were conspicuously absent because they had not been invited. In the Regina Hotel, anxiously awaiting the meeting's outcome, were Voytech Mastny, Czech ambassador to Berlin, and Hubert Masaryk of the Foreign Ministry. They were present in Munich only as "observers."

Hitler spoke first and, according to Ciano, "thanked the participants for having accepted his invitation and explained the situation as it had worsened in the past few days. He confirmed that he had agreed to delay the ultimatum by twenty-four hours following the Duce's intervention but also stated that he would be forced to intervene if no agreement was reached in the shortest possible time." The Führer accused the Czechs of continued persecution of the Germans. Prague had begun a terror campaign that forced Germany to grant asylum to over two hundred thousand refugees fleeing their homes and villages. Hitler proposed a general plebiscite in Czechoslovakia for an accurate count of the people's will. Chamberlain, diplomatically, took note of Hitler's declarations, while Daladier, much more nervous about the situation, declared himself ready to return to Paris if they were to discuss the liquidation of Czechoslovakia as an independent state. Mussolini requested a first break, striving to appear as the objective moderator of the meeting. He then took out a document that summed up in five points his compromise proposal, put together in the minutes just before leaving the Prinz Karl Palace.

The five points were: (1) The principle of transfer of Sudeten territories to Germany must be confirmed; (2) The operations would take place within the first ten days of October, to prevent Czechoslovakia from destroying any military and industrial installations; (3) A four-power international commission would handle all pending questions; (4) The option to choose nationality would be given to the populations within the territories; (5) The questions of the Hungarian and Polish minorities would also be discussed beyond the Sudeten problem. Mussolini had previously asked Hitler if he demanded the Sudeten territories where eighty percent of the population was German and where the last election results had favored the Nazis. Hitler agreed.

Mussolini's proposal could not be rejected by the participants because it contained the wishes of each delegation. The only new element were the other minorities that the Duce had slyly added and that took everyone, including Hitler, by surprise. But for this precise reason, none of the other three could give an immediate reply without running the risk of adding new enemies to Hitler's list besides the Czechs. The question for Hitler was really the integrity of the installations that the Germans wanted. The Czechs did have a modern and motorized army of over two million men plus a fortified line similar to the Maginot Line. Prague could also count on a very efficient light and heavy industry that included the famous Skoda plant.

Chamberlain and Daladier were ready to discuss Mussolini's proposals, but the Duce's document had first to be translated into French and English. Prime Minister Chamberlain also observed that the consensus of the Czechs was also indispensable and the four powers had to include them in the discussions somehow. At these words, Hitler—who had already expressed his satisfaction—literally jumped out of his armchair. Once again, Mussolini proposed another break in the proceedings and suggested that the Czechs be included in the international commission to implement the agreement. It was now 2:30 p.m. and a virtual agreement had been reached among the four participants.

Chamberlain went back to the Hotel Regina, where he was staying and where the two Czech observers were kept waiting. Daladier went to the Four Seasons Hotel, accompanied by Göring. Hitler took Mussolini and some of his entourage with him to his private apartment at 16 Prinzregentenstrasse. The Führer was not very satisfied with the turn of events. He felt he had worked for nothing and that a victory at the conference table was robbing him of his victory parade through the streets of Prague. In his apartment, he was in better spirits. He was angry at Daladier's assistant, Alexis Léger, who he said was from Martinique and, therefore, had to be a Negro. "It should be forbidden to have colored people negotiating European business," he said.

Anfuso recorded his words: "The racial case of Léger made him indignant to the point that he began talking about his own wartime experiences. He did say that the British would attack but they were tipsy from whiskey, as he observed them jumping out of the trenches. Hitler then took us into a very bourgeois room, where some canapés were served, including venison, which none of the seven or eight Germans present touched, including Himmler and Ribbentrop, who certainly were meat eaters, because the Führer was a vegetarian. Only the Italians ate the venison, and they ate a lot of it . . . "

Mussolini made some sarcastic comments about Chamberlain's umbrella and Daladier's love of cognac. Then everyone returned to the Führerhaus.

The second act began at 4:30 p.m. Ciano noted: "Chamberlain said that he accepted the Duce's proposal as a basis for discussion, and Daladier concurred." This was the signal for experts, who had been waiting in the hallways of the building, to enter the room. First the three ambassadors to Berlin: Neville Henderson for Britain, André François-Poncet for France, and Bernardo Attolico for Italy, accompanied by Ernst von Weizsäcker, the German Undersecretary for Foreign Affairs. Some real horse trading began then and there, no longer regarding cities, villages, and roads, but rather, animals, livestock, electric power plants, harvests, and so on.

Hitler acted repelled by all this, saying "these foolish details should not be taking up the time of the most important men in Europe." Daladier revealed himself to be an excellent horse trader, while Chamberlain was intent on reducing the Czechs' losses. Ciano recalled: "The Duce was bored by this vaguely parliamentary atmosphere that always appears at conferences. He walked absentmindedly around the room with his hands in his pockets. From time to time he helped out in finding the right wording for some issue. In his great mind, always ahead of men and events, the agreement was now concluded, and while the others were immersed in formal problems, he had already lost interest. He was on to other things."

The open-air market gave way quickly to mass confusion. Ministers, civil servants, diplomats, secretaries, and typists came and went incessantly. Hitler sometimes looked enviously at Mussolini, who appeared to be the "senior statesman," the mover and shaker, the man who stopped the war, while he himself appeared to be the thief who had been granted a reprieve. Shortly after 8:00 p.m. the conference broke for dinner. The remaining work was to transcribe in a final document the entire agreement in each of the four languages, a task left to the translators. German protocol had scheduled a formal evening dinner for all four delegations. But both Chamberlain and Daladier refused the invitation, as they both felt it would look unseemly if they had banqueted on the evening Czechoslovakia had been cut to pieces. While those two hurried away, the Wilhelmstrasse functionaries scrambled to find replacements for the open seats at the fifty-plus dining room table, and so added minor civil servants to the dinner list.

Mario Luciolli remembers: "Mussolini, with Göring at his right, sat in front of Hitler, who had Ciano at his side. Then came Himmler, Ribbentrop, Keitel, and the other Nazi leaders. Hitler ate very little and was constantly talking. He was visibly in a state of nervous excitement. As was his habit, he constantly repeated the same things with no logical connection. He did not express thoughts, but only feelings or, at this time, hatred of Czechoslovakia. He ridiculed the Czech army, the Czech politicians, and the Czech pride. He indignantly cited repeated incidents of violence by the Czechs against the Sudeten Germans. In the course of the meal, he repeated three times the incident of a German woman thrown out of the window by a Czech policeman. There was no mention of the central political problems, world peace, the ways of assuring European coexistence. . .

"Mussolini spoke very little. His tactic of allowing Hitler to let off steam had worked well until then, and there was no reason to change it. Everyone else remained silent except for Göring, who kept praising the pagan concept of life. He declared that the entire Western, democratic, pacifist mentality was influenced by Christianity, and this spirit was essentially destructive and corrupting. He recalled how he had felt it while visiting the catacombs in Rome. . . 'The Christian world was insidiously digging the moral and material grave of the Roman world.' Göring also seconded Hitler in abuse against the Czechs: 'They give the Czechs as newborns a violin string in one hand and a small coin in the other. Depending on which hand they bring to their mouth, they will either become musicians or usurers."'

The third act in Munich began at 10:00 p.m. with the tired and anxious participants ready to close the proceedings as soon as possible. At 1:00 a.m. on September 30, the final drafts of the agreements were at last ready to be signed. Hitler signed first, then Chamberlain, Daladier, and Mussolini. The document, in eight chapter headings and two attachments, was the summary of the Duce's five points. Various witnesses have recorded the remarks at the historic event. Mussolini told Daladier: "You will be cheered on your return to France." Ambassador François-Poncet, who was about to be transferred to Rome, was overheard to have said: "Voilà le sort qu'on réserve aux amis de la France" (Such is the fate of the friends of France). Ciano said: "Everyone is satisfied, even the French, even the Czechs, according to what Daladier tells me." Hitler, however, never thought the Munich agreement a successful one, and even referred to it as a semi-defeat. One year later, just before the invasion of Poland, he repeated to his aides: "I hope that this time, no clown will step in to upset my plans."

A second verbal agreement, no less important than the Sudenten agreement, was also reached at Munich. Mussolini and Chamberlain agreed, between sessions, to revive the British-Italian "Easter Treaty," whereby Great Britain agreed to recognize the Italian Empire in Ethiopia, while Italy agreed to withdraw ten thousand volunteer troops from Spain. These conversations began immediately, and on November 16, 1938, the British ambassador presented his credentials to Victor Emanuel III, as King of Italy and Emperor of Ethiopia.

Mussolini refused the extended hospitality offered by Hitler and left Munich immediately for Italy. Hitler, Hess, and Göring saw him off at the railroad station. The train left exactly at 2:00 a.m. So ended the fourth and final peacetime meeting between Hitler and Mussolini. The two dictators were to meet again eighteen months later on March 18, 1940, at the Brenner Pass, just before Mussolini's fateful decision to declare war.

Mussolini returned triumphantly to Italy. The King, who was at his country residence at San Rossore, came to greet the Duce at the Florence railroad station. The Duce was cheerfully surprised to see the King on the platform and went with Ciano to greet him. They shook hands at length, and the King said: "Your four-power pact worked without ratification or parliamentary intervention. The nation is proud of you." At 2:05 p.m., the Duce was on his way back to his Roman triumph, scheduled for the evening. In just five hours, teams of workers had set up barriers along the route from Termini railroad station to the Tomb of the Unknown Soldier. Banners, marching music, and songs could already be heard. By 5:00 p.m., one hour before the Duce's arrival, there wasn't a square foot of space to be found along the way. By 6:00 p.m. the Piazza Venezia was filled to capacity, and Mussolini appeared three times at the well-known balcony. On the third appearance he said: "Comrades! You have lived through hours that you will remember. At Munich, we worked for peace with justice. Is this not the ideal of the Italian people?" The crowd roared back with a huge yes. But, in fact, the peace had ended.

Back at his home at Villa Torlonia, Mussolini's family, as usual, asked for his impressions, and his son Vittorio recorded the scene: "When he reached home, he was not as happy as we expected him to be. He was satisfied and even emotional about some of the welcome he had been given, but there was something that made him bitter. He answered all our questions and pointed out how his knowledge of languages was a decisive factor in the success of the negotiations: 'I understood even more clearly the meaning of the confusion of languages represented by the Tower of Babel.' He was full of praise for Chamberlain, while he did not have a favorable impression of Daladier. He said Hitler had shown he could be patient enough to reach the agreement, and I noticed that he described the German leader in more favorable terms than he had done up to then. It was the zenith for my father, the apex of his popularity and political fortunes."

One of the reasons for his bad mood had been the floral arch of triumph that Starace had ordered for the Duce on the Via

Nazionale. When he saw it, he asked Starace: "Whose idea was this carnival float?" A year later, Starace would be sacked.

Peace had been saved for just one short year in Munich. Czechoslovakia, however, had not been saved: it had been parceled off to the "best offer." In Vienna, on November 2, under the agreement supervised by Ciano and Ribbentrop, Czechoslovakia surrendered 12,074 square kilometers and 1,044,438 inhabitants to Hungary, many of whom were not even Hungarians. Hitler then forced Slovakia to proclaim its independence so that he could finally annex Prague itself on March 15, 1939. He entered the city as it was being occupied by the German army without firing a shot, and then proclaimed the German "protectorate" over Bohemia and Moravia, as the former Czech provinces were henceforth called.

Chamberlain was both humiliated and upset. Hitler, he was now convinced, had blatantly lied at the Munich conference in September 1938 when he formally and solemnly declared that "in his plans, there was no room for a single Czech citizen." London's reaction was to offer immediate guarantees to the countries in Eastern Europe: first to Romania, obviously for its oil fields, then to Poland on March 31, 1939. Even Mussolini was offended at having been kept in the dark about Berlin's latest coup and at having been informed verbally by roving Ambassador Philip of Hesse. Hitler was celebrating his bloodless success at the Hradschany Palace, now flying the Nazi flag. The Prince of Hesse explained that Hitler was compelled to act because the Czechs had not demobilized their army, which was still strong, and because they continued to hold secret talks with the Russians.

Ciano wrote in his Diary: "German hegemony is beginning to take on ominous colors." Mussolini was deeply offended at the manner in which his friend and colleague Hitler had treated him, and he forbade that any announcement be made regarding the Prince of Hesse's visit to Rome: "The Italians will laugh at me. Every time Hitler acquires a new country, he sends me a message." To show Hitler his own might and as a consolation prize, the Duce authorized the "family outing," as the Italian occupation of Albania was referred to on April 7, 1939, Good Friday. Ciano wanted to partici-

right
Mussolini failed to convince Franco
to enter the war in 1941.

below
Military conference at Klessheim
Castle in April 1942.

The assault on Malta was approved, only to be cancelled later after the conference. Mussolini, Hitler and Marshal Kesselring were confident in victory at El Alamein in 1942.

above
The 1943 conference at Klessheim was not as
promising after the defeat at Stalingrad.

below
At the 1943 conference, the V-1 rockets and other
"secret weapons" were discussed.

"Usually the Führer did all the talking, while Mussolini, with a sorry look on his face, remained silent and listened patiently and politely." Eugen Dollmann

When the two dictators emerged from their private meetings "they both looked already dead, just like two ghosts," according to Paolo Monelli in his *Roma 1943*.

Hitler called for an emergency meeting
after the Allies invaded Sicily. Mussolini lands at Treviso,
at 8:30 a.m. on July 19, 1943.

At 9 a.m. Hitler lands at the same airfield
for the Feltre conference.

The Feltre conference was held at the Villa Gaggia-Pagani
that Mussolini termed a "nightmare of a place, a labyrinth of rooms".
Rome was heavily bombed during the meetings.

The Grand Council of Fascism met on July 25, 1943. A majority led by
Grandi and Ciano voted against Mussolini.

above

King Victor Emanuel III asked Mussolini
to resign and had him arrested after their
meeting on July 25, 1943 at 5 p.m.

right

Marshal Pietro Badoglio was named by
the King to form a new Italian government
on the same day Mussolini was arrested.

right
Raffaele Guariglia (left), Minister of
Foreign Affairs in the Badoglio government,
had only one meeting with the Germans on
August 19, 1943. Italy was preparing to
sign the armistice with the Allies.

below
On September 9, 1943, after some fighting
with Italian troops, German paratroopers
take over the center of Rome.

above

Luftwaffe and SS paratroopers, led by Otto Skorzeny, land with gliders on the Gran Sasso Mountains, where Mussolini was kept prisoner on September 12, 1943.

below

Mussolini and his Nazi liberators pose for the camera outside the hotel at Campo Imperatore where he was held prisoner.

Mussolini meets with Hitler on September 14, 1943 at Rastenburg where he will agree to create a Fascist Republican regime in northern Italy.

above

Italy was a tough battleground for the Allies, who made slow progress.
The British, near Monte Cassino, capture German paratroopers in1944.

below

Ciano (center) and other fascists who voted against Mussolini
are tried and put to death in January 1944.

Northern Italy was under Nazi-Fascist control.
From the right: SS General Karl Wolff, Alessandro Pavolini
(secretary of the Fascist party), Ambassador Rudolf Rahn,
Justice Minister Carlo Alberto Biggini. Venice 1944.

On July 20, 1944 Mussolini's final meeting with
Hitler was unexpectedly delayed by von Stauffenberg's
failed bomb attempt to assassinate the Führer.

Cardinal Ildefonso Schuster of Milan tried to broker
an agreement between the CLNAI and the Fascists
but Mussolini refused on April 25, 1945.

The bodies of Mussolini, Claretta Petacci,
and other Fascist leaders are on display at noon in
Piazzale Loreto in Milan on April 29, 1945.

pate in the venture even though the whole country was practically already under Italian control. This initiative signaled the decline of Mussolini's political fortunes. Spain provided some solace for the Duce: Franco, having taken Madrid, had finally ended the civil war and freed Italy from the military and financial burden that had depleted the Italian treasury.

Mussolini was feeling under fire. The French kept on making him the target of their scorn in the press, on radio, in parliamentary debates. Despite the dissenting messages coming from his ambassador to Berlin, the Duce, after having rejected the formal alliance several times, decided to agree to it and have Ciano sign, on May 22, 1939, what was to be called the "Pact of Steel," which tied Italy and Germany. At that very moment, Germany was beginning to confront Poland about the problem of Danzig.

Danzig, fated to become the causus belli, was a problem the parties could perhaps have resolved; it appeared certainly a less difficult and grating problem than the Czech crisis. In fact, Hitler at first did not act aggressively toward Poland as he attempted to reach an agreement on freedom of travel in a way that would not have infringed upon Warsaw's sovereignty. As late as March 25, 1939, Hitler told his aides that he "did not intend to use force in resolving the Danzig issue." The root cause of the dispute was the German majority in Upper Silesia, as had been confirmed in a regular plebiscite. The Allies had arbitrarily drawn the region's borders in 1921, giving the richest coal mines in one-third of the territory to Poland.

Then there was the "corridor," giving Poland access to the Baltic, cutting off East Prussia from Germany. Danzig stood on the Baltic, at the northern end of the Polish corridor; culturally and ethnically it was clearly a German city. It had been administered as a "free city" by the League of Nations since 1919. Right after the Munich agreement, the Germans in Danzig made their own demands. Hitler responded by requesting the reunification of the "free city" to the Third Reich and the right to build, at Berlin's expense, an autobahn connecting East Prussia to Germany proper, thus eliminating the need for Germans going to Königsberg to have a passport. This all looked like a reasonable package, not the kind one would have expected Hitler to propose. Even Poland, as it rejected the proposal on March 26, 1939, left open the possibility of an agreement replacing the international status of Danzig with a joint Polish-German administration.

Warsaw was also ready to consider other means of facilitating rail and automobile traffic between the Third Reich and East Prussia, but not the autobahn idea. Any Polish willingness to discuss the issues was erased by Chamberlain, now understandably embittered by Hitler's behavior. He declared to the House of Commons: "Should any action openly threaten the independence of Poland, His Majesty's government will feel obligated to offer the government in Warsaw every possible form of assistance. The Polish government has received precise assurances from the British government, and the French government has authorized me to communicate that its position regarding this matter is identical to that of London."

The British political and military historian, Basil Liddell Hart, made the following comment concerning the British government's decision: "The vaguely generic terms with which the British commitment had been formulated practically delivered Great Britain's destiny into the fluctuating hands of the Polish leadership, men of dubious and changing political intelligence. Furthermore, even though it was clearly impossible to keep the commitment without Russia's help, the British government made no preliminary attempt to sound out Moscow regarding such help or to confirm that Poland would accept it. When the British cabinet was asked to approve the guarantee to Poland, no one was shown the Chief of Staff's report clearly stating that it would be impossible to provide any effective protection for Poland. However, given the prevailing mood, knowledge of this report, even though far from encouraging, would not have changed the final decision. The news that Parliament was about to discuss the question of guarantees to Poland was approved by all political factions in London. The only dissenting voice was that of Lloyd George, who warned the House of Commons that it would be suicidal folly to take on such a burden without first having assured Russian participation with the British.

"The commitment to maintain Polish independence was the surest way to provoke an immediate explosion and therefore a new world war. It was a great temptation and an act of defiance; not only would it demonstrate to Hitler the futility of such a guarantee to a country that had no common borders with the West, but it would also strengthen the stubborn Poles not to make any concessions to Germany, thus making it impossible for Germany to turn back without a loss of face. Why did the Poles accept the British offer? In part because they absurdly overestimated the capabilities of their antiquated armed forces, to the point, even, of dreaming about "galloping all the way to Berlin." But there also were personal factors.

"Shortly thereafter, the Polish Foreign Minister, Colonel Jozef Beck, was to say that he made the decision to accept the British guarantee while he "shook the ashes from his cigarette," and went on to say that during his meeting with Hitler in January, he could not accept the point Hitler made that Danzig must be returned to Germany. When he was offered the British guarantee, he saw in it a way of putting Hitler back in his place. This is a typical impulse of how the destiny of entire populations is often decided. The only way to avoid war was to secure the participation of Russia, the only power that could provide direct assistance to Poland and thus thwart Hitler's aggressive plans. Even though the situation was very dangerous, the British government moved slowly and without much conviction."

Upon returning to Rome from Berlin, where he had just signed the Pact of Steel, Ciano found a congratulatory telegram from the King. Later, at the royal meeting of May 25, Victor Emanuel warned: "While the Germans need us, they will remain courteous and even slavish. But at the first opportunity, they will reveal themselves to be the ruffians they really are."

But Ciano was not yet convinced. He was to have his anti-German crisis three months later. On August 11 at Füchsl, Ribbentrop told him clearly that Germany wanted war. This meeting of the two Axis foreign ministers was the surrogate for a canceled meeting between the dictators planned for August 4. Hitler feared that his war plans could be "deviated" by the Italians. Ambassador Attolico had been pushing for the summit because he could see where the Polish crisis was going, and he kept on sounding the alarm. Even Chamberlain, who by now was used to dealing with Hitler, through his ambassador to Rome, Sir Percy Lorraine, appealed once again to Mussolini on July 7 to use his influence to calm Hitler in the crisis with Warsaw. Neither Attolico nor Chamberlain were to have any luck. Mussolini was by now convinced that he would have missed his appointment with history if he didn't follow Hitler.

In mid-July, following Chamberlain's instructions after Sir Percy's visit, the British Ambassador asked Mussolini to throw cold water on his friend Hitler. In the meantime, from Berlin, Attolico kept sending alarmist messages amounting to an SOS about a general conflagration if something was not done in time. Ciano felt his ambassador to Berlin was just panicking. But in the end, Mussolini began to fear the worst and urged Ciano to go and meet with Ribbentrop. Ciano told Attolico that the meeting should be scheduled after September 1, and left for Spain, where he was to reap the glory of Franco's victory which he had promoted as his own. In Ciano's absence, Attolico's response was given to Filippo Anfuso. It was more a reprimand than an answer from a man tired of playing the Cassandra in a world of empty-headed dandies.

Sir Ivone Kirkpatrick (author of a biography of Mussolini) wrote about this incident:

"The fact that we had picked a date in September, said Attolico, demonstrated that in Rome, in spite of his warnings, no one took the situation seriously. War was now imminent. The Germans had no intention of waiting for Italy's approval to attack Poland. The military preparations were now complete, and propaganda was at its peak. It appeared that the date of the attack was now to be the end of August, and if something had to be done, it must happen immediately, not seven or eight weeks hence. After having cabled Ciano, Anfuso showed the Attolico message to Mussolini, who saw the need for an immediate discussion with the Germans."

With Ciano summoned back to Rome, a meeting was held on July 22, 1939, in Mussolini's office with Massimo Magistrati, Attolico's First Secretary. The situation was deteriorating too fast, said Mussolini; it was therefore urgent to set up a second Munich, drawing in Italy, Germany, France, England, Poland, and Spain. Two days later, Attolico and Magistrati went to visit Ribbentrop at Füchsl near Salzburg to present the idea, but the entire mission failed. Ribbentrop, while stating that Hitler might change his mind, said that the Führer was opposed to a new international conference. "Germany could not give the impression it was weak or ready to give up. The Poles were behaving very badly, but there was nothing to prevent them from becoming reasonable."

To make some kind of progress, the Italian diplomats proposed an immediate meeting between Hitler and Mussolini at the Brenner Pass on August 4. But Ribbentrop reacted negatively to this proposal as well. A week later, the Führer officially replied that, regretfully, he would not be available in the short term for a summit with the Duce. Only four days earlier, he had signed the orders to occupy Danzig. Since every Italian proposal to avoid war had been rejected, Mussolini decided to communicate with Hitler via Ciano, who left for Salzburg on August 10. The next day, he had his ten-hour clash with Ribbentrop. Just before his execution by firing squad in Verona in 1944, Ciano recalled that tragic day:

"It was in his country house at Füchsl, as we were about to sit down for lunch that Ribbentrop told me about the German decision to set Europe on fire. And he said it as though it were a mere administrative detail.

"'Well, Ribbentrop,' I asked, as we strolled through the garden, 'what is it you want? The corridor or Danzig?'

"'Not anymore,' he answered, looking at me with those cold, metallic eyes of his. 'We want war.'"

The next day, with a heavy heart, Ciano went to see Hitler at his Berchtesgaden residence. Even though the Führer was much more congenial than the unpleasant Ribbentrop, the tune remained the same: Germany is already off to war. "He has words of appreciation for the Duce," wrote Ciano, "but he shows little interest when

I tell him the harm war will do to the Italian people. In the end, I understand that the alliance with us is only worth the amount of enemy forces Italy can divert from facing the German army." Mussolini was in a deep personal crisis. He had never felt more isolated and experienced a confusion of contradictory feelings: pride, anger, hope, jealousy, panic, impotence, opportunism, faith, prudence, and courage.

According to Ciano, Mussolini feared Hitler's rage should Italy decide to cancel the Pact of Steel. The Führer could leave Poland alone and turn against Italy. Mussolini also knew that German espionage was in possession of the Austrian archives, which contained proof of the anti-Nazi actions taken by Italy from 1933 to the Anschluss on March 12, 1938. A close reading of these documents could prompt Hitler to justify giving the "Italian traitors of 1914" a brutal lesson. Torn by all these doubts, Mussolini decided to send Ciano back to Germany after hearing his son-in-law tell him: "The Germans, not us Italians, have betrayed the alliance, where we were to be partners and not servants. Tear up the pact and throw it in Hitler's face, and Europe will recognize in you the leader of an anti-German crusade."

Ciano tried to reach Ribbentrop by phone, but the German Foreign Minister was not available. Finally, at 5:30 p.m. on August 21, Ciano was able to speak to him and to request an urgent meeting at the Brenner Pass. Ribbentrop answered: "I cannot give you an answer because I am waiting for an important message from Moscow. I'll call you back this evening." At 10:00 p.m. Ribbentrop told Ciano that if he needed to meet with him, it would have to be at Innsbruck rather than at the Brenner Pass because of time constraints, since he was due to leave for Moscow to "sign a political agreement with the Soviet Union." Ciano quickly withdrew his request and, in view of the situation, asked his colleague to forget about the meeting until his return from the Soviet capital.

"The Germans," noted Ciano in his Diary, "have dealt a master stroke. The entire European situation has been turned upside down." But even though Stalin may have given Hitler "license to kill" in Poland in order to divide the spoils, Great Britain and France will keep their commitments toward Poland. At dawn on September 1, 1939, German armored divisions crossed the frontier and attacked Poland. The Poles fought back with courage and honor, but that would prove insufficient to avoid their destruction within two weeks. On September 3, London and Paris declared war on Germany. On September 1, Mussolini called Attolico to request that Hitler send Rome a document freeing Italy from any obligation toward the alliance. The Führer sent the following cable to the Duce:

"Duce, I thank you most cordially for the diplomatic and political help you have given to Germany. I am certain to be able to fulfill the task ahead with the German armed forces. I therefore do not think that, in these circumstances, we will need Italian military help. I further thank you, Duce, for everything you will do in the future for the common cause of Fascism and National Socialism."

There had been a thick exchange of letters the week before between Hitler and Mussolini. On August 25, Hitler had justified both his refusal to meet at the Brenner Pass and his agreement with Stalin:

"I had not been able to predict the scope of our conversations with the Russians, nor foreseen any chance of success. Now the friendly attitude of Russia toward us in any conflict was assured while Romania will not dare make any moves. Turkey will have to review its entire policy. Finally, the successful negotiations with Moscow created a new situation, all to the advantage of the Axis." Hitler also confirmed his decision to attack Poland without giving the date. Mussolini answered with the expected congratulations, taking note of the German decisions.

As for Italy, the Duce wrote: "If Germany attacks Poland and the conflict remains localized, Italy shall give Germany every political and economic assistance that will be required; if Germany attacks Poland and the allies of Poland attack Germany, I must inform you that I will not take the initiative of military operations given the present condition of Italian military preparedness as repeatedly pointed out to you and von Ribbentrop. Our intervention can take place immediately if Germany gives us the military materiel and raw materials to withstand the attack from the French and

British which would be directed mostly against us. In our meetings, war had been expected after 1942, and by that time I would be ready on the ground, on the sea, and the air according to the plans we agreed to. I believe that the simple measures already taken and other to be taken later will engage in Europe and Africa large numbers of Anglo-French forces. I consider it to be my duty as a friend to tell you the whole truth."

Hitler was anxiously waiting for the letter, and Attolico had never felt happier in playing the part of letter carrier. Interpreter Paul Schmidt, who witnessed the delivery of the letter, said that "Hitler seemed struck by the message as if he'd been hit by a bomb." Enraged, he repeated the old refrain: "The Italians are behaving exactly as they did in 1914." Attolico was summarily dismissed and called back two hours later to pick up Hitler's reply to Mussolini's requests. In closing his message, Hitler requested the list of materials Italy needed to withstand an attack by the Allies. Attolico was ecstatic: Hitler has backed down somewhat, and in order to preclude any false Italian move, the Ambassador cabled Ciano to make sure that the Italian list of its needs would be a complete list in order to impress upon Hitler that these were not requests which can be satisfied from one day to the next. Attolico had also learned that Hitler had just suspended the attack on Poland, scheduled to begin the next morning at dawn. It was to be Berlin's last attempt to win a war at the negotiating table.

The next day, August 26, Italian newspapers published the news: "This morning, the Duce held a cabinet meeting of the responsible ministers and heads of the general staff to discuss military preparedness."

The real story was very different. Mussolini and his staff were preparing at full speed a list of requested materiel to be submitted to Hitler. Ciano had instructed the group before the meeting: "Be as truthful as possible about our needs in every area. This is not the time to be economical."

The total, ranging from steel to oil, from rubber to antiaircraft guns to molybdenum, came to 170 thousand tons requiring 17 thousand trainloads. In transmitting his list, Mussolini apologized, explaining that it could have been avoided had Italy had the time to replenish its stocks. "Without the certainty of obtaining these materials, I must tell you that the sacrifices I would request of the Italian people with the assurance of being obeyed would all be in vain and could be detrimental to my cause and to yours."

Attolico read and reread the document, realizing that he finally had a weapon to cut the Gordian knot of German-Italian relations he had opposed. He went by car to the chancellery. Magistrati went with him and left the following account:

"I asked Attolico on the way if he'd thought of the term during which the materiel were to be delivered, since nothing was mentioned in Mussolini's letter to that effect. Attolico did not answer me, but when Ribbentrop asked him the same question Attolico answered 'Immediately.' Von Ribbentrop ran in to inform Hitler." Italy had temporarily avoided war.

Hitler answered that only part of the requests could be fulfilled: coal, steel, and wood, but nothing else for the moment; maybe in the future . . . Hitler, after having requested factory workers from Italy for German factories being emptied by military conscription, had asked that Mussolini keep the Anglo-French forces engaged through propaganda and appropriate military demonstrations, and concluded: "Since Attolico has presented the immediate delivery of the items required as an absolute condition prior to your military intervention, I can see that unfortunately your request cannot be satisfied for purely technical reasons. In these circumstances, Duce, I understand your position."

That evening, at the Italian embassy in Berlin, everyone was drinking champagne. Mussolini, truly Italian in his style, sent another note to Hitler to conclude "Attolico had involuntarily misunderstood" the need to deliver everything immediately. Italy in any case remained ready.

During the period of "non-belligerency," a term coined by Mussolini himself because he hated the word "neutrality," Italian industry was working to capacity making more money than ever. Italian cargo ships were completely booked, but Mussolini was only half satisfied. The long winter of the "phony war" between the

Allies and Germany, where no fighting really took place, preoccupied the Duce, who was unable to answer the questions "What will happen in the spring? What will I have to do?" These questions were made even more difficult by the constant sniping by the French and British, who did not let a day go by without creating some new problem for Mussolini: stopping ships, blocking merchandise, or wanting to buy weapons to be used in the war against Germany. A new meeting between Hitler and Mussolini to review the situation became necessary, and it was set for March 18, 1940 at the Brenner Pass.

VI

The Axis

Brenner Pass: March 18, 1940

T he fifth meeting between Hitler and Mussolini took place
at the Brenner Pass on March 18, 1940. They had not met
since the night of the Munich conference on September 29, 1938,
when the world still believed that peace had been saved for generations to come. Between March and September 1939, Hitler, having
reneged on every commitment he had made, in public and in private, had destroyed two countries: Czechoslovakia, just politically,
and Poland, politically and physically. The newest summit was
requested by Hitler not only to justify his lightning alliance with
Moscow, which Rome had bitterly criticized, but also to force
Mussolini to take sides within the framework of the Pact of Steel in
view of his secret war plans for the spring.

In addition, one must factor in the anxiety created in Hitler's
mind by the European trip of US Undersecretary of State Sumner
Welles, intended to boost the democracies. Welles had held several
meetings with Mussolini, Ciano, and Italian Ambassador to Berlin,

Attolico, the latter two by now very high on the German "blacklist" as enemies of the Axis. Finally, Hitler wanted to speak to Mussolini for personal reasons, since he was tired of being "scolded" by all of his closest lieutenants, from Göring and Ribbentrop, to Goebbels and Himmler, that he had made a terrible mistake in tying the fortunes of National Socialism to those of Fascism.

These feelings were not limited to the Führer's entourage, as witnessed by an Italian diplomatic note from the Berlin embassy: "Monday March 18, 1940—The Führer left for the Brenner. News of this meeting spreading today among the public creates a feeling of optimism. Everyone is convinced that peace will be the end result. We have, however, been instructed to sound out the opinion of responsible circles regarding an Italian entry into the war. The unexpected and immediate reaction is: everyone thinks we are joking. Some say 'Italy entering the war? Don't say such absurd things! Mussolini isn't so stupid.' And others say, 'Italy in the war? How could she? God forbid! We already have enough problems!'"

Prince Philip of Hesse delivered the invitation to the Duce for a working lunch with the Führer in Rome on February 8. Mussolini agreed, making Ciano somewhat fearful, as he wrote in his Diary: "The Duce is getting excited. Today he used warmongering language with Hesse. He said it was his intention to be at Germany's side as soon as rearmament would allow Italy to be helpful rather than detrimental to the Germans."

Mussolini, besides feeling the need to do something, had been favorably impressed that Hitler would pick the Brenner Pass for a meeting, thus confirming to everyone that the Alpine pass was now the permanent border between Italy and Germany. All this just two months following the searing conclusion of the options within South Tyrol that had been decided by Rome and Berlin on June 23, 1939, to conclude the delicate nationality problem of the inhabitants of Alto Adige. It had amounted to a forced census, having immediate legal consequences in that those having declared themselves Italian stayed in their own homes, while those who chose German citizenship would have to leave for Germany. The enactment of this inhuman diktat had generated clashes between Fascist and local Nazis. The victim of this state of affairs would be Giuseppe Mastromattei, Prefect of Bolzano, whom Mussolini was to fire in deference to Himmler. And it would not be the last of such sacrifices.

The news of Mussolini's agreement to meet at the Brenner Pass set in motion all the Nazi hard-liners who wanted an agreement with the Italian ally on paper before the spring offensive that was expected to solve all the Führer's problems. Hitler had a huge German army to support for more than one year at a staggering cost to the treasury of the Reich. In Poland, the Germans had not discovered gold, while in the west, the front was frozen on the Siegfried Line, waiting for the allies to attack. Weeks and months went quietly by. Hitler had decided to begin moving by April 1940; otherwise his army would be defeated by hunger. By that date, Mussolini would have had to make up his mind.

The most fateful choice would be for Mussolini to take his place alongside the Germans and engage or block any Allied moves in the Mediterranean. To help Italy make this step, it became urgently necessary to force the Duce to overcome his hesitations, fears, and contradictions, especially while Sumner Welles was traveling around European capitals, preaching moderation and peace. It was also important to ensure that the anti-Axis elements within the Duce's entourage were prevented from influencing his decisions. These men were sabotaging every initiative favorable to the Pact of Steel and went so far as to demand its revocation because of Germany's behavior, as Galeazzo Ciano had hinted during his speech of December 16, 1939, at the Italian Parliament, supported by Ambassador Bernardo Attolico.

Ciano noted on that occasion how the Germans had broken their promise of May 1939 to keep the peace for four or five years, while Ribbentrop had brutally told him at Salzburg in August, "We want war now." Furthermore, Ciano was also guilty in the eyes of the Germans of two other anti-Nazi actions: first, on August 31, 1939, of having told British Ambassador Sir Percy Lorraine that Italy would not join Germany in its attack on Poland, thus inducing the Allies to declare war on Germany; second, to have told the

Belgian ambassador to Rome on January 2, 1940 that Germany was planning to attack the Netherlands.

Hitler entrusted Ribbentrop with the preparations of the summit with Mussolini with a precise agenda in mind.

Ribbentrop began by inviting Ambassador Attolico and his wife to his villa at Dahlem, near Berlin. During the conversation, Ribbentrop—Hitler's "Talleyrand," as he liked to describe himself— asked the ambassador, according to Mario Luciolli, if he was to be considered a friend or an enemy of Germany. The Italian Ambassador replied that he considered himself a friend of Germany but that he was first of all a friend of Italy; that way, Ribbentrop would know which side he was on at all times. He then added that in attempting to avoid war he felt he had defended Germany's interests as well as Italy's as best he interpreted them. Ribbentrop diplomatically agreed with the answers but had secretly placed the Italian Ambassador's name on his list of those to be eliminated.

Through the German Ambassador to Italy, von Mackensen, he told Ciano on March 8, 1940 to expect the German Foreign Minister in Rome to deliver a letter two days later from the Führer to Mussolini. Ciano noted his uneasiness at this move in his Diary while he was negotiating with the British regarding coal shipments by sea from Germany to Italy. On March 10, a sunny spring day, Ciano welcomed Ribbentrop at the railroad station.

Ribbentrop immediately began saying how the good weather would favor military success during the operations that spring. "In a few months, the French army will be destroyed, and the only Englishmen left on the continent will be prisoners of war." He repeated that Italy's place was at Germany's side. With the Duce, the script was the same; Mussolini listened and waited, delaying his answer until they met the next day, just before Ribbentrop's return to Berlin. The Duce avoided any declarations, and said he would go to war, but he needed to pick the date. And he agreed to meet Hitler at the Brenner Pass.

The Nazi machine was moving and Ribbentrop told the Führer in Berlin what the results of his mission were: Attolico and Ciano were completely opposed to the Axis. Mussolini needed to be pushed very quickly. That evening, March 13, Ribbentrop phoned Ciano to confirm the date of Monday, March 18. Mussolini reacted nervously: "These Germans are impossible: they leave you no time to breathe or to think." But in the end, he agreed to the date. As was to happen henceforth before each one of those meetings, Mussolini would prepare himself meticulously, putting documents and memoranda in order and preparing the notes of the subjects he planned to discuss with Hitler. He also wanted Hitler to issue a communiqué that would allow Italy not to participate in the war even after the Germans began their offensive in the west.

Mussolini thought that due to the short time allocated to the meeting by Hitler, only ninety minutes, Germany was about ready to attack. This was troubling to him. He didn't want to be ambushed by Hitler. To Ciano on March 16, he said: "I'll behave like Bertoldo*— I'll accept the death penalty on one condition: that I be allowed to pick the tree for the execution. Needless to say, Bertoldo never found the right tree. I'll go to war if I can pick the time and place, I want to be the one to judge, and a lot will depend on how the war unravels." Ciano then commented: "These statements make me feel better but only up to a point. It's easy to push Mussolini forward, but very hard to pull him back."

On Sunday, March 17, at 1:30 in the afternoon, Mussolini and Ciano, with a small group of functionaries including Anfuso, left for the Brenner Pass. Before pulling out of the station, the German Ambassador, ill at ease, told Ciano that the Führer wished to have a private meeting with the Duce before the conference. This was the signal for the purge of anti-Axis elements from the Italian government, and Hitler wanted to resolve the issue alone with Mussolini. The Duce was calm during the trip; he let his imagination run as he planned the positioning of the ships, armies, and air fleets on the left wing of the Axis deployment. Ciano read the cables from various capitals, which commented favorably on the Brenner meeting. Optimists related the meeting to the Sumner Welles mission, with

---

* Bertoldo is a popular peasant figure in Italian folklore, full of cunning and guile.

whom Ciano had met twice just the day before. Was peace at hand? The hopeful question was on everyone's mind.

At 10:00 a.m. on March 18, Mussolini's train stopped about 300 meters from the border. Half an hour later, slightly behind schedule, Hitler's train pulled in. The weather was awful, with a strong wind and driving snow. The Duce was waiting for the Führer on the platform. After the usual long and warm handshake, the two dictators entered the Italian train. Hitler told the Duce, with all the diplomacy he was capable of, how in Berlin there was uneasiness regarding the unfriendly attitude displayed by Count Ciano toward Germany. He added that Ribbentrop was asking clearly for the resolution of the "Attolico case." The Wilhelmstrasse was deeply uneasy when it had to contact the Italian embassy. Had Ciano himself not requested the removal some time before of Ambassador Ulrich von Hassell because he was considered "an uncooperative man, hostile to the friendship between the two peoples founded on the identity of political regimes and a common policy?"

Ciano wrote in his Diary about the departure of von Hassell when he was replaced by Georg von Mackensen on February 4, 1938: "I feel not the slightest remorse in having been instrumental in replacing this individual, who served his country and the German-Italian friendship so poorly." Under the circumstances, Attolico would also have to pack his bags, said Ribbentrop, who had the gall to propose two names as candidates to the new ambassador's post to Berlin: either Roberto Farinacci or Dino Alfieri. Ciano politely reserved his answer until he had time to consult with the Duce.

With Paul Schmidt as interpreter, Hitler then began his monologue, after spreading a map on the table showing the positions of 207 German divisions already in place or about to be deployed. This was a powerful psychological weapon to use on Mussolini, who followed intently the deployment of this tremendous wall of steel and fire ready to be let loose on any new enemy of the Reich. Hitler began by justifying his attack on Poland with the "fact" that Germans living in border areas were subjected to persecution and unspeakable atrocities by the Poles.

Naturally, this attack was made possible by the satisfactory agreement reached with Russia, and, he added with a slight argument toward the Duce (who had criticized the move), that "since there was no conflict of interest between the two countries," he, Hitler, had determined that it was essential to maintain forever good relations with the Soviet Union, since "Stalin had thrown Judeo-Bolshevism overboard to re-launch Slav nationalism." In the near future, a German-Russian agreement would be possible with Italian participation to keep the peace in the Orient and the Balkans.

With respect to the "blitzkrieg" (which he, Hitler was convinced he had invented), the Führer explained that it was a modern use of mechanized divisions together with light bombers, especially the famed Stukas, which had performed beyond all expectation. "Entire centers are blown away in a few hours. The Luftwaffe has been a surprise, not just for the enemy, but also for us. A wonderful surprise. That augurs well for the future." Hitler then analyzed the relations between Britain and France, carefully showing the moral superiority of the Third Reich when compared to the decadent democratic nations.

Then he came to the crux of the meeting. As persuasively and patronizingly as possible, he said that he had not come all the way down to the Brenner to ask for something of his Italian friend, but only to explain how things stood. If Italy was content with a secondary role in the Mediterranean, then she had no need to make any moves; but if Italy aspired to play the role of a great power, then she would always find her path blocked by France and Britain. It was up to the Duce to make the final decision, based upon the objective analysis he had undertaken. The Führer emphasized once again that Italy's and Germany's fates were now irrevocably joined. The defeat of Germany would mean the end of the Italian Empire. But he was a realist and did not wish to push the Duce to do anything that would go against the interests of the Italian people because, "contrary to what the British do, we don't expect anyone else to pull the chestnuts out of the fire." Hitler concluded that the German divisions were poised to attack in the west without saying how and when. "What will you do?" he asked the Duce.

Humbled like a poor relation, Mussolini answered that he too hated the French and the British; he agreed with the Führer that Italy would have to enter the war. The date was the big problem because the depleted condition of the Italian treasury did not allow for a long war. If the expected German offensive in the west could be delayed for three to four months, then Italy could complete some of its preparations. In this way, Italy could participate in the offensive and not just look on from the sidelines at its ally's battles.

Hitler answered that he would not alter his plans to suit Italy.

"I suggest, Duce, an attack that would be less difficult and costly than a direct assault against France over the Alps. I propose that about twenty Italian divisions line up alongside the German army near the Swiss border, facing the Rhone Valley in an attempt to outflank the Italian-French border."

Mussolini showed enthusiasm for this idea but insisted that Italy's role would be to give a coup de grace to the Allies "strong enough to break their legs." However, if the German advance were to be slow, Italy would have to wait.

Hitler, now convinced that his future offensive depended on speed, didn't even consider the possibility of a slower advance, and he formally accepted Mussolini's declaration to come into the war in due course. Having reached this agreement in principle, the dictators had a quick lunch and then parted company with the promise of meeting again soon to celebrate the inevitable victory.

At 1:10 p.m., Mussolini's train journeyed back to Rome. Ciano noted that Mussolini had found Hitler to be as adamant as Ribbentrop had led them to believe. The Duce thought Hitler would hesitate longer before ordering the offensive, and he advised the Führer to make more use of his air force and navy. The meeting had not changed any of Italy's plans. Mussolini reported by cable to the King the next day: "Yesterday's conversation was very important, more than I had anticipated. Hitler impressed me as being in good spirits and excellent physical condition and, in spite of some minor hesitations, certain of victory. I do not think there will be an immediate ground offensive. As soon as more news arrives from

Berlin, I'll send you a report. I wish to offer to Your Majesty my devoted respects."

The press reports from the meeting said very little: "The Duce and the Führer have held, at the Brenner Pass, in the Duce's railroad car, a two-and-one-half-hour meeting with the participation of Count Ciano and von Ribbentrop." The entire German press expressed satisfaction at the friendly atmosphere of the discussions. The *Deutsche Allegemeine Zeitung* commented on the coincidence of the submarine attack at Scapa Flow and the Brenner meeting:

"Our soldiers are taking the war where England does not expect it. Our foreign policy prevents war where England would want it to be. In Berlin, we note that both Germany and Italy are in agreement in preventing the extension of the war to the Middle East and the Balkans. Rumors reported yesterday relating to the possible Russian and German guarantee, joined also by Italy, for peace in those regions continue to be discussed in many circles and are thought by many to be related to the Brenner meeting. It is possible that Hitler and Mussolini have discussed this issue at length."

The Italian embassy in Berlin had a much less enthusiastic assessment: "Tuesday, March 19, the Führer returned from the Brenner Pass but did not want anyone from the embassy staff to be present at his arrival. An obvious condemnation of Attolico's policies. Everyone thinks we are on the threshold of peace; they all praise Mussolini and fail to recognize that, because of Italy, the war is about to become even more intense. Even the few people who know the situation but who are not blinded by the ideas of Ribbentrop and Hitler, think that the Duce, by changing his attitude so radically, may be trying some mysterious move. These same people are absolutely convinced that Italy has no intention of going to war anytime soon. Our military officers show signs of alarm. They had thought we were exaggerating when we told them our fears after Ribbentrop's visit to Rome. Now these same people have seen some evidence and are becoming very uneasy. They show us on paper why it is impossible for Italy to go to war. The Germans know this. They don't believe in our entry into the war and don't even want it. Other indications show that Ribbentrop's March 10 visit to Rome was meant to secure Italy's neutrality just before the Reich's next offensive."

Ciano knew all the secrets of the Brenner meeting, and everyone wanted him to reveal what had really happened. The next day, March 19, he met quietly with Sumner Welles at the Acquasanta Golf Club outside Rome to tell him there were no new developments: "An internal Axis event that leaves everything unchanged."

The American Undersecretary was pleased to note, as Ciano relates:

"There is no immediate threat of a military clash. Roosevelt will thus have the time to ponder Welles's conclusions and possibly make some move for peace. Welles also spoke of a possible meeting between Mussolini and Roosevelt at the Azores: a complicated project with uncertain results."

Ciano was less reticent than usual with the American diplomat in order to position himself, in the eyes of the Western powers, as someone in the know, someone who could play an important role. In fact, hoping to create a back channel to Roosevelt, he told Welles:

"Please give the president the following message. Tell him that I have the greatest personal admiration for him and the utmost faith in what he can accomplish for civilization in Europe. Tell him that as long as I remain Italian Foreign Minister, Italy will not enter this war at Germany's side and that I will do all I can to influence Mussolini in this direction. Tell him that I wish above all to have the opportunity for Italy to cooperate with the United States to reestablish the peace the President is hoping for."

But when the fateful moment arrived, Ciano did not keep his promise and resign from the post of foreign minister. Neither he nor Mussolini had understood the long-term strategy of President Roosevelt, who had already decided to enter the war on the side of the Allies with a series of small steps to provoke a German reaction. All the while Roosevelt was preparing his third-term reelection and attempting to resolve the Depression that still gripped the United States. The New Deal had so far been unable to bring back prosperity and economic stability. Before building 24,000 planes in 1938, Roosevelt said: "War is an illness, and those nations responsible for illegal acts should be quarantined." To secure his voting base, the President had also declared: "Your sons will not be sent to fight foreign wars." Roosevelt dreamed of a peace that would be an American peace after the break up of the British Empire and the substitution of the sterling with the dollar as the standard of world trade: an old settling of accounts between the American colonies and the "old country."

After Sumner Welles, Ciano was at pains to reassure the British ambassador, Sir Percy Lorraine, by telling him that "the Brenner meeting does not precede any new changes in our policy." This was what the British ambassador was hoping to hear. Ciano was less persuasive with François-Poncet, who deplored "the meeting between those two gentlemen at the Brenner," as Chamberlain put it at the House of Commons that same day.

Giuseppe Bottai, the Fascist intellectual, who considered himself in political exile as Minister of Education and aspired to an important diplomatic posting, such as Berlin or London, was careful to maintain his contact with Ciano, who, he thought, could help him realize his ambitions. He was often seen at lunch with Ciano at the Acquasanta Golf Club but managed to avoid being a member of the "friends of Ciano" club, as Galeazzo's group of sycophants was called. Bottai was always seeking access to the center of the power structure and asked Ciano on March 19 about the "real" news from the Brenner.

Ciano answered: "Nothing definite, but we are on the way to a compromise solution. The Führer spoke for two hours and ten minutes. Mussolini for twenty minutes. Hitler, while repeating what Ribbentrop had said about overwhelming German superiority, did not seem so sure of himself, as Ribbentrop tried to be while here in Rome. Mussolini was eager to demonstrate how Italy would not, before or after, align itself with the French and British, and he didn't even discuss the possibility of going to war alongside Germany. But the Germans interpret this omission as a subterfuge, and no matter what, Mussolini is still free to act as he pleases, and he waits for events to show him the way. A Germany victorious on its own frightens him. Contacts with the British and French are maintained through me personally, and Mussolini knows it, since I keep him informed daily, even though I keep taking the initiative so as not to involve him. There is none of the duplicity that is being whispered about."

However, the "Ciano case" became real just two days later, as he wrote in his *Diary*: "There are many rumors that the Duce has decided to replace me as Foreign Minister. I don't think so." But the rumors were correct. They followed the complaints voiced by Hitler. And there was gossip in Rome that Ciano was now proclaiming himself openly as Mussolini's "heir apparent" and pursuing his own policies. But Ciano, who, up until August 1939, had been a key figure in promoting the success of the Axis, had the privilege of being the Duce's son-in-law, the husband of his beloved daughter, Edda. Had Mussolini shifted Ciano to another ministry, foreign opinion would have attributed the move either to a weakening of the alliance with Germany or, after Ciano's speech in December that was critical of Germany, as a necessary move to calm Berlin.

So Mussolini chose the worst compromise: he merely alluded to the problem at a morning meeting without openly saying so, as Filippo Anfuso noted after a conversation with Ciano, with whom he was on quite friendly terms. Toward the end of the meeting, Mussolini showed Ciano the front page of a French newspaper with an article entitled, "Röhm—the man who wanted to succeed Hitler."

The Duce said: "Read this carefully. This man Röhm was powerful. He could do anything he wanted. He played the role of both military and political leader; he had armed followers and faithful troops. Hitler let him be because it seemed he owed him a lot. Röhm was totally unprincipled and had very bad habits. But in spite of his past—"

Ciano interrupted the Duce: "I remember this well . . . "

And Mussolini continued: "Yes, but perhaps in this article, you'll discover some details you didn't know. The most important thing is that Röhm was considered untouchable. Hitler not only got rid of him----some say he even shot him himself, but I don't believe this---he also liquidated all of Röhm's friends, conspirators, acquaintances, all in a few hours. A few hours! It's a very strange story. But read the article, because it's interesting."

Ciano understood the warning and told Anfuso initially that it certainly originated from one of his enemies. But from that day on, he was resolutely opposed to the Duce's policies all the way to the vote against Mussolini on July 25, 1943, a vote that would land him in front of a firing squad in Verona.

The "Attolico case" was resolved very easily, even though Berlin sent a request seeing that one whole month had gone by since the Brenner meeting and nothing had happened. On the morning of April 25, Ciano talked to the Duce about it and proposed naming Dino Alfieri, much more civilized and levelheaded than Farinacci, Ribbentrop's alternate candidate. Mussolini accepted the proposal and personally instructed the new ambassador regarding his mission in Germany: Italy intends to remain faithful to the Axis, but "as for the war, be advised that I will go in only when I have the mathematical certainty of being able to win it."

The substitution of Attolico, Ribbentrop's *bête noire*, did not surprise anyone in Berlin: it had been seen coming for some time, since the end of the summer, in fact, when Germany attacked Poland. The German Foreign Minister, fond of quoting the adage: "Naples is the only African city without a European quarter." aimed all his anger and hatred for the Italians directly at Attolico. Attolico, who had been ill and unable to attend the Brenner meeting, took the news in stride. In saying good-bye to his staff, who had been very supportive in trying to keep Italy out of the war, he said: "There's nothing more to be done." He was right: Italy was now only forty days away from war.

Having closed the "Ciano and Attolico cases," Mussolini began studying the second important point Hitler had made during their meeting: the best plan for an attack on France, which he had accepted with enthusiasm, if not quite understanding what was meant by it. Hitler had demonstrated enough competence and thoroughness in discussing his plan to make anyone envious, even the Duce, who was always wearing his rank insignia as First Marshal of the Italian Empire, a new rank that had become a curse. In practical terms, it had not added anything special, but in personal terms, he had clashed with King Victor Emanuel, who had felt humiliated at being lumped together with his prime minister in the military area, which the King believed to be his exclusive domain.

Mussolini himself was to write about the "marshal issue" in his book, *Storia di un anno,* because it was a thorn in his side. In order to give the Duce his due (having "wanted, planned, and won" the war in Ethiopia), the Fascist Parliament had decided in 1938 to create the rank of "First Marshal of the Empire," awarding the special rank to both the King and the Duce. Mussolini wrote: "Once the law was approved by both houses of Parliament, the King was about to refuse to sign it. In our meeting right after the vote, he was extremely excited. After the law of the Grand Council, he said, this law is another deathblow against my royal prerogatives. I could have conferred upon you as a sign of my personal admiration any rank, but this creates an unacceptable situation because it violates the statute of the Kingdom."

The Duce replied: "You know I have no interest in such honors. Those promoting this wanted to offer Your Majesty the same rank automatically." "No," answered Victor Emanuel, "Parliament cannot take such initiatives. This is really unacceptable! I don't wish to add any oil to the fire in the midst of an international crisis, but in other times, rather than accept such an affront, I would prefer to abdicate! I would rip off this double decoration!" (the insignia worn on the sleeve of the uniform). This had become a joke all over Italy, and Mussolini avoided wearing the uniform of first marshal as much as he could, most of all whenever the King was present and substituted for it the old uniform of corporal of the Fascist militia.

Hitler's "easy" plan for Mussolini to attack France was neither new nor even applicable. It was an operation often studied by the Italian military staff. The Führer, sensing the excitement of the Duce at his suggestion, summoned to Zossen (the headquarters of the Wehrmacht), the German military attaché in Rome to receive instructions.

On April 10, 1940, General Enno von Rintelen, presented to the Italian general staff from its German counterparts a memorandum that detailed "a few possibilities for the engagement of the Italian army: (a) sending twenty to thirty divisions to the south of Germany, where, after the break in enemy lines in the upper Rhine, would see the engagement of the Italian forces on the German left flank; advance into the Vosges towards the Langres plateau with the possibility of moving south and so opening up the Alpine front; (b) offensive on the Alps front; (c) Italian operations in Africa. The German high command considered the first proposal, the one proposed by Hitler as the best one and invited General Mario Roatta to give his opinion on the subject during his visit to Berlin."

Marshal Graziani in his book of memoirs, *Ho difeso la patria*, remembers the incident: "In April, the German high command sent us the following proposal: 'When the German army attacks the Maginot Line, an Italian army corps of 10 to 15 divisions, with modern weapons and equipment furnished by Germany, will take positions at Burgund Gate (Trouée de Belfort) to break through into the Rhone Valley and turn the French army defending the Alps (then about 25 divisions strong).' This plan was a revival of the one created during the Triple alliance, between Germany, Austria-Hungary, and Italy, that the Italian high command still had in its files.

"At the beginning of the First World War, Italy was preparing to follow this plan had it not been interrupted by the decision to remain neutral. Mussolini ordered me to study the plan. A memorandum was prepared by the high command: one copy went to Mussolini and another to General Pietro Badoglio. General Roatta was about to go Germany to reach an agreement regarding the operation. When I explained the project to him, Badoglio listened without making any comment, and to my question as to what should be done next, answered: 'Nothing more. I will take over this matter, and I will let you know what else needs to be done in the future.'"

Graziani continues: "Some time later I was asked to report to the Duce, who was staying at Villa Torlonia because he was not well. He received me in a small study next to his bedroom, looking very angry when he entered. He grabbed the file with the documents and asked me: 'What did you send me to read?' I answered: 'The plan to deploy the troops at the Burgund Gate.' He only said,

'I see.' A real crisis began. A nervous Mussolini, in shirtsleeves, paced rapidly up and down the small space of his study . . . He was nervous at not being able to make a decision regarding the plan for which he'd previously been so enthusiastic. I dared to say: 'Duce, the army follows you faithfully . . . are you as certain about the general staff?' I had hit the bull's eye. Mussolini screamed in a high-pitched voice: 'So be it! If Badoglio doesn't feel up to it, let him leave! Let him leave. This is not about me, but about the interests of the country . . . ! Go, Graziani, I'll let you know what my decision is about this.'" The plan for the Burgund Gate was shelved. The old marshals fought among themselves like old women and enemies under the incredibly loose "command" of the Duce.

According to Badoglio, things went differently and even Graziani rejected the three German plans at first, under the proviso that the problem of troop transports should be solved. Badoglio had in fact rejected them all in writing to Mussolini:

"The German high command is more interested in the positioning of 20 to 30 divisions on the Rhine . . . Naturally, this troop movement should take place only after the beginning of the German offensive along the entire front and after a significant success is certain . . . In conclusion, we would be going in as secondary troops . . . I don't think that you, Duce, who so proudly have upheld Italian prestige in 1935 and 1936 in the face of world threats, could agree to such a use of our armed forces."

The negative effects of the Brenner meeting became apparent on March 31, 1940, when Mussolini, still under the influence of Hitler's pressure, wrote his secret political and strategic memorandum on the world crisis that had started in September 1939. It is the most important Italian document of that period because it explains the philosophical motivations underlying Italy's entrance into the war. Using syllogistic arguments, the Duce recorded in that memo his categorical and final conclusions on Italy's short-term destiny. Only eight copies of this secret memo were printed and sent to the King, Marshals Badoglio and Graziani, the Foreign Minister, the Minister for Africa, the Chiefs of Staff of the Navy and the Air Force, and the Duce's private secretariat.

In his introductory comments, Mussolini wrote:

"In the present, extremely fluid, situation, it becomes difficult, if not impossible, to make any sort of forecast . . . The unexpected is apt to play a large role (see the Russo-Finnish War) and we must consider what might happen to the policies of countries far removed, like the United States or Japan.

"Negotiated compromise peace.

"This possibility must be excluded in the present circumstances. It is true that strong pacifist sentiments are voicing their opinion publicly in England and underground in France, but the war aims of the Allies are such, that any compromise is impossible. It could only begin with the acceptance of the fait accompli of German and Russian conquests in the northeast, but this can't be reconciled with the stated intent to reconstitute Poland, Czechoslovakia, and even Austria. Germany could accept a compromise peace more easily than the democracies. The democracies would not shy away from accepting the Polish booty of Russia if Russia were to leave Germany in the lurch. Mr. [Sumner] Welles has at the end of his pilgrimage concluded that a negotiated peace is still premature.

"Ground military operations.

"Can we can predict that the Franco-British alliance will take offensive operations, meaning an attack on the west wall on the western front? This can be discounted as things now stand. British troop strength in France is minimal . . . The morale of the French army is defensive not offensive. The Franco-British are looking for a ground front that is less uncomfortable than the one in the west . . . But such a front is not readily apparent geographically. The Balkans? The Caucasus? Libya? The Franco-British will continue to avoid the initiative in ground operations; to operate counteroffensively rather than offensively on the sea and in the air, and most of all, to tighten the blockade around Germany.

"German operations.

"For months we have heard about a German operation against the Maginot Line or against Belgium and Holland to reach the Channel. Logic would dictate that this offensive should also be excluded for the following reasons: (1) Germany has already reached its war aims and can wait for the enemy's attack, because it is too risky to bet everything on one operation . . . It's therefore probable that between an attack and the tactic of resistance, Germany will choose the latter; it will do everything to resist the blockade; (2) it will take the initiative in larger naval and air force operations to break the blockade . . .

"Italy's Position.

"If the unexpected happens, that is, a negotiated peace in the next few months, Italy, in spite of its nonbelligerent status, will not be excluded from the negotiations; but if the war goes on, to think that Italy can remain outside the conflict until the end is absurd and impossible. Italy is not in a corner of Europe like Spain, it is not half Asiatic like Russia, it is not far removed from the war zone like Japan or the United States; Italy is in the middle of the nations at war, by land and by sea, and it therefore cannot avoid taking arms. Even if Italy should switch allegiances and go to the Allied camp, she could not avoid immediate war with Germany, a war that Italy would have to fight alone; only the alliance with Germany, a country which has not yet needed our military help and is content with our economic help and our moral support, allows for our current nonbelligerent status. Excluding the possibility of a switch on our part, which even the Franco-British do not expect, and seem to appreciate in us, the other possibility remains: a parallel war to that of Germany's to reach our objectives, which can be summed up in this formula: freedom on the seas, window on the ocean. Italy will not really be an independent nation until it does away with Corsica, Bizerte, Malta, Gibraltar, and Suez, all of which constitute the walls and bars of her prison. Once its frontiers on the ground have been resolved, if Italy wants truly to be a world power it must resolve the problem of its frontiers on the water: the very security of the empire is tied to this fact.

"Italy cannot possibly remain neutral for the entire duration of the war without abdicating its role, without disqualifying itself, without being reduced to a Switzerland multiplied by ten.

"The problem is therefore not to know whether Italy will or will not enter the war, because Italy will not be able to stay out of the war; we need to know WHEN AND HOW; we need to delay as much as possible, in accordance with our honor and dignity, our entry into the war:

a. to prepare, so that our participation becomes decisive;

b. because Italy cannot engage in a prolonged war and cannot spend hundreds of billions as the current warring nations are doing.

"As to the date, during the Brenner meeting, it was clearly established that this is Italy's decision and that Italy must make it alone.

"War plan.

"Working under the premise that war cannot be avoided and that we cannot ally ourselves with the Franco-British (meaning that we cannot go to war against Germany), we must lay down from now on the overall strategy so that detailed studies can be made.

"Ground front: on the defensive on the Alps. No initiatives. Surveillance. Initiatives only in the unlikely case of a complete French collapse under German attack. The occupation of Corsica can be planned but the prize is probably not worth the trouble; however, the air bases on the island must be neutralized.

"In the east, toward Yugoslavia, first cautious observation. Attack in case there is an internal collapse of the nation because of the Croat secession already taking place.

"Albanian front: the attitude to the north (Yugoslavia) and to the south (Greece) is related to what will happen on the eastern front.

"Libya: defensive posture towards Tunisia, as well as Egypt.

"Aegean: defensive.

"Ethiopia: offensive to guarantee Eritrea and operations on Gedaref and Kassala; offensive on Djibuti, defensive and possibly counteroffensive on Kenya.

"Air forces: will shadow the activity of the army and navy...

"Navy: offensive across the Mediterranean and elsewhere.

"These are the directives on which the high commands should base their operational studies . . . without wasting an hour's time, in spite of our intent to delay, for the stated reasons, as long as possible our current status as nonbelligerent, the decisions of the Franco-British or an unforeseen complication that could force us, even in the immediate future, to get into the war.

Rome, March 31, 1940."

This memorandum, written by the Duce and considered by the impressionable King to be a model of geometric precision, set the stage for an Italian war parallel to Germany's war.

Three days later, as if to confirm Mussolini's document, "Operation Weser" began: the occupation of Denmark and Norway by Nazi troops. The lightning speed of this operation took the British completely by surprise. The German success, allowing Hitler to control the North Sea, with its iron ore supply lanes, came at a heavy price: over two months of harsh combat (April 8 to June 8, 1940), the loss of three cruisers, ten destroyers, eight submarines, and twelve merchant ships. The Allies were defeated both morally and materially and lost an aircraft carrier, two cruisers, nine destroyers, and eight submarines. The British were able to rescue King Haakon VII of Norway, his cabinet, and the Norwegian state gold reserves. But Hitler was able to grab seventy-five million dollars in the banks of Oslo and Copenhagen. King Christian X of Denmark, surrendered to the aggressors three hours after the ultimatum was handed in at 8:30 a.m. on April 9, 1940, "to spare his country disaster and destruction." Mussolini was kept in the dark about all these plans: at the Brenner meeting, Hitler had said nothing regarding his intentions in Scandinavia, even though his plan was in effect since March 1.

For anyone else, even as a question of personal pride, it would have been an excellent excuse to show some displeasure towards a cagey ally. But Mussolini once again accepted the humiliation and the Führer's excuse that he had to protect the northern operation from any possible leaks in order to maintain the element of surprise. Hitler kept repeating that the Duce was surrounded by a clique of blabbermouths, like Count Ciano, who learned of the attack on Denmark and Norway at 7:00 a.m. from German Ambassador von Mackensen on the day it was launched. Then they both delivered the Führer's message to Mussolini, who was waiting at Villa Torlonia.

Ciano noted: "Same letter in the usual style to announce what had already taken place. Mussolini said: 'I heartily approve of Hitler's action. It is a move that can have enormous consequences, and this is the way wars are won. The democracies have been beaten by speed. I'll order the press and the Italian people to approve wholeheartedly the German move!' When we were alone, the Duce talked about Croatia. He's itching to get involved. He wants to shorten the timing and take advantage of the confusion that is gripping Europe." Hitler later kept Mussolini informed on the progress of the operations.

General Pricolo remembers: "The Führer wrote a long letter to the Duce, praising the lightning speed and success of the campaign, thus starting the myth of the invincibility of the German soldier. Mussolini, as he read me a few lines from the letter, seemed transformed. He became nervous, impatient, anxious to do something, as he admired the latest proof of the power and precision of the German military machine . . . " Hitler continued his correspondence with Mussolini through the month of April, both to make him swallow the initial lack of trust and to slowly fire up his colleague's growing enthusiasm for war. May was to be Mussolini's longest month. The Germans kept on winning, and the leaders of the democracies continued to exhort the Duce to remain cautious and abandon the "Nazi wolf" to his destiny.

Hitler, excited by his success in Norway, then set the date for the attack in the west. Chamberlain, who cut a pathetic figure with his umbrella as a symbol of peace before being misled and then defeated by Hitler, resigned as prime minister on May 10, 1940. Winston Churchill replaced him and immediately formed a War Cabinet. On the same day, at 5:55 a.m., the German army invaded Holland, Belgium, and Luxembourg. It was the beginning of the end for France. The German attack was another early wake-up call for Mussolini, who at dawn on May 10 once again received Ambassador von Mackensen and Count Ciano at his residence. The ambassador could not hide his embarrassment at the fact that the diplomatic courier who arrived from Berlin had been locked in his hotel room all night waiting for 5:00 a.m., the precise hour set by the Führer to hand over the letter to the Duce.

Ciano described the scene: "Mussolini read the letter wherein Hitler explained the reasons for his move and invited the Duce to consider the decisions he intended to make for the future of his people. Then Mussolini looked at the attachments. Finally, after about two hours, he told Mackensen that he was convinced that France and England were about to attack Germany through Belgium and Holland, and he therefore approved Hitler's decision unconditionally. After Mackensen left, he repeated to me how impressed he was by the quick success of the Nazi armies and of his own decision to go to war."

Hitler had personally drawn up the plan to liquidate France, based on a blueprint by General Erich von Manstein. Three army groups would move west as follows: Army group one, under General von Bock, would enter Holland and Belgium and attract as many French and British troops there as possible. Von Bock would attack with paratroopers and airlifted troops, even using gliders to encircle the Belgian and Dutch defenses and create the impression that the Germans were attacking France from the north. The second group, under von Leeb, with fewer divisions, would cover the line between Luxembourg and the Swiss border to control the Maginot Line.

Finally, the third and most important group, once it was certain that both the French and British had fallen into the trap and run to the rescue of the Belgians and Dutch, was to break through the center of the Ardennes toward Sedan with forty-six divisions, including seven armored divisions led by the young lions of the Wehrmacht: Hoth, Reinhardt, Guderian, and Rommel. It all went so smoothly that Hitler himself, a veteran of the battle of the Marne in the First World War, became fearful of having fallen into a trap as he was setting one up. He even got angry with Guderian, who was racing along, covering forty kilometers a day, and had allowed his tank commanders fill up with gasoline from abandoned private service stations along the way.

It was the darkest hour yet for the Allies. The Franco-British high commands and the governments of both countries were in a state of panic, and within the chaos came accusations, recriminations, and criticism. The first to be criticized were the Poles, who had only lasted two weeks against the Nazis rather than six months as they had promised. Then Denmark because she had surrendered in a single morning, and Norway for not having resisted more vigorously. Holland was absolved because of Queen Wilhelmina, who had been able to reach London with the Dutch treasury and government on a British vessel. But King Leopold III of Belgium, in the midst of the confusion among the Allies, was to be the most vigorously condemned because he surrendered his army on May 27, without informing the British and French.

With little flags pinned on a large map, Mussolini followed the German invasion of France as it swept away everything in its path. In the morning, he was ready to declare war on the Allies, but by the afternoon, he had second thoughts and put everything off until the next day. He was nervous and openly expressed his frustration to everyone. Only the "hawks" were allowed in to see him. The moderates and doubters were left to rot in the anteroom along with the ambassadors of the United States, France, and Great Britain, who were coming with last-minute compromise proposals to keep Italy out of the war. Up to the Belgian surrender on May 27, the Duce kept repeating that he could waste no more time and had to join in Hitler's fishing expedition.

On May 29 at 11:00 a.m. at the Palazzo Venezia, the Duce assembled the Italian High Command. Three days before, he had told Balbo and Badoglio: "Yesterday I sent Hitler a message to assure him that I will not sit on my hands and that starting June 5, I'll be ready to declare war on England." However, there is no trace of this document in the existing correspondence between the two dictators. Mussolini was possibly already lying to himself and to everyone else in order to convince himself that there was no alternative to war.

At the May 29 meeting attended by Badoglio, the chief of staff, and Graziani, Cavagnari, and Pricolo, the Duce gave precise orders for the first day of war: "We'll stay on the defensive. Something may happen in the east: Yugoslavia. Our forces will be concentrated against England, its naval positions and ships sailing in the Mediterranean. As I announced on May 26, 1939, an air and naval war on every front." To clarify and emphasize the authority of his orders, Mussolini sent out a memo on June 4: "The Supreme Commander at war of all the armed forces wherever they may be stationed is the Duce, by delegation of His Majesty the King." The immediate consequence of the meeting of May 29 was the so called "P.R. 12 bis," the mobilization plan in case of war with France and Great Britain, with a hostile Yugoslavia and Greece and Turkey as neutrals.

Yugoslavia's "hostility" was short lived. On May 29, Ciano appeased the Yugoslav ambassador regarding the peaceful intentions of Italy toward his country. The war plan was then modified to "P.R.12," which forecast a neutral Yugoslavia. On May 30, Mussolini gave Ciano the note to be transmitted to Hitler regarding Italy's final decisions. The date of Italy's declaration of war was set for June 5 unless the Führer required another few days' delay. Hitler's written response arrived the next day through the German ambassador.

Ciano wrote: "The news of our intervention is welcomed by the chancellor with enthusiasm. He asks that the date be set back a few days because he intends to attack the French airports shortly. He fears that Italy's declaration of war might prompt the French to move their planes and thus avoid destruction. The Duce agrees."

Mussolini was ready to accept any one of Hitler's wishes as commands at this point, and he even claimed the delay was positive because "it allows for more time to prepare in Libya." Twenty-four hours later, once the date had been set at June 11, Mussolini was told by von Mackensen that Hitler had again changed his mind and now wanted Italy in the war as soon as possible. This time Mussolini refused to change and maintained the June 11 date. Ciano noted: "Even the King finds the date of the 11th to be a good one because it is his birthday and his number as an army recruit was 1111."

The game was finally up, and at 6:00 p.m. on Monday, June 10, 1940, Mussolini went to the balcony of the Palazzo Venezia to announce that as of the next day, Italy would be at war with France and Great Britain. It was not the best of the dictator's speeches. He listed his motives and justified his personal decision, since he had not consulted the government or the Grand Council of Fascism. He spoke of "an hour marked by destiny that flies in the sky of our motherland . . . "; of having his own "conscience at peace" for having tried to avoid the "hurricane that was overtaking Europe"; and he recalled the sanctions directed against Italy by the League of Nations as justifications for his theatrical gesture. He was more realistic when he spoke of "the fight of poor nations with many arms against the exploiters who stringently control the monopoly of all the wealth and all the gold of this earth."

He concluded with a call to arms: "Take up your weapons and show your tenacity, your courage, and your valor." That was it. With mixed feelings, the crowd left Piazza Venezia and the hundreds of other town squares of Italy, where loudspeakers had broadcast the Duce's voice. The wars that are won are the ones the people really want to fight, as the old adage says. But there was no doubt that a majority of Italians sensed that this would not be a short, easy war, because the United States, the Soviet Union, and Japan, still outside the conflict, would certainly not be able to accept momentous changes without having their say. Ciano marked the moment: "The news of the war doesn't surprise anyone and doesn't create any excessive enthusiasm. I am sad, very sad. The adventure begins. May God help Italy."

This sadness was not visible according to General Pricolo: "On June 10, Ciano, who liked to pass for anti-German, was present at the Palazzo Venezia dressed in the uniform of an air force lieutenant colonel, looking fit and satisfied. Shortly before, he'd told us how he had summoned the British ambassador, Sir Percy Lorraine, to inform him of our decision. The ambassador remained unmoved and only asked for a written copy of the declaration of war. It was the same ambassador to whom, on August 31, 1939, even before the shooting war began, Ciano (with Mussolini's approval) told that Italy would never go to war against France and Great Britain." Mussolini, respectful of the old diplomatic customs, gave the enemy a six-hour preannouncement.

Some critics interpreted this as proof of the complete absence of any war plans within the Italian high command. Hitler also was convinced this was the case, as his military attaché to Rome recalled: "He said that when the Duce told him he could not delay the announcement beyond June 11, he, Hitler, was convinced that Italy had prepared a lightning move against Corsica, Tunis, or Malta and that military secrecy prevented a delay." So, after the speech, he obviously expected something to happen. But nothing moved. "He reminded the Führer of what happened in the Middle Ages, when cities exchanged threatening messages and nothing else happened."

Both the French and British were being beaten and humiliated. The Italians also suffered a huge loss at the declaration of war: 220 merchant ships and 1,226,000 tons of shipping were caught in foreign ports, a very costly disaster to Italy. After the war, General Pricolo remembered that when Mussolini told him of the date of June 10 as the official day of the announcement, he begged the Duce to delay for one day at least. On the French border, at Modane, there was a train transporting special steel alloys to Italy, nickel, chrome, lead, copper, rubber, and mica. Mussolini answered: "I perfectly understand, and you are right. But if I give twenty-four hours, I'm sure that tomorrow Admiral Cavagnari will come over to talk about his submarines that are far away from Italy, and then the minister of merchant marine will ask about this or that ocean liner on its way back. And so on." Operationally, the orders for June 10 were to maintain the defensive on all fronts.

Only late that night did Mussolini accept that going to war meant firing a few shots, and he suddenly gave Pricolo orders to attack Malta the next day. During the night of June 11 to 12, the British bombed Turin, the first Italian city to be hit during the Second World War. One week later, after some small skirmishes, Hitler called

Mussolini urgently by phone: the Duce had to come immediately to Munich because the French had asked for an armistice. Paris had fallen three days before and was now under German occupation. The new French government on the run had ended up in Bordeaux, the provisional capital, and was now headed by Marshal Pétain. The Spanish government had been the go-between for the French and the Germans. On the night of June 16, after being head of the government for only one hour, Pétain asked his foreign minister, Paul Baudoin, to summon the Spanish ambassador to give him a note asking Spain to request "the conditions Chancellor Hitler would require to put a halt to military operations and sign an armistice." The message arrived at the Führer's roving headquarters at the village of Brûly-en-Petche, not far from Sedan, at 3:00 a.m. Hitler's aides were uncertain as to whether they should wake him up until finally his valet opened the door where the Obersterkriegsherr was sleeping.

Pétain's message came as no surprise to the Führer, who had been expecting it for days, and he had already planned a spectacular program to record the scene of the French surrender to the Germans for future generations. Hitler also thought it correct to punish the centuries' old enemy by answering their request unhurriedly after a moment to ponder the situation, justified by the "need" to consult the Axis ally. The French had completely forgotten about Italy, as if it didn't exist. The next day Baudoin corrected the situation by calling the Vatican representative, Monsignor Valerio Valeri, to whom he handed the following note: "The French government, headed by Marshal Pétain, requests that the Holy See transmit to the Italian government as quickly as possible the note it has also transmitted through the Spanish ambassador to the German government. It also requests that he transmit to the Italian government its desire to find together the basis of a lasting peace between the two countries."

Rather than a formal request for an armistice, it was a declaration that France was first and foremost negotiating with Germany, its most important opponent. Pricolo remembers: "On the morning of June 17, Mussolini called me to say that Hitler had informed him of the French armistice request and that he was to leave immediately for Munich for a meeting with Hitler the next day. To compose the armistice demands, a commission was created with General Roatta, Admiral DeCourten, and General Perino. These officers left with Mussolini and drafted the Italian armistice clauses."

That evening at 9:00 p.m. at Termini railroad station, along with Mussolini, went Ciano and some functionaries of the various ministries. The Duce was in a bad mood and barely acknowledged the greetings of many Fascist leaders present to see him off. Mussolini obviously was troubled by his image:was he a winner or an opportunist? He was beginning to live the tragedy of his new personal relations with Hitler, where he was to play an increasingly subservient role, the kind that looks like a mere cameo when history is written. Perhaps he was pondering General Custer's words just before the Little Big Horn: "The first is the first and the second is nobody." And Mussolini was traveling to Munich for the third time in very different circumstances from those of September 1937, when he was referred to as the founder of Fascism and of the Italian Empire to the applause of the German people. And then, one year later, when all men of good will had praised him for having saved the peace at the Munich conference. Now he was going to pay homage to the greatest warlord of all time.

VII

France Surrenders

Munich: June 18, 1940

W hile Mussolini's train was speeding toward Bavaria during the night of June 17, 1940, the Italian delegation was busy preparing the list of demands the Germans would present to the French on Italy's behalf. The Duce knew full well that he lacked the arguments to back up his requests. Two days before, on June 15, he ordered Badoglio to attack the French border positions on the Alps, since Hitler, according to the Duce, had refused an Italian armored division on the western front alongside the German army. The chief of the general staff was opposed to this project of Mussolini's because it would be impossible to switch the two Italian armies from a defensive to an offensive posture on the front in just forty-eight hours and because of the need to transfer the artillery to the front lines.

Mussolini had replied harshly: "The decision to attack France is a political one, and I alone bear the responsibility for it." He went on to explain that he could not get his share of the booty after having just been a spectator of France's collapse. Demanding the

Alpine province of Savoy was impossible, but he could not also give up Nice, Corsica, and Tunisia. He was convinced that the army was exaggerating the need for artillery on the line, since the disintegration of the French army had simplified things on the ground. There was no need for artillery, according to the Duce. Mussolini ended the conversation with Badoglio saying suddenly: "In any case I will personally give the orders to the Army Chief of Staff Marshal Graziani." These orders, however, were rescinded in the late afternoon of June 17 at 6:10 p.m. with the message: "Hostilities with France are suspended."

The news was met with enthusiasm in the ranks of the Italian army. Everyone believed that the war was over and that it was time to grab the "spoils." On Mussolini's train, meanwhile, the experts prepared the "Italian point of view of the armistice conditions." Ciano later remembered the race among his staff to lengthen the list of Italian demands to be handed to France. They looked like country bumpkins visiting a supermarket for the first time. Some wanted the entire fleet, others all the colonies, and still others all the locomotives. One even requested the Mona Lisa. At dawn, the document was given to Mussolini.

There was a lot to choose from: ships, aircraft, weapons, railroad rolling stock, military bases in the Mediterranean, Corsica, Tunisia, Djibuti, the occupation of a slice of French territory up to the Rhone. Hitler and Ribbentrop, meanwhile, had reached Munich from the headquarters near Sedan. Paul Schmidt, Hitler's interpreter, wrote: "On June 17 we received a message from the Spanish foreign ministry that the French government now in Bordeaux had requested that Franco's ambassador transmit an armistice request to Germany. We left that very afternoon by plane with Hitler and Ribbentrop for Munich. On June 18, in the very same rooms of the Führerbau, where the conference with Chamberlain and Daladier had taken place in 1938, there now took place a brief conversation between Hitler and Mussolini." The discussion between the two dictators lasted two and a half hours, from 4:00 p.m. to 6:30 p.m., while parallel conversations took place between Ciano and Ribbentrop, and Generals Keitel and Roatta.

The Führer received his guest in his office with unusual levity and the usual deference, while Mussolini was visibly ill at ease. Hitler understood his colleague's embarrassment but did nothing to make him comfortable. At the outset, he repeated the usual program: "Our interests are in the north and yours are in the south." The Führer couldn't help but show his satisfaction for the victories of the German army under his command. Paul Schmidt related: "Hitler was surprisingly peaceful and discussed the need to avoid imposing heavy armistice conditions on France."

Hitler's philosophical attitude upset Mussolini's plans, as he was prepared to show the Führer the Italian demands and began alluding to the French fleet. Hitler cut him short: "If we put this condition on the table, the entire French fleet will defect to the British. It is our interest to see that the French keep hoping to regain their ships after the formal peace is signed." As for England, Hitler repeated his ideas from his book, *Mein Kampf*, saying that he did not wish the destruction of the British Empire, which he considered "an important factor for world order"; and he only wished that London would renounce its anti-German stance and accept the reality of a greater Germany. He felt confident that an agreement could be reached because of certain conversations that were taking place through Sweden.

Mussolini was in shock. He felt all was lost, including honor, and understood that all his dreams and aspirations in the Mediterranean were in danger. A peace between the two "big dogs," Britain and the Third Reich, would be concluded at the expense of the weaker partners, France and Italy. On this subject, Sinrokuro Hidaka, the Japanese ambassador to Rome, who was the last diplomat to meet with Mussolini on July 25, 1943, a few hours before the Duce's arrest, revealed that during that final meeting, Mussolini told him: "It is urgently necessary that Germany and Russia stop making war on one another. It's not that Germany does not want to help us, but she is so bogged down on the eastern front as to be unable to send us any help. On June 18, 1940, when I met with Hitler, I told him: 'Now that you have broken the Maginot Line, concentrate all your forces against the Allies. Even though you may not see eye to eye with the Russians, don't worry about them, they will not cause any problems for you. Don't deviate, don't open any new fronts.' I begged him but he did not want to listen to me."

The final blow came when Hitler, the rabid anti-Semite, as he spoke of the redistribution of the French colonies, came out with the idea: "We could create a Jewish state on the island of Madagascar," reviving an old proposal Mussolini had made some years before. The Duce had also proposed something similar in Ethiopia, generating disgust among the pure racists in Berlin. Hitler also politely but very firmly rejected Mussolini's request to sit at the same table and sign the armistice with the French, because Hitler argued that he had prepared a solemn ceremony for this historical event that could not be changed. But he reassured the Duce that in one of the clauses of the armistice between France and Germany, there was also to be a separate armistice between France and Italy. As for Italy's territorial demands, Hitler proposed that the subject be discussed with the foreign ministers and the generals during the extended meeting that followed and ended at 7:30 p.m., before dinner.

Hitler, previously dogmatic on questions of principle—no further humiliation for France, open door for Great Britain, no common negotiation with the Italians present—suddenly proved very flexible with respect to the Duce's territorial demands. Ribbentrop and Ciano had discussed the Franco-Italian list while the two dictators were alone. Ciano noted in his *Diary*: "I find a very different Ribbentrop: reasonable, seeking peace, cautious. He says right away that France should be given moderate armistice conditions, especially where the fleet was concerned, to avoid it joining up with the British. From Ribbentrop's words, I sense that the German tune has changed; if London wants war, it shall have total, absolute, and merciless war. But Hitler voices many objections to the idea of dismantling the British Empire. . . I ask Ribbentrop point blank: Would Germany rather continue the war or have peace? He has no hesitations: Peace."

Contrary to what many historians have written, Ribbentrop, as Hitler's mouthpiece, agreed to the annexation by Italy of Nice,

Corsica, Tunisia, and Djibuti, making some reservations regarding Algeria, half of which had been promised to Spain, along with half of Morocco if Franco agreed to enter the war on the Axis side. Mussolini's requests for "guarantees" on French territory were limited to the line of the Rhone; however, Hitler suddenly extended Italian oversight to the Saone so that both Axis zones of occupation would be connected.

Franco Bandini described the episode: "Hitler points with his finger on the large military map to the line between Dijon and Chambery. Roatta proposes the railway line Chambery-Culoz-Dijon, but since he does not have his pen on him, Hitler lends him his to draw on the map the demarcation line for the armistice. But that's not all. The chancellor sees what no one else sees: the Italians are still confined to the Mediterranean with an occupation zone that ends at the Rhone. From a strategic point of view, this is an unnecessary limitation, when a southern railway link is obtained from the French that will allow free transit to Spain. He suggests this change as well, and Roatta, full of enthusiasm, accepts indicating the line along Avignon, Nimes, Perpignan. Hitler not only substantially agrees to all the Italian demands, he actually goes beyond the limits requested." The meeting ended with the approval of five essential points: (1) the Reich will communicate to the French government that it is ready to discuss an armistice and requests that a commission be named; (2) the "enemy" is asked to present a similar armistice request to Italy, since the Duce chose not to accept the note transmitted through Monsignor Valeri; (3) both armistices with Germany and Italy will be interdependent; (4) there will be two French delegations to negotiate with Germany and Italy; (5) the Germans are to support with one armored division the movements of Italian forces to Chambery.

Having reached this agreement in principle during the night of June 18, the German response was transmitted to Pétain:

"The German government is ready to communicate to the French government the conditions necessary to stop the hostilities. It recommends sending plenipotentiary envoys to this end. The government of the Reich will communicate the venue to receive the envoys as soon as the list of their names has been communicated. The government of the Reich notes that the agreement regarding the cessation of hostilities can only be discussed if the French government contacts the Italian government through the good offices of the Spanish government."

The French, who had many more urgent issues to handle after a monumental defeat, still wanted to argue with the Italians, as French General Huntziger told the Germans: "Italy declared war on us but did not fight . . . If, in Rome, we are faced with unacceptable demands, all our agreements with Germany will go up in smoke . . . You can trample us and hurt us even more: we'll take it, but we will not sign, and we will take our freedom of action: our navy and air force are intact. Come what may! France has seen worse than this. It believes that honor is more valuable than life itself."

The Italians were frustrated by the Munich summit. Mussolini said: "Germany can be compared to a very lucky gambler who has always won as he doubles his bets. Now he's a bit nervous and wants to take his winnings home. In truth, Hitler wants to negotiate with England, with whom he never wanted to go to war." Hitler told Ribbentrop privately: "I do not wish to have the antipathies between Italy and France influence any of our negotiations."

And Ciano wrote: "From everything Hitler is saying his desire to close all the issues quickly is obvious . . . He speaks with such moderation and insight that appear truly surprising after such a heady victory. I cannot be suspected of having excessive tenderness toward him, but today I truly admire him. Mussolini is visibly embarrassed. He feels that he is playing second fiddle. He relates the discussion with Hitler to me without hiding any bitterness or irony, and he concludes by saying that the German people already have the seeds of their own collapse, because a tremendous clash will take place that will blow everything away. What the Duce really fears is that the hour of peace is at hand and his lifelong dream will once again elude him: glory on the battlefield."

General Roatta: "Ciano was convinced that Germany feels like a poker player with too many chips. Isn't it better to step away from the table?"

General Pricolo: "The people surrounding Mussolini at Munich made the wrong decisions. General Roatta became the most prominent member because of his experience at international meetings and his perfect German. And immediately all questions discussed with the Germans were geared to territory and ground troops, while it was clear that the occupation of this or that part of metropolitan France was of secondary importance. It was obvious that with the fall of France, the war was to continue in the Mediterranean, in Libya, and East Africa. Due to Roatta's importance, the chiefs of staff of the three branches were basically cut off from the discussions. Everything was decided by Mussolini, Ciano, and Roatta with help now and then from Badoglio. General Perino told me that, at Munich, Hitler clearly proposed that Italy would have formulated, as armistice conditions, the occupation of French territory (up to the Rhone), as well as Tunisia and Djibuti."

Before leaving Munich, Mussolini, unhappy in his sidekick role to the victorious Führer, gave General Perino the order to continue air force operations against the French bases. During the return trip, Mussolini called General Roatta to his railroad car and told him, with many omissions and withholding some points, what he had discussed in private with Hitler. To show his power, Mussolini confirmed that he would demand from France, Nice and its surrounding territory, Savoy, Corsica, Tunisia, Algeria, Djibouti, British Somaliland, a corridor to link Libya and Ethiopia, and the neutralization of both sides of the Straits of Gibraltar. Finally, not having consulted the interested parties, he will demand that the Egyptians substitute the alliance treaty tying them to England with a friendship treaty with Italy. Roatta reminded the Duce that as they were leaving, Keitel repeated his promise to support the projected Italian advance into France. While the Duce suffered from the position of inferiority he saw himself relegated to, Hitler was living his days of glory. His success was all the more delectable in that the victory over France was achieved against the recommendations of his generals, who had opposed an offensive in the west.

Raymond Cartier wrote: "This triumph almost made Hitler amiable, easy going, even. He left his modest command post on the

Rhine to set up his headquarters in a village on the French-Belgian border, Brûly-de-Pesche, near Rocroi. Once his vengeance had been fulfilled, he relaxed. With two old comrades in arms he visited the battlefields of 1914-1918, Flanders, and Champagne, where he served in the infantry. Leaving Brûly-de-Pesche, where the flat landscape was no inspiration for his romantic visions, he went on to the Black Forest, near Freudenstadt. Alsace, now reconquered, was close by, and he paid it a visit, excited by its visibly German character... In Strasbourg, the Place Kleber had been renamed Adolf-Hitlerplatz, and in Mulhouse the Rue Sauvage met with the same fate.

"After its long trek, the French government had finally stopped in Vichy and filed a protest against the annexation without a treaty of the provinces. Hitler ignored the matter. His plans went way beyond the recreation of the old Reichsland of 1871. Besides Metz and Strasbourg, he wanted to take back the old German cities of Verdun and Toul. He wanted the "Germans of the sea" (the Dutch) to return to the Reich, and to Germanize Burgundy by sending German colonists from Transylvania and Tyrol to settle there. But it was premature to reveal these projects. First England must ask for peace."

Returning to Rome on June 19 at 6:50 p.m. after his lightning trip, Mussolini rushed to the Palazzo Venezia. During the night, he had thought up a plan show the Germans and the French that he too can make war. His political ambition, in the style of Garibaldi, was to conquer Nice. But luck was against him: snow and heavy rain fell on the border areas while the temperature dropped to below zero. To attack in those conditions would be insane. But the Duce had decided to do something. The general staff proposed once again the plan of June 14, which had been cancelled after Hitler's summons for a conference at Munich. And so at 8:50 p.m. on June 19, General Roatta called the western front to "undertake small offensive operations immediately . . . To make contact with the enemy everywhere, to decisively harass enemy forces as harshly as possible."

On Thursday morning, June 20, Mussolini went to his office early to read the war dispatches. There was no news. Perhaps his orders were not being followed? He called Badoglio urgently and ordered him again to begin a general offensive across the entire front. The meeting quickly got out of hand because the marshal was vigorously opposed to Mussolini's demands. The Duce insisted. Ciano noted: "Then I talked to him. I found very little glory attacking a defeated army . . . The armistice is at hand, and if the Italian army failed to break through the first time, we would end the campaign with a tremendous failure." Then, to one of his close friends, Ciano confessed: "Did you see? He wanted the war and now he has it; but after the bad decision he made, all he gets is one humiliation after another."

A compromise was reached that afternoon. After many solemn declarations of principle, a consensus was reached and an operational order drafted was issued at 9:10 p.m. by Marshal Graziani to the troops: "With partial modification . . . I order that deep action, as already decided, take place by the right wing of the 4th Army . . ." At 3:00 a.m. on June 21, the Italian units moved under snow and rain against difficult French defensive fortifications scattered across the mountains.

General Emilio Faldella wrote: "At the front, near the border, the French forts have the mission of delaying the Italian army from reaching the line of defense, which was made up of steel and concrete fortifications . . . Our infantry will have to advance in the open against well-covered troops through a field under fire from French artillery . . . And all this was to happen in three to four days. In these conditions, Italian manpower superiority is useless . . . It would be a mistake to say that a battle was fought in the western Alps; what took place were only preliminary actions, technically called 'making contact.' It is not possible to speak in terms of victory or defeat..."

Mussolini wanted a victory he could publish in the newspapers by the morning of June 21. Instead, he learned that the Italian army had not moved one inch. He complained to Ciano: "I just don't have the material to work with. Even Michelangelo needed marble to make his statues. Had he only had plaster, he would have only made ceramics."

Meanwhile Hitler went ahead with his choreographed signing of the armistice with France's delegation, headed by General Charles Huntziger, Ambassador Léon Noël, Admiral Le Luc, Generals Parisot for the army, and Bergeret for the air force, and Charles Rochat, the director of the ministry for foreign affairs. The ceremony took place at the open field of Rethondes in Compiègne, in the same railway saloon car where, in 1918, Marshal Foch had told the defeated Germans: "I shall now read the conditions established by the Allies." At that time, the representatives of the Berlin government had to accept everything without discussion. And now, the French, at 6:50 p.m. on June 22, 1940, were given the very same treatment twenty-two years later. The French-German armistice became effective six hours after the signature of the French-Italian armistice. After signing, Huntziger told Keitel, head of the German delegation: "General, as a soldier you know how hard it is for a soldier to do what I have just done. We French military officers hope we will not have to regret this action." Keitel answered: "It is honorable for the victor to respect those who have been defeated." And he invited both delegations to stand in memory of the dead on both sides.

On the evening of June 21, Dino Alfieri, the Italian ambassador to Berlin, cabled the text of the French-German armistice. Ciano noted: "These are very mild conditions, showing Hitler is anxious to reach an agreement. Under these conditions, Mussolini is not prepared to make territorial demands; these could break up the negotiations and cause a serious break with Germany. So he will ask only for the demilitarization of a fifty-kilometer area on the border and wait for the peace conference to make all our formal demands."

On the following day, the same French delegation that faced the Germans arrived to meet with the Italians. "Mussolini would like to delay the meeting as much as possible in the expectation that General Gastone Gambara would take Nice. The armistice signing is being prepared, but without fanfare because the Duce feels there was no real battle and the whole ceremony will take place almost without any press coverage."

This low-key attitude on Mussolini's part proved to have a disastrous effect on the Italian war effort because several important bases controlling the Mediterranean were omitted from the agreement. General Roatta was amazed to see that all the decisions made in Munich by the Italian general staff and the Germans were now shelved. He asked Mussolini: "Are there any new elements?" and the Duce answered that he already sent his modified demands to Berlin on the basis of the conditions of the armistice between France and Germany.

With the occupation of Menton, on the French Riviera, Italian operations ended in the west with 631 Italian troops dead (fifty percent of which were victims of frostbite) and over 1,500 wounded. This was a very high price for an operation that was basically politically inspired propaganda. At three in the afternoon on June 23, flying aboard three German planes, the French delegation that had just been at Compiègne, arrived in Rome. The delegates were accommodated in the private residence of an Italian diplomat. At 7:30 p.m. Huntziger and his colleagues are driven to Villa Incisa all'Olgiata on the Via Cassia. The five-man Italian delegation named by the Duce to negotiate the armistice was waiting: Ciano, Badoglio, Pricolo, Cavagnari, and Roatta. The meeting lasted only twenty-five minutes, enough time for Roatta to read the French translation of the armistice conditions prepared by Italy. Huntziger asked for a pause to communicate with his government, and Ciano adjourned the meeting to the following day.

The French could not believe how cordial the Italian welcome had been and how lenient the Italian conditions were. Not at all the atmosphere of an armistice but more like that of an alliance! Ciano noted: "Badoglio was visibly moved. He wanted to be very courteous with the French; among them was General Parisot, a personal friend of his. In the dining room on the ground floor, there was a long table; we sat on one side, Badoglio at my right and Cavagnari at my left. We rose when the French arrived . . . they showed neither haughtiness nor sorrow. Only Ambassador Noël was white as a sheet . . . I announced that Badoglio would read the terms of the armistice."

The Italians returned to Rome after having presented the document to the French. Roatta found an urgent call from Mussolini and went immediately to the Palazzo Venezia, where he was told that Hitler, having read the Italian armistice conditions, was upset, saying that there was a limit to everything. To avoid exaggerating was one thing, but to ask for practically nothing was too much. The Führer suggested a reexamination of his proposal to connect the two zones of occupation, German and Italian, with a corridor along the Swiss border. Italian troops would move to about twenty kilometers from Geneva. Mussolini discussed the problem with Roatta late into the night, but in the end, the accommodating general said to the Duce: "It's too late. We have already given the documents to the French."

The next day, Monday, June 24 at 7:15 p.m., Huntziger signed the armistice with Italy, after having been authorized by the French government to do so. France kept her fleet, her colonies, cities, bases, and regions (such as Corsica), which had been part of Mussolini's demands in the past. A few minutes before signing, the head of the French delegation asked Badoglio, since Ciano was absent from the signing ceremony, if the clause demanding that the French police turn over Italian political refugees, including the Socialist leader, Pietro Nenni, to the Italian police could be canceled. There was a moment of silence, until Badoglio decided to be safe and called Mussolini, who answered: "I agree. It's best that they stay where they are."

Pricolo remembered: "We were all very moved: one could not witness the armistice, albeit a moderate one, with a nation like France, defeated practically without a fight. Huntziger said to Badoglio, 'Marshal, in the present, infinitely painful circumstances, the French delegation is comforted by the sincere hope that the peace which will follow shortly will allow France to begin its task of reconstruction and renewal and will create the basis for lasting relations between our two countries in the interest of Europe and of civilization.'

At the end of the meeting, wrote Pricolo, "we all went to see Mussolini, who received us in an angry mood. 'The only thing missing was for you to start crying,' he said sarcastically. Ciano quickly informed him, 'Obviously . . . as I said, we were emotional, but this was justified because since Caesar's conquest of Gaul, it was the very first time that Italy was imposing an armistice on France, the nation of *grandeur*, the France of the kings, the France of Napoleon.'"

Robert Aron summed up the French delegation's impressions: "The Italians seemed to be excusing themselves for picking up the spoils of someone else's victory. Count Ciano shook hands very cordially with Ambassador Noël. Badoglio had greatly watered down the original text. The occupation of French territory was excluded except those areas already in the hands of Italian troops, a purely formal clause. The article regarding the handing over of Italian political refugees was canceled . . . Italian control on French territories, namely North Africa and Syria, was reduced to a minimum . . . At the moment of signing, Badoglio said happily, 'I hope France will have a resurgence; it is a great nation with a great history, and I am certain that it will have a great future. From one soldier to another' he said to Huntziger, 'I sincerely hope so.'

Military operations between France and the Axis ended at 12:35 a.m. on June 25, 1940, according to the terms of the armistice with Germany. From the Munich summit between Hitler and Mussolini on June 18 to the general armistice with France in effect on June 25, only seven days had gone by. During this time, the Duce had every indication that Italy had already lost the war, be it on Germany's side or even if she suddenly and slyly had switched to the Allied camp. Italy, an essentially poor country, without raw materials, without a modern army, with a still embryonic unified State, remained, politically and militarily, a "geographic expression," as it had been cruelly defined by the Austrian chancellor, Clement Metternich, when on August 6, 1847, he wrote about Italy to the courts of France, England, Russia, and Prussia.

After having ended, with much embarrassment, the "French comedy" with as little propaganda as possible, Mussolini took time off to visit the battlefields in the west. Lying even to himself in an attempt to justify his decisions, he returned elated by his trip. To

Ciano, he said that the Italian troops were well armed and that in the final analysis, they *had* defeated the French. He wanted to capitalize on the recent experience without delay and had already offered Hitler Italian ground and air support for the announced invasion of the British Isles. Days went by without any news from the Führer, who had gone to Berchtesgaden.

Mussolini began to hope that Marshal Graziani—who had just been named to head Italian forces in North Africa after the unexpected death of Italo Balbo, whose plane had been accidentally shot down by friendly fire at Tobruk—would soon give him the satisfaction of conquering Alexandria in Egypt. Graziani was less optimistic. On September 13, after a long series of disagreements with Rome, the Italian army finally moved toward the east, with five divisions and about two thousand trucks. The Italian columns, after passing the border between Libya and Egypt, progressed quickly along the coast. Graziani had changed the original plan in an attempt to encircle the enemy by traveling inland and thus save gasoline and equipment. At a speed of twenty kilometers a day, the Italians reached Sidi el Barrani on September 16 and stopped. Graziani cabled Mussolini that he could not march forward without first having replenished his supplies, especially water.

Without any real clash, the British had decided to fall back in retreat. The Italians had 97 dead and 270 wounded. British losses were about 50 casualties and a few dozen pieces of equipment. Graziani, having stopped 120 kilometers inside Egypt, began building a new road connecting Libya and the Via Balbia, the coastal highway on the Italian side. He also started the construction of an aqueduct and stockpiled all sorts of supplies and, consistent with the Fascist custom, he even found the time to build a monument commemorating his own glorious enterprise. Mussolini was elated by what he saw as a success against the British that he could claim as his own. He also demanded that Graziani resume his march toward the ultimate prize: Alexandria.

Graziani did not change his plan, even though he sent enthusiastic messages, such as this one, to the Duce: "When will the British begin to understand that they are facing the best colonial army in the world?" The truth, however, was very different. The Italian units had not been able to pin down the enemy in retreat. There was confusion in the forward columns, and on the third day a snag developed in the Italian order of battle. Italian superiority in artillery and tanks had not been fully taken advantage of, with the exception of the artillery units, as observed by the British themselves, fighting with bravery and daring. Mussolini finally accepted the halt of the Italian army at Sidi el Barrani, when Graziani cabled that to begin operations against Marsa Matruh—a British armed camp— he would need the entire month of November, "because, should our communications fail to work, now that the lines are 120 kilometers long, we would have to retreat. And in the desert a retreat is a rout."

The best military news for Mussolini at that time came from the far away and abandoned Italian East Africa. Viceroy, Amedeo d'Aosta, who in July had successfully occupied five important centers, Kassala, Gallabat, Kurmuk, and Gezzan in the Sudan, and Moyale in Kenya, now began an offensive against British Somaliland, occupying it within two weeks. According to some British historians, it was the only real Italian success in World War II and no doubt, it was one of the best-prepared and commanded operations of the Italian army. The attack began on August 3, 1940, toward the north of Somalia: two main Italian forces advanced, one toward Djibuti to discourage any initiative by the French governor, and one toward Berbera, the capital of the British colony. On August 6, Zeila, Dolo, Hargesia, and Oaduenia were occupied, and then all the British forts fell, one by one. On August 17 it was almost the end for the British, who were trying to gain time to evacuate their troops. On the evening of August 19, the Italians entered Berbera. The British, who were masters at strategic retreats, were able to save about 7,000 men. Their casualties were 38 dead, 102 wounded, 120 missing, as well as a large quantity of materiel, from artillery, rifles, and tanks to trucks and food supplies. Italian losses were much heavier: 2,052 dead, of which 184 were Italians, and the others, colonial troops. September 1940 saw the Italian expansion in Africa reach its maximum. It was to last only a few months.

The Italian navy was already the cause of much anxiety clouding Mussolini's satisfaction at these African successes. In the meantime, after his triumphant victory over France, Hitler was trying to find the best way to achieve peace with England. July 19, 1940, had been Hitler's day of triumph. Victorious German troops had marched through the Brandenburg Gate in Berlin for the first time since their victory in 1871. Ranks and decorations had been handed to Göring, now promoted to the new rank of Reichsmarshal. Twelve other marshals had been named: Keitel, Brauchitsch, von Rundstedt, Bock, Leeb, Reichenau, List, Kluge, Witzleben, Milch, Kesselring, and Sperrle. The Führer closed the day with an extremely moderate speech, holding out the olive branch to England.

"My conscience dictates that I should send a new appeal to reason to England. I think I can do this because I am not a defeated enemy who is begging but a victor who has nothing to ask. I do not wish for any reason to continue this struggle. I regret the victims it has created, and I want to spare the English. Mr. Churchill may find in these words proof of my doubts as to the way this war will end. But I have cleared my own conscience . . . "

Hitler's words made a favorable impression worldwide until the British answered through Lord Halifax the next day, throwing cold water on any possible peace overtures: "Germany shall have peace if it evacuates all the territories it has occupied, restores the freedoms it has trampled, and gives guarantees for the future."

A disappointed Hitler retired to Berchtesgaden. Why did the peace move toward London fail? His answer was that Britain hoped Russia would come to its side. The liquidation of the Soviet colossus would serve two purposes: providing *Lebensraum* (living space) for the German people and the elimination of a potential British ally. The main obstacle to any plan is the timing, since it was now midsummer, and even if the German army attacked immediately, it would be stopped by the *Schlammperiode* (the muddy season) in Russia. On July 31, Hitler held a war planning session with his generals, the most crucial military conference of the war. He immediately indicated his determination concerning the "Russian case" and set the timetable for an attack in the east for the spring of 1941: it would involve 120 divisions.

Then he turned to Great Britain and the Mediterranean problems in discussing General Jodl's memorandum, *Invasion oder nicht?* (Invasion: yes or no?). The memo demonstrated that an invasion on the coasts of England was a very risky enterprise, to be attempted only in case of extreme necessity. An alternate could be Operation *Felix*, the conquest of Gibraltar (thus closing the Mediterranean), the occupation of the Canary islands and the Azores, and the dispatching of German armored units to Libya to help the Italians reach Suez. Bitter differences of opinion broke out among the generals. General Brauchitsch, who had set up the colossal *Seelöwe* plan to invade England, was criticized by Admiral Raeder, who began shouting that he did not have enough landing barges to ferry all the men across, nor the kind of naval cover necessary, nor the time to prepare for the operation. Raeder's criticism prompted discussion of a reduced plan, but the proposal did not work.

Hitler hesitated. He saw that the only way to open *Seelöwe* to the army's landing units was the Luftwaffe. The German air force must wipe the RAF out of the sky over England; once this happened, a mass invasion would be successful. The Führer's directive Number 17, to destroy the enemy air force, was compiled. The plan was to destroy RAF installations on the ground, but the bombing of urban centers and terror bombings were forbidden at this time. The Luftwaffe would mobilize 2,669 planes. The offensive was to start on August 5, but it was postponed to August 12, while the invasion date was set for September 15.

At this time, Stalin had bloodlessly occupied Bessarabia and part of Bukovina, with the assent of Germany and Italy, who had both prevailed upon Romania to accept the Soviet demands. And after the failure of his air war against the RAF over Britain, Hitler also had to scrap the *Seelöwe* plan. These reversals forced him to pull back and renew high-level political contacts. On September 19, Ribbentrop went to Rome to discuss Russia and the United States, but his real mission was to explain the pact with Japan and the reasons for the failure of the invasion of Britain.

Ciano noted in his *Diary*: "Ribbentrop was in good spirits. He is happy about the applause by the crowd rounded up by the Italian police commissioner for the occasion. In the car, he immediately talks about the surprise of the military pact with Japan that would be signed a few days later in Berlin . . . As for England, he says the weather has been bad and has been the real winner rather than the RAF, but this will not alter the final result as soon as a few days of good weather come back. The landing plan is ready . . . English coastal defense is negligible: just one German division can make it all fall apart." In a second conversation, Ribbentrop spoke about General Franco and a letter Hitler had just sent to Madrid. At the end of the meeting, the two foreign ministers agreed to the text of the Tripartite Pact with Japan, for a "new order" in Europe and Asia, which was signed in Berlin on September 27, 1940, in the new Reich chancellery by Ciano, Ribbentrop, and Japanese Ambassador Kurusu.

Ciano met with Hitler twice during his brief visit to Berlin. First formally, right after the signing of the Tripartite Pact, and the second, just before leaving. During this second meeting, Hitler spoke about his philosophy regarding the meaning of the Pact, which was intended, according to the Germans, to encourage the United States and Soviet Russia to turn their attention away from European problems and focus on Asia and the Pacific Ocean. The Italian-Japanese alliance would also help awaken Franco and, it was hoped, make him decide to join the Axis and evict Great Britain from the Mediterranean. "I wish to speak about this and other matters with the Duce, and I therefore think we should meet at the Brenner as soon as possible." Ciano answered: "Führer, we can set the date for next week, on October 4."

VIII

Franco and Pétain

Brenner Pass: October 4, 1940

T he Brenner Pass was unseasonably warm on the seventh meeting between Mussolini and Hitler on October 4, 1940. The border between Germany and Italy had been picked for the second time for propaganda reasons and to simplify protocol, so that the discussions between the dictators could take place in a single session in the saloon car of the train. Since the Munich meeting of June 18 regarding the French surrender, Mussolini and Hitler had exchanged a thick correspondence and communicated through their foreign ministers and ambassadors. Among the most important open issues were the Italian demands towards the Allies which Mussolini had put on paper after having been thwarted during the frenetic week following the armistice with the French and the Italian military contribution to victory.

Those demands were handed to the Führer on July 7 by Ciano, who had written in his *Diary* before leaving for Berlin:

"The Duce gave me my instructions before my trip to Germany: he absolutely wants to participate in the attack on Great Britain if it does take place, and he's worried that France may be attempting to join the anti-British camp. He fears this could deprive us of our booty. He wants me to tell the Führer that he intends to land on the Ionian islands, and control Yugoslavia, a typical anti-Italian creation of Versailles. Greece, through its minister, gives assurances of complete neutrality, which the Duce accepts with a wait-and-see attitude . . . " Ciano gave Hitler a document that stated, in effect:

Nice, Corsica and Malta: annexation;
Tunisia and a buffer zone in Algeria: protectorate;
Syria, Lebanon, Palestine, Transjordan: independence with Italian military bases, expropriation of the oil companies;
Aden, Perim, and Sokotra: military occupation;
Egypt and the Sudan: Italy replaces Great Britain; management of the Suez Canal;
Cyprus: given to Greece in exchange for Corfu and Ciamuria;
British Somaliland, Djibuti, French Equatorial Africa up to Chad: given to Italy.

The interpreter Paul Schmidt was present at the conversation between Hitler and Ciano and remembered that the more Ciano spoke, the more demands he made, adding Kenya and Uganda, which were not even in the document. The Führer looked at him in amazement, thinking it was indeed too early to make such vast assumptions. Italy was not just asking for a part of the spoils, but for a large slice of the entire planet earth. However, Hitler accepted the document without any comment.

The other delicate problem was that of Italy's contribution to Germany's war plans, a contribution which had been politely rejected by the German general staff under technical and other pretenses. Ciano noted, regarding this matter, on July 2: "Hitler did not respond to the offer made by Mussolini to send men and planes to take part in the attack on the island. It is actually he who is offering us aircraft to bomb the Suez Canal. There are obviously few expectations of us or our capabilities . . . Hitler sent the Duce a long letter. He announces the invasion of England as imminent, but he politely and firmly rejects our offer to send an Italian expeditionary corps. He explains this refusal because of logistical difficulties in supplying two army corps. Göring, as well, in conversation with Alfieri, said that the Italian air force has too big a task in the Mediterranean to divert forces to other sectors. The Duce, on July 16, was disappointed by this refusal." But a few weeks later, on August 11, Ciano noted: "The German air force has requested that our air force to participate in the action against Great Britain. When we offered to do so one month ago, it was rejected. Now they want us in. Why?"

Ciano's question appears naïve, if not hypocritical. Hitler obviously wanted, against the opinion of his generals, and consistent with his somewhat romantic personality, to give his allies some satisfaction in dispatching an Italian unit to fight alongside the German "professionals." An Italian Air Corps (the CAI) would not have hampered the action of the Luftwaffe, and could even be useful on occasion. The head of the Italian Air Force, General Pricolo, was opposed to this project and was worried when Mussolini told him that Hitler had changed his mind in favor of a collaboration with the Italian air force. The Duce then added, "Listen, Pricolo, Germany refused the Bersaglieri* and the artillery, and asked only for the air force. How can we refuse? Are we allies or not?"

The CAI was a symptomatic episode. Pricolo was against sending the unit for psychological and technical reasons. The general viewed the CAI as a dangerous scattering of energies and opening the possible unfavorable comparison between the Italians and the British and, even more dangerous, a negative comparison between the Italians and their German ally. The Italian flyers chosen for the expedition were more enthusiastic about this adventure. There was even a race within the Italian Air Force to join the squad that everyone felt was destined to cover itself with glory. True to Italian tradition, politicians and well-connected young airmen lobbied to be picked in the unit. The first clash concerned the leader of the CAI. Instead of General Pricolo,

---

* An elite unit of the Italian infantry, known for its speed and courage under fire.

General Rino Corso Fougier was selected. He was a friend of Ciano's and an air ace, who had made his reputation in Gorizia at the beginning of the 1930s, when he created a group of acrobatic flyers.

The CAI left Milan on September 10, 1940, with 181 planes, 75 bombers, and 95 fighters. After one hundred days over the English Channel, few came back, and those who returned were very downcast.

The political consequences were disastrous, especially when, by error, Italian planes, among other embarrassments, went off course and bombed London by mistake, against specific orders.

None of this was on Mussolini's mind on October 3, 1940, as his train took him to the Brenner Pass. He was feeling upbeat, with the CAI in place, a victory in Somaliland, and Graziani's victory in North Africa. As Ciano noted: "I have rarely seen the Duce in such good spirits and good shape as at the Brenner on October 4." The Führer, on the other hand, was at a low point. The Luftwaffe offensive, the "blitz," of August and September had not produced the kind of results that could justify *Operation Seelöwe*, even though it had caused much death and destruction in Great Britain. From Moscow, the first signals of Stalin's intentions in Eastern Europe were beginning to surface. In Spain, Franco was beginning to look like an ingrate to Berlin, and the Balkans were growing restless. The exhausted German treasury still had a huge army to feed, and as for France, a new set of problems had appeared with the proclamation of a new government in exile by General Charles de Gaulle, who, following a heartfelt radio appeal to his countrymen from London, on June 18, 1940, had been recognized by Winston Churchill as "head of the Free French." All these events had discredited the peace initiatives of Marshal Pétain toward Berlin as a prelude to a lasting Franco-German agreement.

Mussolini went to the Brenner Pass meeting accompanied by Ciano; Anfuso went along as Ciano's assistant. Hitler and Ribbentrop were assisted, as usual, by interpreter Paul Schmidt. The two special trains arrived almost simultaneously and stopped at their usual places on the tracks. The reunion between the Führer and the Duce was very cordial. Hitler immediately began his standard monologue, aimed at settling minor issues before addressing the most embarrassing problem: the postponement of *Seelöwe* already decided on September 17. The Führer told the Duce that, according to the *Kriegsmarine*'s high command, the RAF had not been defeated in spite of the enormous losses the Luftwaffe had inflicted. Therefore, not being certain of favorable weather, he had decided to postpone the invasion until a new date was picked. This did not mean, according to Hitler, that he would not keep up the pressure; Göring had orders to continue his attacks on the enemy regardless of the heavy losses of German bombers. After the war, the exact number of losses of German aircraft during the Battle of Britain, from July to October 1940 would be 1,733 planes, while the British lost 915 fighters.

Mussolini said he understood the situation, and the Italian CAI unit would soon be operational alongside the German air force. Hitler complimented Mussolini for the attack on Egypt that had brought Graziani and his army to Sidi el Barrani. The Duce answered that the Italians were organizing for the second act the conquest of the British fortified camp at Marsa Matruh. The conquest of Alexandria and the Nile delta would be the third and final act. Hitler, who had many idle divisions at that time, offered Mussolini a specialized German unit to help Graziani, but the Duce replied somewhat arrogantly that he did not think such a contribution would be necessary just then.

Mussolini then began setting the groundwork to justify his next move—he had already decided to attack Greece—and spoke of the ambiguous attitude of the government in Athens and how it was extending help and safe haven to British vessels and aircraft. He said it was necessary to land Italian troops on the Ionian islands to set up bases directed against the "double dealing" Greeks. Hitler seemed unconvinced by the Duce's explanation and said: "This war can be considered as being won. Therefore, the Axis powers must avoid any initiative that cannot be considered as absolutely useful to the struggle ahead and for which we are perfectly positioned."

The Führer noted that in Eastern Europe, Romania could become somewhat of a problem, and he digressed into an anti-Bolshevik tirade that surprised his audience. He said in part: "Bolshevism is the doctrine of populations in decay." However, the Führer did not speak of his coming moves on the Romanian oil fields scheduled to begin eight days later, and he naturally did not mention

"Barbarossa," the plan, already being prepared in detail to liquidate the USSR in eight to ten weeks. This reticent and ambiguous attitude, made of half-truths and half-lies, disgusted Anfuso, who was somewhat naïve and sentimental about friendships, passions, and human relations. Ciano wrote about this in his *Diary*:

"Anfuso, who has been exposed at length to the Führer and his entourage and is the most pro-German member of my staff, is quite unhappy about the meeting and says that adventurism still pervades the atmosphere with the Germans."

Many years later, in his own memoirs, Anfuso was to correct this notation by his boss and friend, Ciano:

"The truth is I was neither pro-German nor unhappy, but I couldn't understand what was going on: I knew Mussolini had decided to attack Greece, and we weren't announcing anything about that to Hitler, who was now ranting against the USSR in terms reminiscent of his morbid anti-Slav tirades preceding the attack on Poland. As for my own pro-German bias, it was certainly not based on any special love for the Goths but only on the principle that since we were both on the same ship, to hide plans from each other or to willfully mislead each other would have driven both of us to ruin—as it most certainly did! . . . The October 4, 1940, meeting of the two leaders virtually ended any real German-Italian collaboration."

France and Spain were to be the main topics of the meeting. Hitler hoped to increase Pétain's acrimony toward England for having set up de Gaulle and the Free French movement against Vichy. He intended to clarify the situation during an upcoming meeting with the aging French Marshal. Regarding Spain, however, the Führer was disappointed and pessimistic. In September, he had attempted to sound out Franco, who had made impossibly high demands. Back in July, during preparations for the military summit at Berchtesgaden, *Operation Felix* had been discussed as an alternative to the invasion of Great Britain. According to the thinking behind *Operation Felix*, since the main objective was to defeat England, Gibraltar had to be occupied first. With typical German thoroughness, the Führer concluded that to complete the study of *Felix*, he needed a fresh report on the actual situation inside Spain by a knowledgeable observer.

Admiral Wilhelm Canaris, head of the Abwher (German Military Intelligence) since 1935, was ideally suited for such a mission. The little admiral, he was barely taller than five feet, with snow-white hair, was secretly an anti-Nazi and determined to destroy Hitler. This would ultimately take him to the gallows on April 9, 1945. In Berlin, Canaris was considered an expert on Spain, since he had spent much time in that country during his initial missions as a secret agent in the First World War. During the Spanish Civil War, he had built a close relationship with Franco while he set up the nationalist espionage services. At the beginning of July 1940, Canaris traveled to Madrid, where he met the local Abwher representative, Wilhelm Leissner, who was operating under the alias of Gustav Lenz, general manager of the Excelsior Import-Export Company, specializing in precious metals. The company had about one thousand freelance operatives.

By July 27, Canaris had written a very complete report. The admiral concluded that if the Nazi army went into Spain, it would certainly encounter its first serious defeat. The country was deprived of everything, from roads to railroads, from military bases to supplies of food, not to mention a terrain that was very unfavorable to a mechanized army. Canaris, furthermore, was determined to prevent further reckless adventures, and secretly suggested to his friend, Generalissimo Francisco Franco that, in the event of serious negotiations, he demand ten large 381-millimeter artillery pieces, which he knew did not exist within the German arsenal. Hitler was disconcerted by the Abwher report; intuitively, he did not fully trust its conclusions, as many things Canaris wrote did not fit his own knowledge of the situation. Why was Spain suddenly on its knees? Where was all the materiel and the artillery pieces that Italy and Germany had given to Franco at the conclusion of the civil war? Hitler also remembered that Franco had indicated, on June 10, 1940, his interest in entering the war alongside Mussolini.

To find out firsthand what the situation was, Hitler wrote a letter to Franco on September 15 to ask for naval bases for Germany in the Canary Islands, among other places. Franco replied negatively one week later, demanding, as compensation, huge stockpiles of weapons, supplies and part of French North Africa. Such a trade-off would have had disastrous consequences, as the Führer explained to Ciano on

September 27, creating a crisis with Pétain and giving the British an excuse to occupy the Canary Islands. The Führer concluded to Ciano: "Spanish intervention will cost more than it's worth." The Duce, who considered himself the godfather of nationalist Spain and wanted to have another Latin partner to counter the German colossus, answered that another, more personal attempt, was necessary to convince Franco that his interests lay in the Axis camp. Hitler agreed and announced that he would travel to meet the two "Sphinxes" in Spain and France, namely Franco and Pétain.

The Brenner summit was over. Ciano commented:

"Hitler put only some of his cards on the table and mentioned his plans for the future. There is no more talk about landing in the British Isles, and preparations for this operation will remain on hold; they hope to attract France into the orbit of the coalition, because it is obvious that the Anglo-Saxon world is a pretty tough bone to gnaw on; more importance is given to the Mediterranean sector, and that is good for us." The Axis program for October 1940 appeared to be clearly drawn: quiet on all fronts and a search for new agreements with France and Spain to force Churchill into a general negotiation. Within this scenario, Germany would be free to act in Eastern Europe, Italy in the Mediterranean, and Great Britain would keep her empire on all five continents.

This stalemate was to be short lived because, like a "bolt from the blue," on the morning of October 12, Berlin told Rome that, following a specific request from Romania, a German military mission was en route to Bucharest and Luftwaffe planes would be sent there to defend the oil fields. Mussolini was flabbergasted. Once again he felt as if he had been tricked by his friend: after every summit, Hitler would regularly create some surprise that made the Duce look ridiculous in the eyes of the world. He reviewed all his bad memories from the past: Dollfuss, the Night of the Long Knives, the Anschluss, the pact with Moscow, the attack on Poland, the invasion of Norway and Denmark, the offensive on the western front, the flirting with the defeated French . . . And Ciano recorded:

"It is now Romania's turn, a country that Mussolini considered part of his own sphere of influence. He is outraged because the German occupation of Romania made a deeply negative impression on Italian public opinion . . . 'Hitler always puts me in front of a fait accompli,' says Mussolini. 'This time, I will give him some of his own medicine; he'll learn from the newspapers that I have occupied Greece. This way, things will be even once again.'"

Three days later, following a war council meeting at the Palazzo Venezia, Mussolini set the date for the attack on Greece—a crucial move as he noted in his book, *Storia di un anno*. A version of the meeting also exists, by Badoglio, that differs from Mussolini's. The actual debate regarding the so-called "Emergency G" in its detail is rather unimportant. The conclusion that all those present agreed to in the end is what counts: Mussolini, Ciano, Badoglio, and Generals Soddu, Roatta, Visconti Prasca, as well as the governor of Albania, Jacomoni, all decided to hand Greece an unacceptable ultimatum that would inevitably lead to an attack. The only doubts concerned the need to occupy the whole country or only the section on the Albanian border up to the Gulf of Arta. Mussolini was ecstatic at the idea of annexing the beautiful Ionian Islands. Incredibly, the record shows that the chiefs of staff of the navy and air force were not present during the initial elaboration of plan G.

On October 17, after having finally discussed the plan with the navy and the air force, as well as with General Soddu, Badoglio went through a sudden crisis of conscience, a change of heart. He told Ciano that the chiefs of staff of the three branches of the armed forces had voiced opposition to plan G because the troop strength for such an operation was too weak and because the navy doubted it could land in Parvesa due to the shallow waters in the bay. Ciano, who had made the invasion of Greece his personal project, just as he had done a year earlier with Albania, said to Badoglio: "Politically, this is the right moment. Greece is isolated, Turkey will not move, nor will Yugoslavia. If Bulgaria comes in, it will be on our side. I can't judge the military situation. We must speak with Mussolini."

Badoglio hinted at handing in his resignation rather than take on the responsibility of an attack destined to fail. Ciano felt that the chief of staff was much too pessimistic, because he had already said that with Greece, it would not be a question of a real war because, he, Ciano, had already "bought" a few key Greek generals and politicians. According to Ciano, after the first few days of war, there would be a "coup" against the government and the army, while a pro-Italian government would sweep away the "unreliable" government of Ioannis Metaxas. Badoglio was now convinced and limited his demands to two more days to prepare the operation, delaying it from October 26 to October 28. The Duce accepted the postponement: the twenty-eighth was the anniversary of the March on Rome.

While this sordid affair was being cooked up in Rome, Hitler's special train, an amazing piece of ultra-modern rolling stock for its time, was racing toward Montoire-sur-Loire in France on October 22. Hitler told Pierre Laval, the prime minister of the Vichy government, that two days later he would like to meet Marshal Pétain, and the Vichy government should prepare public opinion for this important event. On October 23, Hitler went to the Spanish-French border at Hendaye to meet Generalissimo Francisco Franco, the Caudillo of Spain. The meeting was extremely festive, so much so that it was difficult not to suspect that behind this happy facade which the Spaniards had carefully staged, there were no traps and feints, which were General Franco's specialty as a long-standing master of war in North Africa. The Führer came right to the point: Gibraltar. With Madrid's approval, special German units, which had worked so well in Belgium in similar situations, would storm the rock on January 10, 1941, and deliver it to its rightful owners: the Spanish. What did the Caudillo think of this project, which obviously implied that Spain would declare war on Great Britain?

Measuring his words very carefully, the Caudillo answered that it looked good to him, very good. But there was one important modification he must make to the Führer's proposal: not German, but Spanish troops alone, and without foreign help, should carry out this historic mission. The Spanish people have too much of an innate sense of pride to be able to accept something that is rightfully theirs as a gift from foreigners, even though they were great friends. However, this could be overlooked if the Führer, said Franco, in his generosity could supply the Spanish army with the necessary equipment to undertake the mission. But this would also not be sufficient, because Spain needed the funds to rebuild the roads and the railway lines that had been destroyed during the civil war.

The Caudillo, according to his own experience, pointed out that any war, even the most sacred of wars, cannot be fought by a people on an empty stomach. Could Germany therefore supply Spain with the necessary food for such an undertaking? Politically, Franco was no less demanding. As compensation for Spain entering the war on the side of the Axis, he asked for some border changes with France, and practically all the French colonies in North Africa, including Algeria and Morocco. Finally, Franco said that January 10, 1941, was much too soon to be adequately prepared for the operation.

Hitler lost control. He jumped out of his armchair, exclaiming that his trip had been useless, and on the basis of what Franco was requesting, he could only pack up and go back to Germany. An intense discussion went on for seven more hours, in a very strained atmosphere. The only remaining way out was to come up with a document reconciling the two points of view as much as possible. The foreign ministers were given that task. Coming out of the railway car where the conference had taken place, Hitler told Keitel: "I'd rather have three of my teeth pulled than have another meeting like this one." The official dinner was more like a wake than a celebration. The next day, Ribbentrop had to leave empty-handed, without the draft of the compromise between Madrid and Berlin, because his Spanish counterpart, Serrano Suñer, failed to keep his appointment. Instead, the Spanish foreign minister sent his undersecretary with a paper that made little sense. The German foreign minister told Schmidt, the interpreter: "Franco is a cowardly ingrate, and his faithful Suñer behaves like a Jesuit."

Still upset after his disastrous meeting with Franco, Hitler hoped to fare better with Marshal Pétain at their meeting at Montoire during the afternoon of October 24, 1940. The French marshal was obviously a superior class of military man than that "parvenu" of a Spanish general. In fact, the meeting at Montoire between Hitler and Pétain had a very different flavor than that of Hendaye, and it turned into a subtle duel between two men who knew what they represented and what they wanted from each other.

Hitler began with studied politeness, telling Pétain: "Marshal, I regret, meeting you in such circumstances. I know that you did not want this war that was declared by a French government taking orders from England . . . France has been defeated, and I am certain that soon I shall also defeat England as well . . . She relies on the United States and Russia in vain . . . The United States will not have enough weapons stockpiled until 1942 . . . By then England will already be occupied . . . As for Russia, Germany has signed agreements with that country's government . . . Within one year Germany will have 230 divisions, of which 186 will be infantry, 20 armored, and 12 motorized."

What followed was a polite battle of wits, with Hitler pressing Pétain to join up with Germany and Pétain, pretending not to hear very well answering that the proposal would be studied carefully by his government. At one point, Pétain said to the Führer: "Since we are talking about peace and collaboration between our two countries, it would be interesting to know what destiny Germany has in mind for France. This would be a very good time to measure German good will. There are some very urgent questions to be discussed: the release of over two million French prisoners of war; a more humane set of regulations for the demarcation line and the relations between the occupied and the Vichy-controlled parts of France; and the reduction of the costs of maintaining the army of occupation."

Hitler avoided the trap set by Pétain by saying that all such questions would be settled as soon as Great Britain had been defeated. However, there was nothing to prevent a review of these problems before that time. The Führer concluded: "If Germany and France reach an agreement on collaboration, France can expect concessions on all the issues of interest to the marshal."

The hope of being able to bring back the prisoners of war to their families by Christmas induced Pétain to give his famous radio speech, wherein he invited the French people to collaborate with the Germans. That speech was to become one of the crimes for which the elderly Marshal was condemned at his trial for treason after the war. For Hitler, the meeting with Pétain had been relatively successful and eased the fiasco of the encounter with Franco.

Hitler told Ribbentrop to inform the Italian government regarding the results of the two meetings. Ciano wrote in his *Diary*: "During the evening of October 24, Ribbentrop called from a small railroad station in France. He told me about the Franco and Pétain talks and was optimistic about the results. He said the collaboration program is off to a good start with concrete results . . . Ribbentrop also spoke of Hitler's next trip to a city in northern Italy very soon to meet with the Duce."

The mention by Ribbentrop that Hitler wanted to meet with Mussolini only twenty days after their preceding summit at the Brenner alarmed Ciano. Had the Germans been informed of the Italian plans against Greece? Ciano was right to be worried. His conscience was not altogether clear, having cooked up the "the letter plot" with Mussolini's consent.

When Mussolini learned of the German move to protect the Romanian oil fields at Ploesti, he had harsh words concerning the Führer: "He will learn from the newspapers that I have occupied Greece. This way, things will be even once again." The Duce, set upon countering Hitler's move, took advantage of the fact that the Führer was in France that week. On October 19, Mussolini began writing a personal letter to Hitler which he completed on October 22, when he gave it to Ciano to be dispatched to Hitler. The letter, still dated October 19, remained at the Italian foreign ministry offices in the Palazzo Chigi for one whole day and, on the 24th, was finally in the hands of the Italian ambassador to Berlin, Alfieri, who contacted the German foreign ministry to deliver the document. It was on the same day as the Hitler-Pétain meeting at Montoire and of Ribbentrop's phone call to Ciano relating the results of the trips to Spain and France, and ending with the request for a new summit between Hitler and Mussolini.

At the German foreign ministry, Mussolini's letter was taken very seriously in spite of its vague terms. The Duce, after some generalities, wrote that he was resolved to end the Greek problem quickly and present the government in Athens with an ultimatum, without giving the exact date of this move. The German foreign ministry called Ribbentrop by phone on the morning of October 25 to give him this important news. Hitler was immediately informed of the dangers of this new crisis. He ordered Ribbentrop to call Ciano once again and set the summit for Monday, October 28, in Florence, the Führer's favorite Italian city. Ciano agreed to the date and the venue, noting in his *Diary*: "This rush of the Führer to Italy so soon after his conference with Pétain is not at all pleasing to me. I hope he will not offer us a cup of hemlock because of our claims against France."

Mussolini's actions posed a grave threat to Hitler's short- and long-term plans. According to the Führer, the fragile balance in the Balkans must not be upset before his war with the Soviet Union. Furthermore, the Greek government was then in the hands of General Ioannis Metaxas, a pro-Nazi dictator who had studied at the military college in Potsdam and made no mystery, within limits, of his sympathies for the Axis and his lack of enthusiasm for the Allies. This made it all the more urgent to prevail upon the Duce to stop his absurd plans against Greece. Hitler asked to see the actual text of the letter (it was finally given to him at the station of Yvoir-sur-Meuse).

The train reached Munich during the night of October 27. A cable from the German embassy in Rome, delivered to Hitler, informed him that during the afternoon, Count Ciano had read to Prince Otto von Bismarck the text of Italy's ultimatum to Greece, to be delivered at 3:00 a.m. the next morning. Should no positive answer be received by 6:00 a.m. a state of war would exist between the two countries. The German interpreter Paul Schmidt left the following notes on this episode: "We were not terribly happy after the fiascoes at Hendaye and Montoire, and the news of the Italian initiatives produced as much warmth as the snowy landscapes we crossed by train toward Italy. The police were about to reach the scene of the crime too late, as usual."

Ribbentrop was more realistic, and while the train was speeding toward Florence, he termed Italy's attack on Greece as an insane project because with the coming fall season of bad weather, the Italian army would be easily defeated. But time was running out. Mussolini's "war machine" was in motion, opening one of the worst disasters in the history of the Fascist dictatorship.

IX

Disaster in Greece

Florence: October 28, 1940

T he eighth meeting between Hitler and Mussolini took place
on October 28, 1940, in Florence, at the railroad station
and the Pitti Palace. It was a typical fall day, windy and cold. The
nine-car German train arrived exactly on time, at ten in the morning.

In Bologna, the Führer had been informed that three hours
earlier, Italy had attacked Greece. Mussolini was jumping with joy,
and as soon as the train stopped at the platform, the Duce himself,
in a burst of boyish enthusiasm, began leading the military band as
if he were its conductor. Hitler appeared at the window, wearing a
forced smile as Mussolini walked down the red carpet to greet him:
"Führer, we are on the march. My troops victoriously entered Greece
at six this morning." Hitler remained silent and the Duce added,
"Don't worry, in two weeks, it will be all over." After a strong handshake, the two dictators adjourned to the waiting room of the railroad station to exchange the latest information. Anfuso noted in
his book:

"Hitler took the unexpected news he was given in Florence relatively well . . . it was a sort of modest answer to all those communications after the fact he had given us in the past, ever since the Anschluss. He did not complain but held on to his habit of not communicating any of his plans to us. The meetings with Franco and Pétain were part of a plan to secure the western part of the continent before embarking on an anti-Soviet crusade. The widening of the war to the Balkans was embarrassing to him. His plan was to repeat what he had done in Bucharest: to neutralize the Balkan countries without the use of force and continue wooing Turkey. In coming to Florence, his intent was probably to dissuade Mussolini from any action against Greece . . . He wished the Duce the best of luck in his enterprise, without showing any disapproval, and led us to understand that he thought Italy's action could have been delayed. That was all."

Hitler saved his comments for a letter, a means of communication he found to be much more effective in his relations with Mussolini. Face to face, there were always many difficulties to overcome: language, witnesses, emotions, and personalities. Following the official agenda for his meeting with Mussolini, Hitler opened the discussion in a sitting room of the Pitti Palace on the two issues of the day: Spain and France. The Führer began by saying that Germany would never favor France over Italy and, therefore, any fears Italy may have on this issue were unfounded. At the Montoire meeting, Pétain had made a good impression on him, but he had not been as favorably impressed by Laval, whom he considered a horse trader even though he was pro-German. They were both, however, paralyzed by the political success of de Gaulle, who had British support in arms and propaganda, leading the French people to believe that revenge was close at hand.

Later at lunch, Hitler was to expand upon this idea: "The French are so intent on sitting in every chair at the same time that they may well lose each one of them. This is because the soul of the French people is divided, torn . . . Since France does not have a strong man today, no one is able to make clear-cut decisions, even though there are really only two paths for French policy: give up on Europe and transfer the government to North Africa to continue the war against us, or join the Axis, salvaging most of its European territory and obtaining other forms of compensation for the concessions it will inevitably have to make to Germany, Italy, and Spain at a peace treaty . . . A people faced with such a profound dilemma regarding its own future needs a man at its head capable of clear reasoning . . . Pétain is not such a man. It's true that he does enjoy an extraordinary amount of moral authority, but it is the authority of white hair . . . An agreement, an exchange of views with Pétain, seems useless to me . . . It is deplorable that none of Pétain's closest aides can make quick decisions. Laval, for instance, has only the experience of being a member of parliament. The Vichy government, in effect, is without any real authority, and such governments are always dangerous ghosts."

As for Spain, Hitler told Mussolini that Franco impressed him as a brave man but without the qualities of a statesman. He had no organizational ability and wasted much time in small talk. Franco didn't have what was required to solve the gigantic problems facing Spain without the backing of the Church. Just before the Hendaye meeting, Admiral Canaris had warned Hitler not to be disappointed, because in Franco he would not find a hero, but a diplomat who was a master at the art of procrastination. Hitler then repeated for the Duce's benefit the wisecrack he told Keitel: "Better to go to the dentist than have a second meeting with Franco." The Führer had left the meeting with renewed hope of being able to enlist Spain's participation in the Tripartite Pact. Regarding Greece, in order to please Mussolini and gauge his behavior, Hitler offered his contribution in the form of paratrooper units for an eventual invasion of Crete. The Duce, a bit stung in his pride and not yet informed of the realities on the Albanian front, declined the offer.

The Florence summit ended in the late afternoon, and Hitler returned to Germany, leaving Florence via the Brenner Pass. He was depressed; in six days, he had seen all three Mediterranean dictators and had been unable to coax them into actions that would help his plans in the east. After the war, Paul Schmidt recalled: "Hitler went back north that night feeling very bitter. He had been disappointed three times: in Hendaye, in Montoire, and in Florence. During the long evening discussions in the years that followed, those trips became the recurring themes of rancor toward ungrateful or duplicitous partners: Axis friends and French deceivers alike."

Regarding the Italian attack on Greece, Hitler told Ribbentrop, Keitel, and Schmidt: "How could Mussolini do such a thing? This is pure madness. Rather than attacking a small country, why didn't he mount an assault on Malta? I have decided to do something because, in any case, the Italians won't get anywhere in Greece during the fall rainy season and the winter snow."

Mussolini returned to Rome in high spirits, convinced that he had at last given his German partner a lesson, showing he could also engage in *blitzkrieg* operations. Back at the Palazzo Venezia, he would stare at the phone in the hope it would ring. But hours went by without any news. Only at 5:30 p.m., almost twelve hours after the war with Greece had started, a cable arrived from General Sebastiano Visconti Prasca, announcing that for the first time, the weather was to be blamed for the inability of the Italian army to advance. It was, apparently, an unexpected discovery for the Italian high command and for Mussolini, that at the end of October on that mountainous region of the Greek-Albanian border there could be such a thing as bad weather. Once the enormity of the miscalculation became apparent, Ciano, one of the instigators of this adventure, was among first to seek alibis and excuses.

Historian Giordano Bruno Guerri wrote: "The Ciano *Diary* tends to show that he had little to do with the Greek operation. But the opposite is closer to the truth. It is no accident that the places where Ciano made extensive changes in his 1939-1943 *Diary*, erasing and rewriting passages during the first half of 1943, are the ones dealing with the war in Greece. In the original version, the pages dated October 27 and 28, 1940, had been torn by Ciano himself who then corrected the date on the pages for October 26 and 27, adding a few meaningless lines and doing the same for October 28 . . ."

Greece was destined to play an important, if moderate, part in Ciano's plans in the Balkans ever since he had been named Foreign

Minister. On November 1, 1937, he wrote: "The future is clear: the Serbs will take Salonica, we will be in Tirana and in Corfu. The Greeks sense and fear all this . . . " Ciano had visited Tirana from May 22 to 25, 1940. He told General Geloso, the Italian commanding general in Albania: "Within the next two to three weeks, Italy will declare war, and you will have to attack Greece." Ciano further suggested moving five divisions from the Yugoslav border to the Greek-Albanian border. General Geloso pointed out that he would make no moves without orders from the high command and that, in any case, five divisions were insufficient. Back in Rome, Ciano was able to convince Undersecretary of War General Soddu, and a man beholden to him, to replace General Geloso with General Visconti Prasca, who was more receptive to Ciano's directives . . . Ciano's continuous interference in military operations was one of the most absurd aspects of the war with Greece.

After the Florence summit, Ciano immediately left for Tirana on October 29: "Bad weather," he wrote, "we can't fly . . . Things are proceeding a bit slowly because of the rain." On November 1 the sky cleared. Ciano became optimistic and put on his air force uniform, feeling very much the "warrior." He wrote in his *Diary*: "I take advantage of the sunny skies for a bombing action with all the trimmings over Salonica. On my way back, I am attacked by two Greek fighter planes: all is well and two of them are shot down . . . " Ciano returned to Rome on November 6, after a quick trip to Germany to meet Ribbentrop. He found Mussolini displeased with the war in Greece. The Italian army was in full and shameful retreat, which Ciano attributed to an "Albanian battalion" that began to cut and run away from the front out of fear.

On November 11, the Italian army was close to being defeated, thanks to General Alexandros Papagos, who had inspired his troops and equipped them well with British supplies. The Ciano *Diary* then, while recounting basic events, suddenly becomes a masterpiece of half-truths and cover-ups regarding the Greek campaign. On November 12, while he noted the successful British torpedo plane assault on the naval base at Taranto, which knocked out three Italian battleships, Ciano did not even mention the reelection of Franklin

D. Roosevelt, a disastrous event for the Axis because it was very clear by now that Roosevelt was determined to bring the full pressure of American industrial power to the fight against Germany, Italy, and Japan and in favor of the Allies.

Suddenly, on November 13, after much bad weather and the "retreat" of the Albanian battalion, Marshal Badoglio reappears in the Ciano *Diary* as the scapegoat regarding the disaster in Greece. Ciano defended himself against accusations coming in from all sides: "Farinacci tells me that Mussolini, in speaking about Greece, has said that 'even Count Ciano gave me the wrong information' . . . I can only answer that I had the same information that Mussolini had." He did not repeat his assertions regarding corrupt Greek officials, including generals and high-ranking diplomats, that everyone had heard before the war began.

In this dramatic atmosphere, Ciano was called to a meeting with Ribbentrop in Salzburg, then with Hitler at Berchtesgaden on November 18 and given a list of German demands. The Führer gave Ciano a personal message for Mussolini, listing all the objections he did not voice in Florence. According to Ciano:

"Heavy atmosphere. Hitler is pessimistic and thinks the situation is very difficult . . . His criticism is candid, tight, and merciless. I try to discuss matters with him, but he does not let me speak."

The next day, the German and Italian delegations went to Vienna to sign the Tripartite Pact with Hungary. At the end of the meetings, Hitler told Ciano: "From here in Vienna, I sent Mussolini a cable to assure him that I would not forget his help on the day of the Anschluss. I confirm this today, and with all my strength I shall be at his side." Hitler's personal message for the Duce was full of complaints and criticisms. On November 21, Ciano wrote of his own surprise at the Führer's letter: "Hitler's letter to the Duce is full of worries and criticisms. I expected a violent reaction from Mussolini. But nothing happened. He attaches no importance to the document which deserves much more attention." Perhaps because a few days before, the Duce had told the provincial heads of the Fascist party in a famous speech: " . . . in July 1935, just before the war in Ethiopia, I told you that we would break the Negus' back. Today, with the same absolute certainty, I repeat, *absolute*, I can tell you that we will break the back of Greece."

In his long letter to Mussolini, Hitler feared and anticipated that the Italian military failure in Greece would have dire consequences on Axis morale and the military situation. He regretted, much like an old fashioned patriarch, that he had arrived in Florence too late to stop the unwelcome decision. However, with a good dose of realism, the Führer had now decided to stop any further British infiltration into Greece. The British had landed troops in the Bay of Suda in Crete on October 31, creating a powerful naval and air base threatening the Italian front in Cirenaica. But since the German high command was not given to sudden "impulses" like its Italian counterpart, any large operation could not begin before the weather improved in March. Until then the Axis must concentrate on the Mediterranean, attacking all enemy positions.

Therefore, the Italians should now move again in North Africa and reach Marsa Matruh, the British armed camp, deeper into Egypt, and "from that position it will be much easier and faster for the air forces to reach Alexandria and the Suez Canal. This will set the stage for a massive offensive against Egypt." Axis air forces must also attack the British fleet in the Mediterranean: Germany would send a few Stuka dive bomber units to Sicily to help in this effort. Finally, the Führer promised to resume his political pressure on the hesitant Francisco Franco and announced stronger measures to assure the protection of Romania (anticipating that Yugoslavia would soon join the Tripartite Pact).

On November 22, Ciano noted: "Mussolini is writing his answer to Hitler. It is short and calm. He accepts the political and military proposals the Führer is making." The Duce's comment was more true to life: "Hitler rapped me on my knuckles with a ruler like a schoolboy."

December was to be one of the most painfully disastrous months of that fateful year 1940. Mussolini demanded and obtained the resignation of Marshal Badoglio, held responsible for the Greek debacle, and replaced him with General Ugo Cavallero as head of the general staff. On the same day, December 6, Mussolini called

Alfieri, the Italian ambassador to Berlin, and told him to give a general SOS to the Germans. "What should I request?" a puzzled Alfieri asked Ciano, who answered unhesitatingly: "Any help, as long as it comes immediately. The situation can be changed completely by just a few planes, artillery pieces, and ground units." Such a message conveyed a dramatic situation but did not give any technical details, which were required for military action.

Alfieri hurried back to Berlin and Ribbentrop, who began with a harsh lecture before answering any of his questions: "This crisis has erupted because the Italian government willfully ignored the Führer's warning not to attack Greece." Alfieri met with Hitler the next day, and the Führer was just as hard as his foreign minister and in a terrible mood because of deteriorating relations with the USSR. In addition to chastising Italy for attacking Greece, Hitler also noted the very poor showing of the Italian army. Mussolini, he declared, had to resort to mobile courts-martial and execution squads if he wanted to turn the situation around. He had to go "back to barbaric methods, such as shooting generals and colonels who fled their units and using decimation on the soldiers." After enduring this second tirade, Alfieri was able to phone Rome that the Führer had authorized fifty heavy troop transport planes to airlift fresh units from Italy to Albania. However, Hitler also wanted to have a meeting with Mussolini, but the Duce, on this occasion, was not at all receptive.

On that same December 6, Mussolini met with Luftwaffe Marshal Erhard Milch bearing a message from the Führer. Milch was in Rome to discuss the arrival of German air force units that were to operate in the Mediterranean from bases in Sicily. In his letter, Hitler stated that confidential negotiations led him to believe there could be an agreement with Yugoslavia, while his suspicions concerning Spain were growing rapidly since Franco was changing positions much too quickly. France was also not to be trusted, as Pétain appeared to be double-crossing Germany and plotting secretly with de Gaulle.

Mussolini felt that thanks to German help, the worst dangers had been avoided. In Albania, after the loss of Argirocastro and

Porto Edda, the Italian army had appeared to stop the Greek advance. But bad news was coming in from North Africa, where the British had suddenly attacked the Italian positions. On December 10, they took Sidi el Barrani. Graziani was sending desperate appeals to Rome, saying that he would have to fall back as far as Tripoli. On December 15, the Italian army was overwhelmed in Egypt and in East Africa: in Ethiopia and Somalia, the British were counterattacking vigorously.

Winston Churchill, now assured of American support after President Roosevelt's reelection to a third term, broadcast an appeal to the Italian people during the night of December 23 through the voice of actor Norman Shelley. After recalling the long friendship between England and Italy, he went on to say:

"Now we are at war . . . Our armies are cutting your African empire to pieces and shall continue to do so . . . And why is all this taking place? For what reason? People of Italy, I want you to know the truth. It is because of one man alone. One man and only one man has launched the Italian people in a deadly struggle with the British Empire and has deprived Italy of the friendship and good will of the United States of America. I do not deny that he is a great man, but after eighteen years of unchecked power, he has brought your country to the very edge of ruin. No one can deny that. It is only one man who, against the Crown, the Italian royal family, against the Pope and the Vatican, and the authority of the Roman Catholic Church, against the wishes of the Italian people, who had no enthusiasm for this war, has brought the heirs of the glory of the Roman Empire to the side of the bloodthirsty pagan barbarians."

On December 30, President Roosevelt also touched on this theme during one of his fireside chats, to persuade the American people to follow his policy of eventual war against the Axis and Japan:

"There are dangers on the horizon, dangers against which we must be prepared. But we know we can't run away from danger by getting in bed and pulling the sheets over our faces. Should England fall, all of us here in America will live under the threat of a gun pointed at us, loaded with exploding bullets, both economic and military. We must build ships and weapons with all the energy we have. We must be the great arsenal of democracy."

This hardening of the battlelines was taking place just a few days after Hitler had made another fateful decision with his infamous Directive Number 21 of December 18, 1940, which contained the executive orders for Operation *Barbarossa*, the attack on the Soviet Union. The document, after an introduction explaining the general objectives of the campaign, went on to say: "The German armed forces must be ready to annihilate Soviet Russia with a lightning campaign, even before the conclusion of the war with England." It detailed the specific tasks of the army, navy, and Luftwaffe. All preparations were to be completed by May 15, 1941.

The British attack in Cirenaica, conceived at first as a secondary campaign to relieve the pressure on Egypt, became an all-out offensive due to the weak and inconsistent deployment of the defensive positions of the Italian army. The bases of Bardia, Derna, and Tobruk fell one after the other to the British. The Italian army was completely defeated. King Victor Emanuel III commented tersely, "For much too long in Italy a chair is being called a palace. But the fact is a chair is only a chair. Likewise our divisions, thin and poorly equipped, are divisions in name only."

Mussolini was seized by panic. He cabled the Italian military attaché in Berlin, General Efisio Marras, to "purchase immediately all you can in tanks and artillery at any price." On the morning of December 23, Mussolini told Ciano: "I am now like one of those country innkeepers who draws the picture of a rooster on the wall and says, 'When this rooster crows, I will start extending credit.' I shall also extend credit to the military leaders when they will prove to me with facts that the situation has changed." The Duce was alluding to the optimistic pronouncements of Cavallero, the new head of the general staff, who had been announcing for weeks that the Italians were about to break the encirclement of Valona in Albania.

During those weeks, Italian personnel at the embassy in Berlin noted: "The Germans are worried about the British advance in Egypt and the situation in Albania. All this will have negative diplomatic consequences and will surely provoke insurrections in occupied territories. Various indications are that the Germans, in their methodical manner, are carefully studying the Italian problem. They are of the opinion that our army has already done all it can and must be considered liquidated . . . How can the situation be reversed? The Führer is once again speaking about the need for a meeting with the Duce, who is again rejecting the request."

Mussolini obviously was in need of some time and space to recover from his own behavior on October 28. In Florence, by aping Hitler in the technique of an ultimatum followed by a surprise attack, he wanted to believe for a day that he could liquidate Greece in two weeks. His attitude worried Hitler somewhat, and the Führer quickly dispatched the Prince of Hesse to Rome. On January 3, 1941, Hesse asked Ciano how to read Mussolini's attitude toward the Führer at that time. Ciano replied: "The Duce has never been more grateful toward the Führer than he is today for his friendship and solidarity."

A few days before, the Italian embassy officials in Berlin were up in arms against Ambassador Alfieri, who was about to send a report to Rome recommending that the Italian government accept, without criticism or reservations, the help offered by the Führer and its humiliating conditions: no raw materials but only finished goods would be shipped, while Italy would be required to send more workers to Germany. Embassy personnel demanded that some negotiations take place to preserve Italian dignity. Alfieri finally tore up the document, due to new developments announced in the form of Italo-German military agreements.

The daily diary of Ambassador Alfieri's assistant noted: "Sunday December 29 at about 5:00 p.m. there was a call from Ribbentrop. He's very worried by the news from Albania. Valona appears threatened; Alfieri answered that he doesn't believe such information to be correct. The German minister sarcastically replied that he hopes it will be so. Then Ribbentrop stated: 'Ciano was telling Mackensen that between eight and ten thousand men a day were landing in Albania.' The Germans, however, have calculated that, at the most, only five hundred troops were actually arriving per day. Ribbentrop would like to know if the ambassador of the Reich misunderstood. If not, then Italy should have enough troops to stop the Greeks. Why then are they still advancing?"

General Favgrossa arrived in Berlin on Monday, December 30, on a mission to finally discuss the problem of supplies. His experts and he did not expect a positive outcome and, in case of success, they did not think the situation could even be improved. The Italian diplomat's diary continues: "The current crisis, they say, is based on a lack of confidence by the soldiers toward the officers and of the country toward its leadership. Ciano should be eliminated as well as a few others. Badoglio should become head of the army to impose 'honesty' as a motto and apply it energetically . . . But Ciano, shielded by the Duce, does what he pleases, and Mussolini doesn't do anything anymore; he looks like an empty canvas."

Bilateral discussions took place in the presence of General Keitel. Their objectives were to dispatch armored units to Libya, and to supply Italy with weapons and raw materials. Keitel began with "a presentation of the points that were to become the basis for negotiations, alluding to the fact that this would have to be a long-term program . . . the need for Italy to send to the front all her existing materiel, the need in Italy itself to impose necessary restrictions on consumer goods and on production that would be required to attain favorable results; the requirement to factor in the problems of transportation.

The problem of sending armored units to Libya had been studied by General Jodl, who made a candid assessment: "There had developed between Italy and Germany a crisis of confidence which had prevented the dispatch of an armored division to Cirenaica. The declaration of war on Greece had been a colossal political mistake . . . This being said, there would be no limits placed on Germany's willingness to help Italy; the Führer wanted to avoid at all costs German units being placed in conditions that would result in any loss of prestige; Germany was certain it would win the war, and, therefore, Italy, its ally, was also assured of final victory."

Jodl further described the situation as follows: "(a) the naval and air war against England would continue vigorously . . . ; (b) Germany will march against Greece. Two divisions, one armored and one mechanized are already stationed in Romania. The campaign will require twenty divisions, two of which will be mountain troops commanded by Marshal Wilhelm List. Starting on January 1, fifty trains a day will transport these troops to Romania . . . The operations will begin during the first two weeks of March; (c) necessary forces are being prepared to complete the occupation of all of metropolitan France . . . ; (d) troops destined to occupy Gibraltar are being trained in southern France . . . The Gibraltar operation should only last three days. However, Spain is not yet committed to entering the war . . . ; (e) in the Italian sector, the Luftwaffe Xth Air Corps, is already in Italy but will only participate in actions against British forces."

Jodl insisted, in particular, that "we must not lose Albania, and we must save Valona." He then asked: "Why not send in the Taurinese alpine division now on the French border? There is nothing to fear from the French sector . . . " Finally, he invited the Italians to "hold in Libya and not allow the British to link up through French Africa . . . " Jodl's presentation shows that Italy was now militarily practically under German administration. Hitler was still unclear regarding Spain's final decision. As if to confirm the failed adventurism of Mussolini and Ciano in their attack on Greece, Germany was preparing over twenty well-equipped "real" divisions to begin operations in the spring rather than the fall. The East African Italian Empire had finally been abandoned to its own destiny by both Germans and Italians alike.

The results and the promises made at the Berlin meeting buoyed Mussolini. Ciano cabled Alfieri that the Duce was now ready to meet the Führer anytime between the twelfth and the nineteenth of February. Ciano noted that Mussolini did not wish to meet Hitler "under the weight of many failures not even partially resolved." On January 10, the final date for the meeting was set for February 19 at Berchtesgaden. Mussolini was again in high spirits after hearing the news from the eastern Mediterranean, where the Xth Air

Corps had successfully engaged the British fleet. It was the first appearance of German forces in the area. Hoping to be able to bring some good news to his meeting with Hitler, Mussolini went to Foggia on January 14 to preside over a war council regarding Albania. Two days later, he returned "dark and pessimistic." In spite of the "Cavallero recipe," the front did not stabilize at all, and a new Greek attack was always possible. He vented his displeasure the next day by ordering the mobilization, as of February 1, of all the Fascist party leaders, the government, and the Grand Council and parliament to go and fight on the Greek front.

Anfuso commented on Mussolini's "morale hostage taking": "During the war in Ethiopia, many Fascist leaders had volunteered to participate in the campaign: during the initial phases of this operation, the same party leaders had gone to Albania and did their best. The new orders from Mussolini now hit the inner sanctum, the untouchables: the cabinet ministers, the members of the Grand Council, the people he saw every day! It was a decision that would cost him dearly in the future, much more even than the decision to declare war on Greece. It lined his men up with Badoglio, made them unhappy, exacerbated them, and placed them in front of their own promises of sacrifice, transforming them into soldiers for an operation where they suffered the bitterness of being ordered to go.

"Hatred of the dictator began festering in the mud puddles of the Albanian front, a hatred that would eventually orchestrate his undoing. The sudden decision left the cabinet ministries in the hands of bureaucrats: I had to take over Ciano's work while he went to Bari to command an air force fighter group. What was Mussolini thinking as he said good-bye to his comrades, those he had elevated to the highest levels of the state administration over the past twenty years? . . . To give a positive example to the country? Anyone who saw them leave would not have been impressed. They were critical and began using the same critical vocabulary they were to repeat during the meeting of the Grand Council two years later on July 25, 1943."

Giuseppe Bottai, the minister of national education (and one of the future conspirators of the Grand Council), gives a good example of the inner thoughts of the leadership in his *Diary*: "January 17, 1941. There are rumors of the departures for the Albanian front ordered by the Duce to ministers and leaders. At five minutes to eight, my direct line with Mussolini rang. 'When must you leave for Germany?' It was a visit to the German schools. 'Monday,' I answered. 'You can call your German counterpart and tell him that the trip is canceled until after the war.' 'Fine.' 'As for you, you have just been redrafted.' 'Fine.' I hung up mechanically. I look into the nothingness around me. This is how this war reached me, in a sort of dehumanized way. Through an office memo; not between the chief and myself, man to man. What I would have given voluntarily was imposed upon me by force."

Bottai, now feeling "politically raped" by his former idol, wrote on January 20: "Obedience has the strangely bitter taste of revolt. Mussolini's last sortie, and he was very proud of it, was: 'I'll show the country how to govern with civil service directors!' We are the guinea pigs of a dictatorial experiment."

Ciano sounds even more pathetic complaining about being "rounded up" for military service. In his *Diary* he quoted the complaints of those sitting in the Duce's anteroom: "There is something in all of this that just doesn't work, and we must not pretend it doesn't exist. Some, like Bottai, even talk about a real *coup d'état* by the Duce to liquidate Fascism and base his power on other political forces. I don't believe any of this . . . But it is a drastic decision, and this is certainly no time for experiments on the home front." On January 25, Ciano showed some bitterness: "I take leave of the Duce; tomorrow evening I will be with my unit in Bari. It was not as friendly as it should have been. But these days Mussolini is feeling that the order to send the cabinet ministers away from Rome has not been well received, and, as usual in such cases, he persists in his determination, and his manner becomes surly. He made some comments in saying good-bye to me that he could have kept to himself."

Another Fascist leader to be ordered to Albania was Dino Grandi, the great conspirator and third man of the July 25, 1943, coup. Grandi was at the time justice minister and president of the lower house of Parliament. He did not expect and did not welcome the news. Lieutenant Colonel Dino Grandi, Major Giuseppe Bottai, and Major Galeazzo Ciano would never forgive Mussolini for being penalized in such a manner. It can be surmised that the "conspirators" of July 25, 1943, reached their "pact" while serving in Albania together. Grandi himself would say as much:

"Mussolini wanted both Bottai and me dead. I was very upset when my Alpine troops went to their deaths with their feathered caps flapping in the wind as they cursed the Duce by name. We had to get out of the war. The sooner the better. I made contact with my friends and jotted down, then and there, in the trenches of Greece, the agenda that was to place Mussolini in a minority position at the Grand Council of Fascism." Having written the document, Grandi would take two more years to improve and update it. He no longer felt the haste that had gripped him in Albania.

Mussolini was able to show Hitler the kind of power he still exercised over the Fascist party, with the novel approach of dispatching "the leadership to the front" as well as proving his commitment to the war. The Duce also proceeded to complete the first purge of the army high command. He had encountered a few problems when he replaced Badoglio. In the end, he ignored the advice of those involved and, above all, bypassed the sacred seniority list of the officer corps when he picked General Ugo Cavallero. Cavallero had been an opponent of Badoglio ever since the defeat at Caporetto in 1917 and had three positive "virtues" on his side: he was an iron clad optimist; he spoke fluent German and English; and for twenty years he had successfully commuted between the armaments industry (such as Pirelli and Ansaldo) and the army high command. In short, Cavallero was someone everyone feared and respected, and bad-mouthed behind his back.

Just before leaving for the Albanian front on December 6, 1940, Cavallero suggested to Mussolini a change of leadership in the naval high command. After seven years on the job, navy chief of staff, Admiral Domenico Cavagnari handed over his command to Admiral Arturo Riccardi, while Admiral Angelo Iachino replaced his superior, Admiral Inigo Campioni, of whom he was a leading critic, as commander of the fleet. Campioni was however promoted to deputy chief of staff. Within this entire purge, Mussolini also took the opportunity to get rid of Cesare Maria De Vecchi, who had created problems as governor of the Aegean Islands. General Soddu replaced the purged General Visconti Prasca, who was held responsible for the debacle in Greece. General Cavallero had personally taken over the command of the front.

The only issue Mussolini had been unable to prepare for in advance of his meeting in Germany was the "Russian mystery." The Duce resented having been kept in the dark until the eleventh hour regarding the German-Soviet nonaggression pact. He also saw himself rightly, as something of a prophet with respect to relations with the USSR. Mussolini asked Ciano to probe in that direction, to sound out the Kremlin for a possible understanding. Everything proceeded better than expected, so much so that Molotov accepted a dinner invitation at the Italian embassy in Moscow. The Italian ambassador to the Soviet Union, Augusto Rosso, sent a message to Rome on December 31, 1940, with three questions from the Soviets to take the conversations one step further—what was Italy's position on Romania, the Danube, and the Straits?

Italy's reply was that the guarantees offered to Romania were in no way directed against the USSR; Italy was ready to accommodate the USSR on other issues as much as it could; as for the Straits, their importance and sensitivity made it necessary to include Berlin in the discussion. Ciano then asked Alfieri to inform Ribbentrop about the ongoing Italian conversations in Moscow. It was as if the roof had fallen as Ribbentrop violently berated the Italian ambassador. How was it, roared the Nazi foreign minister, that the Italian government had decided to meddle with problems in Eastern Europe that were the exclusive domain of the Third Reich? Had not Mussolini and Ciano understood that the USSR was attempting to obtain through Italy what Germany had repeatedly and categorically denied it?

Ambassador Rosso was immediately told to break off the discussions. Two weeks later he wrote to his colleague Alfieri in Berlin: "The foreign ministry kept me in the dark about your conversations with Ribbentrop. Any comment or criticism on this subject is useless. The notes regarding your meeting of January 6 put everything in perspective for the first time. They confirm what I had already suspected, that we went into the Moscow discussions without having secured Berlin's agreement. I can't understand why Rome did not do this before ordering me to begin discussions with Molotov. Perhaps Palazzo Chigi thought it could simply reach an understanding with these gentlemen on the basis of a generic agreement to update the pacts of 1933 . . . When a December 28 cable from Ciano ordered me to begin talks, I was convinced that Rome was ready, this time, to discuss the problems Molotov had mentioned in June: Romania, the Balkans, and the Straits . . .

"I always thought that in June we had been forced to stop the discussions that we had started on our own initiative because the Germans asked us to do so . . . I could not believe that we would risk this once again . . . All these conjectures based on logic turned out to be wrong. Hoping that my suspicions were unfounded, but needing reassurance, I cabled Rome the day after meeting with Molotov on December 30 to ask if the German government was informed of our reopening political discussions with the USSR. Only on January 5 was I told that you had been given instructions to inform Ribbentrop . . . Molotov has been waiting for an answer for eighteen days now, and he is probably beginning to think that we might be playing the same game as last June: to start discussions only to let them drop suddenly. If this is the end result, it would mean a renewed crisis in Soviet-Italian relations, a crisis that Germany, at this time, should be interested in avoiding."

Mussolini wanted to send his answer to Ambassador Rosso after his meeting with Hitler. In brief, the Berchtesgaden meeting was held between two swindlers: Hitler, without informing Mussolini, had given his orders for Operation *Barbarossa*; the Duce was secretly moving to reach an agreement with the Soviet Union behind the back of his Axis partner. Both were playing an underhanded game with each other.

X

The Italian Crisis

Berchtesgaden: January 19-20, 1941

The last thing on Mussolini's wish list was to spend a winter weekend with Adolf Hitler, even in the dramatic mountain landscape around Berchtesgaden. Mussolini was frustrated by the rout of Graziani's army in Cirenaica and ashamed of his boastful behavior on October 28, 1940, in Florence, when he told Hitler the Italian army would liquidate Greece in a fortnight.

The special train left Rome for Germany late Saturday afternoon, January 18, 1941. Mussolini was in a dark mood, worried by the news coming from Albania as Ciano noted: "Nothing tragic happened, but once again, we fell back, losing many prisoners." The worst part was that a special unit with a long tradition was the hardest hit: the *Lupi di Toscana* (wolves of Tuscany), a crack paratrooper division that had just reached the front, carrying the hopes of the Italian high command. The Duce could not understand why all this was happening and kept repeating: "If anyone on October 15 had prophesied what actually took place, I would have had him shot."

Officially the train was going to Salzburg, but the next morning it stopped at a secondary railroad station near Berchtesgaden. The small village had become the capital of the "Adolf Hitler district" since 1925, when he first rented, then purchased, a chalet called Haus Wachenfeld, built on the great salt mountain, the Obersalzberg, which dominated the valley. By 1935, Haus Wachenfeld became known as the "Berghof," or the "Berg," after Hitler enlarged the structure into a residence worthy of the Führer of Greater Germany.

Hitler's architect, Albert Speer, wrote: "Hitler wanted to pay for the new construction out of his own pocket; but it would be a futile gesture, since Martin Bormann used other, much larger funds than Hitler had planned to lay out to construct the additional buildings. The Führer did more than just produce a drawing of what he wanted for the Berghof. He asked me for a drawing board, a ruler, a drafting triangle, and other drawing instruments, and he personally set the plans, the exposures, and the sections of the new house, rejecting any kind of help. The old house was not destroyed but simply built into the new one. The new living room was joined to that of the old house through a wide opening."

Hitler was very proud of the large sliding picture window on the lower floor living room: an enormous window with a magnificent vista of the Untersberg, Berchtesgaden, and Salzburg. Facing the Berghof, on a hill called the Mosslahnerkopf, was the site of the Teehaus, a small structure with three rooms and a verandah, the usual place where Hitler took his afternoon stroll. The Berghof quickly became a symbolic fixture of Third Reich iconography. Since the Nazi "Sun King" spent much of his time on the Obersalzberg, his entourage, Göring, Speer, Hess, Bormann, and Goebbels quickly proceeded to build their own more or less luxurious residences in the vicinity, each one a reflection of their personalities. Göring's house was the most outrageous, though he rarely used it; but its mere presence was enough to show everyone that he was Germany's number two man.

Bormann was the real lord of the district, and he had forced all the local peasants to sell their land at extremely low prices. At the end of the operation, having "bought out" all the fields and barns, the Hitler was the owner of the side of a mountain almost 2,000 meters high, sloping down 600 meters lower into a valley covering almost 2,000 acres. Speer commented: "With complete disregard for the beautiful landscape, Bormann crisscrossed the countryside with various roads . . . Just as it happens in a resort that suddenly becomes popular, many different buildings suddenly appeared: barracks, an enormous garage, a hotel to accommodate Hitler's guests, a farm, a village for the Führer's employees."

Carried away by his own grandiose visions, Bormann even had the gall to spend some thirty million Reich marks, a monumental sum at that time, to build a cabin and observation point on the top of Mount Kehlstein 2,000 meters high, that was to named the Eagle's Nest. In Bormann's mind the cabin was to be used by Hitler to entertain important visitors. To reach it from the Berghof, he built a seven-kilometer paved road that took two years of backbreaking work by hundreds of workers to complete. The winding road ends at the entrance of a three-hundred-foot-long tunnel burrowed into the side of the mountain. At the end of the tunnel, an elevator took the visitors up the mountain.

The elevator arrived in a small entrance leading into a dining room. From the other rooms, the eye can see way out into Germany and Austria, Hitler's sacred domain. Beyond these rooms are bathrooms, a kitchen, and storage rooms. (A large terrace is now available to visitors and the German Alpine Club. The current owner of the Eagle's Nest makes a profit managing the facility, thanks to a restaurant and bar for tourists, who come regularly during the summer season.) Hitler, contradicting Bormann's expectations, almost never went to the top of the Kehlstein; perhaps the high altitude bothered him.

In any case, the Führer, whose tastes differed from Bormann's, preferred to receive his important guests at Klessheim Castle, whose majestic structure could be seen on the Salzkammergut, from which one had an excellent view of Kehlstein. The old Klessheim manor was near both Salzburg and Berchtesgaden, so the Führer could easily meet with his guests and return to his residence. Hitler and

Mussolini were to meet several times at Klessheim. On January 19, 1941, however, the meeting place would be the Berghof with its glorious views. The Führer, well aware of the agitated state his Italian colleague was in, attempted to create a family atmosphere to their conversations. And Eva Braun, by now the de facto lady of the manor, had expressed the wish to be formally introduced to the Duce. Mussolini was given Villa Bechstein as his residence, even though the Berghof had fourteen guest rooms. Eva Braun referred to it as the "Grand Hotel."

The morning of January 19, 1941, was not too cold, the air was clear, and the snow gave a festive mood to the scenery. The meeting between Hitler and Mussolini was quite friendly, without any of the "expressions of sympathy" Mussolini had worried about since he left Italy. Ribbentrop and Ciano went into a private meeting while Hitler met with the Duce. The Sunday meetings were exclusively dedicated to political matters, and the Monday conferences were to address the military situation. There was a strange incident concerning gossip that greatly disturbed the Duce. The Führer handed him a secret document, a report from Rome by SS Lieutenant Colonel Rudolf Likus, stating that Galeazzo Ciano was in fact a playboy and a dedicated anti-Nazi, who systematically bad-mouthed those Italian officials who were favorable to the Axis. To avoid any embarrassment for Ribbentrop (who had issued the document), Hitler identified Himmler, the head of the German police and the SS and another one of Ciano's powerful enemies, as the author. The material came from Prince Colonna's drawing room set, which Ciano used as his preferred social meeting place. There was no trace of this "Likus report" in either Italian or German archives, but it was certainly the result of an espionage mission, as pointed out by historian Giordano Bruno Guerri. Ribbentrop made a mistake in including Ciano's wife, Edda, who happened to be Mussolini's daughter, in these accusations of marital infidelity. This fact definitely played a role in prolonging Ciano's tenure as foreign minister until February 1943.

There are several possible explanations as to the reasons Hitler made such a gaffe with Mussolini. The gossip had it that Hitler bore a personal grudge toward Ciano ever since he first visited Berchtesgaden. Eva Braun had requested an introduction to Mussolini's son-in-law. Hitler refused, saying that protocol and the tight schedule would not allow such an introduction.

The truth was apparently different: Hitler was extremely jealous of Ciano, according to Nerin E. Gun, author of a biography of Eva Braun. "Hitler's mistress found Ciano 'adorable' and avidly collected his photographs. She would blush when she spoke of how attractive he was, how young and stylish he looked, and she chided Hitler for not dressing with equal elegance. Eva also considered Italy her second homeland." In Eva Braun's household, Italy was the fashion; most of her clothes therefore came from Florence and Rome. Her older sister Ilse (who had flirted with an Italian naval officer at La Spezia, thus getting into trouble with Himmler's policemen, who were always looking for spies and traitors) fell in love with Mussolini's son, Bruno, who would perish in an airplane accident at Pisa airport later that year.

Historian Duilio Susmel concluded that the SS report against Ciano that Hitler gave to Mussolini was only a warning, not intended to provoke the dismissal of the foreign minister. The Führer was convinced that Dino Grandi would have then succeeded Ciano, and Grandi was an even more dangerous foe of Nazi Germany. Ciano was, in the final analysis, only "an unstable friend."

When the Germans informed Ciano of this machination, he commented: "Von Ribbentrop stabbed me in the back. Behind Himmler there is Ribbentrop. I'm told that the memorandum also requests that I be fired. If Mussolini hands Ribbentrop my dismissal, he will show what we all know he is: a coward . . . Mussolini will never give my head to anyone. He's afraid. He knows full well that the Italian people are on my side. The Italian people know that in Italy I am the only one with the courage to counter Mussolini." In view of the final tragedy of Galeazzo Ciano, these may seem pathetic illusions on his part. It was obvious that the relationship between the two, father-in-law and son-in-law, was not as close or as affectionate as it may have appeared.

During the first two-hour meeting Hitler launched into a violent anti-Soviet tirade, in which he accused Stalin of preparing the invasion of various eastern European countries. Moscow's domination tended to spread like an oil slick all the way to the Straits and the Dardanelles. Hitler, however, remained completely silent about his orders regarding the Barbarossa plan. This vituperation against the Soviets was enough to convince Mussolini that he should stop his own discussions with the Kremlin, begun the previous December. As for Great Britain, Hitler confirmed his doubts and uncertainties on how to conclude a war he had "never wanted." Any discussion of a landing was out of the question for now, even though the project had only been postponed and not canceled.

The Führer said: "I am like a man with only one bullet in his rifle. As long as he keeps it, he's strong, but if he shoots and misses the target he's disarmed. I am able to neutralize England by threatening it, while a failed invasion would give the British freedom of action for a very long time . . . " On the other hand, the problem posed by Gibraltar—Operation *Felix*—could easily be resolved. Hitler continued: "Closing the Straits of Sicily doesn't amount to much compared to my plan for Gibraltar. Only the ingratitude displayed by Franco has made the operation impossible. If, even at this point, you could persuade him to enter the war, it would be a great help to our coalition. The situation within the Mediterranean would be completely altered in our favor . . . "

It was a difficult task, said Hitler, because Franco is under the control of the Church and the clique led by Serrano Suñer, his brother-in-law and foreign minister, who is pro-Axis in words only and is secretly plotting in favor of the Allies. Spain was a sore point for the Duce, but he agreed to meet with the Caudillo within the month to sound him out. He understood Franco was difficult to deal with, and he wanted to show his complete support for Hitler's policies. There were only two possible results: either Franco would be willing to join the Axis or he would remain neutral. In case he failed, Mussolini could always point to the Führer's own failed meeting at Hendaye; if he succeeded in swaying Franco, his success would be that much greater.

Mussolini had little to add to Hitler's presentation. He confided that King Victor Emanuel III was ambiguous in his attitude, though not openly hostile to the Axis and that he had fired Badoglio because he was convinced that the chief of staff had sabotaged the war against Greece. After the first discussions, Ciano noted: "The Duce appears generally very pleased. I am not so pleased, mostly because Ribbentrop, who so far had always been so boastful, now, to my pointed question as to the length of the war, said he couldn't see it ending before 1942. And what were we to expect?" Italy and its fate would be discussed at the military meeting the next day.

Again, Hitler spoke nonstop for two hours, illustrating the Marita plan, which assumed that Yugoslavia would join the Axis, allowing the German army to attack the Greek-British defense line from the rear during the spring. In this way, the Axis could turn the tide of the unsuccessful Italian initiative. Ciano was impressed by what he felt to be the clarity of Hitler's analysis: "I must say that he does this with exceptional skill. Our generals are impressed. Guzzoni (whose wide girth and tinted toupee made a terrible impression on the Germans) noted with some surprise the depth of military expertise displayed by Hitler." Ciano never focused on the hard facts in such circumstances.

Guzzoni requested some tough Bavarian alpine troops for Albania and an armored division for Libya that Mussolini had denied Badoglio only a few weeks before. Hitler answered with a double refusal: "We are not yet at war with the Greeks. If our troops go to Albania and do nothing while the Italians fight, it will create a morale problem. If they were to become engaged, we would risk the intervention of Turkey, widening the war prematurely in the Balkans . . . I will not dispatch the armored division to Libya. Our commitments are so vast that I cannot spare extremely valuable units to locations where they will not be fully effective."

Mussolini was now displeased. The Marita plan actually assumed Yugoslavia becoming a full partner of the Axis in the operations against Greece. This was a scenario the Duce had always rejected. He requested that, at the very least, no intervention by Yugoslavia should take place before the spring offensive, which was intended to reverse the negative trend in Albania. Hitler made no commitments; a prudent move it turned out, because of the bitter surprise Yugoslavia was to be; but he did give the Italians a tactical lesson on how to reorganize themselves in Libya to avoid losing the entire region. The Führer said, in sum, that the Italian army did not even know how to employ the weapons it had. It became a humiliating and mortifying scene, too much even for Mussolini, who was ready to accept the "moral punishment" of the double failing mark in Albania and Cirenaica, as he later told Ciano: "It was a tormenting scene. I can't wait to leave." But on the return trip to Rome, as after every meeting with Hitler, he became euphoric and optimistic. In the end, as Sir Ivone Kirkpatrick observed, there had been no recriminations or questions, and the Führer's arrogance convinced him that soon the situation would reverse itself favorably for the Axis.

The only task for Mussolini coming out of the conference was to bring Franco back to the Axis fold. Ciano was convinced that the Spanish estrangement from the Axis was essentially due to misunderstandings caused by the Germans and their attitude in dealing with Latin countries. From Rome, Ciano wrote a letter to Serrano Suñer, suggesting a meeting with Mussolini near Genoa, in northern Italy's Ligurian region. Before taking his leave, Mussolini, still in shock after Hitler's scathing comments regarding the front in Cirenaica and the measures adopted to halt the British advance in North Africa in general, confirmed his plan to bring up to strength by February 20 the three divisions already in Libya and the transfer of two more divisions, one armored and the other motorized, from Italy.

However, German participation in the North African war was still not resolved, mostly because the German high command was opposed to the idea. Long before the British offensive began, the Germans had sent General Wilhelm von Thoma to survey and report back on the local situation. Von Thoma's report was extremely negative and discouraged any attempt to land units of the Wehrmacht in Libya, the main reason being that the operation would require at least four armored divisions. The corollary problem was the need to continuously supply these units when the Italians had been unable to secure complete control of the Mediterranean. British author Desmond Young interviewed von Thoma after the war and the general related that he convinced Hitler, based upon his own experiences during the Spanish Civil War, that Italian troops were not to be trusted, that "one British soldier is worth twelve Italians" and that "the Italians are only good workers." On January 21, when Hitler and Mussolini parted company, they could not foresee that during their next meeting, some four and a half months later, on June 2 at the Brenner Pass, the situation would be almost completely altered, politically and militarily.

On January 22, back from his weekend in Hitler country, Mussolini was rudely awakened by the fall of Tobruk. Eight days later, Derna was lost, and within seven more days it would be Benghazi's turn. The Führer was now forced to make a momentous decision, overriding Mussolini's pride and the hostility of his own high command.

On February 3, in a meeting of his closest aides, Hitler stated: "The loss of North Africa could be acceptable militarily, but it would have disastrous psychological consequences in Italy. Great Britain would have a loaded gun drawn against Italy itself . . . British forces would not be engaged. The British, having about twelve divisions, could use them effectively in Syria. We must be sure to avoid all this."

The Fifth light motorized division was ready and was to be transported, according to the plans, by air and sea, between February 15 and 20. This unit alone would be insufficient to block the British mechanized units. So Hitler added an armored division, the fifteenth, which had been recently assembled. This was to be the nucleus of the famous Deutsche Afrika Korps (DAK). The first candidate as commander was General Hans von Funk. But von Funk had returned from a visit to Libya with such a pessimistic attitude that the Führer decided to name Erwin Rommel as the commander instead. He had been the HQ commander in Poland and a brilliant tank commander in France.

Erwin Rommel was not yet fifty years old. On February 6 at general staff headquarters, he was given his orders. Just one month before he had been promoted to the rank of lieutenant general. Field Marshal von Brauchitsch told him that his mission was specifically to "assist the Italians," who were blocking the British advance on Tripoli. The German units were to play the role of extreme defenders—in effect, a stopping unit. In order for everyone to have a clear view of the situation, it would be necessary, said Brauchitsch, for Rommel to make an inspection tour of Libya and then return to Berlin to present a comprehensive assessment. General Schmundt, the Führer's aide de camp, would accompany him on his tour.

Rommel accepted the mission with enthusiasm. He wrote to his wife that he was happy to go to a warm climate to cure his arthritis. After a short stop in Rome, he flew to Tripoli on February 12. Three days later, he surveyed British positions by plane to get a first-hand view of the enemy. He didn't know it at the time, but luck had it that Rommel found the British divisions at El-Aghelia in disarray. Expecting a German attack Churchill, committed one of his many military mistakes of the war, and ordered his British commanding general, Archibald Wavell, to divert his troops to Greece to shore up the exhausted Greek army. This massive British intervention—the Lustre plan—had been made possible by the sudden death of Greek dictator General Ioannis Metaxas, the pro-German leader who kept hoping Germany would eventually intervene and stop the Italians. Metaxas, who died of leukemia, was replaced by Alexandros Kortzis, head of the state bank of Greece.

Raymond Cartier analyzed the Greek situation this way: "The weakness of the Greeks, the pulling back by the Turks and the Serbs, did not divert Churchill from his Balkan plans. He forbade General O'Connor—who had previously defeated Graziani—from advancing toward Tripoli and ordered General Wavell to reorganize a mobile reserve in the Nile delta. The British Seventh armored division and the Australian Sixth division—which had been victorious—returned to Alexandria, leaving only small units in place with two larger replacement units improvised around them, the Second British armored division and the Ninth Australian division. They organized a web of advanced positions—the ones Rommel would observe from the air on February 15—and surrounded themselves with barbed wire, thus losing the freedom of movement just as Rommel, the genius of mobile warfare, appeared in North Africa. Churchill would eventually abandon the strategic advantage of controlling the entire African coastline in favor of a European adventure that was bound to have a disastrous outcome because of the imbalance of forces in the field. He turned away from the possibility of threatening Italy directly, as Hitler feared."

Rommel's good fortune continued after Churchill's ill-fated decision. Wavell discovered only after February 21 that German units were appearing in the desert, and declared to his staff: "Even if they are Germans, we have little to worry for about two months. They can't attack us. They will need time to get organized." But on March 31, after having forced the British out of their El-Aghelia advanced position a week earlier, Rommel, on his own initiative and without clearing his decision with Berlin, attacked the enemy with three columns. Benghazi was retaken on April 4 amid the applause of local Italian residents. The "Rommel myth" had just been born, while the myth of General Graziani melted away as he was replaced with General Gariboldi.

Just two months earlier, on February 9, the British air force, flying in from the sea, executed a bombing raid—named Operation Grog—on the port of Genoa. It was not clear whether the raid was intended to impress the visiting Francisco Franco or was simply a coincidence. Three days later, in keeping with his promise to Hitler, Mussolini met with the Caudillo at the resort town of Bordighera, not far from the French border. The meeting was held at Villa Margherita with Anfuso replacing Ciano, who was forced to remain on military duty in Bari against his will. Mussolini answered Anfuso when he was asked if Ciano should be advised of the Spanish-Italian summit: "Count Ciano is a military flyer and will remain with his squad. You are either fighting in the war or are foreign minister. Count Ciano will remain in Bari!"

As he prepared the agenda for his meeting with Franco, Mussolini said: "The Germans will never understand the Spaniards. The Spanish soldier is one of the very best in Europe, but he's not in uniform or at least not wearing the kind of uniform the German high command has in mind. The participation of Spain at this time would have effectively ended the war. I'll talk to Franco today as if I were a lawyer; yesterday I could speak to him as friend. The Greek campaign will never encourage him to enter the war; Franco is careful about the fate of his people ... I will tell him all that has to be said, but I have no illusions—he'll have made up his mind before I open my mouth. Had General Visconti Prasca taken Greece in the time frame we had set for ourselves, Spain would have forgotten Hitler's refusals. The war against England will be won in the Mediterranean: at Suez and Gibraltar. This will not be the time Franco comes into the war with us."

This forecast turned out to be correct. At the meeting, Franco was careful to be as deferent and sympathetic as possible toward Mussolini, whom he was meeting for the first time. However, he was firm in his position, essentially the same one he took with Hitler at Hendaye. According to Anfuso, at Bordighera, Franco concluded that he would definitely not enter the war. Mussolini who had few illusions on the matter, closed the Spain issue himself, by sending Hitler the minutes of the meeting via diplomatic courier. His only private comment was: "It's hard to fault Franco on his decision."

Within the framework of the new military cooperation between Italy and Germany, a naval conference was held in Meran, in northern Italy on February 13 with Admiral Arturo Riccardi and Admiral Dönitz. The end result, due to many factors, including lack of proper communications and intelligence, was the Italian navy's defeat at Cape Matapan, where three cruisers and two destroyers along with 2,300 sailors were lost. At the same time, the East African Italian Empire was its final agony. One after the other, the British took Somaliland, Eritrea, and Ethiopia. The Duke of Aosta surrendered to the enemy on May 18 and was to die of cancer as a prisoner of war on March 3, 1942, in Nairobi. Mussolini's promise to both Hitler and the Italian people—to teach Greece a lesson with the approaching spring weather—now had to be kept.

As General Pricolo remembered: "At the beginning of March, the decision was made to take the offensive on the central part of the front, before the Germans intervened, with a limited objective at Suka, or if possible at Klisura. Mussolini, whom I accompanied, went to Albania on March 3 and toured the front lines several times, where, to his own surprise, the soldiers cheered him enthusiastically almost everywhere he appeared. The attack began at 8:30 a.m. on March 9 after a violent artillery barrage by hundreds of pieces; along with bombing raids. In spite of the first optimistic reports, Mussolini, who was watching the offensive from an observation post at of Komarit, concluded, after four hours, that things were not going well.

Lying on the ground alone near some bushes, he was eating a biscuit with some rations from a tin can. He called me over and asked: 'What do you think about it, Pricolo?' 'I think we're doing all right, Duce; several positions have already been taken.' 'No, no, the attack has failed.' He asked if I had ever been in the infantry, since I looked puzzled. I said no, I had not, and he answered, 'I served in the infantry, in the trenches, and I know these things; if the attack doesn't succeed in two to three hours, it will never succeed.' Unfortunately, this was the case. A second general assault took place six days later, after careful preparation but with equally disappointing results. Some insignificant territory was taken but not a single prisoner. The troops had no fighting spirit: too many sacrifices, too many disappointments, too much suffering. The offensive was now losing momentum."

Mussolini made the following statement to Pricolo on March 20 at Devoli: "I have decided to return to Rome tomorrow. I am disgusted with the atmosphere here. We have not made any kind of progress; I have been deceived until now. I deeply despise all these people. I sent a report to His Majesty, the King, last night." At 10:30 a.m. on March 21, Mussolini's plane landed at the Centocelle airfield, near Rome. He was coming back empty-handed. On April 6, the Germans attacked on the Metaxas line toward Salonika as planned. The Italian army, with its terrible sacrifice, and careless planning, had worn down the Greek ability to resist, after five months of attempting to contain the aggressors, thus paving the way for their German allies. Just as in Cirenaica, the Germans quickly took credit for the victory of the Axis. However, the Yugoslav situation suddenly upset Nazi war plans to create a spider web and control the entire Balkan peninsula.

The Yugoslav crisis began on February 14, when the prime minister and foreign minister of Yugoslavia, as well as Prince Regent Paul, went to visit Hitler at Berchtesgaden. Germany wanted Yugoslavia to join the Tripartite Pact and become an active member of the Axis. In exchange, Germany would guarantee Yugoslavia's borders, including the Italian-Yugoslav border and extend economic assistance. A pact with Germany was not to the liking of the Yugoslav ruling classes, who had been influenced for some time by various British agents bearing the necessary funds. Even though the Yugoslav Crown Council approved the agreement with Germany on March 20, it would only be signed on March 25 in Vienna, after much hesitation.

On the night after the signing, General Dusan Simovic staged a coup against the government, and at first attempted to convince the Germans that it was simply an internal Yugoslav matter and not at all directed against Germany or Hitler personally. The putsch was carried out during the night of March 26. By noon of March 27, the Führer had already decided to take the necessary steps to punish the "betrayal" by the Yugoslavs. Hitler considered the matter as a personal insult, since he had orchestrated the entire negotiation with Yugoslavia and was mistakenly convinced that no one could resist his powers of persuasion and his "charisma." But suddenly another painless victory for the Führer was about to turn into a serious political and military setback, since the Barbarossa plan timetable was now entering its critical phase.

Hitler, in a state of hysteria, screamed that Yugoslavia must be wiped out, first militarily and then as a state. Its punishment would be an example for every one of his less trustworthy friends. He informed Mussolini, through General von Rintelen, to refrain from stirring things up in Greece any further before the Yugoslav matter was disposed of. The plan to crush Yugoslavia was set up in Directive Number 25 and contained a sentence that would have far-reaching consequences for the final results of the Second World War: *"In diesem Zusanmmenhang muss der Beginn der Barbarossa Unternehmung bis zu vier Wochen verschoben werden . . .* " ("Under these conditions the start of Barbarossa must be delayed for at least four weeks.")

The attack on the Soviet Union planned for May 15 now slipped to June 15. In other words, the conquest of the USSR, which was to be effective by September, would be prolonged into the month of October. Hitler had just signed his own defeat. Those four weeks would, in the end, mean the difference between victory and defeat for the German army. Bad weather would force the Wehrmacht to stop in the snow in front of Moscow, which fell early that year, mired in mud and freezing temperatures with its soldiers wearing summer uniforms. The German high command had rejected a proposal to issue winter clothing and supplies so as not to tip off the enemy and in this they succeeded in tricking Stalin into disbelieving his spies.

Mussolini bore a heavy responsibility for the misery of the world during the 1940s, but it is exaggerated, as some have insisted, to say that the ill-conceived Greek campaign was the root cause of the German reversals in Russia. By the time Hitler was ready to attack, the Greek problem had been resolved, and the Greek armed forces were completely engaged on the Albanian front facing the Italians. Even with the short-term British reinforcements from North Africa, Greece would have probably collapsed in the face of a Nazi threat of invasion. The Yugoslav surprise was what upset Hitler's plans, and Belgrade was subjected to a brutal bombardment for three days, between April 6 and 8. The capital was practically destroyed, with thousands of civilian victims buried under the rubble. The war was over in eleven days, and General Simovic disappeared, while a new government signed the surrender. Greece was also overrun in the next few weeks, even though it attempted a heroic resistance to the German forces. The British units were then forced to leave Greece in conditions similar to Dunkirk in 1940, abandoning all their supplies and weapons. Churchill blamed Yugoslavia for not being able to hold up the Germans a little longer.

Roosevelt had succeeded at this time in getting the momentous Lend Lease legislation passed by Congress, providing the necessary help for the democracies to survive and thus taking a few more steps toward entering the war against the Axis. Great Britain was the first country to benefit immediately from the legislation, in the form of thirty anti-submarine PT boats. The bill also vastly expanded the powers of the president. Greece was intended to be the second country to benefit from Lend Lease, but it was now much too late for that: the swastika was already flying over the Acropolis.

Heavy bombing actions were exchanged by Germany and England. London was bombed on March 19, while the British, attacked Berlin on April 10. The Luftwaffe returned by bombing on May 10 setting fire to the House of Commons. Suddenly, on Saturday, May 10, Hitler's own deputy, Rudolf Hess, took it upon himself to negotiate peace with the British. Flying alone in an ME 110 from Augusta airfield, he bailed out near Glasgow in Scotland, where he requested to be taken to the Duke of Hamilton, whom he had met during the 1936 Olympics in Berlin. The Hess "peace mission" landed him in a British prison and later to a life sentence at the Nuremberg trial.

This fiasco, coming right after the Yugoslav problem, was a severe blow to Nazi pride. Hitler was told of Hess's flight while conferring informally with Ribbentrop and Göring. The Führer unhesitatingly composed a press communiqué explaining the Hess flight as the result of his deputy's stressed mental condition, especially aggravated in the last few months. The Russians, and Stalin himself, were immediately convinced that the entire affair had been concocted by Hitler, together with Hess, to set up an Anglo-German alliance aimed against the Soviet Union.

In May 1941, German army paratroopers led by General Kurt Student landed and successfully occupied Crete in what was known as Operation Merkur. British forces resisted bitterly and destroyed scores of enemy planes and landing craft but suffered enormous losses in men and ships. On the sea, British battleship *Hood* was sunk by the new German battleship *Bismarck*, which itself was to meet the same fate only three days later, on May 27, at the hands of the British fleet.

On April 24, after his short war service Ciano returned to his former job. Both the Greek and Yugoslav problems had now been solved. In his absence, Mussolini had responded to Hitler's request and given, on March 23, the list of Italian demands against Greece: the complete occupation of the country by Axis troops; annexation to Italy of Ciamuria up to Prevesa, which had a predominantly Albanian population, and the islands of the Ionian Sea, Corfu, Cefalu, Zante, other smaller islands, for obvious strategic reasons. In Vienna on April 21 and 22, Ciano attempted to increase the Italian booty at the expense of Yugoslavia, but his plan backfired completely.

G. B. Guerri notes: "Ciano was convinced that he could annex the entire Adriatic coast from Istria to Albania, but he was bitterly disappointed. First of all, Ribbentrop told him that the borders of Slovenia, the northern part of which will be annexed to Germany, had already been drawn: this borderline goes all the way to the outskirts of Ljubljana, a city that was under Italian control and included the electric power plant and the radio station . . . As Ciano attempted to object that the German borderline was not where Rome understood it to be, that is, much further south, Ribbentrop cut him short, 'The border is to be considered permanent because it has been drawn irrevocably in this manner by the Führer himself.' On the new Bulgarian-Albanian border, Bulgaria was given the most territory, while on the frontier between Serbia and Montenegro, it was Serbia, a country outside the Italian sphere of influence, that was favored.

"As for the Italian-Croatian border, Ribbentrop stated that he was not involved in its discussion but suggested that Italy allow the new Croatian state an opening on the Adriatic. Croat leader, Ante Pavelic, assured of German support, created many problems for Ciano during the discussions. Ciano, on the other hand, fearing that Croatia, an essentially Italian client state, might slide voluntarily into the German orbit, made larger concessions than expected to the new country. The Dalmatian coastline was divided between Italy and Croatia, while Ciano was able to secure the Croatian crown for a prince of the Italian House of Savoy. However, due to the ambiguous attitude of Germany regarding Croatia, it was very difficult to maintain order in the country."

The Yugoslav chapter would end with Italy obtaining some portion of Slovenia and Dalmatia, a protectorate over Montenegro (the homeland of the Queen of Italy), and direct control over Croatia, thanks to the naming of Aimone of Aosta, a cousin of the King of Italy, as King of Croatia.

The subject of Greece was to be much more complicated, and negotiations were conducted by Filippo Anfuso on the Italian side. The Greeks, following the French example, had attempted to place their fate in the hands of the Germans rather than the Italians. Hitler would not allow these discussions to drag on too long and, by the end of the talks on April 23, gave Italy the opportunity to annex the Ionian Islands and Ciamuria. Italy was also to administer Greece along with the Germans, but with more responsibilities as to food supplies in particular.

Mussolini sent General Cavallero a cable: "At this time of victory, I recognize your efforts in preparing, over the course of four months, the necessary conditions to attain it. These conditions required, as you have done, breaking the enemy's capability to mount a counteroffensive and give everyone the necessary material and moral support for success." Only one month had passed since the Duce's bitter complaints against the generals in Albania during the past March. Now, all was forgotten in his moody disposition.

Mussolini did not mention the German contribution in Greece in his cable to Cavallero. There now existed a crisis within the Axis, with problems mounting in the daily workings of the alliance. There were incidents and clashes between Italians and Germans in Greece. In North Africa, Rommel, all wound up by his easy victories over the British in Cirenaica, began to neglect Italian units and even threatened revenge in some instances.

An Italian diplomatic observer in Germany wrote at this time: "The Nazi leaders are declaring at the top of their voices that they have no interest in Croatia, but then they begin showering the [Italian] embassy with suggestions that actually read more like orders ... In the meantime, there is a subject no one talks about but precisely because of this silence and other specific clues, I am more and more convinced, it is dominating the Führer's thoughts: Russia. A German cabinet minister told me: the Russian problem is one of political regimes. It cannot be tolerated much longer . . . " Italian ambassador Alfieri in Berlin was worried: "The Führer and the Duce must meet as soon as possible." But what do these meetings achieve if nothing precise comes out of them?

The Hess mystery deepened by May 13 with the sudden visit by Ribbentrop to Rome. He spoke with Mussolini and offered a sanitized version of Hess's flight to England. Ribbentrop assured Mussolini that Hess was physically and mentally sick and had become a convinced pacifist. The Duce played the role of the noble and understanding patriarch who offers his support. But with Ciano, Mussolini was privately delighted: "This is a tremendous blow for the Nazi regime!" And he declared himself happy because it "lowers the prestige of the Germans in the eyes of the Italians." The real reason behind Ribbentrop's visit to Rome was the German fear that there would be damaging consequences stemming from the Hess adventure. The deputy Führer knew all about Hitler's plans against the USSR. It would have been disastrous if he had talked, both for the still officially correct German-Soviet relations, as well as for the relations within the Axis, since Rome knew absolutely nothing about Barbarossa.

The German-Italian relationship was just about to boil over. Suddenly, on May 31, Hitler urgently requested a meeting with Mussolini, either the next day or no later than June 2. The Duce was unhappy, both with the invitation and the manner in which it was handed down to him. "I'm tired of being called to appear with the ringing of a bell." But he agreed to meet at the Brenner Pass on June 2 in one of those railroad rituals that were by now quite familiar. As usual, Berlin did not present an agenda, and this angered Mussolini even more because he disliked messy, unplanned meetings.

The next day the Duce's special train left Termini station in Rome for the Brenner. The train also carried Prince von Bismarck, who accompanied the Duce and passed on to him the news that Göring was losing favor with the Führer, while Ribbentrop was increasing his influence, and Himmler was all-powerful. Mussolini confided to Ciano that he could not understand the reason for this "urgent meeting." His fear was that France may be pressing the Germans for an agreement, behind Italy's back of course. But that night as the train moved north, there was only deep silence throughout the convoy.

XI

Rudolf Hess
and *Barbarossa*

Brenner Pass: June 2, 1941

The tenth meeting between Mussolini and Hitler took place at the Brenner railroad station on June 2, 1941, and lasted for five hours, from 10:00 a.m. to 3:00 p.m. When the two special railroad convoys stopped side by side, the Duce left his train to give the Führer the usual warm welcome. The two dictators then went together into Mussolini's saloon car for their meeting.

Hitler spoke uninterruptedly until lunchtime; the topics were the same ones he had covered many times before. The truly new element was the embarrassing "Hess problem." With tears in his eyes, Hitler told Mussolini that his former deputy had kept him completely in the dark regarding his intentions and had left behind a letter in which he attempted to justify his flight: "My Führer . . . you can imagine that the decision to take this flight was not an easy one, since a forty-year-old man has different ties to life than a twenty-year old . . . " He then listed details of his "mission" that, he said, he had already attempted several times before. Hess was careful to state that his flight was not the result of cowardice or weakness but motivated by the high ideal he was pursuing, which was peace between England and Germany. Hess reminded the Führer about the specific question regarding German policy toward England and Hitler's answer that an agreement between London and Berlin was the solution he favored. Hess was convinced that he was the right man for such a historic mission, since he knew the British well, having been born in Alexandria, Egypt. He ended his letter by writing: "And if, my Führer, this project, which I must confess, has few chances of succeeding, ends in failure and destiny turns against me, this should not create any adverse consequences for you or Germany; you will always be able to deny all responsibility. Just tell everyone that I am a madman."

This was exactly the course of action Hitler and the Nazi leadership decided to follow as they repeated that Hess was indeed mentally ill. The line chosen by the Nazi party in the press release dated May 12 announced that "Rudolf Hess, who had been suffering from illness for several years, and in spite of the fact that he was forbidden to fly, was able to commandeer an aircraft, a Messerschmitt 110, on Saturday, May 11. He left the airfield at Augusta and never returned. The letter he left behind demonstrates, by the way it was written, that he was suffering from mental illness . . . The Führer has ordered the immediate arrest of those who helped Hess . . . Given the circumstances, we must conclude that party member Hess either bailed out by parachute or was involved in an accident." Having been classified as "crazy" by just about everyone, Hess withheld his biggest secret from the British: the imminent German offensive to the east. Hitler, apart from the shame he had to endure because of Hess's attempt, was only worried about the coming war with Russia.

On May 12, after the first reactions to the Hess flight, Hitler finally confirmed June 22 as the final date for Barbarossa. While Hitler conferred with Mussolini, the Hess image was being systematically tarnished within Germany by various Nazi party luminaries, such as Himmler, Goebbels, and even Martin Bormann, who owed Hess his job. All sorts of strange anecdotes and unknown episodes began to surface. Hess was a sex maniac, a homosexual, he suffered from a deep inferiority complex, he was a mediocre person, a man without real culture, a follower of Oriental religious rites. A few jokes began to circulate, such as this one from Vienna: "Hitler is always threatening to land in England. But the one who goes there, Hess, is accused of being crazy."

Mussolini, in words and gestures, commiserated with the Führer and declared that the "Hess case" was closed as far as Italy was concerned. Hitler then turned to the subject of naval warfare and voiced his confidence in the submarine strategy of Admiral Karl Dönitz, who was convinced that with improved weather conditions, the U-boats let loose in wolf packs, would cause severe losses to British merchant shipping in the Atlantic. Hitler was proud of the success of the *Bismarck* in destroying the symbol of the British navy, the *Hood* even though, due to mistaken radio communication, his battleship had been intercepted and was immediately sunk by the enemy.

Hitler dropped no hints about the USSR and repeated his usual oratory against Stalin's tendencies toward hegemony, seeking to succeed where the czars had failed. It was always the old Russian dream for warm water ports in the Mediterranean that the Kremlin wanted to achieve at the expense of the Eastern European countries. Hitler then voiced his dissatisfaction with the entire Yugoslav affair, even though he did suspect something when the Yugoslav leaders hesitated in joining the Tripartite Pact. He was pleased with the agreements reached between Ciano and Ribbentrop on Slovenia and Croatia. He repeated his unhappiness concerning Spain and considered that Franco was, in retrospect, a bad investment.

The meeting went into an executive session with the foreign ministers and the military leadership. Ciano noted: "Mussolini was convinced that the Germans were by now satiated with victories. They were seeking the victory that came with peace." Ciano also said that on June 2 the Duce was satisfied with the meeting because he noted "there had been no changes of attitude in German-Italian relations." The next day, while Mussolini made disparaging comments on Hitler's verbosity, he felt that the relationships must be reinforced from now on by the coupling of counterparts on a personal basis: Ribbentrop-Ciano, Keitel-Cavallero, and so on.

But just one week later, this optimism faded when Mussolini told Ciano: "Personally I am fed up with Hitler and his behavior. I don't like these meetings where I am summoned by the bell like a waiter. And then what kind of meetings are these? I must endure a five-hour monologue that is as useless as it is boring. At the Brenner, he spoke for hours and hours about Hess, the *Bismarck*, of things more or less pertinent to the war, but without an agenda, without examining a problem, without making a decision." But at no point, even during their private discussions, did Hitler confide any of his Barbarossa plans to Mussolini, even though the Duce did say that in case anything new happened in the east, Italy would be ready and happy to set up an expeditionary army corps against the USSR.

And so ended the third and final railroad summit at the Brenner. Late that afternoon, the two convoys took each dictator back home: Hitler to his colossal and suicidal campaign against Russia, Mussolini, more low key, to his planned speech on the first year of war to the Italian parliament.

The June 10 speech was expected by the parliamentary audience to be an uneventful one. Twelve months of military operations were suddenly lined in red ink, and no fancy slogans could change that reality. After a long introduction restating the events, Mussolini attempted to explain his motivations in declaring war on Greece. "Beginning in August of last year," he said, "Italy had proof of secret agreements between the Greeks and the British (he was referring to documents discovered in Paris after the armistice with France), and we had to step in before it was too late. It is absolutely mathematical that as of April, even if nothing else had happened in the Balkans, the Italian army would have overwhelmed and annihilated the Greek forces." This statement elicited mechanical applause, and the Duce went on to the biggest bitter pill—the loss of the Italian Empire in East Africa, about which he exclaimed vociferously: "This is a personal vendetta that cannot have any kind of influence on the final result of the war. Italy will return to the lands that in a few years it transformed by building hospitals, schools, houses, aqueducts, factories, roads: those large roads, the envy of the entire African continent, where the mechanized armies of the enemy were able to advance quickly."

He then spoke to the people, praising their resistance: "Even if the war should last longer than we can foresee, even if new complications should appear, England cannot win because all its positions in Europe have been destroyed, and America, despite its efforts, cannot replace her. I firmly believe that in this terrible battle between blood and gold, the just God, who lives within the soul of the younger nations, has chosen. We will win!" The Duce's presentation remained unconvincing.

Three days before the speech, Bottai had noted in his diary: "Cabinet meeting. Mussolini is wearing his white summer dress uniform, and he is clearer and happier than usual. There is a law to curtail internal emigration. He reveals its true significance: to slow and finally stop altogether the emigration of our workers to Germany. He became excited: 'We will not send any more workers to Germany. Enough! Now they want 100,000 more. One hundred thousand and not one less. We will answer no! I don't want to make comparisons, but we should remember the groups of workers we used to send to France years ago, during the First World War. They were hated by the soldiers. And then the Germans must forget about thinking of us as useful laborers and not as soldiers. They think of themselves as a nation of soldiers, who know how to handle weapons, compared to our people, who, they think, are only capable of hard work and of giving their lifeblood for everyone else.

"In their eyes, [the Germans] are the Herrenvolk and we are the Slavenvolk . . . What's more, these workers are well paid in Germany, and the good pay makes them optimistic. They see everything through rose-colored glasses and come back home with endless praise for Germany. They only see the facade, behind which there is a tired people, very tired of this war! . . . ' This doesn't sound like the man who only five days before had beamed and lunched with the man responsible for his awful behavior toward the Italian people. Maybe this was Mussolini's way of criticizing himself."

The Russian question remained in the air. Ciano and Ribbentrop met in Venice on June 14 and 15 to sign the Tripartite Pact with the new state of Croatia. The Nazi foreign minister was "exceptionally jovial and in good spirits." At the restaurant, he actually winked at the waitress, leading Ciano to ask if there was anything new, while from the Hotel Danieli, they took the gondola to go to the reception offered by Count Volpi at his palace. With a studied slowness, Ribbentrop answered: "My dear Ciano, I can say nothing yet. Every decision is locked within the impenetrable chest of the Führer. But one thing is certain. If we were to attack, Stalin's Russia will be erased from the map in eight weeks." While they were enjoying this short vacation mixed with some work, Ribbentrop was suddenly summoned back to Berlin. Perhaps something had changed in the Führer's viewpoint? He explained that he must return ahead of schedule because of the further deterioration of relations between Russia and Germany, adding that "the Führer will be compelled by the end of the month to make some final requests to the USSR. If they are rejected, Germany will find ways of seeking its own justice."

The real reasons for Ribbentrop's recall to Berlin were much more precise and were part of his duties as foreign minister. Molotov, fed up with all the rumors and hints from every part of the world regarding the aggressive intentions of the Germans, had called German Ambassador von Schulenburg to the Kremlin to hand him the text of a declaration to be broadcast on radio that night and printed the next day by the press of the interested countries. The note stated that the British ambassador was the only party responsible for the rumors circulating concerning the imminence of war between Russia and Germany. The Soviet government declared that these rumors were only "obvious absurdities and propaganda moves attributable to the enemies of the Soviet Union and of Germany."

During the evening of June 21, while Mussolini was on the beach at Riccione, the German embassy signaled Palazzo Chigi that it expected an important message from the Führer. Ciano, informed in due time, just after midnight, received Prince von Bismarck, accompanied by Anfuso at his private residence, bearing a letter from Hitler for Mussolini. Even though the Duce was sound asleep in his villa at that hour, Ciano had to wake him up. The declaration of war on the Soviet Union was worth the trouble.

The document was the usual essay in Hitlerian rhetoric, stating that "England has already lost the war; like a drowning man, it now seeks to hold on to any branch . . . the branch is the Soviet Union, where British warmongers have always attempted to direct the conflict. Now they will both be served: the drowning man and his branch. It will be a final blow that will drown them both together. We cannot trust France. Spain is unable to decide, and I am mathematically certain that it will wait until it knows for sure what the name of the winner is; an attack on Egypt is impossible before next fall; Great Britain is being helped by the United States and is not interested whether the Americans enter the war or not, since the British are getting everything they need anyhow.

"Even the supplies from the Atlantic become more and more difficult. London's two hopes are the United States and the Soviet Union. We cannot defeat the USA but we can beat the USSR, and once the USSR is defeated, even America will hesitate before entering the war. Japan will also have greater freedom of action in the Far East and the Pacific. For these reasons, I have decided to write the word 'end' to the hypocritical comedy the Kremlin is playing. I feel spiritually liberated for having untied an absurd alliance that was completely circumstantial." The Führer closed by thanking the Duce for his understanding and for the promised Italian expeditionary corps for which he had no urgent need.

Anfuso, who was present at the Ciano-Bismarck meeting, left the following description: "Counter to what Ciano is said to have stated . . . the German intention of invading the USSR was known by the Palazzo Venezia some time before it occurred, but still a short enough time to prevent any leaks coming from the Palazzo Chigi. In any case, no date was given . . . The German HQ was sensitive that no unpleasant incidents harm Italian personnel at the Moscow embassy and that we not be tempted to cable, even in cipher, causing an alarm and allowing the Russians to be ready for the invasion. The final announcement came at night as usual. Ciano was having dinner with the Marchesa Balestra Mottola, a niece of

Benedetto Croce. Bismarck had been warned to stay awake . . . At about midnight, he reached the Ciano house with an envelope bearing the image of an eagle and the Führer's name. Ciano opened it in the presence of the German diplomat and me.

"We sat on the sofa, and I translated the message from Hitler into Italian: when Bismarck felt that I gave the wrong translation, he would elbow me and translate the sentence again into English . . . Even though we hadn't known the date, our military attaché in Berlin had predicted a new operation just one week before. This nighttime method continued but was not welcome, as Ciano told Bismarck. Bismarck was happy to hear this, since whatever Hitler did was automatically a mistake for the descendant of the Iron Chancellor . . . Mussolini, therefore, had had time to examine an Italian participation in the Russian campaign some days before; Hitler's letter was an answer to that proposal.

"One could see that the German chancellor wanted to conclude the Russian campaign in eight weeks before the Italians could arrive . . . Mussolini's first reaction on the telephone as Ciano gave him the news was: 'We must be present on the Russian front as soon as possible!' Ciano told me: 'He wants to go looking for trouble in Russia!' Bismarck did not understand the Italian expression Ciano used ["cercare rogna," literally, "look for trouble"], but in any case, he approved. Mussolini wanted to win the war with Hitler." The rejection of Italian military assistance was enough to put Mussolini in a bad mood, and the Führer knew this perfectly well, so much so that it seemed to be a planned provocation.

This latest adventure immediately excited the Duce, and he gave instructions to inform the Soviet ambassador in Rome that Italy considered itself at war with the USSR that very day and that very hour. Ciano had difficulty locating the ambassador because he was spending that Sunday at the beach in Fregene. Finally he was brought to the Palazzo Chigi at full speed. Ciano noted: "The meeting lasted two minutes. Stalin's ambassador showed only indifference at the news . . ."

The next day Mussolini wrote to Hitler: "The liquidation of the Russian problem brings the following advantages: it deprives Great

Britain of its last hope on the European continent; it frees us from any worries in the immediate future; it takes us back to the ideological positions we had temporarily set aside for tactical reasons; it attracts to the Axis all the anti-Bolshevik feelings around the world in general, including the Anglo-Saxon countries; it can bring back a renewed Russia reduced in size into a circle of economic cooperation with the rest of Europe and give us the raw materials we need, especially if the Anglo-Saxons make it necessary to prolong the war. The above will illustrate, Führer, how your decision has been received with enthusiasm, especially among the older party members, who would have accepted another kind of solution with much regret. In a war that takes on such a character, Italy cannot remain on the sidelines."

And Italy unfortunately did not stand aside. Mussolini's order was: "Get to the Russian front as quickly as possible. Our presence in numbers in Russia is essential. That is where Hitler believes he will win the war. Should we be absent, even the fact that I was the first one to fight Communism, will not count in the face of the realization that the Italians were not present in Russia."

At 3:30 a.m. on June 22, the German army, the most powerful military force in the world, moved east along a 2,000-kilometer front. The Russians were taken completely by surprise. The Barbarossa plan was developed along three main lines. To the north, the army group of Field Marshal von Leeb, with twenty-nine divisions, including three armored and three mechanized divisions, moved from East Prussia, to take over the Baltic states and occupy Leningrad. In the center, the army group led by Field Marshal von Bock, with fifty divisions, of which nine were armored and six mechanized, was to march to the north of the Pripet marshes and along the Amin-Minsk-Moscow road. In the south, the army group led by Field Marshal von Rundstedt, with forty-one divisions, five armored and three mechanized, was to cross the southern part of the Pripet marshes toward Kiev. There were also twenty-six reserve divisions, and in the north, twelve Finnish divisions would help in the attack against Leningrad, while in the south, seventeen Romanian divisions would support von Rundstedt's army.

The Germans seized the Baltic states and, in just a few days, the territories of Poland and Romania that Russia occupied, according to the German-Soviet Pact of August 1939. On the one side, there was the Red Army, now applying the traditional Russian response to any invasion from centuries past: withdrawing, to force the enemy to scatter its forces in the vastness of the land and, at the same time, to destroy behind enemy lines whatever could be useful to the invader, from bridges to factories, from roads to railway tracks. It was the scorched-earth policy.

On the other side was Hitler's Wehrmacht, crushing everything and everyone, and was initially receiving the warm welcome of the occupied populations who thought they were being freed from Soviet domination. They did not expect the SS murder squads and the units specializing in requisitions that would move in the next day.

On May 30, as if to confirm that he knew of Hitler's plans, Mussolini told General Cavallero: "We must assemble one new motorized division between Ljubljana and Zagreb and a second one to be attached to the Grenadier division." On June 22, in expectation that the Führer would accept the Italian contingent, General Francesco Zingales was named commander of the Italian expeditionary forces in Russia, the CSIR, or Corpo Spedizione Italiano in Russia. It would operate on the border between Romania and sub-Carpathian Russia. The CSIR included the Italian mechanized divisions, Pasubio and Torino; the third armored division, Principe Amedeo d'Aosta; the Sixty-third Blackshirt Legion Tagliamento; the Thirtieth Artillery group; and units of engineers, supplies, and antiaircraft batteries. It would also have its own air force unit, including fifty-one fighter planes, twenty-two reconnaissance and twenty transport aircraft. In all, Zingales would have 58,000 soldiers, 2,900 officers, 5,500 cars and trucks, 4,600 horses and mules, and 83 planes.

Impatient to get involved and wanting to reach the fait accompli without even having the Führer's approval, Mussolini, on June 26, giving the event the maximum publicity exposure possible, reviewed the Torino division in Verona and was completely satisfied.

He phoned Ciano to say that the division was perfect. Finally, on June 30, Berlin officially transmitted to Rome the invitation to attend the "party." The CSIR was given a geographic area that should have milder weather than the northern areas. It was the B zone under von Rundstedt, within the German Eleventh Army, which after having taken Bessarabia had stopped along the southern banks of the Dnieper River.

The movement of the Italian forces began on July 10. Verona became the launching pad for the Russian front. From that railway station, 225 trains would take thousands of men along a distance of over 2,300 kilometers across the Brenner, Austria, and Hungary—up to the border of Romania.

Cristano Ridomi, the Italian press secretary at the embassy in Berlin, wrote: "The small station of Schwechat, near Vienna, usually has little traffic. Some big, yellow-haired horses from the local brewery are usually parked in front of it. . . . The German authorities have allowed a brief stop here to the trains taking the first Italian units to Russia . . . Ambassador Alfieri had wished to salute the passing troops and offer refreshments to the soldiers during that hot day in July. Some Italians living in Vienna were called. It was very sad. Our participation in the war against the USSR was not even the result of a request from Hitler. He had accepted Mussolini's proposal and let the Duce understand that it would be a long campaign, and there would be plenty of time to send in Axis troops. But once again, Italy was fearful of arriving too late and somehow being kept out of the action. Then the trains arrived with huge delays . . . The Italians from Vienna tried to help. Our soldiers appear almost disdainful. Perhaps they are tired. It's a long and very slow journey. When General Zingales arrived, his aide came over to say that the general was unable to leave the train. He whispers some words to our military attaché. Good God! The commander has suffered a heart attack, and we have to secure a gurney to take him to the hospital. A pretty bad omen."

The CSIR would go into battle during the first days of August. Hitler's aggression had even pushed Stalin to rediscover "the ways of the Lord." On July 4, 1941, American newspapers were full of news that the "Red Czar" had requested prayers be said in the few remaining churches after asking the Russian Orthodox clergy to bless the Red Army units that were going to fight to save "sacred Russia." Leninism was not emphasized during that time. While the Germans were encircling Smolensk in a deadly vise, Moscow was bombed for the first time on July 12. General Messe received the order to head the CSIR on July 13 while he was in Padua. He was to go to Vienna and take over from General Zingales at the hospital.

While he was still enthusiastic about the "perfect" review of the troops in Verona on June 26, Mussolini received a letter from Hitler on July 2 about the lightning success of the operations in the east. But by then the Russians were beginning to shake off the surprise effect and were putting up stiffer resistance. The Duce was ecstatic: "I hope that in this war in the East the Germans will lose a lot of their feathers. It's wrong to talk about an anti-Bolshevik struggle. Hitler knows that Bolshevism disappeared a long time ago. No code of law protects private property like the Russian civil code. He should admit that he wants to knock out a continental power that had fifty-two-ton tanks and was getting ready to wring his neck."

The letter contained a flattering nod toward Mussolini—who was still unhappy at having been rudely awakened on the night of June 22—in the form of an "historic" invitation to come to the Führer's HQ on the Russian front. Since he would go alone, without risking an encounter with King Victor Emanuel III, the Duce could finally wear his fancy uniform of First Marshal of the Italian Empire with the double insignia on the sleeves. The invitation was immediately accepted and his wife Rachele prepared her husband's military wardrobe.

In his own twisted way, Mussolini continued to root for Stalin in private conversation. He told Bottai: "The Russians are fighting well. There have been moments of heroism: surrounded tanks that explode, having been mined from the inside. Soldiers killing one another to avoid being made prisoner. The Germans are using their tried and true strategy: they enclose the enemy in tighter and tighter pockets until he suffocates. It's the strategy of space, of masses, of daring. Italy cannot stay out of the war against Russia. We could have been present at inception had the German high command asked us. For the moment we will send three divisions. No volunteers. The Germans don't like volunteer units. This troop movement will also serve as a sort of comparison. I have given precise orders to the commander of our expeditionary corps: unimpeachable conduct, fraternize with the Germans, but otherwise keep apart. Now, there will be the question of proportions between what the Germans have done in this war and we have done and will do. . . . We will have to reconquer Ethiopia by ourselves."

Stalin again was a source of anxiety for Mussolini. Upon learning that Great Britain and the USSR had signed an alliance on July 16 in Moscow, the Duce was now skeptical of the successful conclusion of Barbarossa before the winter, "and this will open the door to many unknown factors." But he immediately stated: "We must hope for two things: that the war will be long and exhausting for Germany and that it will end in a compromise, which will preserve our independence." The Duce's trip to the Führer's HQ was in the preparation phase, when suddenly, on August 7, 1941, Mussolini lost his beloved son Bruno, the child he loved the most.

Bruno, born in 1918, was an air force captain with the 274th Escadrille BGR in Pisa. His unit had been given the new four-engine P.108B for which the Italian air force had high hopes. At the time, it was more or less like an American "flying fortress." During a test flight, the heavy plane crashed, killing Bruno and two other members of his crew, while the remaining five survived. The accident was caused by a broken pump and the flooding of the engines as the pilot suddenly gave more power while attempting to land.

Through a bizarre coincidence, Bruno, had been speaking about Stalin shortly before the fatal accident. His older brother, Vittorio, who was also an air force officer, remembered: "Early on the morning of August 7, 1941, Bruno and I left the Hotel Nettuno, facing the Arno River. The night before, my brother had a dream, and we talked about it during our trip to the airport. 'I dreamed,' said Bruno, 'that I was in Moscow. He invited me to come to the Kremlin, which instead of being made of stone was made of wood. Stalin received me in a room that was also made of wood. It looked like a giant box. He made a proposal that surprised me; I was to stay in Russia as his personal pilot. Naturally, I refused, in spite of his friendly insistence. When I went to the door to leave, I noticed that the room had no exits. I beat on the wooden walls without any result. Stalin was looking at me and smiling. . . . I kept banging on the walls and then I woke up.'

"Bruno and I laughed when he finished his story. When we reached the airport, I went to the cafeteria to have breakfast, then, by bicycle, I went toward the hangars. It was my turn as the day officer to handle the requirements of my unit. The four propellers of the P.108 were already spinning happily and Bruno was putting on his flight gear. I did not witness his takeoff. About ten minutes later, we saw the silhouette of the plane quickly losing altitude in the distance behind the airport buildings. Bruno said just before dying, 'Dad, the airfield.' Then it was all like a bad dream. My father came by plane from Rome, and later, my mother arrived from Forlí. My father stayed all night at the wake with the rest of the family . . . The Holy Father, the King, the crown prince, Hitler, Franco . . . and many other well-known personalities, even some enemy leaders, sent flowers and cabled their sympathies. Bruno was buried in the cemetery at San Casciano.

"In October of 1943, I went with my father from the Rocca delle Caminate to visit the grave. Inside the mausoleum, father meditated for a few minutes and then, as if speaking to himself, he whispered: 'Bruno was the lucky one, he doesn't suffer anymore, and he died at the right time. He died young, and he will continue to live in our memory and in the memory of those who loved him. I would have liked to die that way, unexpectedly. Remember that I want to be buried here as well.'" A discreet message from Berlin to Rome informed the Italian government that the Duce's visit could be canceled if necessary. Anfuso pressured the Duce to delay the trip, but Mussolini rejected the idea. He honored the memory of his son with a sad and well-written book, _Parlo con Bruno_.

The German aggression against the Soviet Union had given new hope and vigor to Winston Churchill. On August 4, in Argentia Bay, off the coast of Newfoundland, aboard a warship, President

Roosevelt and the British Prime Minister announced the Atlantic Charter, which was to contain the statement of freedom for all peoples. The eight-point document declared: "the United States and Great Britain do not seek any territorial or other form of gain in this war; they do not wish any other territorial changes that would not be sanctioned by the freely expressed desires of those concerned; they respect the right of all people to choose the form of government they desire . . . ; they will strive to give all states, large and small, winners or losers, the possibility of participating as equals in world trade, with access to raw materials which are necessary to achieve prosperity; they wish to promote the maximum cooperation between nations . . .; after the end of Nazi tyranny they hope for a lasting peace that allows all nations to live in security . . . ; a peace that will allow all men to cross the seas without obstacles; they feel that all nations in the world, for material and spiritual reasons, must agree to renounce the use of force . . ."

It was the answer of the democracies to the New Order promised by the Tripartite Pact in Europe and Asia. The Atlantic Charter immediately took on a public relations character, as intended by its authors.

After Bruno's death, the Mussolini family came together for ten days at Riccione. One evening, as the Duce's trip to Russia approached, he called his oldest son, Vittorio, to ask him to pack his bags and accompany him on his tour of the CSIR, which had already been engaged successfully in battle on the Dnieper and in the Donetz basin.

Mussolini, who had more practical political instincts than Hitler, was worried about France. French Communists had tolerated the Pétain government because of the German-Soviet nonaggression pact. But after June 22, things had suddenly changed. De Gaulle, according to the French left wing press, was no longer a general in the pay of British imperialism, but an authentic French patriot fighting to free his country. On August 21, 1941, a Communist commando killed a young German naval officer at the Barbés Rochechouart metro station in Paris. This was the opening shot of the partisan warfare that would paralyze the Axis forces in occupied countries. At the same time, in France, Italian anti-Fascists resumed their activity after a long silence following the Spanish Civil War and the German-Soviet pact. In October 1941, Italian Communist party leaders Sereni and Dozza, Socialists Nenni, Saragat, Trentin, and Fausto Nitti of the "Giustizia e Libertà" movement, created a joint committee issuing an appeal to the Italian people that ended with these words: " . . . from common action on everyone's part, from our common sacrifices, from the coordination and development of every struggle, the will of the people will erupt in an irresistible wave from which must and will arise the new Italy of peace, of independence, of freedom, of work."

Every evening from England, anti-Fascist proclamations were echoed by the voice of "Candidus," who was broadcasting from the BBC a relentless series of anti-Fascist talks in the propaganda war. Candidus was Joseph John Marcus. Born in England in 1903 of Italian parents, he had studied in Venice and Padua. After working as a newspaper editor on the staff of the *Gazzettino*, he had returned to England in 1938, and the BBC, impressed by his perfect Italian, had hired him for its Italian language section. His first broadcast on April 13, 1941, was a direct attack on Mussolini: "Tomorrow's historians will have to solve one of the most absurd mysteries of our times, that of Mussolini's foreign policy. They will need to explain why a statesman whose program was to turn his country into a world power has succeeded in reaching the opposite result, reducing his nation to the rank of a German protectorate."

XII

The Long
Shadow of Napoleon

Rastenburg: August 25-29, 1941

O n Monday, August 25, 1941, after traveling for three days, the special Italian convoy arrived in East Prussia at Görlitz, the false name given to the railroad stop known as Rastenburg, to keep the true location secret because the real Görlitz was located in Saxony. About eight kilometers beyond the station, at the edge of a thick forest of fir and pine trees, was the famous "Wolf's Lair" (*Wolfsschanze*), the headquarters where Hitler was directing operations against Russia.

Mussolini, during his trip to Rastenburg (now the Polish village of Ketrzyn), was accompanied by a large delegation of diplomats and military men: Anfuso, having replaced Ciano, who had been ill since July 23, Ambassador Alfieri and military attaché Efisio Marras with press secretary Cristano Ridòmi; Army Chief of Staff Ugo Cavallero; and General Antonio Gandin. With the Italian group were the German ambassador to Rome, Hans von Mackensen, and

SS Lieutenant Colonel Eugen Dollmann, acting as Himmler's representative in Italy. The Duce's son Vittorio was also part of the trip as a VIP. In anticipation of Operation *Barbarossa*, construction of the Wolf's Lair had begun in 1940. Millions of marks had been spent to create this palatial complex, built by thousands of workers, technicians, and engineers. It was a well-protected area of eight square kilometers, surrounded by mine fields and barbed wire, spread over three separate sections, where giant bunkers had been built, covering a vast underground fortress that housed the Führer's HQ, the *Führerhauptquartier*, and the HQs of the key branches of the German high command. A maze of corridors connected various offices and services. Every possible requirement had been covered: a powerful radio and telephone exchange, a hospital, kitchens and mess halls, supply depots and archives. On January 24, 1945, when the moment came to retreat, Hitler ordered the destruction of his labyrinth. However, there was not enough dynamite to be found to pulverize that masterpiece of iron and concrete. What remains of the Wolfsschanze today is a tourist attraction, and Polish authorities have built restaurants, bars, and even a small hotel around the area.

Hitler had invited Mussolini to visit him when everything seemed to be going according to plan for the German armies. At the beginning of August, a series of disagreements surfaced between the Führer and his generals regarding the most immediate objectives of the current operations. The high command recommended heading directly for Moscow, while Hitler, following the teachings of Clausewitz, wanted to destroy the enemy armies in battle first and not be distracted by prestigious objectives. He had his own priorities, and the capital of the USSR was at the bottom of his list. At the top was Leningrad, not for its symbolic value as the cradle of Bolshevism, but because of its key position on the Baltic. In second place was the Ukraine with of its grain reserves, and then, the Crimea, because of its proximity to the Romanian oil fields. The argument lasted for about three weeks.

Hitler's answer was aimed at securing the support of General Heinz Guderian, head of the armored divisions and a strong advocate of the "Moscow objective": "Had I known the Russians had as many tanks as you suggested in your book, *Achtung Panzer!* I would not have started this war." On August 23, just as Mussolini's train was approaching East Prussia, the Führer made his final decision: the main objective would be neither Leningrad nor Moscow, but the Ukraine and at full speed. Hitler said: "My generals must understand that war is above all an economic event." On August 25, the army group center, which had been pointed toward Moscow, was in the process of making a ninety-degree turn as the commanders became more and more critical of the Führer's order: the generals feared they would have to fight a winter campaign to take Moscow, as it would happen after having expended their energies in fighting for the Ukraine.

The Duce knew little or nothing of all these delays and behind-the-scenes debates. Hitler had hoped to welcome Mussolini at Moscow itself. A photograph of the two dictators walking near the smoldering ruins of the Kremlin would have been the best propaganda for the Axis cause. That was the reason why the day after the death of the Duce's son, Berlin had sent signals to delay the visit to a better date. But Mussolini understood that behind the sympathetic suggestion coming from the Führer there was some kind of political motivation. On the morning of August 25 on the platform of the station at Görlitz, there appeared a low key Hitler, who, as the consummate actor that he was, showed no signs of disappointment. Vittorio Mussolini wrote: "My father and his entourage were welcomed with all the usual honors and demonstrations of friendship while respecting the stiff protocol customary within the German military. Hitler said a few words of sympathy as soon as my father got off the train, then he introduced the German military leaders he had kept a short distance away. At the *Führerhauptquartier* in East Prussia, near Rastenburg, my father had long conferences with Hitler, sometimes alone or in the presence of Cavallero, Keitel, Ribbentrop, Anfuso, Mackensen, Alfieri, Jodl, Gandin, and Warlimont."

The program of the visit, the longest Mussolini would make during the entire war, had been the result of a series of compromises between Hitler and the high command, which resented this type of "tourism" while the Wehrmacht was locked in a deadly duel with the Red Army. The difficulty for the German army can be surmised by the strange itinerary that had been set for the "Duce's five days" on the eastern front, from Monday the twenty-fifth to Friday the twenty-ninth of August. Mussolini was ferried from north to south and back, over thousands and thousands of kilometers by train, plane, and automobile without much regard for his age and status as well as a very un-German disregard for logistics. The high point of the trip, the inspection of the CSIR, had been well organized, up to a point.

As Cristano Ridòmi noted: "Mussolini arrived on a long train with a presidential sitting room coach, a restaurant car, sleeping cars for his entourage, which included high officials, generals, colonels, and the German ambassador to Rome, von Mackensen, with his big cigars that stank up the entire train. There were no newsmen, not even the correspondent of the Stefani agency. Naturally I brought along my faithful typewriter. . . . Alfieri told me to take notes because I would be, if not the historian, at least the chronicler of this expedition. What I did see on this trip is difficult to describe beyond my summary for the Italian press. Everything appeared unreal, strangely fantastic—starting from the Görlitz station, where the train engineer stopped the convoy *exactly* at a stripe painted on the platform so that Hitler would be *precisely* in front of the door the Duce would emerge from.

"The real town of Görlitz is located, as we know, in a different part of Germany . . . Something false, but with a tragic meaning. Here, reality ends, and now begins a detached and solitary world, where among the trees of an ominous forest are enclosed, protected by barricades and barbed wire for kilometers and kilometers, the accommodations of the "war lord" and his commanders who simply transmit his orders. Small huts are dug into the ground, protected by huge slabs of concrete. The inside rooms are all in wood paneling, like the 'Stuben' of the small mountain hotels or Alpine chalets. Buried deep into the ground are the water and heating ducts, telephone lines, and telegraph wires. A few hundred people live in this mysterious village surrounding Hitler, cut off from the rest of the world." During their first conversation, Hitler confessed to Mussolini that in August of 1939 he was in shock when he had been forced to reach an agreement with the Soviet Union to attack Poland. Hitler would continue to repeat this refrain during the entire trip."

Anfuso wrote: "The language he used that day and then repeated during the next few days appeared to conceal two main worries. The first, a visible one, was that his great *Entescheidung*, his great "decision," to attack the Soviet Union had been made very recently and at the last minute . . . The second, hidden worry, concerned the growing difficulties of the *Kreuzzug* (the crusade against Bolshevism) and the new obstacles that began to confirm the prophesies in the reports sent to Berlin by the German ambassador to Moscow, F. W. von Schulenburg, which had been burned in the fireplace because they contradicted Hitler's own wishes at the time."

Hitler's own arguments to justify his crusade were not very different from those used after the war by the United States and Western Europe to underscore the need to contain Soviet imperialism. Hitler complained to Mussolini that the Western democracies, especially Great Britain, had misunderstood him and had quickly signed an alliance with the USSR after the German attack. He saw the Atlantic Charter as an aggression against his policies, an instrument forged by Roosevelt and the circles of international Judaism that were supporting Roosevelt in his struggle against Nazism. But the Atlantic Charter, the Führer said, would save neither the British Empire nor Mr. Churchill's own career.

Hitler was also angry because he had been informed that an Anglo-American mission led by Lord Beaverbrook and Averell Harriman was in Moscow to discuss the first massive aid to the Soviet Union. The agreement was to be signed on October 1, 1941, with the United States and Great Britain agreeing to supply Moscow, by July 1942 with 3,000 aircraft, 4,000 tanks, 30,000 trucks, 100,000 tons of fuel, and other supplies. Hitler's continuous complaints convinced Mussolini and his staff that German expectations for a blitz-type war in the east had been, for the most part, frustrated: the Russians were vigorously fighting back, with tremendous courage, taking advantage of their two oldest and best trump cards: vast open spaces and brutal weather.

After meeting with Hitler, Anfuso quickly gave a puzzled Mussolini his own impressions. "Duce, the truth is that the Germans have discovered that Russia is big, too big for them to grab in one single effort." After the meeting, the guests adjourned to a chalet for luncheon with their respective staffs. The Führer kept on talking. He revealed that he had met Lord Beaverbrook in the past and thought that he had a reasonable attitude toward Germany. Yet at that very moment, said Hitler, this British gentleman was in the Kremlin, plotting against the Nazi crusade. The Führer then praised the Duce and returned to his most vexing problem, Russia, emphasizing that he had proof of Stalin's aggressive intentions; had the German armies failed to attack on June 22, 1941, they almost certainly would have been attacked by the enemy. He also described the martyrdom of his own soldiers when they fell prisoner to the "Asiatic hordes," and he insulted the Western countries who fought the German people by becoming the allies of the Soviets. The endless complaint about the war in Russia, which would be repeated constantly by the faceless bureaucrats in Rastenburg, was: "War in Russia is good but only during four months of good weather."

By August 1941, Hitler began his physical decline. He became stooped, round shouldered, and lost that image the world was accustomed to seeing, an image cultivated by Heinrich Hoffmann, the wealthy Munich photographer who had befriended Hitler during the 1920s.

On Tuesday, August 26, Mussolini went to Brest-Litovsk by plane to visit the scene of a recent battle. He was welcomed by Field Marshal von Kluge, commander of the Fourth army, who exhibited some annoyance at having to entertain the Italian ally, described the actions that had led to the fall of the city. The Duce then went to the HQ of Marshal Göring, and the meeting between the two, who had known each other for almost twenty years, was friendly. That evening Mussolini flew back to Rastenburg.

Anfuso, who had stayed behind at Rastenburg, wrote: "When the two dictators met again that evening, I found that Mussolini was extremely interested in Russian history; the history of Brest-Litovsk; an old fort he had seen showing signs of recent fighting; the type of buildings the Soviets had erected: hospitals, barracks, and schools that he expected would be imposing structures were actually very modest, in disrepair, and old. Mussolini's train set forth that night, turning south to Leopolis (Lvov), following a strange itinerary. Across the Polish corridor, the train went to Kattovice, Krakow, Rzeszow, and Lvov. During this interminable journey, Vittorio Mussolini asked his father about his conversations with Hitler. The Duce answered: "If the German armies continue to advance at this pace, and are able to solve their supply problems, their success is almost certain. But we are very close to the fall, and the winter comes to Russia much sooner than to us. Napoleon, whose very name Hitler cannot bear hearing, had his own bitter experience with the weather.

"The presence of our troops on this front is essential, not just from the ideological point of view, but also because Hitler is convinced that the war will be won in Russia. He has praised the energy, the courage, the fighting spirit of our expeditionary force. Our soldiers and officers are capable of carrying out the mission we gave them. Keitel, as any good Prussian, is always skeptical of the military qualities of the Italian soldier, but this time he said he couldn't find any differences between our troops and theirs. If we had the equipment and the transportation the Germans have, there would be no difference between our soldiers and theirs."

The Führer's train was closely following Mussolini's. On the morning of August 28, from an airfield very close to the location where both trains had stopped just north of Lvov, a four-engine Condor took Hitler and Mussolini to Uman to review the CSIR units.

The CSIR began its movement into Russia on July 16 from Botosani, on the border between Romania and Bessarabia, toward the zone of operations that had been assigned by the German high command. On the evening of August 12, units of the *Pasubio* division had made contact with the Red Army rear guard; the fighting continued into the night. Lieutenant Colonel Benigno Crespi wrote: "News from Russian prisoners confirms that the enemy is now in full retreat toward the south in order to cross the Bug [River] as quickly as possible; other Russian units are marching toward Odessa. The Bug is still 150 kilometers away. The weather is excellent. The roads and tracks are dry and our movements are very easy but the heat has returned. The main worry for an army advancing for hundreds and hundreds of kilometers with motorized units deep into enemy territory, as we are doing, is the problem of gasoline supplies. Gas, diesel, and lubricants are the CSIR's main concerns.

"On Sunday, August 17, mass was celebrated in the public gardens of Oligopol which during the week are used as a marketplace. Near the soldiers there were, as usual, local inhabitants watching. They have not seen a religious service in twenty-four years, and they make the Russian Orthodox sign of the cross. Every Ukrainian *isba* ("hut") has its own icons depicting the thin and inspired faces of the Virgin and the saints. The Ukrainians are peaceful people, and after the first days of occupation, they overcame the suspicion Bolshevik propaganda had instilled in them, and whenever possible, they were helpful and hospitable. Our commanders had to forbid excessive fraternization between Italian soldiers and the population. But the real misery our soldiers saw was too moving to remain indifferent, and soon, they were sharing their rations with women and children. The Italian units succeeded in creating good will among the population in Russia and, perhaps because of this, were usually spared attacks by partisan fighters.

"On Sunday, August 24, after mass, we were informed that in the next few days Mussolini and the Führer would inspect some of the units of the CSIR."

Aboard the Führer's Condor, piloted by Hans Baur, were Ribbentrop, Himmler, Otto Dietrich, Alfieri, Anfuso, and other adjutants. The weather was clear and hot, and the mood was serious. "They were all thinking of the front pages of the newspapers had we all crashed together," commented Anfuso. The plane flew over the vast and fertile Ukraine, at 10,000 feet, surrounded by

Messerschmitt escort fighter planes. After about two hours, the plane landed near Uman.

Marshal von Rundstedt welcomed the Führer and the Duce on the field, and he looked very much annoyed and disturbed by the occasion. The German soldiers, on the contrary, were enthusiastic about getting close to Hitler, who seemed to have forgotten his guest and saluted the troops by himself. Then Mussolini and Hitler boarded a powerful Mercedes to reach the area where the Torino division, the same one the Duce had inspected at Verona two months earlier, was bivouacked.

The good weather was over, and during the night heavy rains had transformed the entire region into a vast mudpit. The tracks were now impossible to use. General Messe was unable to use any kind of vehicle to cover the five-kilometer distance to the southeast of Uman, at the Tecucza crossing where the meeting with Mussolini was to take place. He had to take a cart pulled by a mangy horse to reach the meeting in time. Fortunately, the heavy wind had, in the meantime, firmed up the roadbed.

Benigno Crespi wrote: "At noon, we saw a lot of cars coming from Uman. After the command car, came the big vehicle with Hitler and Mussolini followed by other cars carrying marshals and generals, Keitel, Rundstedt, and Cavallero, and followed by the diplomats. General Messe and his staff saluted. The Führer and the Duce came out of their car and spoke briefly with Messe and invited him to get into their car. Our troops are lined up along the road in perfect order in spite of the narrow pathway."

Anfuso described the scene this way: "I had the impression that the motorization of our units had been somewhat difficult. The troops looked good, and the infantrymen looked like Italian soldiers, not stone-faced, but all smiles and changing expressions. On their faces their joy at having been seen by Mussolini was obvious since he had ordered all of them over there. The fading names painted on the tanks that reminded the soldiers of home: *Birra Peroni* or *Fratelli Gondrand*.

"General Messe looked just like his men: the face of a make-believe tough guy, with sharp eyes. He stayed in Russia until November 1942, and just like his men, he had a rebellious streak, constantly fighting and arguing with the Germans. When the Italians were not fighting the Russians they argued with the Germans, as if it were a favorite pastime. Ribbentrop, who had to accompany me, had a darkly immobile look on his face, as if he was the one being reviewed. I said more than once while he remained silent: 'Beautiful troops!' He nodded from time to time, and when we reached the *bersaglieri*, he said finally '*Schöne Truppen*' ("beautiful troops"). Hitler was much more enthusiastic, probably wishing to please Mussolini, who craved Hitler's approval."

Dino Alfieri, who was riding near Vittorio Mussolini, commented: "It's not the first time the bersaglieri fought in Russia. Cavour had sent them to the Crimea, and even then we could not be absent if we wanted to gain some advantages later." The vision of Hitler and Mussolini disappeared as fast as it had arrived. The Italian troops, having been rewarded with the visit by the Duce, went back to digging themselves out of the mud, avoiding the rain and the cold as they faced their terrible and tragic adventure.

The two dictators were on their way to Uman for a "healthy" German-style meal of military rations. A photograph of the Uman airfield shows some German aircraft in the background and a thick group of German soldiers looking on, while the dictators sit on a bench at a rough wooden table. Mussolini is in the middle, Hitler on his left, and von Rundstedt on his right. The menu was a challenge for the Italians. A mysterious vegetable soup was served with a small orange that must have been a relic, in view of the season. Everyone felt sick on the way back. Mackensen accused Alfieri of not tasting the soup, thereby insulting German cooking. Alfieri answered: "True, I didn't try it, but it's also true you are not such a good friend." After the argument, Hitler said to Mussolini: "Too bad the Italian soldiers are not here with us."

Before returning to Lvov, von Rundstedt dragged his guests to a hangar, where there was a blackboard set up in the center. He illustrated, with a pointer, the progress of the operations that had taken his forces to Uman at the end of July and the beginning of August. When the field marshal concluded his presentation, everyone gathered around a table where maps had been spread. Photographer Heinrich Hoffmann took pictures of this historic moment. In the afternoon, the entire group boarded the planes back to Lvov. Soon after the Führer's plane left the airfield, Mussolini, in a strange moment of exhibitionism, asked to pilot the aircraft. Hitler was so surprised that he said nothing and only made a face intended as a strained smile. The Führer had never learned how to drive a car, let alone fly a plane and in spite of his enthusiasm for both means of transportation he thought both activities unworthy of a great man. Mussolini got out of his seat, went to the cockpit and flew the plane for over an hour, making the copilot, and everyone else on board for that matter, quite anxious.

Anfuso noted: "I'm sure the joke was not at all to Hitler's liking. The SS must have thought of it as an attempt to murder the Führer. Not knowing what to do, they stared blankly at Himmler, who kept silent. When the time came to land, Hitler's pilot, who had given his seat to Mussolini, told the Duce that landing was not such a good idea. Mussolini turned and saw the convulsed faces of the passengers, who having so far avoided death at the hands of the Soviets did not want to die because of an Italian, however famous he may have been. Back in his seat, Mussolini was congratulated by Hitler, but not with the same kind of words he used to praise the Duce for eradicating Marxism."

In high spirits, Mussolini, unable to talk about recent Italian military victories that could compare with those of Germany, used Roman history for a worthy comparison, namely the successes of Emperor Trajan. Dollmann recalled the episode: "The Führer had to patiently endure the description of the victorious battles of Trajan, the conqueror of Romania. No detail was omitted, not even the great ability of the Romans to build bridges across the Danube, an art that remained unsurpassed by modern armies." Mussolini also pointed out that Trajan was famous not only for his military and strategic ability but also as a builder of great public works and great works of art. The only thing Hitler wanted was for his plane to land, and he probably made the silent decision never to share an airplane trip with the Duce again.

The convoy went back north from Lvov in a real arm-twisting trip. On Friday morning, August 29 in Rastenburg, Mussolini told Anfuso that it was time to discuss the communiqué with Ribbentrop, which would necessarily stress, as an answer to the Atlantic Charter, what was to happen to Europe after the disappearance of the USSR. "It was a way of forcing Hitler to say publicly that he was not conducting a colonial war within Europe and not a war just for the Herrenvolk, but for the new Europe."

Ribbentrop was visibly unhappy with Anfuso's request, even though the matter had been presented as Mussolini's personal wish. Then Anfuso took a draft communiqué out of his briefcase and made the mistake of saying it had been corrected by Otto Dietrich, the head of Hitler's press office. This was compounded by a second mistake: Anfuso suggested that Ribbentrop should discuss it with the Führer. In any case, in the end, after many changes and additions, the document was finally published.

On the final evening of the trip to Rastenburg, an outdoor party was organized in the Duce's honor and it included a typical scene of Hitlerian theater. At one point a general approached the two dictators and announced: *"Mein Führer, Reval ist gefallen!"* ("My Führer, Reval has fallen!") A triumphant wind was blowing over all the Italians present, and it was very clear that the wind was intended only to be a German one.

Everyone ran up to congratulate Hitler, who was requesting details of the operation. Keitel began playing a sort of duet with the Führer, who was now cast in the role of the great war lord. Hitler recited the names of the generals and the units which had been used in this operation. Then, obviously feeling satisfied, he began staring silently at the moon.

Mussolini suddenly asked Anfuso: "Do you really believe in this story about Hitler being the technical and strategic military genius?" Anfuso replied that he more or less thought Hitler was genuine but that he was also capable of memorizing things before a "performance." The Duce then asked: "What about the communiqué?" Anfuso told him that after many changes the final document was very similar to the original and Ribbentrop had authorized its release to the Italian press as soon as they crossed the Italian border at Tarvisio. Mussolini could also consider himself satisfied with the meetings just as much as Hitler, if not more, on the political side, especially after Hitler confided that General Gehelen's informants had significantly underestimated the real troop strength of the Red Army.

Mussolini's train was quickly traveling south with an additional antiaircraft car with multiple barrel guns as a gift from the Führer. At Klagenfurt, the train suddenly came to a halt. The Minister Plenipotentiary Urach, who represented the German foreign office's press section with the Italian delegation told Anfuso: "The communiqué doesn't work." "What does that mean? We were all in agreement. Everyone agreed: the Führer, Dietrich, Ribbentrop. We spoke of nothing else at Rastenburg, didn't we?" Urach replied: "The Reich foreign minister has asked me to suggest how the communiqué can be improved." "Ah," said Anfuso, "you go and tell that to Mussolini." After many such exchanges and with the very small margin to negotiate that Urach had been given, a new draft of the document was typed while Mussolini kept cursing everything and everybody. The Duce felt bitter about the incident. Anfuso suspected that the document had been stopped by Ribbentrop when he noticed that his name was mentioned following General Keitel's.

Dated from Berlin on August 30, the much-altered message was finally issued. It said: "The Führer has received the official visit of the Duce at his HQ on August 25-29. During the discussions that took place from the 25th to the 27th, Hitler and Mussolini studied in great detail all the military and political problems concerning the length and development of the war. At the close of these discussions, an official communiqué was published stating, among other things: 'The conversations were held in light of the will of the two nations and their leaders to conduct the war until final victory. The new European order that will be established after this victory will seek to eliminate the causes that have been, in the past, at the origin of previous European wars. The eradication of the Bolshevik menace on the one hand and of plutocratic exploitation on the other will allow a peaceful, fruitful, and harmonious collaboration in all sectors, political, economic, and cultural of the populations within the European continent. During the course of his visit, the Duce was accompanied by the Führer to the most important locations on the eastern front and reviewed the Italian divisions engaged in the struggle against the Russians. Hitler and Mussolini met with Field Marshal von Rundstedt on the southern front.'"

Cristano Ridòmi had typed the communiqué, since he was the only person on the train with a typewriter. He had added the name of Vittorio Mussolini to the text of the Italian version but the Duce crossed it out. These ridiculous behind-the-scenes gyrations concluded the eleventh meeting between Mussolini and Hitler, the third and final conference in the year 1941. The dictators would meet again eight months later, at the end of April, in Salzburg, when the possibility of an Axis victory was still considered realistic, even after the United States entered the war following the Japanese surprise attack on Pearl Harbor on December 7, 1941. The German offensive toward Moscow stopped twenty kilometers short of its objective, paralyzed in the mud and snow of the Russian winter. Stalin had been able to throw well-trained and fresh divisions against the Wehrmacht during this first winter crisis, divisions which had been previously deployed in the Far East facing the Japanese, after receiving assurances from Tokyo that Japan would not attack the USSR.

Great Britain took advantage of the lull the Führer had created with the Russian campaign to increase war production and reduce Atlantic convoy losses. In North Africa, Churchill had also tried to put together, between November and December 1941, an offensive against Rommel by the new Eighth army, which had some initial success. The Axis, however, took the initiative at the beginning of 1942, when it started the buildup of the wild race that would take it all the way to El Alamein. The weak spot in the German-Italian forces was the naval supply line to the armies in Cirenaica. Only by eliminating the British from the island of Malta could that problem be permanently resolved, since the Pétain government was opposed to allowing the Italians to use the well-organized French bases and communications in Tunisia.

After Mussolini's trip, rumors about him began to surface in Rome and Berlin, many of them spread apparently by Galeazzo Ciano, who had returned as Foreign Minister on September 22, and by Italian ambassador Dino Alfieri.

A member of the staff of the Italian embassy in Berlin had overheard a high-ranking German official refer to the Duce as: "Here is our Gauleiter for Italy." Mussolini, upon hearing this, told Ciano: "I can believe that. In Germany there are many recorded messages. Hitler is the only one to record each one of them. The others repeat them. The first such recording was 'the faithful Italy, an equal partner, the queen of the Mediterranean, just as Germany is the queen of the Baltic.' Then came the second recording, the one after the victories: 'Germany will dominate Europe. The defeated countries will be mere colonies. The partner states will be confederated provinces. The most important of these will be Italy.' We had better accept this status because any attempt to react would push us down from the category of confederated province to that of colony, which is infinitely worse. Even if tomorrow they were to demand Trieste to be within the German sphere of *lebensraum* we will have no other choice but to acquiesce. There is finally the possibility of a third recording: should increased Anglo-American resistance make Italy's collaboration more useful to Germany. That recording has not yet been published."

The analysis Mussolini offered on October 13, 1941 was more or less realistic at the time. The Duce then made another fateful decision during that same period: to increase the size of the Italian army on the Russian front despite the lack of equipment and the objections of the German high command. The plan was to send another twenty divisions by the coming spring: "In order to align our war effort with Germany's, and once victory is achieved, since it is absolutely certain that there will be victory, prevent Germany from laying down the law as if we were a defeated nation."

Marshal Messe who was at the time commander of the CSIR, wrote about this delicate episode: "On October 25 and 29, 1941, political discussions took place between Italian and German officials at the Oberkommando der Wehrmacht (OKW). During these meetings, Ciano, who was personally opposed to the plan, was insisting, under orders from Mussolini, to commit more Italian troops to Russia, including a division of Alpine mountain units to be deployed in the Caucasus. Hitler was giving vague answers, saying that he knew the Alpine divisions were excellent units."

One month later, on November 24 to 27, Ciano was again invited to Berlin to a conference of all the countries that were part of the anti-Comintern pact. He spoke with Hitler "first and foremost of the question that was of greatest interest to the Duce—the Italian participation in the war on the Russian front." This time, Ciano was offering armored divisions that Italy did not even have. He wrote that the Führer replied that the presence of Italian armored divisions seemed neither necessary nor even desirable, since Italian tanks used completely different ordnance from German armor, which would further complicate supply problems. If Italy was able to form new divisions, they should be deployed in Tripolitania, where a French threat cannot be ignored.

Following ever more insistent requests by Ciano, Ribbentrop added that "we will welcome the contribution of Alpine divisions in the southern sector of the Russian front. The Führer knows these Alpine troops are excellent, and together with the German army and the current Italian forces, which he praised once again, they should take part in the attack on the Caucasus."

Mussolini quickly wrote to the Führer on December 3, 1941, saying he had given the order to prepare an Alpine army corps of three divisions plus an army corps of mountain infantry for the Caucasus. But, in a note dated October 3, Chief of Staff General Cavallero, who was against sending troops into Russia, pointed to the problem of a lack of transportation, in addition to the threatening situation in France and the Balkans.

Messe continues: "On January 6, 1942 following Mussolini's letter to Hitler, Cavallero was insisting that the six divisions intended for Russia be subordinated to a normal state of affairs in Europe, so that in the spring, Italy could dispatch only three divisions, thus improving the equipment and supply of the army corps already stationed in Russia, as I had been requesting. Keitel, who at first was opposed to having any Italian troops in Russia, relented in February, and on the eighteenth of that month, Cavallero informed him that the two army corps would arrive, but that he could not provide the necessary vehicles for supplies and support. Cavallero was attempting to delay the departure of those troops but he failed because Mussolini was now adamant, and as usual, the general acquiesced. On June 2, 1942, as I was in Italy for a few days' leave, I was received by Mussolini. I wanted to tell him of the high risks we run in deploying an army in Russia without proper equipment for the special conditions within that theater of operations, as I had personally experienced.

"I told the Duce: 'It's a mistake to send an entire army to the Russian front. Had I been consulted, I would have taken a position against it, just as I was opposed to sending a second army corps last year.' Mussolini answered very calmly: 'We just can't do less than Slovakia and other smaller countries. I must be at the Führer's side in Russia, just as the Führer was at my side in the war with Greece and now in Africa.' And since I kept on insisting, he cut me short: 'Dear Messe, at the peace conference the 200,000 men of the army corps will weigh much more than the 60,000 of the CSIR.' I was unable to discuss this issue further. And so, in the summer, not six, but seven, divisions with two army corps commands left for Russia to become the Italian Eighth army. It required many vehicles for transportation and supplies that could not function in the condition of the Russian front. The Eighth army, besides 25,000 horses and mules, deprived Italy of 16,700 vehicles, 4,470 artillery pieces, and 1,130 tractors."

The problem of Malta was again on everyone's mind. Hitler thought Italy would solve the Malta issue with a lightning attack of Italian naval and air forces on the very first day of the war. The problem had dragged on unresolved until October 14, 1941, when General Cavallero had ordered that plans be completed by the army chief of staff for the occupation of the island with the cooperation of the navy and the air force. Cavallero also ordered that special units be trained to participate in the operation. Rommel was increasingly concerned that his supplies reach Libya intact from Italy. The Führer's HQ was also taking an active role on the issue.

Field Marshal Albert Kesselring, commander of all German forces in the southern sector, which included Italy and the entire Mediterranean, was the prime supporter of an operation against Malta. In April 1942, Kesselring went directly to Hitler to explain the advantages of an attack on Malta. This was no easy task, since the Führer was opposed to such landing operations because of the difficulties in the operation in Crete. But Kesselring was persuasive and obtained Hitler's approval. On April 22, the German commander gave Mussolini the good news and two days later, Ambassador Mackensen brought the Duce an urgent request by the Führer for a meeting to be held at Salzburg.

Mackensen told Mussolini that Hitler wished to discuss various issues (Malta among them) which were increasing sources of worry. Unprepared, the Duce answered that he would prefer to delay the meeting until the first days of May. But over the phone, Hitler was adamant that "this is not possible for reasons beyond my control." The Palazzo Venezia had to accept the dates without any discussion, April 29 and 30, 1942. Once again, on the evening of April 28, the Duce's convoy went north. Ciano, who was with Mussolini on this trip, complained that, as usual, without a precise agenda, he was entering a dark tunnel. Cavallero was also on the train, and he took the time available to explain to the minister of foreign affairs the "Malta plan," which would most certainly be discussed the next day. In his *Diary*, Ciano wrote: "Cavallero understands that Malta is a tough objective. The preparation is now being carefully carried out with the understanding that the attack will take place. This gives additional energy to those involved. But if and when the operation actually does take place is another story. Cavallero is noncommittal on this issue, and he characteristically hides behind many 'ifs' and 'buts.' He speaks of the future course of the war. We must win this year or at least be in a position to win. If not, the dangers will continue to grow."

XIII

Rommel and Malta

Klessheim: April 29-30, 1942

On the morning of April 28, 1942, Mussolini's special train arrived at Puch, near Salzburg. The Duce and his staff, Ciano, Cavallero, and diplomat Mario Luciolli had accommodations in one of the wings of Klessheim Castle, the former residence of the Prince Archbishop of Salzburg, now refurbished as a luxurious hunting lodge for the Führer's most illustrious guests. Ciano was convinced that the Germans were using art treasures stolen in France to decorate the castle.

Hitler stood six paces in front of the rest of the German welcoming party waiting on the platform. Mussolini stepped off the train, quite curious to discover the reasons for such an urgent meeting. Right after the effusive greetings, the groups left for the castle, where the first discussions began at once. Hitler and Mussolini were alone at first, while Ribbentrop and Ciano, and Cavallero and Keitel, met separately. Military matters were on top of the agenda with three major issues on the table: the Italian contribution in Russia, operations in Cirenaica, and the Malta operation. On the first issue, after attempting to keep the Italian effort as low as possible with the CSIR at 60,000 men, Cavallero in the end had to accept Mussolini's position to increase the number of divisions for political reasons. But as a final, desperate argument, Cavallero had insisted that there was hardly any transportation, which made the problem of supplies all the more acute.

This final attempt to stall the operation was settled immediately in the conference next door between Hitler and Mussolini. Hitler at first began by praising the German soldier during the awful winter just passed on the Russian front. He also congratulated himself for his own strategic and tactical intuitions and was asking the Duce about the Italian divisions the OKW could count on in view of the renewed offensive on the Russian front. Hitler also talked about the courage displayed by the Romanians and the Hungarians who had committed 27 and 12 divisions, respectively. Mussolini answered that, as he had repeatedly promised, the brave CSIR would grow during the coming summer to a total of 227,000 men.

There would be several crack Italian divisions in the new army corps that would bear the name "Armir": three Alpine divisions, the Tridentina, Julia, and Cunense, those very troops, Mussolini pointed out, that the Führer admired. To these would be added three infantry divisions of the Second Army Corps: Ravenna, Cosseria, and Sforzesca, plus the reserve division Vicenza. The CSIR of General Messe with its divisions, Pasubio, Torino, and Celere, which included the Bersaglieri and the Savoia cavalry, would stay in place as the Thirty-fifth Army Corps. Finally, the Black Shirt Legion was to be formed out of four groups: Leonessa, Valle Scrivia, Tagliamento, and Montello. Even after requisitioning everything available, the Italian army was still short of vehicles. The Führer immediately replied that the German logistical services would make up the difference. The fate of tens of thousands of men was quickly decided, and by August 10, as planned, they would be deployed in the bloody Russian tragedy according to the plans Adolf Hitler had prepared.

The Malta problem dominated the discussions because it was closely tied to the question of the invasion of Egypt. Cavallero, with General Gandin at his side, as well as military attaché to Berlin General Efisio Marras, repeated his point of view that the operation should take place as soon as possible. The Italian chief of staff sent a message to Keitel prior to the meeting in which he stated: "We must make some sacrifices to eliminate this threat. Combined with possible enemy actions in 1942 and, more realistically, in 1943, its continued presence could seriously damage Axis operations. While it is obvious that the heavy bombardment of the naval and air bases on the island has given positive results, these must be exploited before the enemy has a chance to recover or before sudden changes on the ground could alter the balance of the forces facing us."

Cavallero's analysis was correct. During the month of March alone, Axis bombers pounded Malta with ten times more bomb tonnage than the city of Coventry, which had been leveled in 1940. Churchill was aware of the threat looming over the island, and wrote in his diary: "Malta was up for grabs." Cavallero, sensing a favorable reaction from his listeners, spent some time detailing "Esigenza C.3" the operational plan that would lead to the occupation of Malta. The plan had been written by General Gandin, with Admiral Girosi and air force General Cappa. German and even Japanese technicians specialized in island landings had also participated in its elaboration.

Kesselring spoke right after Cavallero, confirming his support for the C.3 plan (renamed "Hercules" after its approval). Keitel, still uncertain about Hitler's final decisions, answered that he would not be able "to immediately provide the required naval landing crafts and paratroop units." Only the Führer could unlock the situation. Kesselring repeated to Hitler: "Malta has been neutralized by my bombers, but until it is occupied by the Italians we will be unable to stop the British air force. Our plan is now complete and has the approval of both Italians and Germans. We need your final approval." Hitler, always sensitive to requests coming from his generals, approved Hercules on condition that it be synchronized with Rommel. A final compromise was then reached: in May, Rommel would be given the green light in Cirenaica. Once certain Axis objectives had been reached, such as the taking of Tobruk, Hercules would begin in mid-July, after the full moon on the thirteenth. The units that would be part of Hercules were the Italian fleet under the command of Admirals Iachino, Tur, and Barone. The air force would deploy 1,506 aircraft, 666 of which would be German. General Vecchiarelli, the supreme commander, would have under him Generals Sogno and Cesare Rossi, as well as German Generals Student and Ramcke, who specialized in paratrooper and other types of airborne units. Right after the Klesseheim meeting, all units intended for the Malta operation began their transfer to Sicily. The operational plan required that it begin immediately, to be ready at day X plus 20. Naval and air attacks on the island were progressively increased.

But Hercules was destined to never see the light of day, and Malta was spared complete destruction, thanks to Rommel. On June 29, Rommel occupied Tobruk and took 35,000 British prisoners, including seven generals. He was convinced that the British Eighth Army was practically destroyed, since it had lost over seventy-five percent of its strength. Cavallero was well aware of the professional weaknesses of the Afrika Korps commander and, on the evening of the great victory in Tobruk, quickly submitted the following letter addressed to Hitler, for Mussolini's signature:

"Führer: in the naval and air offensive just completed, the enemy has endured a major defeat. The same can be said for operations in Marmarica that are about to reach a positive conclusion.

"It is my opinion and certainly also yours, Führer, that we must consolidate the current results as quickly as possible. At the center of our strategic picture, there is Malta, which we have previously settled. I wish to tell you that preparations for the Malta operation are very advanced. It becomes more urgent than ever before. To make the most of the results we have achieved in the Marmarica and to prepare for future requirements, we must be able to channel our supplies in complete security. The occupation of Malta, besides solving transportation problems in the Mediterranean, would give us full use of our air forces, now stationed and committed to the Mediterranean theater as long as Malta is controlled by the enemy. The freeing of the air force, along with the other advantages stemming from the occupation of Malta (for instance, the problem of fuel), would allow us to regain freedom of movement, a crucially important factor to achieve victory. The problem of fuel for the Italian Air Force must be examined in relation to the Malta operation, and discussions on the issue are taking place within the Italian high command. The occupation of Malta will create opportunities in this area that we will best examine once the operation is completed.

"I have every reason to believe, Führer, that in spite of the considerable difficulties that I can imagine, your personal intervention will also ensure a favorable solution, since it is of vital importance for our position in the Mediterranean and its future developments. Mussolini."

The naval and air battle Mussolini was referring to was known as the "mid-June" operation and was in fact to be the swan song of the Italian navy. Two months later, as historian Aldo Fraccaroli pointed out, during the mid-August operation, in the midst of another, larger effort by the British to resupply Malta, Italian battleships were unable to sail because of a lack of fuel. Many naval commanders took credit to having led Italian forces during the victorious battle of mid-June, Mussolini among them.

The Italian navy had been successfully engaged, as evidenced by a rare British admission at the time: "Only two ships of the eastern convoy reached Malta, while the western convoy had to turn back to Alexandria after losing a destroyer, three cruisers, a support ship, and three merchant men." This battle saw the one and only sinking of a British warship by an Italian torpedo plane. The destroyer *Bedouin*, after being heavily shelled by Italian destroyers, was sunk by a torpedo fired by an S.79 plane. During the "mid-August" battle, the Axis had even greater success in spite of the absence of large caliber guns; the Allies lost an aircraft carrier, two cruisers, a destroyer, and nine merchant ships, while another aircraft carrier, two cruisers, and seven more ships were heavily damaged.

The letter from Mussolini and Cavallero was sent to Berlin on the evening of the Axis victory at Tobruk, and was preceded by a message from Rommel requesting permission to continue his advance to the Nile and the Pyramids, following in the steps of Napoleon. Hitler examined the entire matter for two days, and on June 23 he answered Mussolini with one of the most crucial documents of the entire war.

"Duce, at this time, when militarily historic events are in the offing, I would like to explain my thoughts to you as concisely as possible regarding a decision that may have a decisive impact on the course of the war. Destiny, Duce, has given us an opening that will not appear again in the same theater of operations. The fastest and most totalitarian exploitation of this advantage is our best military opportunity at this time. Up to this moment, I have always ordered our forces to pursue a defeated enemy in retreat for the longest possible time as our troop strength would allow. The British Eighth army is virtually destroyed.

"At Tobruk, with its harbor and piers practically intact, you have, Duce, an auxiliary base that is all the more important in that the British themselves have built a railroad line all the way to Egypt. If we fail to pursue the remains of this British army now with the utmost effort of each soldier, we will follow a fate identical to that of the British when they lost their advantage very close to Tripoli because they diverted troops into Greece. Only this capital mistake of the British high command made our effort in reconquering Cirenaica a success.

"If our forces do not march forward to the extreme limit, into the heart of Egypt, we will be faced with new, long-range American bombers able to reach Italy. At the same time, British and American forces can link together from all sides. In a short time, the situation would turn against us. But the continued pursuit of the enemy will bring about its disintegration. This time, Egypt can, under certain conditions, be taken from England. The consequences of such an event will have vast repercussions all over the world. Our own offensive, helped by the occupation of Sebastopol, will determine the fall of the entire eastern structure of the British Empire.

"If I, Duce, can give you, in this historic moment which will not be repeated, my most heartfelt advice, it would be this: order the continuation of operations to seek the complete destruction of British forces to the very limits of what your high command and Marshal Rommel think is militarily possible with their existing troops. The goddess of fortune in battle comes to commanders only once, and he who fails to seize the opportunity at such a moment will never be given a second chance. The fact that the British, contrary to every rule of the art of war, decided to interrupt their advance on Tripoli and divert their units to another battlefield was enough to save us . . . Please, Duce, accept this request only as the advice of a friend, who has considered for many years that his fate is tied to your own and is acting in consequence. In faithful comradeship, Adolf Hitler."

Mussolini read and reread the letter. Between the lines, it ironically tried to be provocative. But in substance, it was an out-and-out order. Unsure how to react, the Duce summoned Cavallero for advice. The Italian commander arrived at the Palazzo Venezia with Kesselring. They both remained unmoved by Hitler's prose and begged Mussolini not to make any decision before they both had a chance to inspect the front in Cirenaica. The next day they flew to Africa.

Concerning this event, Carlo Cavallero, son of the Italian military leader, wrote: "At a meeting in Derna, on June 25, 1942, Kesselring and my father attempted to convince Rommel that because of the long distance separating them from their objectives, an advance under such conditions would not allow the Axis to fully take advantage of its success. In fact, Rommel would face a refreshed enemy, close to his bases, with a reduced and ragged Axis army that would be dangerously low in supplies.

"Kesselring pointed to the difficulty of effectively supporting the Axis ground forces with the few planes he had, hundreds of kilometers from their bases. The enemy would have the advantage of being very close to his own bases. He concluded by stating: 'I am very skeptical of a deep advance. If I am given the order, I shall obey, but the end result of the battle in this case is very much in doubt.'"

Rommel told Mussolini's two envoys that it was now too late to alter the battle plans. He said he had already given the green light to the units to take Marsa Matruh. However, he continued, given the very persuasive points he had heard, he would consider each of his movements nothing more than a series of "jumps" forward; he was not willing to become engaged in a "deep operation." Rommel only spoke this way to get rid of the emissaries sent by Rome to upset his plans. Rommel also knew that the Führer was definitely on his side, so much so that from Berlin, he had been forewarned that the OKW was preparing an underhanded slap at the Duce.

On the evening of June 25, with typical Nazi arrogance, Keitel phoned the Italian high command to inform them: "The German high command cannot furnish the minimum fuel requirements which have been requested for the Malta operation." Without even waiting for the return of Cavallero and Kesselring, Mussolini, with this piece of information, cabled Rommel that he had a free hand to move forward. The Duce was now beginning to dream of the Nile and the Pyramids. The shelving of the Hercules plan was a German decision and must rest with Marshal Rommel himself. In this entire matter, Mussolini only played a cameo role already imagining himself on a white horse, making his own triumphant entrance into Cairo.

General von Rintelen, German military attaché in Rome, confirmed that at the Salzburg conference, Cavallero had termed the occupation of Malta a prerequisite to any successful campaign in Africa, but the Führer, after Operation Merkur over Crete, had become skeptical about paratroop landings into enemy camps that were well protected and well armed. For Hitler the supply of bridgeheads was the most difficult of all military operations. For this reason, he concluded that it was preferable to let the British remain in Malta so that the Axis could inflict even greater damage to enemy merchant shipping while it was supplying the island. Based on this analysis, confirmed by the recent victories in Africa and the Mediterranean, Hitler approved Rommel's plan. The Field Marshal, well aware of Hitler's views, had told him, before resuming his march toward El Alamein, that in taking Tobruk he had seized enough vehicles and fuel to reach the Nile at the enemy's expense.

The Field Marshal's enthusiasm also convinced Mussolini, who traveled to North Africa on June 29, remaining until July 20, waiting in vain to make his own triumphant entry into Alexandria. This was destined to become one of most humiliating episodes in Mussolini's life. Rommel virtually ignored the Duce's presence in Cirenaica even though he had been invited more than once to report in person to the man who was, at least nominally, his direct commander in the Mediterranean. Cavallero, even though he cut a rather understated presence, consoled himself with his promotion to Marshal of Italy.

Vittorio Mussolini was at Derna at the time and wrote about the Duce's trip: "I reached Berta on July 1 and went straight to the small villa where my father was staying. He was in a sitting room. I hugged him affectionately and he smiled without interrupting his work. I asked him how he felt, because I saw him push his belt below his waistline and assume his usual slumped position, resting deep into the back of the chair. 'Not too well, but maybe it's the change of climate. If Professor Castellani were here, he'd say that I have amoebae. He specializes in diagnosing the amoebae bacteria in anyone who has visited Africa.' At that time, Mussolini would answer questions about his health this way: 'My ulcers are the convoys that leave Italy and never reach Libya.'

"He was in a bad mood," wrote Vittorio, "because he had to cancel his flight to Tobruk due to the weather. I asked about his impressions of the prisoners: "Impressive looking soldiers, tall and strong, almost all of them Australians and New Zealanders, with a few British and South African units. I also saw a lot of Hindus, blacks—a few thousand in all. The commander of the camp told me he had to separate the colored troops at the request of the whites. And then *we* are the ones accused of being racists.'

"Something was bothering him, and in harsh tones he asked me: 'Why is it that our command is located in positions so far re-

moved from the front line? There are some 600 kilometers separating the fighting from the first commanding general. It's good to
be cautious, but I think they are exaggerating . . . ' 'The advance
came faster than they could move the command post.' I replied, in
attempting to justify the situation. 'You're probably right, but the
troops want to see the faces of their generals, and that's why I admire Rommel, who is always extremely active at the front lines. He
may be stubborn, rude, and gross, but he's always among the troops
and they appreciate it.'

"Of the situation on the front, Mussolini said: 'Rommel has
assured me that we will soon be in sight of the Nile. You know how
much I hate silly optimism, but this time I want to believe it. Cavallero
also thinks we're not doing so badly even though we're losing precious time because of transportation problems. Rommel is insisting on taking advantage of the initial success as much as possible
even if it means reaching Alexandria with only one *panzer*. Kesselring
and Bastico, the Italian supreme commander in Libya, are much
more cautious; they feel we must consolidate our positions in the
El Alamein depression.'

The next day the Duce received at his villa headquarters not
Rommel, who was still avoiding him, but Minister Plenipotentiary
Serafino Mazzolini, who was to become civilian high commissioner
of Egypt once the Axis forces had taken Alexandria. This was a
premature appointment, as events were to show. Mussolini justified
this move ahead of time: "The Germans will be full of Teutonic
pride when they reach the Pyramids, like Napoleon. The presence
of the Duce in the area will serve to demonstrate that on these
shores we are the ones in command." Then Mussolini said: "I didn't
come here to be confined to this little house and wait. Rommel
doesn't show up. He has the good excuse of being engaged in battle
on the front. I told Cavallero that I would like to go over there, but
he doesn't recommend it because of the rapidly changing lines. I
don't like to receive second hand information. And when there is
no one around me, it means things are not going so well."

Mussolini's analysis of the situation at the front was far from
wrong. To go and seek out Rommel would have been a humiliating

gesture for him as the "Duce." Fortunately, Cavallero was able to avoid this with a plausible excuse. Mussolini was killing time by traveling around and handing out decorations and harvesting wheat with the Italian colonists at Barce and Borgo Baracca. He finally visited the bombed-out town of Tobruk. On July 16, he held a military conference in his quarters with Cavallero, Kesselring, and Bastico. Cavallero made a pessimistic assessment: at El Alamein the attacks by Australian and New Zealand infantry had made better progress than expected. Afrika Korps tanks were now reduced to about thirty, as many as the Italian divisions Ariete and Littorio.

The breakthrough that would begin on October 23 with the offensive of General Montgomery's Eighth Army was not far away. After meeting with the generals, Mussolini said to his son: "I have decided to go back to Italy as soon as possible, possibly tomorrow." The crisis of the Axis had begun.

After Mussolini accepted Hitler's veto to attack Malta, Cavallero, on July 7, transformed the Hercules plan into the C4 plan—the occupation of Tunisia. General Messe wrote about this change: "The cancellation of the occupation of Malta was one of the major mistakes of the war. The materiel and supplies which had been put together at great cost for the operation and were ready at the beginning of July were immediately assigned to other tasks. The excellent paratroop division was thrown into El Alamein and used as an infantry division. The German paratroopers of General Ramcke had the same fate."

At the end of April 1942, during the Klessheim conference these dramatic events were still to come. The atmosphere of the meetings around Berchtesgaden was almost idyllic, so much so that Hitler invited the Italians to come and have tea at his residence at the Berghof. Mario Luciolli, aghast at the news that fresh Italian divisions were to go to the Russian front, was part of that group.

"We ran into snow as our cars took the mountain road toward Hitler's residence. The German general who had just returned from the Russian front and was sitting next to me suddenly became angry and cursed the snow. It took him a few minutes to calm down, and then he said: 'You know, when you have seen too much of something . . . ' He was obviously thinking about the eastern front. That ride awakened some poetic memories in my case . . . As we had tea, I noticed that the 'Satan' [Hitler] who was responsible for the bloodiest battles in history, was playing host with the simple courtesy of an Austrian *petit bourgeois* . . . "

Ciano, worried by the excessively friendly atmosphere, became suspicious: "The cordiality of the Germans is always in reverse proportion to their good fortune . . . On the second day, April 30, after lunch, we had said all there was to say—on Great Britain, the United States, Russia, France—Hitler spoke uninterruptedly for one hour and forty minutes. There was not as single topic he did not touch upon: war and peace, religion and philosophy, art and history. Mussolini kept looking at his wristwatch, I was lost in my own thoughts, and only Cavallero, who is a model of servility, pretended to listen in rapture and nodded repeatedly. The Germans were much less able to withstand this than we were. Poor people: they had to listen to this every day, and I'm sure there wasn't a word or gesture they didn't know by heart. General Jodl, after a brave fight to stay awake, fell asleep on the couch. General Keitel was groggy, but he was sitting much too close to Hitler to let himself go as he would have wished."

Cavallero, servile as he needed to be to get his way, was privately celebrating his success after having obtained from the loquacious gentleman his approval for the operation against Malta. This was worth the small sacrifice of being the Führer's audience for more than an hour. Had Cavallero known that Hitler's promises had no value perhaps he would not have been so compliant. Mussolini was very happy to leave Klessheim, probably because he could see the problems besetting the Führer. He summed up the two days of meetings this way: "The German war machine is still extremely powerful, but it has suffered wear and tear. Now it will make another gigantic effort . . . "

Mussolini left the following note: "Magnificent valor displayed by the Germans in Russia. But strategic difficulties are growing in the east for the Führer. We spoke with him about defensive actions: "We will need only a few forces to defend this front in prepared positions. The mass will be turned toward the west. Perhaps Great Britain will finally become convinced that it cannot win and will ask to negotiate.' These are the Führer's thoughts. For the rest, a stepping up of the submarine war, and containment on other fronts. Some hope about Turkey."

Mussolini further confided to his son Vittorio: "The Führer is fully convinced of victory and is counting on Anglo-American resistance in the face of Stalin, a useful but dangerous ally who keeps on demanding the opening of a second front. As far as we are concerned, soon we will begin our action in Libya, and immediately after that, we will snatch Malta away from the British. The Germans will start their offensive for Leningrad and Sebastopol in June with huge troop and artillery concentrations. The very difficult winter crisis seems to be over now, and the German high command is confident in the success of the coming operations."

On May 1, a joint communiqué was issued: "The Duce and the Führer met in Salzburg on April 29 and 30. The conversations were held in the spirit of close friendship and brotherhood-in-arms of the two peoples and the two leaders. The result has been a complete agreement regarding the situation created by the victories of the powers of the Tripartite Pact and the future course of the war by both nations. Once again, on this occasion the iron-clad decision by Italy and Germany and their allies was reaffirmed to insure the final victory with all the power of their arms."

At the Rome cabinet meeting of May 2, Mussolini gave his version of the "two days in Salzburg" as Bottai noted: "Very long talks, on a single day up to twelve straight hours. There was a polite mention by the Duce about the Führer's loquacity and his fluent oratorical style. The main issue was the Russian campaign where the Germans were experiencing a collapse similar to that of Napoleon. According to Hitler, Russia is the only worthy foe we have been facing. Bolshevism did, in fact, create something serious: an army that can qualitatively compete with that of Germany."

After meeting four times in 1940 and three times in 1941, the Salzburg summit would be the only one in 1942 and marked the end of a certain sense of balance in the relationship between Hitler and Mussolini. The Führer and the Duce would meet one year later on April 7, 1943, once again at Salzburg. This meeting preceded the events of July 25 that were to overthrow Fascism. But before its unstoppable decline, the Axis was to live through the victorious summer of 1942.

The Germans had overcome the winter crisis, and went back to defeating and annihilating dozens of Soviet divisions. On June 30, 1942, Sebastopol surrendered. One week later, the German army crossed the Don River, and by June 28, Hitler's first armored groups reached the suburbs of Stalingrad, crushing the stiff Russian resistance. Azov too fell at this time. In Africa, Rommel was sipping coffee in a tent on July 2, only a few dozen kilometers from Alexandria, while the Italian army recaptured the strategic oasis of Djarabub, deep in the Libyan desert. At the beginning of July, Admiral Dönitz' U-boats sank almost an entire convoy on its way to supply Stalin. Over twenty-three ships on their way from Iceland were sunk by the end of the attack. German submarines had virtually complete supremacy in the Atlantic and Mediterranean. Compounding all this bad news for the Allies, on August 19, 1942, British forces, on a mission that was the brainchild of a nervous Winston Churchill, were soundly defeated on the French coast at Dieppe, where they had attempted a poorly conceived landing with a few thousand men and two hundred vessels under Lord Mountbatten's command. After about ten hours, the fighting that had begun at dawn suddenly stopped. General Southam surrendered his remaining 2,000 men, leaving 3,500 dead. Only 591 survivors returned to England.

Then suddenly, in the fall, the fortunes of war turned against the Axis. On October 23 at El Alamein, the British Eighth Army began the race that would take it to Tripoli exactly three months later, on January 23, 1943. At the beginning of the British offensive, the Axis order of battle was 69 infantry battalions, 540 artillery pieces, 530 tanks, and 30 armored cars; the Allies had 104 infantry battalions, 2,180 artillery pieces, 1,200 tanks, and 858 antitank and antiaircraft guns. The British air forces outnumbered the Axis three to one: 2,100 planes versus 700. When the offensive began, Rommel, as it would happen again during the war, was in Germany on sick leave. Hitler ordered Rommel back to Egypt immediately by plane the next day, because the German commander replacing him had been killed in battle. Rommel was back in command in the field on the evening of October 25, 1942. While the battle of El Alamein was in full swing, at dawn on November 8, 1942, five hundred American and British ships began landing troops in Morocco and Algeria, finding only token French resistance and initiating a wide encirclement of the Axis in North Africa.

On November 17, a counterattack began on the Russian front. The Soviets, with large forces, and equipment that included the famous Katiusha rocket launchers, began a counteroffensive along the Don River. The Italian army, the Armir, began its terrible odyssey in December. On January 2, 1943, the German Sixth Army surrendered at Stalingrad, because the Führer had ordered it to remain in place rather than break out of the Russian encirclement. General von Paulus had been ordered to hold Stalingrad and not retreat just as Rommel had been forced to wait at El Alamein many more days than necessary.

Mussolini was in poor health after his disappointing trip to Libya. He had lost a lot of weight; there was talk of gastritis, ulcers, or even "amoebae." On October 25, Ciano wrote: "The Duce canceled a big meeting of the Fascist party leadership planned for the 29th where he was to speak. Why? There are three interpretations: (a) The doctors have forbidden the effort required by a long speech; (b) He doesn't want to make any statements until the offensive in Libya has been broken; (c) he wants to make a deep change in the leadership and speak, as would be logical, to the new leaders."

On November 1, under the pressure of events, Mussolini wrote to Hitler, proposing a meeting in Salzburg at the end of the month. The Führer called during the night of November 8 after the Allies had landed in North Africa. Under the circumstances, Mussolini preferred not to leave Rome and decided to send Ciano instead. Ciano left immediately for Munich with Mario Luciolli, who noted: "On the evening of November 10, we walked up the steps of the Führerhaus. At the top a tired and unhappy Hitler shook hands

with us. A very different man from the coldly aggressive Hitler whom
Mussolini had met in that very same building four years before. It
was immediately decided to occupy southern France and Corsica.
In December, Ciano, again representing Mussolini, whose health
was failing at the time, went to Rastenburg to meet with Hitler a
second time, and I was among his entourage. Ciano, according to
Mussolini's instructions, was to convince Hitler of the need to reach
an armistice with the USSR to avoid the decimation of German
forces, since the war could no longer be won in the east. It was
obvious that this proposal would not be accepted. Ciano also did
not present his position forcefully enough, not because he did not
believe in it, but because he was unable to have a meaningful discussion with a Hitler by now on the edge of madness. The enemy
had just broken through on the eastern front in the sector held by
Italian units, and the Germans had accused the Italians of not holding the line. The claim would later be denied, but during the battle
itself, it did have a strong psychological effect."

Even though Luciolli was not present at the private Hitler-Ciano
conversations, he remembered the heaviness of the atmosphere.
Ambassador Alfieri and his secretary, Michele Lanza, were also at
Rastenburg. The Italian embassy in Berlin had prepared, given the
tense state of affairs, a plan to take Italy "out of the problems of
the Axis." Luciolli thought that neither Mussolini nor even Ciano
would have the courage to accept such a plan, and the document,
even if it was in part utopian, revealed the thinking of Italian diplomats regarding the dramatic events that the Axis was facing.

The memorandum stated in part: "It becomes necessary for
Italy to immediately disengage from the alliance with Germany. The
disengagement must take place in such a way as to include not just
Italian interests but also those of all the states that are allied with
Germany, to insure a rapid resolution of the war. The event should
take the form of a natural consequence made inevitable by the situation and possibly with Germany's consent. It appears necessary
that Italy should act in such a way as to preclude any accusation of
treason and actually bring about an increase in our diplomatic prestige within Europe." The paper follows with details of the project,

which was quite complicated, since it was to conclude with the support of Turkey and Spain in leaving an "isolated" Germany to its own destiny, while Italy, Hungary, Romania, and Bulgaria would be removed to the sidelines.

After the war Luciolli commented on this initiative by saying: "Today I am convinced that the disengagement from Germany would have been impossible without the prior collapse of the Fascist regime. When I remember my thoughts at that time, I believed that once the Fascist dictatorship was swept away, Italy would reach an agreement with the Anglo-Americans."

Back in Rome, on December 22, Ciano wrote his report of the meetings with Hitler. He underlined his part in following Mussolini's suggestion regarding the need to seek an accord with the USSR and the negative response from the Führer. Ciano also thought that all this would be useful for his own future and position in history. The "big son-in-law," as he was dubbed, was well aware that his days as foreign minister were numbered. The Duce had saved him from the Germans several times before, ever since the firing of Ambassador Attolico. On February 5, 1943, Ciano was called to the Palazzo Venezia at 4:30 p.m. to hear the Duce ask him: "What do you want to do now?" Galeazzo, who knew the moods of his father-in-law, had prepared a request for a new sinecure: "Ambassador to the Vatican." Mussolini fired Ciano, along with Bottai and Grandi and almost all the other cabinet ministers. A real "purge." On February 1, after the fall of Tripoli, Cavallero had been relieved as chief of staff of the armed forces and was replaced by General Vittorio Ambrosio. In the new cabinet, Mussolini took the ministry of foreign affairs himself and named Giuseppe Bastianini as under secretary of foreign affairs.

Hitler was very concerned by the political changes in Rome. He wrote a sixty-page letter to Mussolini and sent Ribbentrop to Rome to explain and discuss its contents with the Duce. Hitler's main message was his announcement of another massive offensive in the summer against the USSR, where the Germans were being forced out of those cities they had taken so easily in 1941. He also addressed the growing partisan movements in Yugoslavia, where

Mussolini was siding with the Serbian Cetnik partisans. The Führer was convinced that the situation in the Balkans was explosive, especially in view of a rumored Allied landing in the area.

On January 23, 1943, General Giovanni Messe, who had been recalled from Russia during the past November, was summoned to Mussolini's office at the Palazzo Venezia along with Marshal Cavallero, who was about to pass on his duties as chief of staff. The Duce told Messe: "Your period of leave is over. You must go to Tunisia [which had been occupied by the Axis after the Anglo-American landings of November 8, 1942], replace Marshal Rommel, and take command of the Italian First Army. The army you are to command is in good shape and still has excellent firepower, seven hundred artillery pieces and seven thousand vehicles."

On March 9, Rommel left North Africa to go back to Germany, leaving the command of the Afrika Korps to General Jürgen von Arnim. General Messe wrote: "This recall was the logical consequence of the events that took place from El Alamein to now." On March 14, Hitler wrote to Mussolini " . . . Rommel came to my HQ. I have put him on leave for now because according to the doctors and my own impression he urgently needs rest . . . In any case, Duce, I must ask that the news of Marshal Rommel's leave must be kept secret at all costs. In Germany such changes of command are never publicized as a matter of principle and then only after a period of several months. In this case especially, I feel the spreading of such news would be dangerous to us . . . No matter how posterity will judge, Marshal Rommel was loved by his men . . . And for the enemy, he represents a commander they still fear. What is most tragic is that this man, who is one of my very best officers and has exceptional qualities of courage and ability, was led to failure because of the supply problem that can only be solved with better transportation . . . " The secret of Rommel's departure was so well kept that the Allies continued to mention his name in official and unofficial documents. In his letter, Hitler made no mention of Malta or of his decisions to pursue the mad race to El Alamein and kept it secret from the Italians and Marshal Kesselring.

When, on April 6, 1943, at 2:00 p.m., the Duce boarded his train to retrace his steps back to Klessheim, where he had last been on April 29, 1942, the great Axis leaders no longer had dreams of offensives in Russia, Africa, or Malta. The agenda was now quite different. Along with Mussolini went a large group of German and Italian officers and diplomatic staff divided into four groups. The Italian diplomats were under the direction of undersecretary Bastianini, high-ranking diplomats, such as Luca Pietromarchi, Leonardo Vitetti, Francesco Babuscio-Rizzo, and Luigi Silvestrelli, who were to be joined at Klessheim by Ambassador Alfieri and his closest deputies. The military group included General Ambrosio, General Gandin, Colonels Montezemolo, Gallo, and Jannuzzi, and Captain Hausbrandt. The German team was headed by Ambassador von Mackensen, military attaché von Plehwe, and SS Lieutenant Colonel Eugen Dollmann. The Duce's personal staff included his secretary Niccolò de Cesare, medical doctor Arnaldo Pozzi, Guido Leto, the head of the OVRA, the Italian secret police. Police Commander Giuseppe Stracca and Police Commissioner Vincenzo Agnesina, a cook, valets, and other aides.

In a letter dated March 14, 1943, Hitler invited Mussolini to the meeting, mostly to help the Italian dictator overcome a morale crisis as he witnessed the crumbling of all his imperial dreams. The Duce accepted the loss of his African empire and the inevitable landing of Allied troops in Italy itself soon after. The only unknown factor was the location: Sardinia or Sicily? Hitler wrote in his letter: "Duce, if we can hold the Mareth line, or at least the Chott position, and solve the supply system, no power in the world can get us out of our positions in North Africa . . . if we solve the supply problem I have no doubts that sooner or later the North African adventure will be the worse mistake the Americans and the British have made and they will realize its terrible consequences." The Führer expressed the hope of another meeting with the Duce and then concluded: "Perhaps it will be best for you to leave your environment, if only for a few days, and it will be a joy for me to leave the utterly horrible east where I have been uninterruptedly for many months. I can see Salzburg once again, a city that for us Germans, with its buildings and art, represents the bridge between the ways of Italy and those of Germany."

Mussolini always reacted positively to Hitler's entreaties and thought it would serve to placate and please the Führer and his entourage by accepting the invitation. This meant, in effect, that the entire organization of the Reich's chancellery would have to migrate, after the enforced exile of Rastenburg, for a short working vacation in the south of Germany with its beautiful spring scenery. As soon as the train left the station, interminable meetings took place in the saloon cars of Bastianini and Ambrosio in an attempt to extricate Italy from the difficult military and political crisis it was in.

The diplomatic meetings were attended by Eugen Dollmann: "The Salzburg-Klessheim meeting was the first following Stalingrad, and Mussolini's staff had fully understood its importance. I had never found a more united front among the Italians than during the journey by rail from Rome to Salzburg. Starting with the very cautious De Cesare, Bastianini, and his staff of functionaries led by Count Pietromarchi, the brother of Countess Attolico, to the heads of the police escort, Stracca and Agnesina, each one in his own way showing unusual energy and initiative.

"In its main points, the program, elaborated mainly by Pietromarchi and another very able diplomat, Count Vitetti, was simply that Germany must either begin peace initiatives immediately with Russia and accept the reality of heavy losses, or help Italy in an all-out effort by creating a new southern army with modern equipment and organizing an efficient defensive safety net against air attacks and ensure that any landing that would take place on Italian soil after the fall of Tunisia would inevitably fail. Italian diplomacy is ready to establish contacts for negotiations, since it had excellent contacts and back channels mostly in the Balkans . . . This is the program. And since I had the least to lose in all this, it was my job to support it . . . They thought that since I knew the Italian situation, I could, as lieutenant colonel, go to Hitler and, in a friendly voice, tell him: 'Either peace with Russia or a new southern army; otherwise, Italy will leave the Axis.' It would not fly. I pointed out that the Duce was present in the train and that role was his to play. De Cesare maintained that this time Mussolini would bang the table with his fist, but the others shook their heads and smiled uneasily.

"Finally I promised to approach Himmler, who was more accessible to me, to explain the conspiracy that I witnessed on the train. But the Duce would need to see Himmler, and I would have to prepare him for the meeting in advance; the rest would take place during the conversation. The Italians approved, since the Duce was extremely nervous, but Ambassador von Mackensen was opposed to this scenario and to Himmler's being approached and what I would have to tell him. The ambassador did not consider the general situation to be so dangerous."

The military meetings were focused on immediate problems, since the Allies were not letting up their offensive actions everywhere, on the sea, in the air, or on the ground. Colonel von Plehwe was representing General von Rintelen, who was recovering from an injury in an airplane accident. Von Plehwe recalled: "During the evening, I was invited to a long conversation between officers in Ambrosio's car. Ambrosio only participated intermittently in these talks. A synopsis of the Italian issues that General von Rintelen had briefed me about was taking place.

"The picture looked like this: the bridgehead by Axis forces in Tunisia, which began on October 10, 1942, would be overwhelmed by the Allies in a short time, even though Hitler and the German high command kept repeating the contrary. In such a battle, the African theater would be lost to the Axis along with the best units of the Italian army. Furthermore, the battles that for years had taken place in North Africa had meant the loss of almost the entire Italian merchant fleet as well as small- and medium-sized navy vessels, with a few exceptions. These had been sunk while escorting convoys. The larger units of the navy could only be used for a few hours due to the lack of fuel . . . The Italian air force had had little impact because of the antiquated planes that it still used . . .

"After the fall of Tunisia, the Allies were bound to land on Italian territory. The remnants of the Italian army were too weak to be effective . . . The lack of raw materials in Italy had not allowed

enough of a stockpiling of supplies and other cautionary measures
. . . The war in Ethiopia, the action in Spain, and finally the war
itself had all literally bled Italy, one of the poorest countries of
Europe in raw materials, completely dry . . . There could not be a
general rise of the people to arms after the conflict had beaten back
the Italian army all the way to the mainland itself . . . The Italian
high command was of the opinion that if the German ally still
wanted to change the course of the war it must at last decide to
place the Mediterranean at the tactical center of the war effort.
Germany must transfer into Italy enough units of the army and air
force to thwart any possibility of success of an Allied invasion.

"The shipment of supplies must be stepped up dramatically . . .
But the needs of the German army in Russia made this Italian request impossible to satisfy. Since the catastrophic conclusion of
the battle of Stalingrad on January 31, 1943, the enemy had also
taken the initiative in the east. The Italians repeated that now the
proposal Mussolini had put forward at various times to Hitler in
1942, to come to an understanding with the Russians, was all the
more correct . . . Therefore, this possibility would again be put on
the table in the upcoming discussions . . . The Italian high command had given Mussolini detailed material on this issue and begged
him to speak about it candidly with Hitler . . . "

While all these meetings were taking place, Mussolini was locked
up in his compartment. He was a sick old lion with no bite left in
him. At dinner with Bastianini, he discussed how to end the war
with the USSR and prepared plans to submit to Hitler to push back
the coming Allied offensive against Italy itself. Before nightfall in
the Alps, the entire convoy stopped and parked on a side track. It
stayed there for eight hours so that the Duce could rest until dawn.
The shaking of the train prevented him from sleeping, but that was
not the only reason.

XIV

The Secret Weapons

Klessheim: April 7-8, 1943

O n the morning of April 7, 1943, a suntanned and stiff but visibly thinner Mussolini walked up the steps of Klessheim Castle, where the Führer hoped the Duce could spend a relaxing two days away from his problems in Rome. He was given the usual "Cardinal's" apartment, named after the Bishop Prince of Salzburg, who used it for his evening entertainment, surrounded by beautiful women and the music of the young Mozart. Inside as well as outside, the weather was wintry.

Press secretary Ridòmi wrote: "Once again we come to a cold Salzburg, not just in the deep valley surrounded by mountains covered with snow. The situation is difficult for Italy . . . First it was Greece, now Africa, and soon it will be Sicily. During the preceding meetings with the Führer, Mussolini, when pressed by Ambassador Alfieri to take up some of the sore points with Hitler of importance to the alliance, answered that he had nothing to ask the Führer. This time the situation was reversed. Italy had much to propose and even to demand, both on the political and military levels.

"It was impossible to forget Stalingrad in just a few months. Not only because of the magnitude of the defeat but also because a field marshal who had just been promoted in the thick of battle a few days before, had dared disobey the Führer's orders to fight on to the last man. Von Paulus decided to surrender to avoid the carnage of his remaining cold and decimated soldiers, isolated and without supplies or any hope of survival. What Mussolini wanted was clear to his entourage: an end to fighting a war on two fronts and a proposal to seek an agreement with Moscow to end the war in Russia. But how? And who would dare open the subject with the leader of the Third Reich?" The Duce eventually did try but only for a few seconds, because he was silenced and effectively buried under a torrent of words and incomprehensible sentences by the Führer.

Hitler stood at the head of the staircase, surrounded by about sixty of his staff and cabinet, and welcomed Mussolini to the old castle. The two dictators immediately went into a private meeting in one of the sitting rooms, accompanied by Ribbentrop, Bastianini, Keitel, and Ambrosio for an initial exchange of views. Mussolini told Hitler that, due to his health, he would have his meals alone in his room to avoid disturbing the customary banquets. A special refrigerator was made available to the Duce's cook to store the special rice, oatmeal, fat free milk, and fruit.

Hitler took advantage of the occasion to engage in a show of "deep affection" toward the Duce, with words full of sympathy and encouragement. "Duce, I would like you to accept the services of Dr. Theodor Morell, a true scientist, who has succeeded in restoring my health, strength, and will power in such difficult times." Mussolini was suspicious and let the proposal drop because he was well aware that "witch doctor" Morell based his cures on concoctions of every type of narcotic mixed into strange multicolored pills. The doctor was generously handing out such pills to everyone in Hitler's entourage who wanted them. But Mussolini was disturbed that in refusing the services of this miracle doctor, he might possibly offend Hitler. "I would not want the Germans," said the Duce, "to turn this into a political problem." As usual the meetings split into three groups: the political discussions were carried on by Mussolini and Hitler, the diplomatic issues by Ribbentrop and Bastianini, and the military problems between Keitel and Ambrosio.

Dollmann also recorded the events: "The Duce was visited every day by his friend Hitler, without an interpreter. I was able to find out what went on during those duets through the Führer's adjutant. We knew that usually the Führer did all the talking, while Mussolini, with a sorry look on his face, remained silent and listened patiently and politely. A very timid allusion by the Duce regarding the Russian front brought about an interminable flow of words on the absolute certainty of victory on that front—the main argument was that the Russians could not possibly replace the huge losses of the preceding campaigns, the consequences of which, as demonstrated by the numbers produced, could only be catastrophic."

At the close of the first private meeting with Hitler, lasting over two hours, Mussolini told his staff, who were waiting anxiously to know what steps he had taken in the direction desired by the Italians: "Today, there was a monologue by Hitler. Tomorrow, it will be my turn to speak." But, in fact, Mussolini would speak very little in the next few days. A year later, reminiscing about this meeting at Klessheim with his son Vittorio, the Duce would blame his failing health for having prevented him from illustrating, as he had promised Bastianini and Ambrosio the day before, the Italian political and military plan to overcome the current crisis. But he also blamed his staff and experts for the failure of the meetings: "They had come from Rome with strongly worded resolutions and long lists of all sorts of requirements. And they failed to get even a toothpick."

However, as was reported indirectly by other observers, Hitler did confide something important to Mussolini, within the limits of military secrecy because the Germans were wary of any secrets shared with the "loquacious Italians." Goebbels noted in his *Diary*: "When Mussolini got off the train, the Führer thought he looked like a broken old man; when he left, he was back on his feet, in perfect condition ready for anything. The Duce well realizes that there can be no other path for him: either to win with us or die with us."

We can guess what Hitler told Mussolini in confidence during their meetings based on Ribbentrop's memorandum right after the Klessheim talks during the latter part of April 1943. The Führer explained to the Duce certain details regarding Operation Zittadelle against the Russians, which, when successful, could lead to talks with the Russians from a position of strength. Hitler also alluded quickly to the murderous "secret weapons" Germany was completing and which would be instrumental in securing the final victory. Naturally he did not specify what these weapons consisted of. Actually, they were the secret rockets that during the spring of 1943 had captured the Führer's attention. Up to that time, Hitler had been skeptical as to their effectiveness, not because of their quality, but because they would be available too late for his blitzkrieg offensive. The German weapons program in April 1943 was concentrated on four diabolical weapons, the equivalent of science fiction for the time: the Komet fighter plane with a jet-propelled engine, the Me.163B; the Fiesler flying bomb, soon to be known as the V1 rocket; the surface-to-air Wasserfall missile that was to knock Allied bombers out of the sky; and the long-range missile A-4, later to be known as the V2 rocket.

During the discussions, Ridòmi asked Bastianini for some item he could transmit to the Italian press. Bastianini replied: "The situation is what it is. There are three ways to end the war: first, we impose peace on the enemy; second, we negotiate peace with the enemy; third, the enemy imposes his own peace. We do not believe in the first possibility. We are trying to explain that the second possibility was to be attempted if we are to avoid the third one. That's what we were working on." After agreeing to set the Russian case aside in anticipation of new developments, Mussolini brought up the subject of Spain to at least secure the right of passage of Axis troops to attack Gibraltar and North Africa. Hitler was disgusted as

Hitler meets Mussolini for the first time on
June 14, 1934, in Venice.

left
Austrian Chancellor Englebert Dollfuss was assassinated in a failed Nazi coup in 1934.

below
Mussolini in civilian clothes and Galeazzo Ciano behind him (white cap) the day before Ciano became foreign minister, June 9, 1936.

Hitler and Mussolini leave the podium in Berlin, 1937.

left
Italo Balbo visited Hitler at Berchtesgaden in 1937 but was opposed to the alliance with Germany.

below
Hitler and King Victor Emanuel III on the reviewing stand in Rome, May 1938. Protocol kept Mussolini behind the two heads of state.

Hitler and Mussolini in Rome, May 1938.

above
Reinhard Heydrich of the SD (far left) and
Guido Buffarini-Guidi, Undersecretary of the Interior,
salute the Unknown Soldier in Rome, May 1938.

below
Hitler was greatly impressed by the Italian navy.

left
Pope Pius XI shortly before his death in 1939.

below
Eugenio Pacelli became Pope Pius XII in March 1939.

above
Mussolini and Ciano leaving for the Munich conference,
September 29, 1938.

below
The Axis leaders on their way to the conference hall in Munich,
September 30, 1938.

Chamberlain and Halifax, hoping to lure Mussolini
away from the Nazis, visit Rome in January 1939.

above

Ciano signs the "Pact of Steel," turning the Axis into a military alliance. Berlin, May 22, 1939.

left

Roosevelt's envoy Sumner Welles toured Europe and met with Ciano (left) and Mussolini in 1940.

right
FDR was reelected to a third term in 1940.

below
One of many train meetings between
the Axis partners.

above

Hitler and Ribbentrop were furious because of Mussolini's unannounced attack on Greece when they met in Florence on October 28, 1940

below

The Axis leaders were all smiles later on for the Florentine crowds.

above
Hitler at Berchtesgaden in 1940, rebuffed Princess Marie José of Savoy in her efforts to seek favorable treatment for her fellow Belgians, who had just been overrun by Nazi armies.

left
Claretta Petacci, Mussolini's mistress.

above
On June 22, 1941 Ribbentrop announced that
Germany had attacked the USSR.

below
Hitler and Mussolini tour the Russian front
in August 1941.

Soviet cartoon during the winter of 1941 when
the German army failed to take Moscow.

Soviet poster calling for the defense
of Moscow, 1941.

he remembered his past experiences with Francisco Franco and replied that all political contacts between Germany and Spain were suspended, but if Italy wanted to try on her own, she would be welcome to.

The military meeting that included Keitel and Marshal Göring was aimed at giving General Ambrosio assurances that, after taking care of the needs of the Russian front, the German high command would examine the possibility of increasing its presence in Italy, now threatened by Allied landings and carpet bombing of Italian cities. Besides the flaws in the German military system, it did not take a great strategist to figure out that Hitler's aim was to gain as much time as possible by keeping the Allies bogged down in the south, on the Italian front. The Führer was not interested in ephemeral successes in that area; in his view, the war would be won or lost in Russia. After examining the three major issues, Russia, Spain, and help for Italy itself, Ambrosio was hopeful in discussing the situation in the Balkans. The Germans were demanding that the Italians act with extreme brutality to wipe out any resistance in those countries. Ambrosio was against that kind of plan and said that it was in the interest of the Axis to continue supporting the Serb Cetnik nationalists and their commander, Draja Mihailovic, who was fighting against the other partisan units, such as the Communists. But any agreement on the Balkan question became impossible because of the deep differences of opinion within the Axis.

During the diplomatic talks, Bastianini "insisted that it was essential to show that there was some hope of peace among the European countries that were under German and Italian occupation; a sensible definition of a new order for the continent should be put forth in an open document that would serve to promote a minimum of confidence in both Italy and Germany." echoing Hitler, Ribbentrop answered, that this was absolutely out of the question. According to the notes of Italian diplomat Silvestrelli, Ribbentrop, after agreeing with the Italians that the war was not just then going well, kept repeating the current propaganda line: the German high command assures us that soon there will no longer be a Russian front, because the glorious German army will have annihilated the Soviet army. Therefore we must show the enemy, and the smaller countries that were part of the Axis, firmness and energy so that the morale of the German and Italian people would not be disturbed by unfounded promises of an illusory cease-fire.

Ribbentrop openly despised the governments of Romania and Hungary, calling them "Hypocritical, unreliable, and scheming individuals." Even on this issue, there was no possibility of reaching an agreement. The trip to Klessheim was useful after all: it would demonstrate to the Italians that there would be nothing positive coming from the Germans in the future. The Germans themselves, with their negative attitudes at Klessheim, actually set in motion the "bomb" that would explode on September 8, 1943, when Italy signed the armistice with the Allies.

During the final meeting, with all the participants present, Hitler, well aware that he had conceded almost nothing to Mussolini during the conference, declared: "Duce, I can assure you that Africa will be defended. The situation there is serious but not desperate. I have recently read the history of the siege of Verdun during the last great war. Verdun was able to withstand all the attacks of the very best German units. I don't see why this could not happen in Africa. With your help, Duce, my troops will turn Tunis into the Verdun of the Mediterranean!"

Just before the end of the meeting, the approach to Himmler, which Italian diplomats had discussed with Dollmann during the trip to Germany, took place. At Klessheim, the news that Mussolini wished to meet the powerful and much-feared head of the police forces created some embarrassment within the Ribbentrop entourage of the foreign ministry. What could Mussolini possibly want to discuss with Himmler?

Dollmann noted: "Himmler arrived late in the afternoon, and I briefed him as to what he should expect, given the discussions which had taken place on the train. As was to be expected as far as Russia was concerned, the Reichsführer of the SS was in complete agreement with Hitler. He appeared more candid as to what would be the critical situation of the Italian forces after the expected fall of Tunis . . . He was prepared to help Mussolini . . . The Duce received Himmler in a very friendly way . . . After the initial small talk, the Duce asked four specific questions: 1. What provisions had the German police made in case there should be internal unrest due to the lengthening of the war (in Italy, there had been strikes for largely economic reasons in the heavy industries of the north); 2. Senise; 3. Ciano; 4. The Italian royal family and Philip of Hesse."

Himmler, like a schoolboy in front of a demanding teacher, answered each question immediately. To maintain public order he prescribed massive use of concentration camps. He proposed that the Duce accept the suggestions of expert SS officers, after mentioning some misgivings about General Enzo Galbiati, the commander of the Fascist Black Shirt militia. Himmler was cautious in answering the Duce about Carmine Senise, who was the head of the Italian police, saying only that he appreciated his professional know-how, but not discussing his political allegiance. Regarding Ciano, Himmler expressed the satisfaction of Hitler and Ribbentrop for the firing of the Italian foreign minister who had opposed the policies of the Axis for many years.

Dollmann went on: "When he had to respond to the fourth question, Himmler broke out into a violent attack against the monarchy in general, and the Italian royal house in particular, warning of future dangers from that quarter for the Duce and for Fascism. This being said, Himmler wanted to offer Mussolini instructors chosen from the best of the SS as well as the necessary equipment to set up a very modern Italian division, whose mission it would be to ensure the Duce's personal security. Concerning Prince Philip of Hesse, Himmler said that in spite of the very real contributions he made to the Nazi regime, he did not doubt that he could very well be playing a double game in every field." Even though the issue had been settled, Mussolini asked again: "How are things in Russia?" Himmler answered with a long description of Soviet losses and the inevitable victory of the German army. In private, Mussolini told his staff: "Let's hope he's right!"

Himmler had a low opinion of the Duce. He told Dollmann: "We can't count on Mussolini anymore because we can't count on the entire regime. This means that in a short time, at the most within a few months, Italy will drop out, and in the best case, we will have to hold the southern front by ourselves. If the condition the Duce is in today is a reflection of the condition of the Italian people and the Fascist regime, then the end is near. The crack division that I offered him is his only hope for survival."

There was an epilogue to the Klessheim meeting. By the evening of April 9, the conferences were over. The next day, the Duce and his staff would leave for Rome and other locations. Suddenly, Mussolini went to bed. There was talk of an ambulance to take him to his special train, and the illness caused problems for protocol. As Ridòmi noted: "Protocol had planned for a two-day visit by Mussolini. When the visit had to be lengthened, a lot of German officials left and the organization had stopped functioning; even the extremely well-organized service of the SS came to a halt. The castle was now enshrouded in a glacial silence . . . The halls were darkened; in our hallway there was only one small lamp still on." At one point, a janitor who was tired of waiting around, told the Italians: "Don't you realize how late it is? I must shut everything and close the place. I was wounded in the war you know."

On April 11, Mussolini left. The return trip was excruciating. On the way up to the conference there was some hope within the Italian camp. After Klessheim, everything looked dramatically bleak: it was all over for Italy. Von Plehwe wrote: "Ambrosio was even more silent than usual, and he made himself unavailable. The other foreign ministry officials, Pietromarchi and Vitetti, were evasive and hid their concerns at dinner with us. The only one who was in good spirits was Mussolini. He felt better physically, and he had allowed himself to be influenced and propped up by Hitler once again."

Back in Rome, Mussolini, for an entire week, attempted to draw the most from his Klessheim visit by making some decisions intent on influencing public opinion. He told Bottai on April 14: "They say I'm finished, absentminded, over with. Well we'll see. Beginning next Saturday, the third wave will start." In a few hours, he fired Senise, head of the Italian police, and replaced him with Renzo Chierici; then he replaced the young secretary of the Fascist party, Aldo Vidussoni, with an old party comrade of the "squadrismo" days, Carlo Scorza. He also summoned Dollmann, to say that after much thought, he decided to accept Himmler's offer of an armored division for his personal security.

The dismissal of Senise was somewhat rough. In the presence of Umberto Albini, undersecretary of internal affairs, Mussolini criticized his absence of energy in fighting the strikes in northern Italy and his lack of vigilance against the black market, as well as the weak political indoctrination of the police forces in the wake of the momentous events that were sweeping over Italy. "For these reasons you will hand over your duties to General Chierici," said Mussolini. The outgoing commissioner answered that he was paying for other people's lack of efficiency and that he was being sacrificed to the Fascist party militia, whose leadership rejected his new plan for public order coordinated between the army and the ministry of the interior. Senise went to King Victor Emanuel and told him what had just happened. The King said: "We shall see each other again soon." The prediction was correct: Senise was reinstated by Badoglio on July 25, 1943. The reason Mussolini gave for firing Vidussoni was that Scorza had a better speaking voice. This prompted Scorza to give one speech a day, much to Mussolini's annoyance, and making him regret Scorza's appointment almost immediately.

Another spectacular sacking, known only to a handful of people, was that of Claretta Petacci, the romantic and often weeping mistress always waiting to be called to the Duce's side when the dictator wished some moments of relaxation during his busy schedule. During those tragic weeks, Claretta, who was to be arrested and persecuted for no reason after July 25 by Badoglio, failed to realize that the Duce had fallen into a state of indifference, typical of someone who was resigned to accepting the worst. In spite of this, Claretta kept on writing Mussolini long messages every morning, messages that would have taken a few hours for him to read.

On the morning of April 24, after his return from Klessheim, Mussolini found an envelope from Claretta on his desk. It contained a letter written the evening before: "Ben, just a few words because I feel terrible. The painful tension of these last few days and the dramatic moments of this evening have broken me . . . If my love is a comedy, after these conversations you are right to treat me like this; if my suffering is also a comedy you are right to humiliate me and to refuse to understand me. You are correct, it's not modern to suffer as I do, it's not elegant and, above all, it's useless." Promising to write only a few words, she continued her self-pitying for pages upon pages. She suspected that he had found another woman. She concluded: "I only know that for everyone else you are human, patient, understanding, good; more than good, and when it comes to me you are hard, rude, violent, bitter, indifferent, and cruel; you always have an excuse for everyone, even when you shouldn't, for me you only have words of blame, reproach, and threat . . . Forgive me if I have bored you, you cannot waste time with me, you can't, you have no time for me because whatever I do is just an act . . . "

These accusations were the only truly legitimate complaint in the long letter and prompted Mussolini to make a drastic decision. On May 10, Claretta went to the Palazzo Venezia for her usual afternoon tryst with the Duce. Their meetings always took place in the "Cybo" apartment, named after the cardinal who had commissioned the construction of the palace, a sort of small bachelor's hideaway that had been used since the fall of 1936, accessible through a rear door to the Palazzo Venezia, opening onto Via Astalli. Claretta was stopped at the door by a police officer who very politely requested that she return home because the Duce had denied her access to the apartment. In shock because of this unexpected official order from Mussolini, Claretta, in tears, ran back to her villa, the famous "Camilluccia," to fight back. She succeeded in being readmitted in the Cybo apartment a week later. Afterwards, she would tell the story that Mussolini begged her to forgive him. However, "Ben" once again barred her from his palace in June, then relented, probably to avoid yet another deluge of letters and suicide threats from his unhappy mistress.

The war went on relentlessly. On May 5, 1943, Mussolini gave his last speech from the balcony of his office in the Palazzo Venezia. It was the anniversary of the occupation of Addis Ababa, and he said to the Fascist crowd assembled below: "I feel the tension in your voices of the old and unshakable faith. I feel that you, just as I, are certain that the bloody sacrifices of these hard times will be rewarded with victory if it is true, as it is, that God is just, and Italy is immortal. I know, I feel, that millions and millions of Italians suffer from an illness that is called the 'African illness.' There is only one way to recover from this: to go back and that's what we shall do." In his closing words, Mussolini made some dark threats against "the draft dodgers" and "the traitors of all ranks and races" for whom he promised the firing squad.

These last threatening sentences in Mussolini's speech caused much alarm in Rome, where there was not, at the time, a government office, barracks, association, or fraternal group that was not, in some way, setting up its own conspiracy to overthrow the Duce and kick his German friends out of Italy. The most important of all these groups was the court of King Victor Emanuel III, with the minister of the Royal House, the Duke Pietro Acquarone, a rich financier, as the main organizer.

Acquarone had been minister since January 16, 1939, and, in the climate of the times, where many Italians felt the need to cleanse their past of any association with the Fascist regime, even the King found it necessary to write a letter to his minister, dated June 1, 1944, to defend his own record: "Dear Acquarone, I authorize you to declare that since January 1943, I made the irrevocable decision to end the Fascist regime and dismiss the head of the government, Mussolini. This undertaking was made more arduous because of the war and consequently required very detailed preparation in absolute secrecy that I had to maintain, even in speaking with those people who came to inform me of the extreme discontent that was surfacing around the country. You were informed of my decision and of my personal orders, and you know that beginning in January 1943, they made possible the events of July 25. Please receive, dear Acquarone, my best regards, V. E."

This document would not prevent the King from losing his crown, since the Allies demanded that he announce his retirement on April 12, 1944, and then abdicate in May 1946 in favor of his son, Umberto II. Among the many visitors who spoke to the King about the malaise within Italy, was Dino Grandi, the leader of those Fascists who were against Mussolini, and who was to be the organizer of the last dramatic meeting of the Grand Council of Fascism during the night of July 24-25, 1943.

On June 3, 1943, Grandi, at a meeting with the King, made the following offer: "There are no options, either Novara,* which means abdication, or reversing the alliances, as your ancestor Victor Amedeo II decided to do once he realized the mistake of being the ally of the King of France. He saved Piedmont and the dynasty at the last minute by switching to the side of the Empire. Your Majesty, I have no other ambition but to be the man to do it." The King answered: "The time is very near now. I know I can count on you. Let your King choose the right moment, and meantime help me find the correct constitutional mechanism." The real liquidators of Mussolini were to be the Allies, with a series of decisive military initiatives, beginning with the landings in Sicily on July 10 and the first bombing of Rome on July 19.

Five days after the fall of Tunis and Bizerte on May 8, the last Axis troops surrendered on Cape Bon. The Italian units were the last to lay down their arms under the command of General Messe, who had led them with great skill. General Messe had sent the fol-

---

*In 1849 the King of Savoy, Carlo Alberto, preferred to abdicate after losing the Battle of Novara against Austria and went into exile in Portugal. "Novara," thereafter, became the code word for "abdication."

lowing message to the Italian high command on May 12: "The First Army, which has had the privilege of being the last and final defender of our flag on African soil, will continue to fight to the end. The enemy is now closing in from all sides. The enormous disproportion of the forces in the field and the steady drop in supplies and artillery ammunition lead us to conclude that resistance cannot continue for very long."

At 7:35 that evening Mussolini, with a very different sense of ethics and humanity than those displayed by Hitler toward the defenders of Stalingrad, cabled Messe: "Stop the fighting. You are promoted to Marshal of Italy. Honor goes to you and your brave men."

The same day Admiral Dönitz arrived in Rome on a fact-finding mission at Hitler's request. The famous head of the German U-boat fleet had a long conversation with Mussolini, who "spoke so that Hitler would get the message." The Duce restated his opposition to the dispatch of more German divisions into Italy without a prior working plan between the two high commands. He was clearly worried about the tasks these German units were to perform once they were on Italian soil.

Hitler's response was to draw up emergency plans for the occupation of Italy in the event of a sudden collapse of Mussolini's government. The first of these plans, involving the occupation of northern Italy with an army group under the command of Marshal Rommel, bore the code name "Alarik," after the Visigoth King who led his barbarian tribesmen into Italy to looting and murder. Alarik was also responsible for the plunder and burning of Rome. After having imposed a huge payment in gold and silver on the population and having humiliated the Romans, saying that he was unafraid of their many legions because "the thicker the hay, the easier it is to mow down."

Hitler had been "diverted," thanks to Allied disinformation, into believing in a planned invasion of the Balkans, while Mussolini had told Dönitz that the Anglo-Americans would land in Sicily. The Führer wrote a violent letter to the Duce. The letter was carried by

Marshal Kesselring, who at the same time brought an invitation for a new summit between the two dictators that was to take place immediately. Mussolini, who could not even stand on his feet (so much so that he just went from his bed at his residence at Villa Torlonia to a couch in his office at the Palazzo Venezia), did not answer his ally and left the matter undecided.

On June 9, the Duce was unable to get out of bed. Two eminent physicians, Professor Frugoni and Dr. Puccinelli, came to his bedside. The X-rays made by Dr. Milani were clear and showed that Mussolini had acute gastritis and duodenal ulcers. His condition worsened when he was informed the next day that the commanders on the islands of Pantelleria and Lampedusa had surrendered to the Allies even after they had declared their intention to resist.

General Giacomo Zanussi wrote after the war: "'Mussolini's island,' Pantelleria, the anti-Malta, the unsinkable battleship, as the press had dubbed it, with its twelve thousand men, forty-gun emplacements, underground airplane hangers on two levels, bomb-proof shelters and supply stores, Pantelleria surrendered to the allies without firing a shot. All it took were the terrifying Allied bombing runs to frighten the defenders, and its commander, Admiral Pavesi, declared the surrender inevitable."

On the afternoon of June 14, against his doctor's recommendation, Mussolini called for a "war council" at his residence. He read a memorandum regarding the strategic situation to General Ambrosio, the heads of the three branches of the armed forces, and the minister of war production. After rejecting a possible political solution to end the war, the document stated that the Italian army could no longer take the initiative. The strategy was now to be defensive, but, he emphasized, a stubborn defense intended to wear down the enemy forces. The spearhead of this strategy would be the air force. With these words, the Duce ended the meeting.

Mussolini had specifically excluded any political solution to the conflict during his meeting with Italian military leaders, not so much because he did not believe this was the way out of the war but rather because of a new course set by the United States. President

Roosevelt, by 1943, was playing an increasingly dominant role in the Allied leadership, especially in his personal relationship with Churchill, in a manner strangely similar to Hitler's influence over Mussolini. But because of the contradictions between these two couples, Roosevelt-Churchill and Hitler-Mussolini the real winner was to be Joseph Stalin.

In November 1942, Roosevelt felt the need to leave Washington. In the United States the Democratic party was on the defensive, despite the real economic benefits the war was bringing to industry, by now reaching full capacity. In the last elections, the Democrats had seen their majority reduced to just a handful of votes. Troubled and somewhat bitter that the American public did not appear to accept his world view, Roosevelt—just as Hitler would do with Mussolini—invited Churchill to a working vacation, somewhere warm and pleasant. Churchill, for whatever reason, perhaps influenced by the film with Humphrey Bogart, proposed Casablanca. The location sounded attractive to the tired and sick president, who was happy to take a spectacular plane trip in the process. Roosevelt's closest associate, Harry Hopkins, was skeptical of a summit without Stalin's participation. The Soviet dictator had replied to the invitation by saying he had no time for small talk. Hopkins concluded: "Casablanca was one of the president's whims; he wanted to take a trip."

It would be at Casablanca that the formula "unconditional surrender" was announced, and it remains a mystery to this day as to the real reasons and the state of mind of the man who uttered it. The conference took place from January 15 to 24, 1943. Apart from an excursion to Marrakesh, Roosevelt and Churchill met for ten days. They succeeded in bringing together the two rival French generals, Henri Giraud and Charles de Gaulle, each one having proclaimed himself savior of France. At the end of the meeting Roosevelt had them shake hands in front of the photographers. As Churchill would later say: "Those pictures cannot be seen again without causing some merriment."

Then the President and the Prime Minister held the closing press conference. That's when the surprise announcement was made.

Roosevelt said that "the United Nations will only accept from their enemies an unconditional surrender." The formula was not the president's, but belonged to General Ulysses S. Grant, who answered Confederate General Bricker that way when Bricker requested a truce during the American Civil War. Churchill, surprised by FDR, shifted in his chair but remained calm. He could not openly disagree with such a policy in front of his powerful and financially important ally.* Later he would attempt to play down the real threat of total annihilation of Germany that was implied in Roosevelt's words.

For German propaganda genius, Joseph Goebbels, the "Casablanca declaration" was a godsend, as interpreter Paul Schmidt revealed: "My heart started racing as I had to translate for the Führer the exact meaning of the formula. I could measure immediately how much it would reinforce the Nazi position. Even the German opposition was to be heavily damaged by those words." From then on, the Germans felt more united than ever against the Anglo-Americans because the only alternative offered to them was to accept total defeat.

After Roosevelt's death in April 1945, Churchill attempted to justify the move even with regard to Italy, as he wrote on January 20 in his daily report to London on events at Casablanca: "Roosevelt and I proposed to draft a declaration on the results of the conference to be given to the press . . . I would be pleased to know the opinion of the War Cabinet as to the inclusion of a sentence in that document that would confirm the adamant intention of the United States and the British Empire to continue the war until we obtain the 'unconditional surrender' of Germany and Japan. The omission of Italy would send a signal to those favorable to a separate peace in that country. Roosevelt approved this idea; it would be an encouragement for all those favorable to our cause in every country."

---

* Churchill was ambivalent about "unconditional surrender" because he feared it might prolong Germany's willingness to fight on and discourage those opposed to Hitler within the German army.

The next day, Churchill received the reply: "The War Cabinet, after weighing the pros and cons, is unanimous in feeling it unnecessary to omit Italy, because it would raise some worry in Turkey, the Balkans, and elsewhere. We are not convinced that the omission would provoke positive reactions in Italy. It is probably just as effective, where the Italians are concerned, to show them what kind of trouble is in store for them in the near future." It was not difficult to discover the identity of the author of this reply: Anthony Eden, the principal mover of British opinion against Italy in the past.

On June 24 at the Palazzo Venezia, the leadership of the Fascist party held a meeting presided over by Mussolini, who in his speech attempted to lift the low spirits of those present. This was the famous "water's edge" speech that was to be published only on July 5 after many discussions and hesitations. The Duce said: "The Italian people deserve all our love, because it gives a marvelous example of resilience and I for one do not see what more we could ask of our people . . . It gives us its soldiers, its money. It tightens its belt and withstands enemy bombing . . . Naturally there are misunderstandings, disturbances, misdirected persons with the wrong attitude that are for the most part objective in character . . . The enemy must play a card. He has proclaimed high and low that he will invade the continent. This invasion must be attempted because otherwise the enemy would face defeat even before fighting. This is one card that once played cannot be played again. Caesar was able to invade Britannia a second time, after a storm destroyed his ships during the first attempt. And then again, one must distinguish between 'landing,' which is possible, 'penetration,' and finally, 'invasion.' Clearly this attempt will fail . . . Those who isolate each episode are poor judges of this war. As soon as the enemy attempts to land, he must be frozen at the line the sailors call 'the water's edge,' that line in the sand where the water stops and land begins . . . "

The myth and the political joke of the "water's edge" ended just five days later. At 1:00 p.m. on July 10, the radio bulletin of the Italian high command informed the public that, "the enemy has begun his attack on Sicily during the night, with the support of tremendous naval and air forces and the landing of paratroopers. Axis forces are heavily engaged in stopping the enemy; the fighting is taking place along the southeastern part of the coast."

For Italy, this was truly the end. Mussolini was awakened during the night by the high command. Despite events, he refused to make any changes to his program for the morning: at 10:00 a.m. at about forty kilometers outside Rome, at Sette Vene on the Via Cassia, he reviewed the M division, which was being trained by the SS officers Himmler had sent along with thirty-six Tiger tanks, as he had promised at Klessheim. The Duce then returned to the Palazzo Venezia. The first German reports from Sicily stated the poor showing of the Italian army under the command of General Guzzoni. For example: "Up to now there have been no enemy attacks against Augusta. The British were never even there. Nevertheless, the Italian commander decided to scuttle his artillery and ammunition and set fire to a large supply of gasoline . . ."

The Allied armies, General Patton's Seventh US Army and the British Eighth Army under General Montgomery, were advancing everywhere. Despite the real heroism displayed by Italian forces, they were too weak to stop the military colossus of the first Anglo-American landing in Europe. It was an incredible mass of planes and ships, the exact number of which remains unknown. The ancient and beautiful Sicilian cities just opened up to the enemy. Only in the valley of Catania was there any significant resistance.

On the evening of July 12, Hitler dispatched an angry message to Mussolini, saying that he would send no more German units to help if the Italian army did not put up a real fight in Sicily. The Duce ignored the threat and called Ambassador Alfieri in Berlin to tell him: "Have Marras go to the Führer immediately and request the urgent engagement of German fighter aircraft in Sicily. Without this help, we cannot hold the island." This appeal was also ignored. Mussolini did not know, or pretended not to know, that since July 5, Hitler was playing his final card against the Russians in the Zittadelle plan. At a certain point, he had to stop Zittadelle because of a Soviet counterattack and the sudden and unexpected landing in Sicily.

The Soviets were kept well informed by anti-Nazi spies who had infiltrated the Führer's high command. To recapture Kursk, which Field Marshal von Manstein had considered a limited objective, the German high command, beginning July 5, had committed over 600,000 men, 10,000 artillery pieces, 2,700 tanks, and 1,860 aircraft. On July 11, after the most brutal armored battle of the Second World War in Kursk, the Germans were able to advance only 50 kilometers. The next day, having learned the disastrous news from Italy, Hitler held a meeting with his generals at Rastenburg to brief them on the new strategic situation. "We must stop," Hitler told von Manstein, who then argued correctly: "The heavy sacrifices of Zittadelle will be for nothing if we turn away from a battle we can still win." It was useless. For the third consecutive year, the German army had been stopped on the road to Moscow.

Alfieri was unaware of the delay in the Zittadelle operation and sent a cable to Bastianini: "Setting aside the isolated incidents and the polemics, the situation between Italy and Germany, after the landings in Sicily, can be summed up as follows: (1) Germany is completely engaged in its struggle in Russia with vast offensive plans still operational. (2) In the meantime, Germany wishes to save as many available forces as possible and train fresh troops to forestall any direct attack on the territory of the Reich. For this reason, Germany considers the territory of occupied or allied countries bordering it as bastions of the German fortress. (3) Italy is one of these bastions . . . "

Alfieri was very clear in his explanations. So clear, in fact, that in Rome, various conspiracies began planning the overthrow of the now bothersome figure of the Duce, who was the only obstacle to getting the Germans out of Italy and reaching a peace agreement with the Allies. On July 16, the King received Marshal Badoglio, who was ready to take Mussolini's job. At the same time, Mussolini met with Scorza and fourteen other Fascist leaders and agreed to their request to hold a meeting of the Grand Council of Fascism, which had been inoperative since 1939.

The Italian high command was also plotting at the same time to set up its own "Mussolini plan"—for his capture and arrest. The mission was given to General Giuseppe Castellano, who wrote: "Ambrosio ordered me once more to draw up the plan to arrest Mussolini—since I had destroyed the first version of the plan—and bring it up to date in its details. The first part of this plan was to take measures to prevent a possible German and Fascist reaction . . . The German reaction seemed to be less dangerous than the Fascist one because there were four divisions in Sicily, two in Calabria, one in Sardinia, one brigade in Corsica, and one partial division in Orvieto, which was the only unit that could march on the capital. In Northern Italy, there were no German troops. But the SS, a few thousand in all throughout Rome, clearly appeared much more dangerous . . . We could count on the carabinieri since their commander, General Hazon, was totally devoted to Ambrosio. We were also reasonably confident that the police would not react since the new chief, Chierici, was for the most part on our side. But we did expect resistance from the agents who were under the command of Prefect Stracca, who headed Mussolini's bodyguards."

While the King and Badoglio finalized an agreement on the formation of a cabinet that would replace the Fascist government; while Dino Grandi was preparing for the King a "constitutional opinion" to fire Mussolini instantly; and, finally, while the army prepared its own plan to arrest him, Mussolini, on July 18, signed a letter prepared by Ambrosio and addressed to Hitler: "The rapid success of enemy landings in some parts of Sicily is not due to lack of courage of the troops defending the coastline but rather to the size of the firepower and equipment the enemy was able to land, supported by large naval forces just a few miles off the coast and the limited means of our own air force and artillery. The coastline defense did all it could with the weapons it had . . .

"My orders gave the air force the main mission, in the plans regarding attempted landings, to attack and destroy enemy naval vessels. The air force acted as ordered, going beyond the limits of the possible. But the modest forces at our disposal, compared to the massive forces of the enemy that dominated the skies, would not allow us to have decisive results against the merchant and military fleets the Allies have concentrated in the Mediterranean for an operation where America and England have engaged their own prestige in front of Russia and the world. With the continued worsening of the war in the Mediterranean, your generous help has been insufficient . . . I cannot agree with your comments regarding the conduct of Italian authorities as to the manner in which the air forces were displayed on the ground; these officials always have done more than they could for their German comrades . . . The ground organization in Calabria is quickly being completed. I can assure you, Führer, that Italian forces in Sicily have always acted according to my orders, and continue to do their utmost for the defense of the island. The enemy has opened a second front in Italy, where the powerful offensive capabilities of England and America will be engaged to occupy not just Italy but . . . also the Balkans at the very moment when Germany is strongly engaged on the Russian front.

"My country's sacrifice *must not* have as its goal to delay the attack aimed at Germany. Germany is militarily and economically stronger than Italy: my country, which entered the war three years ahead of the agreed-upon date and following two other wars, has burned out its resources in Africa, Russia, and the Balkans.

"I think, Führer, that the time has come to carefully examine the situation together, to draw the necessary conclusions in the common interest and in the interests of each country."

Finally, a candid letter. Unfortunately it was to remain within the Duce's secretariat, since Mussolini, after having given Ambrosio the satisfaction of adopting his words, decided not to transmit it because it was overtaken by the fact that he was meeting with Hitler the next day. In effect the answer had come from Berlin to have the "truth summit" in Italy, because the last few meetings had taken place in Germany, except for the June 2, 1941, meeting at the Brenner Pass. The Führer was to stay three or four days, so the protocol office had picked a wonderful location that was discreetly hidden: the Villa Gaggia-Pagani at San Fermo, a magnificent seventeenth century Venetian palace , only eight kilometers from the town of Belluno. The villa, named Socchieva, had been prepared by the prefect with the permission of the owners, who had decided to vacate the grounds for the occasion, but left their servants behind.

In this villa took place the final meeting of the Duce and the Führer, on July 19, 1943, when Mussolini was still head of the Italian government. The meeting, which lasted about four hours, from 11:00 a.m. to 3:00 p.m. was mistakenly recorded as the meeting at "Feltre" because Mussolini himself gave that title to a chapter of his own memoirs. The correct location is San Fermo, or, at the very least, Belluno. Mussolini arrived in Rimini during the evening of July 18 by plane to spend the night in Riccione. With him traveled his physician, Dr. Pozzi, his private secretary De Cesare, and Police Commissioner Agnesina. At about the same time, General Ambrosio arrived with his staff and the diplomats from Rome, including the Germans, led by Ambassador von Mackensen.

Secret information made public thirty years after the end of the war by historian Giorgio Bonacina revealed that the July 19 meeting was never to have taken place. There were British plans to kill Mussolini, but his life was spared, certainly not out of generosity, by his archenemy Anthony Eden. The idea of killing the Duce came from General Arthur Harris, the head of the British bomber command and nicknamed the "Butcher," by his flight crews.

On Tuesday, July 13, RAF Chief of Staff General Charles Portal wrote the following note to Churchill: "Top Secret—To the Prime Minister—Harris has requested permission to bomb Mussolini at his office in Rome as well as his private residence on a given day in case he were late. The plan had been prepared last year but had been shelved due to the prohibition of bombing Rome at that time. Harris would assign the 617 Lancaster Squadron, the same unit that had bombed the dikes during the May 16, 1943 attack on the Ruhr basin. The mission is entrusted to well-trained and discreet men for such operations. The bombing run would take place at very low levels, just above the roofs of buildings, allowing us to destroy both buildings without causing any other damage. The Palazzo Venezia and the Villa Torlonia can easily be recognized without the danger of making mistakes and are far enough removed, over 1,500 yards, from Vatican City and the churches belonging to the Vatican. Strict orders will be given to forbid any action other than the one related to those two objectives. I feel that should Mussolini be killed or at least shocked at this time, we could more easily and quickly force Italy's ultimate surrender . . . In the meantime we will keep ourselves as well informed as we possibly can regarding the Duce's most recent personal schedule and habits. 13 July 1943 - Signed: C. Portal."

Churchill was puzzled by the RAF document. How should he respond? The only person capable of giving him an objective answer was Eden, who had advocated the physical destruction of Mussolini a number of times. Eden coldly weighed the pros and cons of such action and came to the following conclusion: if British flyers succeeded in killing the Duce, they would certainly make him a martyr, something no one wanted; if the pilots missed their objective, Mussolini would proclaim his own immunity by God's grace and revive some hope of victory in the Italian people. The end result of the entire mission would be a loss. Eden then answered Churchill: "Regarding the note by the chief of staff of 13 July that you sent me, as to the bombing of Mussolini's office and residence, I do not like the idea. There are certainly few probabilities of killing Mussolini, and to shock him into surrender even less. Should we fail to kill him, we will not reduce his prestige and could, in fact, revive his sagging popularity. We would also run the risk of being hated for bombing the most ancient part of the city and causing casualties among the civilian population without reaching any military objectives. My opinion is to ignore the proposal because its goal is too difficult to achieve militarily, while its adverse psychological consequences would certainly be felt if it did not fully succeed. Anthony Eden."

Churchill, even though he was a practical and sometimes unscrupulous politician, approved the position of his top associate and filed away the paper after noting in writing "I agree." However, the tactical need to bomb Rome was raised by General Eisenhower, Supreme Allied Commander in the Mediterranean theater. The action was to take place on July 19 and target the railroad and airport network in order to prepare a landing on the Italian peninsula itself. And so, ironically, July 19, 1943, was to be Mussolini's lucky day.

XV

The Conference at Feltre and the Fall of Mussolini

San Fermo: July 19, 1943

On Monday morning, July 19, 1943, at 8:30 a.m. Mussolini's plane landed at the airfield at Treviso on a flight from Rimini. Present at the airport were Bastianini, Ambrosio, Alfieri (who had just arrived from Berlin by plane as well), and German ambassador to Rome, von Mackensen. Alfieri approached Bastianini and asked: "What kind of mood is Mussolini in?" The undersecretary for foreign affairs replied: "He looks indifferent. He has wrapped himself in total silence." A short time later, at 8:50 a.m., Field Marshal Keitel and General von Rintelen arrived. Both generals approached Mussolini, who was wearing dark sunglasses, to pay their respects. While the Italians welcomed the Germans, the Führer's Condor aircraft landed at 9:00 a.m. Hitler immediately informed his hosts that his plans for an extended trip of several days had been canceled because he had to return immediately to his eastern headquarters to direct a decisive battle against the Russians.

Mussolini has left a biased and highly selective account of this meeting (writing about himself in the third person) in his book, *Storia di un anno*,* dedicating less than one page to such a crucial conference: "Since the Führer had to return to Germany that afternoon, time was of the essence. Rather than at Feltre, which was located three hours away on a round trip, the talks could have easily taken place in the airport command building or at the municipal building at Treviso. But protocol had established its program, and no power in the world could change it. The Führer, Mussolini, and their staff took a one-hour train ride followed by another hour's ride by car to Villa Gaggia.

A beautiful, shaded park, and a labyrinthine building that made an eerie impression on one's mind. It resembled a crossword puzzle cast in stone. After a few minutes, the meetings began: the participants were the Führer, the Duce, Undersecretary Bastianini, Ambassadors von Mackensen and Alfieri, the Italian Chief of Staff Ambrosio, Marshal Keitel, Generals Rintelen and Warlimont, Colonel Montezemolo, and a few other minor officials. The Führer began speaking at 11:00 a.m. He opened his presentation with a clear and complete description of raw materials and the territories where they were located and the need to defend them. He then spoke of the air force, its current deployment, and its present and future capabilities. Regarding the battle unfolding in Sicily, he assured everyone that new reinforcements would be sent, especially artillery and troops.

A private conversation between Mussolini and Hitler then took place, where Mussolini underlined the need to dispatch reinforcements to Italy. They continued talking during the return trip by car and on the train, and in parting, Mussolini said to Hitler: "We have a common cause, Führer!"

---

* The book, *Storia di un anno*, was first published as a series of articles by an "anonymous" author, accounting for the references to Mussolini in the third person. The book was published in 1944 and translated as *The Fall of Mussolini: His Own Story*, New York, 1948.

If the meeting went just as the Duce described, it is difficult to understand why the two dictators did not simply talk over the phone. The proceedings were in fact very different, so much so that it can be considered among one of the most crucial conferences between the two Axis partners. On the one hand, the Führer revealed his immediate strategy regarding Italy, while on the other hand, Mussolini simply confirmed by his silence that he was now passively expecting events to provide the solution to the problems that confronted the Fascist regime and Italy itself.

Before the string of cars reached San Fermo, General Keitel was able to confide to Rintelen that the real objective of the meeting was "to concentrate all power in the Duce's hands, to erase the influence of the House of Savoy, and to send Nazi reinforcements into Italy to place the country firmly under the control of the German high command." If what Rintelen reported was true, then the Duce displayed considerable courage, on July 19, 1943, in opposing, by his passive behavior, an absurd threat by Hitler, while keeping the entire matter completely secret. According to historian Ruggero Zangrandi, Mussolini's dignified behavior can be explained either by the Duce's devotion to the King or by his long-meditated-on decision to quickly take Italy out of the Axis alliance. These motivations were certainly legitimate, especially the first one, if only because during those very hours the King himself was plotting with Acquarone and Ambrosio to remove Mussolini.

In his memoirs, Bastianini relates that during the train trip, Keitel had a heated argument with Ambrosio concerning German short-term plans on the eastern front and in the Mediterranean. The German general could barely restrain himself under a pressing question from Ambrosio: "I could see his cheeks redden even more and his hairy hand continuously wiping his forehead and temples, both dripping with perspiration, with a handkerchief. Ambrosio was constantly challenging him: 'You declare that you are not worried by the situation in Russia, that your reserves are fine, that all your losses have been replaced, and then you say that you do not have the necessary supplies to allow Italian soldiers to defend their own soil from the enemy. The truth is that you do not have those reserves and the Russian front is far from secure.' Keitel had obviously not been authorized by Hitler to deal with the Italians. At one point he cut short the dramatic skirmish and said: 'All these issues will be handled by our leaders among themselves.'

At 11:00 a.m. in the vast ballroom of Villa Gaggia, after a somewhat unfriendly comment; _"Nein, Duze, so geht es nicht"_ ("No, Duce, it doesn't work"), the Führer began his customary soliloquy with interpreter Paul Schmidt at his side. His presentation began with a strategic and political premise. The main issue requiring immediate attention was that of raw materials, without which, of course, no war could be won. For this reason, his priority was to defend all those territories under German military occupation that could deliver the means to bring about victory. The principle of this philosophy was to keep all German lands as far removed from the fighting as possible. It was true that there were some fearful individuals in Germany who would have welcomed an understanding with Russia. "And I," said Hitler vehemently, "will reject their suggestions for the simple reason that not even 300 hundred years from now would Germany produce another leader like myself, capable of solving the eastern problem."

Hitler then went on to examine the question of armaments' supply, arguing that the air force and submarine fleet would have to fulfill decisive tasks in the near future. Germany was about to introduce new aircraft into the war having exceptional performance capabilities, as well as U-boats equipped with special instrumentation. New tanks would soon appear, the gigantic _Panther_ was going into record production and would soon confront the Russians. In the spring of 1944, forty-six newly formed and perfectly trained and equipped divisions would be ready. To further sweeten the good news he was giving his audience, Hitler mentioned two powerful new weapons, which would be used against Great Britain during the winter. The Führer had kept this announcement for the end of his introduction, perhaps to prepare his listeners for some unpleasant remarks concerning the behavior of the Italian army.

His revelations regarding the diabolical weapons were true. The project had progressed since his meeting with Mussolini at Klessheim in April. Twelve days before the conference at San Fermo, there had been a historic meeting at German headquarters that included the Führer, General Walter Dornberger, Dr. Werner von Braun, and the builders of the world's first military missile, known as the V2 rocket. They were the "magicians" of Peenemünde, the ultrasecret base of Usedom on the Baltic. Since May 1937, Peenemünde was the location of the new weapons engineering built and managed by Luftwaffe and Wehrmacht personnel. Suddenly, at 11:30 a.m. on July 7, 1943, the directors of the project were ordered to report to Rastenburg. Dornberger and von Braun quickly boarded a Heinkel III, piloted by another expert from the plant, Commander Ernst Steinhoff. The plane landed near Rastenburg at 1:00 p.m. but the group had to wait seven hours before being introduced into the Führer's study. Von Braun remembered the moment this way:

"Hitler appeared, accompanied by Field Marshal Keitel, General Jodl, General Walter Buhle, the Army Chief of Staff and Armaments Minister Albert Speer. Hitler's physical appearance was frightening. I had last seen him in 1939. He looked tired but still radiated an almost magic strength. His eyes had something diabolical in them, but his face was pale, and he looked like a beaten man. Dornberger was also concerned by Hitler's looks. Stalingrad had taken place just six months earlier. The Don River front had buckled. The Kursk offensive, the Zittadelle plan, which had started two days earlier on July 5, had already stopped. The hit-and-run war in the Atlantic was over. The Allies were fighting in Sicily, and the air war was considered lost."

The program was to show Hitler a film about the successful experiment of October 3, 1942: a thirteen-and-one-half-ton rocket—called "A4"—had effected the trajectory from the ramp to point X in the open sea about 200 kilometers from Peenemünde.

After giving Dornberger and von Braun a warm greeting, Hitler sat in the front row between Keitel and Speer. The documentary described the details of the experiment, and von Braun illustrated the images as they appeared on the screen. When the lights went on, no one spoke for a few minutes; there was absolute silence. Suddenly Hitler jumped out of his seat and went over to the two men from Peenemünde, shook their hands and said as emphatically as possible:

"I thank you. Why did I not believe in the success of your research? Had I had these missiles back in 1939, we would never have gone to war. In the face of such a missile, we can only say that Europe and the world, now and in the future, have both become too small for a war. With such weapons, war will become impossible for humanity."

He then asked the question that was foremost on his mind: "Is it possible to increase the payload of the missiles from one to ten tons?"

Dornberger and von Braun replied that they would need another four years to make a missile such as the Führer described. Hitler was satisfied and after promoting von Braun to "full professor," on July 25, 1943, he signed an order giving Peenemünde absolute precedence over all other armament programs. Four days later, Propaganda Minister Goebbels said in a speech at Heidelberg: "By the end of the war, the German people will have to get on their knees to thank their technicians, builders, inventors, and researchers. The British will be amazed . . . " But the road to success would be very long. The technicians of Peenemünde had to overcome many obstacles, and in those weeks they also became a target of enemy bombers. The first V1 "flying bomb" was scheduled to be fired on London at 4:18 a.m. on June 14, 1944 (eight days after the Allies had landed on the beaches of Normandy during the D-Day invasion). The firing of the missile would take place only fourteen months after the July 7 meeting. The first V2 rocket would be launched on the London suburbs of Chiswick and Epping at 6:43 p.m. on September 8, 1944. But by then Germany had already lost the war.

Hitler was in the middle of his monologue, when in the ballroom of the Villa Gaggia appeared an emotional and very pale De

Cesare, who whispered to Mussolini: "Rome is under violent bombardment by the enemy." The Duce gave De Cesare's interruption only a few lines in his own chronicle of that day: "The news was given to Hitler and the other participants by Mussolini himself, and this created a very painful impression. During the rest of the Führer's presentation, more news kept coming about the Allied bombing of Rome."

Mussolini was somewhat disguising the truth. Hitler was not so much displeased by the fact that Rome was being bombed, as he was annoyed at being interrupted during his talk. He had little reason to be unhappy about the fact that the Eternal City was under fire when Berlin and the largest German cities were by now under constant attack and reduced, in many parts, to rubble. The Führer had no reaction to the Duce's news.

"Probably," as von Plehwe wrote, "Mussolini expected some kind of statement of sympathy from Hitler in the face of extensive destruction of the city. Hitler appeared not to have heard what had been said. He just continued with his plans on the future conduct of the war."

It was close to noon and the time for reprimands was at hand. Hitler said that according to his information Italian soldiers had not really fought in Africa or Sicily. The Italian high command had not been able to fulfill its mission. The civilian administration had shown itself to be weak. There was defeatism everywhere. The notes made by interpreter Schmidt show that, in spite of these remarks, Hitler gave his Italian allies assurances that the Reich would do its utmost to help on the southern front. Obviously Italian requests for equipment and supplies, said the Führer, were much too great to be satisfied. To transfer two thousand aircraft to the Mediterranean was out of the question. On that issue, he criticized the lack of well-equipped air bases and the atrocious assistance given to units of the Luftwaffe, operating in Italy for some time. The Italian government must lengthen the landing strips and expropriate the necessary land without any regard for the owners. The discipline of the troops had to be improved through military courts martial. As for Sicily, he would examine the possibility of sending new reinforcements and other artillery. Hitler then went on to the problem of communications between Sardinia, Corsica, and the islands of the Dodecanesus, overlooking the fact that Italy did not need advice but, rather, merchant ships, warships, and fuel.

Sicily was the most urgent problem demanding a solution. The Führer said that with the necessary supplies, a counterattack could be launched. Should this become impossible, then the best course of action would be to withdraw from the island. Hitler said he was aware of the consequences such a decision would have on morale, adding that to protect the influx of reinforcements, Marshal Göring was ready to concentrate a significant number of antiaircraft artillery at the Straits of Messina. A final decision was necessary: should the decisive battle take place on the Italian mainland, therefore making it useless to dispatch more units into Sicily, or was it imperative to hold on to the island with all the consequences it would imply, including a unified command structure? Germany would then transfer other excellent divisions to the south. Finally Hitler concluded: "The struggle of the Fascist revolution and the National Socialist Party for victory is a task that cannot be left to the next generation."

It was by now 1:00 p.m. and Mussolini, up until then, despite his strong resolutions of the day before, had said virtually nothing. He had remained seated, with his legs crossed over the edge of the armchair that was too wide and too deep, listening patiently and impassively to Hitler's endless sermonizing. According to eyewitnesses, he appeared to be indifferent to what was going on in the ballroom. He shifted positions from time to time to avoid sliding with the cushion. He would draw his left hand behind his back and press on a spot that obviously hurt him. He stared at Hitler with a tired and beaten look, while the German dictator, in an increasingly high-pitched voice, continued to shower the Italians with all kinds of recriminations.

Mussolini could only interrupt Hitler's monologue to read the short dispatches that De Cesare would slip him about the bombing of Rome. Like a radio journalist, he would read them in Italian, then translate them into German. One such message made the Duce very anxious: "The violent attack continues. Four hundred bombers are flying at low altitude. Suburbs and buildings in the center are destroyed. Little reaction from the antiaircraft guns."

It was finally time for lunch. Hitler and Mussolini were in a living room alone, with the windows shut. There were no direct witnesses to this lunch, but it appears that the Duce did not eat at all, while the Führer displayed an excellent appetite as he ate white rice with béchamel sauce, cooked vegetables, cake, and fresh fruit. During the meal, Hitler reiterated his decision to pursue the war against Russia, rejecting another attempt by Mussolini to negotiate an armistice or a cease-fire with Moscow. He also spoke about the secret weapons, stating that some could be used as early as the end of next month, and of the new submarines with special equipment that would make it difficult for the enemy to locate them. Hitler concluded with a demand that the Duce liquidate the traitors of Fascism and beware of the King.

Mussolini did not share confidences with his friend and kept silent on the difficult political times he faced in Rome. He did not even mention the promise he had made to the hierarchy of the Fascist party to call a meeting of the Grand Council of Fascism. The German proposal to move all Italian divisions to southern Italy, leaving all the German units to guard the Alps and the Po Valley, was not really touched upon during the Führer's conference or the private meetings with the Duce, and not even during the clashes between Keitel and Ambrosio.

After lunch, the two dictators went to their rooms to rest. Hitler was given the room of the daughter-in-law of the owner, Senator Achille Gaggia. The Duce went to the main bedroom. It was now 2:00 p.m. While Hitler's footsteps could be heard down the marble hall as he went to his room, Mussolini was stopped by Alfieri, Bastianini, and Ambrosio, all three extremely excited by the news from Rome. The Duce stopped them by saying: "I am very unhappy to be away from the capital at this time. I would not like the people of Rome to think . . ."

will give this any thought, because every Italian expects a momentous decision to come out of these meetings. Did you hear what Hitler is saying? It's your turn to counterattack, Duce. How much longer must Italy passively follow Germany and be transformed into a bastion?" "A supporting wall," corrected Mussolini. Alfieri went on: "For this reason you must answer Hitler with the same kind of brutal candor. The situation is serious. And if our army is in no condition to resist effectively, as General Ambrosio says—"

"I can absolutely confirm what you are saying," Mussolini interrupted. "We must have the courage to face reality. If we must break away we should do it immediately. As long as the carabinieri are in control.* Tomorrow could be too late." Mussolini looked at the two men and, after a few moments, continued: "Don't you think I have thought about this problem and it has haunted me for some time now? Behind my mask of apparent indifference, there is a deep, troubling anxiety. I can accept the idea: break away from Germany. What would the consequences be? The enemy will rightly demand a capitulation. Are we ready to erase twenty years of this regime? To accept Italy's first military and political defeat? And then what would Hitler's attitude be? Do you really think he would simply give us our freedom of action?"

Alfieri replied: "I know of some neutral countries that would be willing to assist us in opening up discussions." Bastianini concurred: "There are possibilities in this direction. This very night, if I am authorized to do so, I can begin to make contacts. In the next twenty-four hours, I could inform you in detail." But this was not to Mussolini's liking. He turned away from his staff and went into his room.

The meetings were over. An hour later, the Duce had the Führer informed that whenever he was ready, they could return to Treviso. At about 3:00 p.m. the cars went back to the railroad station at

---

* In time of war, they are the Italian army's military police. In peacetime, the carabinieri are one of the civilian police forces.

Feltre. Hitler's plane left Treviso at about 5:00 p.m. As they said good-bye, Mussolini shouted over the noise of the propellers to Hitler: "Führer, we have a common cause!" Then turning to General Keitel he said: "Send us everything we need, since we are all in the same boat."

Hitler's plane was still in the air when Ambrosio, Bastianini, and Alfieri approached Mussolini, who, as soon he saw them, said: "There was no need for that discussion with Hitler, because this time he promised to send me all the help we requested." The Duce's three assistants at San Fermo had hoped that, having explained their position, and Ambrosio having even spoken of giving the Germans a two-week ultimatum, Mussolini would at last tell Hitler during the train trip back to Feltre, what he had not said during the morning. A long silence followed Mussolini's words. Ambrosio thought there was no sense in wasting any more time with a man he already considered the "former" head of the Italian government.

According to German military attaché, Rintelen, the Duce pointed out during the return trip by train the critical situation Italy was in, only to repeat his request for help, since he could not bring himself to admit that the war was now lost. Hitler reassured him, saying that he would quickly dispatch new divisions because the defense of Italy was in Germany's interest. A conversation that took place in another compartment of the train, between Keitel and Ambrosio, turned out to be more significant. The German general, emboldened by what had been said at San Fermo, declared that Italy could not expect more help if certain conditions were not met: increasing troop strength dedicated to an efficient line of defense, each country to contribute two divisions; using the narrow area between Calabria and Puglia as the best place to stop the enemy; reaching an agreement to effectively control southern Italy militarily. Ambrosio responded evasively. These conditions assumed the complete evacuation of Sicily. Ambrosio told Bastianini: "Mussolini is still harboring illusions and did not take my words seriously. I tell you he is crazy, completely crazy. What I told him is a very serious matter."

Just as the Italians were leaving Treviso, to return to Rome, the Eternal City was being hit by a second bombing raid. Mussolini was thoughtful; he was preparing both his coming moves and especially what he would tell the King. Ambrosio was also worried, not just because of the results of the last conference, which actually facilitated the task of those who were planning to rid Italy of Mussolini and Fascism, but because he had been informed of the death, during the bombing raids, of the commander of the carabinieri, General Azzolino Hazon, one of the main conspirators in the anti-Duce plot. Ambrosio was worried that Hazon could accidentally have left sensitive documents in his office, thus compromising the plotters. No one yet knew the name of his successor, a choice for Mussolini to make. These worries turned out to be unfounded because Hazon had not made the kind of mistakes Ambrosio feared and because the chief of staff was able to secure the nomination of the trustworthy General Angelo Cerica as commander of the carabinieri and have him report to Acquarone during the evening of July 22.

In the meantime, the official communiqué of the San Fermo meetings was made public. It turned out to be a very understated and misleading document, given the usual rhetoric used on such occasions: "The Duce and the Führer have held a meeting at a location in northern Italy. The discussions covered military issues." It was said that Mussolini wanted to avoid its publication, but that he changed his mind when he became convinced he had to justify his absence from Rome while the city was being pounded by American bombers. The Duce's plane landed at 7:00 p.m. Centocelle airfield, since the other two airports had been damaged in the bombing. Mussolini wrote in his memoirs:

"Just before flying over Mount Soratte, the city of Rome appeared to the crew of the Duce's plane, as if it were covered by a huge black cloud. It was the smoke emanating from hundreds of burning railway cars at Littorio station which had just been bombed. The airport hanger had been destroyed and the landing strip was damaged. Flying over Rome, from Littorio to Centocelle, one could see that this was a massive attack and that the damage was extensive. Few high-ranking officials were at the airport to greet Mussolini. He went to the Villa Torlonia by car. On the streets, were throngs of men, women, and children, in cars, on bicycles, or on foot, burdened with luggage and home necessities, all going toward the suburbs and the countryside. Not just a throng, but rather a river of people."

Rome had been warned by thousands of paper flyers scattered by Allied aircraft over the suburbs and the airports during the night of July 16-17 that a massive air raid was in the making. Italy's capital had been left untouched by bombing raids for over three years of war for a number of reasons. There was the Pope and Vatican City, and the fact that British aircraft were unable to cover the range over the Mediterranean. And even when US long-range bombers were finally available, President Roosevelt initially withheld his approval, mostly for electoral reasons relating to the Catholic vote in the United States.

But the changes in the war after the Sicily landings had prompted General Eisenhower to request Roosevelt's approval to hit Axis sanctuaries, such as railroad depots and airports in Rome: those key traffic points for north-south communications in Italy. Eisenhower's thinking was that no monument however beautiful or historically valuable was worth the life of even one of his men. The British had no objection to the American request. The operation included 270 bombers, 158 Flying Fortresses of the Twelfth Allied Air Force stationed in Tunisia, and 112 Liberators from the Ninth Air Force in Benghazi.

According to historian Giorgio Bonacina, Eisenhower gave orders to pick flight crews that would have no anti-Catholic prejudice and exclude any Catholics who wished to be excused from this mission as well as any other bomber crews who did not think of Rome as a very special objective. At 11:13 a.m. on July 19, 1943, just as Hitler was beginning his monologue at San Fermo, American bombers began hitting the districts of the Prenestino, the Tiburtino, the university center, some parts of the polyclinic, the cemetery of Verano, and the basilica of San Lorenzo Fuori Le Mura that was bombed into rubble. Railroad stations were also hit and so severely damaged that it took several days to reestablish normal rail traffic. More tragic was the high number of civilian victims: over 1,500 dead and wounded.

During the afternoon there was a second wave of 321 twin-engine bombers, Marauder, Mitchell, and Lightning, that were concentrating their bombing on the airports of Ciampino and Littorio, forcing the Duce's plane to land at Centocelle. There were a total of 591 Allied planes engaged over Rome on July 19. During the morning, Italian fighter planes were almost paralyzed by the surprise attack, but that afternoon some thirty of them took to the air, and a Mitchell and a Marauder were shot down. Galeazzo Ciano followed the scene from his living room, hurrying to pass drinks around to his guests. Filippo Anfuso, on leave from his post as ambassador to Budapest, was present:

"Ciano was staying at home due to 'political' illness with his hands deep into many conspiracies. From the windows of Ciano's apartment, I could see the dark clouds of smoke from the bombing by Eisenhower's planes fade slowly toward the west . . . Ciano made a sweeping gesture at the whole scene and asked me 'Did you see that?', as if accusing me of having somehow been responsible for this particular bombing raid, but also to include those he felt were responsible for the war in general, including myself. Countesses and princesses were walking around the room; Galeazzo never gave up his role as the center of Roman social life.

"The ladies said very little and were amused to see who would be on his blacklist. He began to criticize Mussolini so much that one countess decided to close the windows…Then he turned on me: 'And what would you do now?' The countesses looked to see how I would respond to the challenge. 'Well,' I replied timidly, 'first I would defend Sicily! At all costs. There is nothing else to do.' He laughed heartily at my words. The countesses were also amused, but their laughter was subdued."

The following morning Mussolini went to visit the areas that had been bombed. "I was always received with warmth by the people everywhere I went," he later said. The pope and the King had also made the rounds the day before, right after the raids. The King, as his Adjutant General Paolo Puntoni was to write, was welcomed by insults and boos as he passed through a hostile and silent crowd. Pius XII was much more successful—after invoking God's help for the city of which he was bishop.

The eyewitness accounts of the San Fermo meeting varied, depending upon the participant. Dino Alfieri replied to questions from embassy staff in Berlin:

"We have decided to draw the line in Sicily. But absolutely no breaking away from the Axis. The two leaders spoke to each other cordially like old comrades. Hitler made a complete description of the current situation. He promised to transfer several divisions into Italy. He is certain of victory. All of us, myself, Ambrosio, and Bastianini spoke our minds very clearly with the Duce. I think the Führer told him some important things in confidence, possibly the reasons for his being absolutely certain of victory."

The Reich chancellery also wanted news on the post-"Feltre" meetings, as the San Fermo conference was erroneously being dubbed, because the Germans, always precise and respectful of protocol, were thinking about the Duce's sixtieth birthday celebration on July 29, 1943. The Führer was preparing a valuable gift for Mussolini and planned to be present while Goebbels, knowing it would please Hitler, had prepared an impressive program of events in Germany to honor the founder of Fascism.

The King was briefed in advance about the conference at San Fermo by General Ambrosio and Montezemolo. On the evening of July 19, as soon as he was back in his office, Ambrosio wrote a memorandum of the conference ending with the following words:

"Since the German units will not be ready for about two months, and since the most urgent measures are to reinforce the defense of southern Italy, it becomes necessary to move all the Italian army units in northern Italy to the south, including the Alpine divisions and those divisions that are currently being reorganized. These units will be replaced later with German units as mentioned above."

Ruggero Zangrandi observed correctly: "These proposals by the Italian high command on the evening of July 19 came after the decision had been made to do away with Fascism and to end the relationship with the Germans. Ambrosio already knew his orders from the King, and one may wonder whether the coup d'état could not have had much worse consequences than it did."

Mussolini had also decided to set the final date for the meeting of the Grand Council of Fascism, moving it from July 21 to Saturday, July 24 at 5:00 p.m. The invitation was delivered to the twenty-eight Fascist party leaders. A postscript requested that the interested parties wear "…Fascist uniform: black bush jacket and gray-green riding breeches." The Duce's decision was interpreted by some as coming as a result of a meeting with the King, to whom Mussolini had reported that morning about the Feltre conference. A year later, Mussolini would write:

"Mussolini met with the King, who was nervous and in a bad mood. 'A very tense situation,' the King said. 'It cannot last too long. Sicily is lost by now. The Germans will deal us a low blow. Discipline among the troops is deteriorating. The airmen at Ciampino field fled all the way to Velletri during the attack. They call this "spacing out." I followed the attack of the other day from Villa Ada, with bombers flying overhead. I don't believe, as it was said, that there were four hundred planes. The number was half that. They flew in perfect formation. The fiction of the "Holy City" is over with. We must tell the Germans about this."

On August 19, 1943, during his imprisonment under the Badoglio government, under the title "Musings of a Dictator,"* Mussolini wrote the notes which were the raw material for his book, *Storia di un anno,* regarding the Feltre-San Fermo conference:

"My week of sorrows, if I may refer to it in this way, began exactly one month ago during my meeting with the Führer. That meeting was supposed to last four days, just like the preceding one

---

* Wilhelm Höttl, *The Secret Front,* Ch.XIV Praeger 1954.

at Salzburg, and Feltre, near the border, had been chosen for security reasons. The date had not been set. Following the events in Sicily, we chose July 19 . . . Right on time, at 9:00 a.m., the Führer landed at Treviso airport, reviewed the troops, and then we left for the railroad station. We took the train, and one hour later we got off before the station at Feltre. From there, we drove in an open car under a broiling sun for an hour to the villa owned by Senator Gaggia: a nightmarish labyrinth of large and small rooms. I exchanged only a few meaningless words with the Führer . . . He spoke first for about two hours . . . After his presentation, I had my first meeting alone with him.

"He told me two things: The submarine offensive would start anew with updated equipment, and at the end of August, the air force would begin retaliatory raids over London, which would be destroyed within one week. I replied that while we waited for these attacks, Italy's defense had to be greatly reinforced . . . During the hour I spent with the Führer on the return trip by train, I explained to him that Italy had to withstand the power of two empires, Great Britain and the United States, which threatened to crush us. And the bombing of cities not only damaged the morale of the population but war production as well . . . I repeated to him once again that the African campaign would have ended differently if only we had air power at least equal to that of the enemy. I also told him that tension among the population was now very high and becoming dangerous in the country. Hitler said that, in his view, the Italian crisis was one of a lack of direction and that he would order air reinforcements and new divisions to defend the peninsula . . . The conversation was always very friendly, and we said good-bye like old comrades . . . At 6:00 p.m. I went back to Rome . . .

"That evening, from Villa Torlonia, we could still see the lights of the fires in the sky. Rome had just endured a terrible day of fire, and the bombing had destroyed what little hope there was and created an unpredictable situation. During the next few days, I visited the worst-hit locations . . . I gave orders not to mention it in the papers. The enemies of the regime were spreading rumors within

Rome that the Feltre meeting had been a failure and had yielded no results, that Germany was leaving us in the lurch, and that after taking Sicily, the British could reach Rome with little or no opposition. All this increased the nervous tension that preceded a collapse."

It should be noted that when a very superstitious Mussolini celebrated alone in captivity the first month's anniversary of the July 19 meeting at San Fermo he wrote: "Every time I met Hitler in or near Venice, some disastrous events followed." Actually the first meeting, on June 15, 1934, was followed both by the failed Nazi attempted coup in Vienna and the assassination of Chancellor Dollfuss, the Duce's personal friend and ally, and the liquidation of Ernst Röhm. The second meeting in the Veneto region, at Feltre on July 19, 1943, was followed by Mussolini's own overthrow and the dissolution in a few hours of the Fascist party itself. This anti-Hitler pronouncement could have cost Mussolini dearly. Right after his liberation on September 12, 1943, Mussolini was taken to Vienna. That night, the Gestapo was able to steal his personal diaries from his room at the Hotel Continental while he slept. The documents were quickly translated by the SS and transmitted to the Reich chancellery. In the confusion, the Duce had not noticed the theft.

A few months later, through a priest, Don Giusto Pancino, Mussolini would learn the truth just before a meeting with Hitler. It was a bad surprise for the Duce. Shortly before his death, Don Pancino told the author, he remembered that once with bravado, Mussolini had written a very foolish note but actually attributed the anecdote to the King, who in anger had told the Duce: "Hitler is a jinx: every time he comes to Italy, something awful happens." Mussolini had also written that Bottai called Hitler "a ridiculous mouse." In any case, Hitler never made any mention of all this to Mussolini, due either to lack of time or inclination.

According to Dino Grandi, Mussolini's decision to call a meeting of the Grand Council of Fascism was the result of the conference at Feltre and not because of the situation in Rome: "It may seem incredible, but it was Hitler himself who pushed Mussolini to call the Grand Council meeting. Hitler said he was convinced the Duce was surrounded by traitors within the government and in the Grand Council. But it was because of the Führer that the Duce, as soon as he returned to Rome, ordered the Fascist party secretary to call a meeting of the Grand Council. It may seem an unlikely story, but it is the truth."

Mussolini received Grandi at 5:00 p.m. on Thursday, July 22, for a purely administrative reason. But it was in fact an extreme attempt by the "rebels" to convince Mussolini to withdraw voluntarily and not be voted down by the "Grandi Agenda," which was by now well known in its main points.

Grandi wrote: "Mussolini listened to me without interrupting or objecting, as I anticipated, and without expressing any kind of anger. When I finished, he only said these words that I shall never forget: 'You will repeat everything you just told me at the meeting of the Grand Council. It could be useful to the country if it is in fact true that the war is lost. I cannot reveal to you some extremely important military secrets; but just be aware that very soon Germany will come out with an extremely powerful secret weapon that will completely reverse the course of the war. Germany and Italy will win this war. Everything else we shall discuss at the Grand Council." According to Grandi, Mussolini had been well indoctrinated at Feltre with information about the V2 missile which was to reverse the course of the war in favor of the Axis once again. That the Führer had asked Mussolini to keep the information secret is proved by the fact that the Duce also withheld this information from the King during their July 21 meeting, when he could easily have hinted at some big new weapon being prepared by the German war machine.

Perhaps the Duce told the truth about Feltre to his old friend, Manlio Morgagni, president of the Stefani News Agency and the only person to commit suicide at the news of Mussolini's arrest: "The Germans are strong and could very well effectively intervene to plug and possibly resolve the situation in Italy, which has become very difficult. But they don't trust us. Before they come in, they are demanding the command of the entire Italian front, including the home front. This is a precondition that neither the Italian people nor I can accept."

During the afternoon of July 21, Roberto Farinacci, the "leader" of Cremona and one of the extreme pro-German fascist diehards, was given a brief but accurate forecast events to come by retired Marshal Ugo Cavallero: "Be more and more careful. Grandi and his group—Bottai, Ciano, and others—are conspiring to overthrow Mussolini, but their game will not succeed, because the Crown is conducting its own struggle in the same direction with Duke Acquarone." A few hours later, Fascist Party Secretary Carlo Scorza, was informed by a police detective that during a tapped phone conversation, Marshal Badoglio and Duke Acquarone agreed to "bundle up the Duce as he leaves Villa Savoia." Mussolini became angry when he was told of these conspiracies but said only: "I hate mystery stories," making the mistake of not believing what he felt, were alarmist messages that were reaching him. In reality, the King had already agreed to a meeting on Monday, July 26, during the routine visit that took place at the beginning of the week, the second visit would always take place on Thursdays.

Mussolini was confident that his own charisma would be sufficient to overcome any kind of trap that had been set for him, and that he, in a sense, had also set up for himself by calling the meeting of the highest institution of the Fascist party. To Chierici who had just been named to replace Senise as chief of police, he said:

"Believe me . . . these Grand Council members are of low, very low intelligence, wobbly in their convictions, and without much courage. These people live in someone else's shadow: if the source of light should disappear, they too would be cast back into the darkness from whence they came . . . they just want to believe that I can easily bring back to the stable a Grandi, a Bottai, and even Count Ciano, who I feel is being too obvious in his impatience to replace me."

At this time, Grandi was "campaigning" for his agenda in advance of the Grand Council meeting, which would place Mussolini in a minority position after a vote. He enlisted men like Federzoni, De Vecchi, Bastianini, Albini, De Marsico, Bignardi, De Stefani,

Balella, and De Bono. The Crown was looking at the post-Mussolini era in much more practical terms. Acquarone was handling the details of a military coup with Generals Ambrosio, Castellano, and Cerica, as well as former Chief of Police Senise, who was to be reinstated in his old job. Had this entire matter not been the most devastating and far-reaching crisis of modern Italian history, it could be described as a light comedy.

The main beneficiary of the coup, Marshal of Italy Pietro Badoglio, was sitting on the sidelines. Everyone was working for his success while he played bridge with friends in his magnificent villa in Rome, built on land donated to him by the city as a gift from the grateful people of Italy for his wartime contributions. The seventy-two-year-old former chief of the general staff was concentrating on the list of names of those who were to be arrested once he replaced Mussolini as head of the government. According to dozens of witnesses, chroniclers, and historians, during the evening of July 19, 1943 the King made the final decision to remove Mussolini, after Rome was bombed and after learning that the summit at San Fermo had not produced concrete results either for the breakup of the Axis alliance or the serious defense of Italy itself. General Castellano wrote in 1963, even though this was to be contradicted by many other sources: "While the meeting was taking place at Feltre, the big news was that the King had finally made up his mind and lifted the uncertainty we had been living with for so many months. Acquarone told me, since Ambrosio was attending the conference, that the King would replace Mussolini with Marshal Badoglio."

General Castellano's version of these events and their timing places the decision to effect the coup more or less at the same time as the meeting of the Grand Council. Castellano further states that at noon on July 24, five hours before the meeting, Ambrosio, Acquarone, and he himself, all went together to see Marshal Badoglio.

"I was meeting the marshal for the first time. Acquarone told him that the King had finally decided to replace Mussolini and would name [Badoglio] head of the government. He showed him the proclamation, written by former Prime Minister Orlando, that Badoglio would read on radio and asked for the marshal's opinion. Badoglio agreed." The proclamation included the famous phrase: "La guerra continua..." [The war goes on...]

Badoglio showed little interest in all these formalities and relished his nomination to be the next head of the Italian government.

It is therefore surprising at this point that the coup would remain a mystery only to the Germans in Rome, as it appears from a telegram sent by Rintelen from the German embassy to Berlin, commenting upon the Feltre conference: "The Italian high command is very much worried that more German troops are not available to hold the front in Italy. It had always been thought that the opening of a second front in the Mediterranean would have triggered the dispatch of a heavy German contingent, especially armored units. The population is constantly depressed. The public doesn't believe in even the minimal chances of victory and rejects any attempt to be influenced by the press or the radio. We have reached the point where the people only hope in the future generosity of the enemy."

The German high command was not satisfied with this report and requested that Rintelen provide more details as to the Italian political situation, a source of concern for the Führer. Rintelen cabled back at noon the next day, while the King was informing Badoglio of his nomination: "After the meeting at Feltre, the main question on the minds of all competent political and military groups is the doubt that Germany will be able to help Italy enough in its defensive battle against the invaders. The Grand Council of Fascism is meeting on July 24. Given the situation, this meeting is to be considered extremely important. There is a rumor that a group within the Grand Council will request a stronger, more energetic government. It is also rumored that the Duce will be invited to give up the direction of all three defense ministries."

For some time, the German embassy in Rome had been undergoing an internal crisis. It started in March 1942, when the Italian secret police, the OVRA, caught one of the embassy's officials, Kurt

Sauer, in the act of spying for the Soviet Union. The Germans had reacted badly at being humiliated in the eyes of the Italians, who had decided to apply the letter of the law and promptly executed the traitor by firing squad, over German protests. The German delegation was a microcosm of German society of the times. All social strata were represented: Ambassador von Mackensen was the son of a field marshal; he was seconded by Prince von Bismarck, von Plehwe, and Rintelen, all three of whom were assisted by a group of brilliant and very aristocratic young men from the best families in the country. There was also a very strong group of newly arrived Nazis, including SS Lieutenant Colonel Eugen Dollmann, powerful enough to influence the cautious Prussian, von Mackensen, who was always careful to convey a picture of Italy that corresponded to the Führer's fantasies. Von Mackensen went overboard when, on the evening of July 25, he sent a cable to Ribbentrop, stating that the situation in Rome was, in the final analysis, under Mussolini's control. Much to the ambassador's bad luck, the message reached Berlin at the same time as the news that the Duce had been arrested. Von Mackensen was to pay for his bad luck thirteen days later during the meeting at Tarvisio, the only post-Mussolini Italian-German meeting. The ambassador was ordered back to Germany by Ribbentrop on the spot. Dollmann wrote:

"On the platform of the railway station at Tarvisio, Dr. Schmidt whispered to me that the true reason for von Mackensen's recall was due to Ribbentrop's outrage at the cable of July 25, where the ambassador used information from Buffarini-Guidi in a conversation that took place in my presence, where he stated that the situation was serious but not really dramatic. Von Mackensen was replaced with Rudolf Rahn, who represented the 'new line' of the Wilhelmstrasse."

At 5:00 p.m. on July 24, 1943, Benito Mussolini was about to make his entrance at the Grand Council meeting. The situation in Rome was complex and confused. Every conspirator was living with the fear that he would suddenly be attacked by the wounded "target." The history of the Grand Council session has been described in great detail by many participants, friends and foes alike.

One of the most important chapters of Mussolini's _Storia di un anno_ describes the events as follows: "In Mussolini's mind, the Grand Council was supposed to be a confidential meeting, where everyone could ask for and obtain explanations, a sort of secret committee. Since a long discussion was to be expected, rather than beginning at 10:00 p.m. as usual, the meeting began at 5:00 p.m." After describing the military situation and criticizing the behavior of generals and admirals who had not held the line and defended their positions in Africa, at Pantelleria, and now in Sicily, he went on to say: "I must be the most disobeyed man in Italy."

He did not hesitate to reprimand Rommel for the decisions that had driven the Axis to defeat at El Alamein. Mussolini said the German commander was a brave military leader, always on the front line, and a great tactician, but when it came to strategy, he had nothing to teach the Italian generals. In closing, he posed the dramatic dilemma: war or peace? Mussolini told the Grand Council members the risks they faced in the event of easy, last-minute choices which could not change the situation. Then came a long debate where Grandi, Bottai, and Ciano played the most important roles. An attempt to adjourn the meeting to the next day was rejected and the Council came to a vote. The Grandi Agenda, which, in effect, stripped the Duce of his power and returned it to the King, carried the vote with nineteen in favor, seven against, and two abstentions.

Before the vote was counted, however, Bastianini said that the war could only have a political solution and requested permission to begin talks with the Allies. Alfieri, in support of the proposal coming from the undersecretary for foreign affairs, said: "In Germany, the certainty in victory has been shaken. We will not get a single plane, tank, or gun from the Germans. If Berlin were shown an acceptable way to end the conflict, they wouldn't even think about us and have no further hesitation to seek peace." Offended in his pride, Mussolini replied: "What Alfieri is saying is in direct contradiction with what I was told at Feltre by the Führer himself. However, we must take it into consideration."

Finally, Mussolini commented with some disgust on the point in the Grandi Agenda that said: "We invite the head of the government to ask His Majesty the King to accept the offer to take effective command of the armed forces that . . . " Mussolini had asked: "What does this sentence mean? Let's assume that the King agrees to resume his command of the armed forces. The question is whether I agree to be decapitated. I am sixty years old, and I know what certain things ultimately mean. It's therefore preferable to speak to each other very clearly!" And, according to Bottai, he uttered the mysterious sentence: "And then I tell you I have in my hand a key that can resolve the military situation. But I shall not tell you what it is." He was clearly referring to the new secret weapons about which Hitler had sworn him to utmost secrecy.

Once the results of the vote had been read, "everyone left in silence," wrote Mussolini. It was 2:40 a.m. on July 25, 1943. The Duce went to his study, where he was quickly joined by the small group who had voted against the Grandi Agenda. At 3:00 a.m. he left the Palazzo Venezia. During the night that went down in history as the "Night of the Grand Council," the discussion lasted ten hours. Almost everyone spoke and some more than once. It is probable that a crisis would have taken place even without the meeting and the vote on the Grandi Agenda, but impossible to say. Perhaps the cup was full, but it was the famous last drop that made it overflow.

The biggest surprise would be in store for Grandi himself, the first Fascist leader the King would actually remove, even before Mussolini. The King made the decision rather quickly and gave the task to the accommodating Acquarone, who would inform the interested party. Right after the Grand Council meeting Grandi went to his office at Montecitorio, the parliament building, where he presided. He found Acquarone waiting in a car at the gate requesting an immediate meeting, which took place at 4:00 a.m. at the house of the Marquis Zamboni. Grandi was satisfied about his success and handed the representative of the King the text of the Agenda that had ended Mussolini's dictatorship.

"It's the constitutional tool the King had asked me to provide. Now Victor Emanuel can act directly and freely . . . " Acquarone then asked, not without some cynicism, "What do you think we should do?" The words sounded very positive to Grandi, who thought he understood in Acquarone's question the possible opening for a new political career. Grandi enthusiastically proposed the dissolution of the Fascist parliament and the reconvening of the old parliament that would give a vote of confidence to the new "government of peace." Acquarone then asked who should be prime minister? Grandi answered: "Marshal Caviglia, the only military leader without ties to this regime. As foreign minister, Alberto Pirelli; the other names could be De Gasperi, Cappa, Soleri, Paratore . . ." But Acquarone interrupted him to say that the King had already named Badoglio as prime minister.

The dawn of July 25 was appearing slowly. It was now 6:00 a.m. Grandi understood. He was about to be forever shunted out of power. The King attempted two months later to have Grandi approved as foreign minister by the Allies, but they were opposed to the idea.

At 9:00 a.m. on July 25, Mussolini went to his office as he had done every day for twenty-one years. At 1:00 p.m. he received the Japanese ambassador, to whom he said: "Please tell Tokyo urgently of my decision to send a note to Berlin on Wednesday that will say that if Germany does not furnish all the war materiel Italy has requested, we will be forced to declare that we can no longer fulfill our duties within the alliance. I ask that the Japanese ambassador in Berlin support my request very forcefully. Unfortunately, this is the situation, and Berlin must understand. In order to fight, one must have weapons." In the meantime, upsetting the plans of the Crown, Mussolini requested a meeting with the King that same day, rather than waiting for the next day, Monday, as planned. The meeting was then set for July 25 at 5:00 p.m. at Villa Savoia.

By 5:17 p.m. the royal audience was over; it had taken the King only twenty-one minutes to fire the prime minister who had "managed" his kingdom for twenty-one years. Italy exploded with joy: the Germans would leave, the bombing would end, freedom would return to political life. The only epitaph for Mussolini came from Winston Churchill, his friend turned enemy:

"And so would end the twenty-one years of Mussolini's dictatorship, when he saved the Italian people from Bolshevism . . . to have Italy reach a position in Europe that she had never known before. The country was inspired by a new kind of energy. He founded the Italian Empire. His regime was too expensive for the Italian people, but it must be said that during his moment of success, he did attract a large number of Italians. He was, I had occasion to write to him after the fall of France, the 'legislator of Italy' . . . His greatest mistake was to declare war on Britain and France after Hitler's victories in June 1940. Had he not done so, he could have kept Italy in a position of equilibrium, as she would have been courted and rewarded by all sides, deriving great prosperity and wealth from the struggles of other countries . . . "

It is naturally impossible to imagine what would have happened had Italy remained neutral. The words of praise coming from the British statesman for Mussolini long after the war placed Italy's position in the world in perspective at the outbreak of the World War II.

Mussolini was arrested as he walked to his car following his meeting with the King at Villa Savoia. At 5:25 p.m. he was taken to the carabinieri barracks in Via Legnano in Rome. The only person who complained about the manner in which he was treated that evening was the Queen, because Mussolini had been drawn into a trap in the very house of the Savoy family. At 2:00 a.m. on July 27, the Duce was taken aboard the corvette, *Persefone*, to the island of Ponza. Then, on August 7, he was transferred to the island of Maddalena.

The news of the arrest reached the Führer's headquarters like a bolt from the blue. The messages between Rastenburg and the German embassy in Rome became nervous and dramatic. Hitler was screaming betrayal even though the message Badoglio read to the Italian people over the radio gave assurances that the change of government in Italy did not alter the course of the war with the famous line, "La guerra continua..." (The war goes on . . .) Ambassador von Mackensen saw his patient work to maintain good relations with Italy go up in smoke in a few hours. As Badoglio began his arrests and others approached the Allies to negotiate an armistice that would be as honorable as possible for Italy, Hitler began his hunt—Operation *Eiche*—to find the Duce. For propaganda and emotional reasons, as well as to avoid retaliation from his enemies, Mussolini had to be liberated. Hitler was also convinced that the Duce would have been very useful to Germany if a new Fascist government could be created and the monarchy abolished. Furthermore, there were many signs that the new Italian government was trying to break away from the Axis.

At 9:30 p.m. on July 25, the Führer told his entourage: "We must prepare everything so that we can quickly grab this crowd, I mean those bastards who dared arrest the Duce. Tomorrow I will give the order to the head of the Third Panzer Grenadier division to enter Rome with a special unit and quickly capture the King, the entire government, the Prince of Piedmont, and Badoglio. Then you'll see them disintegrate and two days later, there will be another change." The next morning the Führer was asked what should be done about the Vatican. "Who cares? I'll go into the Vatican immediately. That's where the whole diplomatic corps is. I don't give damn. That's where the rabble is. We'll apologize afterwards."

This mopping-up operation inside Rome had been code-named *Student*, after the general who was to be in charge of the operation. On July 26, von Mackensen was ordered to transmit to the Führer's HQ "a list of the thirty most important persons in the army, politics, and the Crown who are well-known opponents of German policies." Mackensen listed some notorious anti-Nazis, such as Ciano, Grandi, Volpi, Cerruti, Suvich, and Princess Isabella Colonna, none of them being a surprise to the Nazis. As for the generals, he thought it to best consult General Rintelen, the military attaché, who in fact refused to comply with these requests and said that in the higher echelons of the Italian army there were no elements hostile to Germany.

Rintelen had decided to put a stop to Operation *Student*, which he thought would forever dishonor the German army, and asked for a meeting with the Führer. On August 1, before leaving for

Germany, Rintelen, responding to a request, went to see Badoglio, who made the following comments:

"I have called you because we have been friends for seven years and you are a person to whom, soldier to soldier, I can open my thoughts . . . The Fascist government disintegrated by itself . . . On Sunday, July 25 at 5:00 p.m., the King called me in and offered me the position as head of the government. For me it was a spur of the moment decision. At seventy-two years of age, my only wish is to spend the rest of my life in peace and quiet. As an old soldier, I must answer my King's call. Once I accepted, we discussed the proclamation with its main message: 'The war goes on . . . ' This was the precondition to my taking office. On Wednesday, July 28, I sent a message to the Führer, General Marras handed him a proposal for a meeting at Treviso, which would include the Führer, the King, and myself. The Führer rejected the idea because he had just had the meeting at Feltre and was unavailable at the moment.

"On August 6, there will be a meeting between the foreign ministers, including Keitel and Ambrosio . . . It is necessary that you let us know what kind of help Germany can provide us with . . . We have made no moves toward the Allies . . . Should the German army attempt to remove the King and myself, it will experience what forty-five million Latin men who are easily excitable can do . . . If I must continue this war I must have the trust of our ally . . . The situation is very serious . . . The bombing of Rome and, even more, of Hamburg has demonstrated the overwhelming superiority of the Anglo-Americans . . . Please let us reestablish a common trust . . . "

In the meantime, the Germans were streaming down through the Brenner Pass into Italy in larger numbers. During the morning of August 2, Rintelen left for Rastenburg in a special plane carrying a box of fresh fruit for the Führer, a personal gift from Field Marshal Kesselring. Upon arrival, he was told that he was to be in the dark regarding Operation Student when he spoke with the Führer because Hitler had ordered that very few generals should be in the know. Rintelen found this situation impossible because it was the very reason for his trip. Von Plehwe, Rintelen's number two in Rome, wrote: "Hitler's state of mind was a mixture of outrage, wounded pride, thirst for revenge, and complete mistrust toward the new Italian government. He was also convinced, after a message from Ambassador Oshima, that the Badoglio government had been dealing with the Allies long before the coup . . . Rintelen, with his way of presenting the facts, succeeded in making Hitler think the situation through. . . . It is obvious, and much to his honor, that Rintelen's report was instrumental in delaying, then completely canceling, Operation Student. He played all his cards on the professed attachment to the alliance that Badoglio had assured him before he left Rome. He was to pay for this unconditional faith in the word of the aging marshal with his job, since he was to be immediately recalled to Germany.

Hitler had decided to liberate the Duce just two days after the coup d'état in Italy and summoned to Rastenburg five officers trained in special operations. Among them was Captain Otto Skorzeny, a six-foot-four thirty-five-year-old Viennese engineer with a long dueling scar (a "*mensur*") across his face, a sign of virility among German youth. He was given the mission, when in response to the Führer's question about what he thought of the Italians he said simply, "I'm Austrian." The other four candidates had made long speeches about the Axis, loyalty, and the duties of an ally. Once the right man had been picked on July 27, Hitler told him in private: "I have a very important mission for you. Mussolini is under arrest. Italy today is wide open to Allied invasion, and Rome could fall at any moment into enemy hands. The King of Italy plotted with Marshal Badoglio against the Duce. These two are now planning to go to the Anglo-Americans with Mussolini on a silver platter. I cannot and will not abandon the Duce to his fate. He must be freed before those traitors can hand him over to the enemy. You, Skorzeny, will rescue my friend."

Skorzeny, along with General Kurt Student, his direct commanding officer, flew to Rome the next day on a plane piloted by the very experienced Captain Heinrich Gerlach. Three days later, the commando from Germany arrived in Rome to set up the operation that was top secret even for high level German circles. Skorzeny realized very quickly that the Italian government was taking new measures every day to throw off any possible attempt to rescue the Duce. In the end, the Germans were able to find out where Mussolini was being hidden: at the Villa Weber on the little island of Maddalena, off Sardinia. On the morning of August 18, Skorzeny, on a reconnaissance flight, flew over the area in a small plane that had to be ditched into the water because of engine trouble. An Italian PT boat rescued the German crew. But on August 28, when negotiations between the Badoglio government and the Allies had reached their final stages, Mussolini boarded a Red Cross sea plane and was first taken to Lake Bracciano and then, on the same afternoon, to the Gran Sasso mountain in an ambulance.

The way Italy reached the point of signing the armistice of September 8, 1943, is well known. Several groups in Italy made various attempts to contact the Allies over time and in different circumstances. The approaches can be divided into two periods: before the fall of Mussolini and after July 25, 1943. There were three different groups: within the first category were the Crown, Badoglio, and the Fascist leaders. The Crown made its first moves in Geneva during the fall of 1942 through Consul General Alessandro Marieni, representing Aimone, Duke of Aosta Spoleto. This overture appeared serious enough to the Allies and was followed by other contacts by Marie José, Princess of Piedmont and wife of the heir to the Italian throne, who succeeded in setting up a meeting on July 21, 1943, in Lisbon between her representative, Alvise Emo Capodilista, and Prime Minister Salazar of Portugal. The monarchist group wanted peace to save the Savoy dynasty.

In December 1942, Badoglio, in agreement with Marshal Caviglia, sent a message to the British via Switzerland, a message that was extremely vague, except for the idea of replacing Mussolini and his regime with a military government. The more moderate Fascists sent two timid signals proposing an armistice under the auspices of Mussolini himself. The first contact took place in Lisbon, with Ciano's agreement, through Italian diplomat Francesco

Fransoni, but had not been cleared by Mussolini immediately following the Allied landings in North Africa in November 1942. This overture was rejected by both London and Washington. After the landings in Sicily, Fransoni, in Lisbon, tried again to contact the British on behalf of undersecretary Bastianini, who had Mussolini's agreement. But by that time it was too late.

The peace feelers initiated after July 25 can be divided into two groups: by diplomats and by the military. The diplomatic efforts that took place on August 2, 1943, in Lisbon by Blasco Lanza d'Ajeta and a few days later in Tangier by Alberto Berio, convinced the Badoglio government that the Allies wanted to negotiate first and foremost a military armistice. This was why on August 12, General Giuseppe Castellano left for Madrid and Lisbon. On August 24, General Zanussi was sent to assist Castellano. After many long discussions, the armistice was agreed upon and signed on September 3, 1943, at Santa Teresa Longarini in Sicily, south of Siracusa. This was known as the "short armistice" of Cassibile, erroneously it turns out, because this small village is six kilometers away from the olive grove where the "peace tent" had been set up for the occasion. There still is a commemorative stone bearing an inscription in English: "Armistice signed here. September 3, 1943, Italy-Allies." The stone was stolen by a newspaperman in 1953, who was subsequently caught and convicted by a court in Siracusa a year later.

On the evening of September 3, after a dinner to celebrate the armistice, General Castellano was given the text of the Long Armistice, which explained in detail the points of the Short Armistice that had just been signed a few hours before. It would not be of great interest to follow all the behind-the-scenes details of these two documents, but suffice it to say that they did point to serious disagreements between London and Washington regarding the political conduct of the war. It also demonstrated how Great Britain was, in effect, handing over world leadership to the United States, repeating on a different level, the same subordinate relationship that existed between Italy and Germany. In brief, the Short Armistice was strongly advocated by General Eisenhower because he felt that an immediate Italian surrender would facilitate the landings on Italian soil on September 8 and 9. The Long Armistice was pushed by the British, who wished to quickly humiliate Italy for having declared war on the British Empire. It should be added that the Long Armistice was to be signed in Malta on September 29 could be condensed to even shorter terms than the Short Armistice. The forty-four articles could be summed up in one sentence: from now on Italy no longer existed. But thanks in part, to the Americans, Italy would be able to reintegrate the ranks of free nations slowly. Among the clauses of the Long Armistice, number 29 specified Italy's obligation:

"Benito Mussolini, his most important Fascist associates, and all persons suspected of having committed war crimes or similar crimes whose names are on the lists prepared by the United Nations and who are now or will be in territory under the control of the Italian military command, will be immediately arrested and handed over to the forces of the United Nations. All orders issued by the United Nations to this effect will be followed."

The issue of the "Big Devil," as Roosevelt referred to Mussolini, had been the subject of a long correspondence between the president and Churchill, who wanted to know in advance what the Duce's fate would ultimately be. Roosevelt, who had other problems to handle, said at one point that the problem would be decided calmly after Italy's surrender. The British prime minister, dissatisfied with that answer, wrote a letter to his American partner:

"The capture of the Big Devil and his most trusted associates must be considered an objective of the greatest importance. We must use all the means at our disposal to reach such an objective . . . . It may happen that these criminals will flee to Switzerland or Germany. They could also turn themselves in voluntarily or be handed over to us by the Italian government. In case they should fall into our hands, we will have to decide after consulting with the United States and the Soviet Union . . . Still, some of us will think that an execution without trial would be the best solution, limiting the proceedings to identifying the criminals. Some others will insist that they be kept as prisoners until the end of the war, delaying the decision. Personally I am quite indifferent. Winston Churchill."

The need for retribution had given rise to point 29, which Mussolini learned about on September 11 while he listened to the radio in the evening in the dining room of the hotel at Campo Imperatore on the Gran Sasso mountain, where he had finally been transferred after his stay at the island of Maddalena. One of Mussolini's keepers, captain of the carabinieri, Alberto Faiola, said:

"The news made a big impression on Mussolini, who called me that night, since he knew I had been a British prisoner of war. He was very concerned about this and preferred to commit suicide rather than undergo such humiliation. I took it upon myself to inform him that no such order had been given to us and to promise him, and actually swear, that if that were the case, I would have protected him and guided his flight across the mountains. Only after I made such a declaration did he feel able to go to sleep . . ." As a precaution, Faiola took away Mussolini's shaving equipment to prevent a desperate act in a moment of depression.

Skorzeny pursued the mission the Führer had given him. Hitler was pressing even more urgently for his friend's liberation after the announcement of the signing of the armistice at 6:00 p.m. of September 8, 1943. After the failed mission to Maddalena, the Germans quickly discovered the new hiding place where the Duce was a prisoner. At 2:00 p.m. on September 12, Skorzeny, with a few planes and eight gliders, landed on the short flat strip in front of the hotel. The German commando, meeting no resistance, was able to go straight up to Mussolini's room. Skorzeny told him: "The Führer sent me to free you." Mussolini answered: "I knew that my friend Adolf Hitler would not abandon me."

A perilous flight took the three men, the pilot Gerlach, Skorzeny, and Mussolini, from the Gran Sasso to Pratica di Mare in a single-engine Storch. Mussolini then switched to a Heinkel III to fly to Vienna where he was taken to the Continental Hotel. He looked like a ghost and dragged himself to the elevator with difficulty. Ten hours before, he was still Badoglio's prisoner on top of the Gran Sasso. Now he was the guest of the Führer in a luxury hotel in the former capital of Austria, whose independence he had once championed. He fell into bed completely dressed, but only for a few minutes because the phone rang almost immediately. The Führer was on the line to congratulate him on his liberation. Mussolini answered: "I'm tired, very, very tired. I need some sleep. Please take care of my wife and children." Hitler had also thought about this and had made sure that Rachele Mussolini and her children were escorted from the house at Rocca delle Caminate to Munich, where they would be safe.

The next day at noon, the Duce was reunited with his family after a hazardous flight from Vienna to Munich. He told Rachele: "I never thought I would see you again. Tomorrow I must visit the Führer at his headquarters." "What will you do next?" his wife asked him. To which Mussolini replied: "I don't know yet. I must speak with Hitler. It's very urgent." A German officer brought some news: "The weather is awful. Flying is not possible. While we wait for some improvement in the weather conditions, you will be accommodated with your family at the palace of Prince Karl. These are the Führer's orders." Germany was on holiday. The liberation of Mussolini was seen as a sort of sports event and met with widespread enthusiasm. The next day, September 14, Mussolini arrived at Rastenburg for his fifteenth meeting with Hitler. He wanted also to thank Hitler for the sixtieth birthday gift. It was a gift that had made him proud as a prisoner and as a man, so much so that he mentioned it specifically in his *Musings* under the date of August 19:

"This morning Admiral Brivonesi returned to La Maddalena. He broke my isolation by bringing me a letter from my wife dated August 13 and a large box containing the complete works of Nietzsche in twenty-four volumes that the Führer had sent me through Kesselring for my sixtieth birthday. The admiral also informed me that my son Vittorio had been declared a deserter, since the end of July he was the guest of the Führer at Rastenburg."

Kesselring wrote the following note to the Duce: "The Führer will be pleased if this work of German literature will bring you, Duce, a bit of comfort and if you will consider it as the expression of the deepest personal feelings the Führer has for you." According to what a former high-ranking SS officer told the author, the box of books was the clue that enabled the Germans to trace Mussolini to Maddalena. German agents had never lost track of the box of books ever since it had been given to Badoglio. They spotted it the day it was seen being loaded on board a small truck, which Skorzeny's men then constantly followed.

XVI

A Fascist Republic

Rastenburg: September 14-16, 1943

Hopes for an Axis victory that was to begin in the Middle East and extend north into the USSR and south toward the Red Sea, during the summer of 1942 were dashed by the failure of Rommel's offensive into Egypt. The Führer's HQ had never seen excitement such as that of September 14, 1943, when it expected the arrival of Benito Mussolini, just liberated from his prison at the hands of Badoglio. As usual, Hitler had planned the reunion scene down to its most minute details. The first one to approach the Duce would be his son Vittorio, who had been the Führer's guest since the end of July, and was now living in a hotel at Königsberg. Mussolini left Munich that morning and landed in the early afternoon at the Rastenburg airstrip. Though his wife had carefully prepared his clothing and pressed his shirt to improve his appearance, the effort was futile: the Duce looked thinner and smaller, very much a diminished figure as he came out of the door of his plane. He had lost almost fifty pounds during the past year and it showed dramatically.

Vittorio described the scene:

"My father came out of the Junkers transport plane smiling and giving the Fascist salute. He wore a black fedora and an overcoat that looked like it belonged to someone twice his size. His face was pale and sickly, unshaven, and he was thin and obviously tired. Only his eyes had kept their lively expression. I had a deep sense of pity and anger: how harsh those forty-five days of painful isolation, rough treatment, and fear must have been. I hugged him and he patted my cheek . . . The Führer then came up to us, and both of them, deeply emotional, shook hands at length. Then he was greeted by the other German officials . . . I was the only Italian present. We went by car to the HQ, where my father was given a room in one of the huts."

Vittorio had learned of the Duce's liberation two days earlier from Hitler himself, who said emphatically: "This is an historical day for the German people and for honorable Italians." The daring rescue at the Gran Sasso became golden material for Goebbels and a very powerful propaganda campaign. In fact, that very evening of September 12, a flash newswire had been sent from Berlin: "German paratroopers, men of the security service, and the SS have successfully completed today, Sunday, a daring mission to free the Duce, who had been kept prisoner by a group of traitors. The raid was successful: the Duce was freed. The conspiracy planned by Badoglio to hand Mussolini over to the Anglo-Americans has failed."

However, there are some doubts regarding the project by his Italian captors to hand Mussolini over to the Allies. It was well known that the British were hoping, like many others, to keep the Duce locked in a prison cell as a hostage for international peace. But it is necessary to take a step backwards and examine the other phases of the negotiations between Badoglio and Eisenhower in August and September 1943. The aging Italian marshal was moving toward an armistice to save whatever was left of Italy, while all Eisenhower wanted from what he called "this dirty business" was a smooth entry into the Italian mainland, mostly by neutralizing the Italian fleet. Eisenhower was not interested in Mussolini, who was not even mentioned in the text of the Short Armistice, signed on September 3, at Santa Teresa Longarini. The problem of Mussolini and his main Fascist associates appeared in the text of the Long Armistice, which General Castellano read for the first time after signing the first document. Then, on September 8, the King and the Italian high command left Rome and went to the south; the Germans immediately occupied all of Italy; Mussolini was liberated after being abandoned in his hotel on the Gran Sasso. When Badoglio signed the Long Armistice at Malta on September 29, the clause relating to the Duce was moot. That all this intrigue was a Machiavellian move by Badoglio or the King, is impossible to ascertain. The facts remain: the Italians made no attempt to hand Mussolini over to the enemy and agreed to deliver him only once it became a promise they could no longer fulfill.

Mussolini, after a short rest, had his first two-hour meeting with Hitler. The Duce retraced the history of his decision to call a meeting of the Grand Council and of the events that followed the "July 25 conspiracy." The Führer listened to him with morbid attention, discovering, in the dramatic adventure his friend had experienced, clues as to how he should defend himself from the internal opposition that was growing inside Germany. He then told Mussolini that the time had not yet arrived for the "Duce of Fascism" to retire. First, there was a war going on that had to be won. Afterwards there would be time for other decisions: "It's necessary to set up a government to administer Italy, which is now a no-man's-land." "But Führer," said a puzzled Mussolini, "I can never be a 'Quisling.'" This reference to the notorious Norwegian Nazi collaborator using such a negative connotation caught Hitler off guard. Mussolini did not understand why Hitler had grimaced at his remark until later, when he was told that the Führer held the Norwegian leader in high esteem as the man who allowed Germany to control Norway. After the uneasy moment passed, Hitler got down to business.

"We can't waste a single day. It is imperative that as early as tomorrow you speak on the radio to announce the end of the monarchy and the foundation of a new Italian Fascist state whose powers will be concentrated in your person. That will be the guarantee, and no other guarantee will be acceptable, of the full validity of the alliance between Germany and Italy. You shall be, as I am, at the same time head of state and head of the government. A new constitution shall be necessary within a week. I don't doubt you will agree with me that one of the very first acts of the new government will be to condemn to death the traitors of the Grand Council. I judge Count Ciano a traitor four times: traitor to his country, traitor to Fascism, traitor to the alliance with Germany, and traitor to his family. Had I been in your position, nothing would have stopped me from doing justice with my own hands. But I will hand him over to you. It is best that the death sentence and execution take place in Italy."

"Count Ciano married my daughter. He's the father of my grandchildren," answered Mussolini, who was very troubled.

"His betrayal is all the more serious because of these facts," replied Hitler, "and you must be very clear about this. The Italian betrayal, had it been used to their advantage by the Anglo-Americans, could have meant the sudden collapse of Germany. I had to give an immediate example as to what fate would befall any one of our Allies who would be tempted to follow in Italy's path. I delayed a very detailed plan only because I knew that I could free you and prevent your being handed over to the enemy. But should you disappoint me, I will have to give the orders to implement the punitive plans I had prepared." Then he turned to Ambassador Rudolf Rahn, who was named Mussolini's "political advisor" and was present at this phase of the discussion, and said: "You will facilitate the birth of the new Italian Republic." The first round had ended, and the meetings would continue the next day. The Duce had one night to accept or refuse.

Late in the afternoon, Mussolini phoned his wife to tell her she should be calm and that all was going well. "The Führer welcomed me like a brother. He wants me back in power as head of the Republic." "Do not accept, Benito," said his wife. "Listen to me. Don't accept." "I must accept. If I don't, the Germans will burn and destroy all of Italy," the Duce answered, already resigned to his fate. "I must see this through to the very end. I must." After this phone call he had dinner alone with Vittorio. Father and son had many things to talk about. Mussolini wanted to understand why everyone was angry with Ciano. Rachele and the most extreme Fascists, such as Alessandro Pavolini, were demanding that the former minister be arrested immediately and put on trial. The Germans wanted the same thing, according to what Hitler was saying, and had already condemned him to death. The only person defending Ciano was his wife Edda, who wanted to "close" the whole matter by getting passports for herself, her husband, and her children and leave for South America.

Vittorio Mussolini: "My father ate very little because his stomach pains had grown worse during his confinement . . . He needed news. He hadn't read a newspaper in forty-six days, and for him that must have been worse than torture . . . We first spoke of our family, my mother, my brother Romano, and my sister Anna Maria, who were all in Munich. Also there were Edda and Galeazzo with their children Fabrizio, Raimonda, and Marzio. I told him that the Cianos were well and, except for a few bothersome incidents, that they had been treated decently."

Edda, Galeazzo, and their children had succeeded with German help in leaving Rome by plane with Spain as their destination. Munich, which was to be a refueling stop on their way to Madrid, suddenly became a permanent stop. On August 27, the Ciano family was taken to a villa on Lake Starnberg and treated very courteously. After a few days, the villa became a house arrest. Edda demanded to speak with Hitler, who saw her on September 1, after sending her a beautiful bouquet of flowers for her birthday. He said: "The trip to Spain could have been dangerous for the Ciano family. It's not a secure country. There are many British agents there and the Spanish attitude is far from clear. I need to consider your request further."

Vittorio told his father that Hitler had been sitting on the request of the Cianos for over two weeks. Edda was angry and suspected the worst. The Duce, still anguished after his meeting with the Führer, said: "It would have been much better to follow a different way out. The Germans will never forgive Galeazzo for his anti-German attitude." And they did not. Ribbentrop first and foremost was accusing his former colleague Ciano of having pushed Great Britain and France to declare war on Germany, after having tipped off the ambassadors of the two powers that Italy would not go to war in August 1939.

Ciano himself, just before his execution, wrote that the Germans "were certain the British and French would look passively on while Germany slit Poland's throat. On this issue, Ribbentrop, during one of those mournful lunches we had together in Salzburg, insisted on a wager. I would give him an Italian painting in the event of Anglo-French neutrality, and he would give me a collection of antique weapons if they would indeed decide to go to war. There were many witnesses present at the wager . . . Ribbentrop preferred to forget the wager and never did deliver on it, unless I consider what will happen shortly to be his form of payment: a bunch of good-for-nothings in the pay of foreigners."* He wrote those words on December 23, 1943, nineteen days before his execution.

The truth is that Ribbentrop, one of the more unsavory characters within Hitler's entourage, did not like Italians in general and Ciano even less, whom he considered an untrustworthy gossip.

Two other German officials, Nazi ideologue Alfred Rosenberg and Field Marshal Rommel, were adamantly opposed to any revival of the Italian alliance and the restoration of Mussolini. Rommel still harbored a grudge against Mussolini because of the Duce's criticism of the conduct of the battle of El Alamein. Rommel had answered Hitler when he was asked about the operation to free the Duce: "It is best to have the Italians as enemies than as friends. If the Duce is freed, our own freedom of action in Italy will be limited." There were similar reactions from other officials, such as Admiral Raeder: "Mussolini behind bars is better for us and will spare us more unwelcome surprises." General Guderian: "Mussolini in jail gives us more guarantees than a Mussolini running free." The only two German leaders who saw some advantages were Field

---

* Ciano is referring to the Fascist firing squad that would shoot him and the other "conspirators."

Marshal Kesselring, for entirely tactical reasons relating to logistics, and Hermann Göring who was more sentimental about the matter: "To abandon Mussolini is to betray the common cause."

Vittorio informed the Duce about the activities of the Italian Fascists who had been transferred to Munich by the German embassy in Rome after the July 25 coup. Then he recounted the episode of the Führer, calling him to Rastenburg to greet his father after the liberation by Skorzeny. Mussolini interrupted his son to say: "Once Hitler cabled me to say 'Duce, I shall never forget this.' Today I was telling him that I would never forget what he did to avoid my being killed, which I don't care about, or, more importantly, the dishonor of being handed over to the enemy." Mussolini gave some more details to his son about the meeting with Hitler:

"The situation in Russia is not good, but the Germans are certain they can contain the breakout first and then stop it later and thus get through the winter. The resistance and courage displayed by the Russians has been a huge and unpleasant surprise for the German high command. The other surprise came from the secret weapons factories, undetected by German espionage, that had been built behind the Urals. To this you must add the enormous amount of weapons and supplies sent by the United States, and you can easily understand the difficulties the Germans are facing. But at Stalingrad, the Russians alone were responsible for encircling and crushing the armies of von Paulus. Peace negotiations? Hitler doesn't even want to hear about the possibility. He says it's a question of life and death for European civilization . . . For us Italians, there is only one solution: go back to the fighting.

"Our land is full of soldiers of all religions and races who are destroying everything. From July 25 to September 8, the Allied air force has destroyed more houses where poor people live than at any other time during the war. There is no pity for those who are defeated. It also appears that Badoglio, who is becoming more aggressive in his old age, is reportedly preparing a small monarchist army that will be under Allied command. It's even more shameful than any switch of partners. Bismarck used to say that when Italy adheres to a military alliance, it is already scheming as to how to get out of it and requires a clause to that effect in the pact itself. Unfortunately, the Italian army no longer exists. The Italian navy was able to find enough fuel to go to surrender at Malta. The honor of Italy demands that we get back into the war.

"Hitler told me very clearly that the German people are disgusted by the Italian betrayal and will not tolerate a weak attitude by the Führer toward Italy. The German high command, which had always been critical of Hitler's faith in the Italians, is now saying it was right in its analysis. We have nothing to celebrate. But we must do whatever is possible to gain a minimum of confidence in order to avoid any German thoughts of revenge on the Italian people. He told me that the Wehrmacht will soon have deadly weapons which will change the course of the war. It's top secret. The lack of confidence in the Italians is also affecting me. Hitler is unaffected by that kind of suspicion, but his entourage has become negative and hard. Do you know what Ribbentrop is thinking? That the July 25 affair was some kind of Italian comedy involving the King and myself."

In a second meeting, the following day, Mussolini gave Hitler his answer. The Duce would agree to form a new Italian government with some minor conditions. One of these was that the new Italian state would have its own army. British historian Sir Ivone Kirkpatrick wrote: "Caution also encouraged Mussolini to accept the German proposals. Mussolini knew Hitler well enough to imagine that if thwarted he could seek a cruel revenge and so he saw himself as a shield for his people in the face of German brutality." Regarding these ideas of revenge, it seems that Hitler told the Duce during their first meeting: "Northern Italy will have to envy the fate of Poland if you refuse to bring back the Axis alliance . . . It's up to you to decide whether we should test our secret weapons on London instead of Milan, Genoa, and Turin . . . "

The Duce's office would remain in Germany for the moment. In the meantime, the German army would complete the movements that would give it complete control of central and northern Italy. Goebbels wrote in his *Diary*: "All our police measures are to remain unchanged. The Führer has insisted that nothing be altered.

The Duce wants to begin by rebuilding the Fascist party . . . and then call for a constitutional assembly that will do away with the House of Savoy. The Duce still hesitates on this issue . . . All in all, I am pleased that the Führer has remained consistent with his initial intentions. It is now clear that emotional and sentimental considerations no longer have any influence upon him."

Those "initial intentions" had not been communicated to Mussolini. These were the measures taken by the Germans on September 10, two days after the Italian surrender, which Hitler had announced in his speech concerning Badoglio's betrayal. The speech was full of fiery threats against an Italy accused of the worst kinds of evil deeds. The first result was the de facto annexation of Alto Adige/South Tyrol and Venezia Giulia by Germany. Two Nazis had been named Gauleiters: Franz Höfer in Innsbruck and Friedrich Rainer in Trieste. Goebbels was dreaming of a confederation of the two regions that would also annex Venice to Germany.

On Wednesday, September 15, one week after the Italian surrender, the announcement of the foundation of the Italian Republic and the rebirth of Fascism was made from the famous Wolf's Lair in the Black Forest. Five decrees were issued that also named Alessandro Pavolini as secretary of the Fascist Republican Party and ordered the persons in positions of authority on the eve of September 8 to return to their posts. Renato Ricci was named commander of the Fascist militia.

Following a pathetic and stressful meeting with Fascist leaders who had reported to Rastenburg, all of them demanding that the Duce act ruthlessly to punish the traitors of the Fascist ideal, Mussolini had his third and final meeting with Hitler on September 16. The Duce said how much he wished to go back to Rome if the German high command decided to hold the line of Monte Circeo-Majella. Hitler left all future plans regarding the location of the Italian government and military operations to the technicians. Mussolini insisted on the need to keep Rome: "To lose the capital after losing Naples would have disastrous consequences in Italy and the rest of the world. That is from the political point of view. Militarily, the enemy would control the thirty airports in central

Italy, which would allow Allied bombers to reach southern Germany, the Danube basin, and the Balkans very easily."*

Mussolini traveled back to Munich with Vittorio. When they parted, Hitler very affectionately told the Duce to take care of his health and dispatched a German doctor, Georg Zachariae, to be at the Duce's side. He also told him not to show the weaknesses of the past toward his enemies or his friends: "Duce, you must show no regard for anyone." During the flight, Mussolini drafted the first speech he was to make as the head of the new Republic on the evening of September 18 on Radio Munich. Vittorio remembered: "His voice was tired but always recognizable, even though many thought it was some kind of trick concocted by the Goebbels propaganda machine."

The main points were well known: Italy would get back into the war as the ally of Germany and Japan and reorganize its armed forces; the traitors would be eliminated along with the "plutocratic parasite countries" that would be annihilated, and work would become the foundation of the new economy. Mussolini addressed the Italian people:

"Black Shirts, Italian men, and women! After a long silence, here once again is the sound of my voice, and I am sure you will recognize it . . . The word 'loyalty' has a deep, unmistakable meaning, an eternal meaning I should say, for the German people . . . The dynasty, the Savoy family, during the entire period of the war in spite of the fact that the King declared it, has been the main promoter of defeatism and anti-German propaganda . . . The King, by his own acts, has created within Italy a situation of chaos, shame, and misery . . . We must annihilate the parasite plutocracies and make work the subject of the economy and the solid base of the state itself . . . Peasants, workers, and employees! The state that will emerge from this terrible catastrophe will belong to you . . . !"

Up to September 23, Mussolini's temporary office was five kilometers outside Weilheim, between Garmisch and Munich, at Waldbichl Castle. Pavolini and Ricci were sent to Rome, followed

---

*Naples was taken by Allied forces October 1, 1943.

quickly by the man who would become Mussolini's "military consultant," SS General Karl Wolff. Over the Weilheim-Rome direct phone line, the new Republican government was set up. In spite of all the risks that being associated with a new Mussolini regime represented, candidates outnumbered the available jobs. Mussolini had problems for the ministries of defense and foreign affairs, and, in the end, he became his own foreign minister, while as defense minister, he brought back Marshal Graziani, whose actions in North Africa had been under investigation. And Graziani's name, tied to past victories in Ethiopia, where he became known as the "Lion of Neghhelli," also turned out to be useful because of his long-standing rivalry with Badoglio.

Reunited with his family in Munich, Mussolini had to face the Ciano problem, which had the makings of a tragedy, due to the orders given by Hitler at Rastenburg that Mussolini had to accept. After the Matteotti assassination in 1924, Ciano was the second political murder to be attributed to the Duce. In both cases, he overcame the problem badly damaged, mostly because of other people's decisions and the course of events. Like any military or political leader, he always feared appearing too weak in the eyes of the public; he wanted his historical self to appear implacable, befitting his position as the founder of Fascism. Yet unknown to a lot of people, behind this implacable facade were moments of real generosity typical of his peasant upbringing. Two examples were to be the steps he took to beg the forgiveness of the Matteotti family and of his own daughter, Edda.

On September 19, Edda attempted a family reunion at a Sunday dinner to put everyone at peace. All the Mussolinis and the Cianos were present. Vittorio wrote:

"My father sat on an antique armchair at the head of the table. He wore a dark suit, and his tie was askew . . . There was a window behind his back, and the light shining through masked his tired and pained expression. He had lost a lot of weight and was not well . . . They served a rather diluted vegetable soup. Father took only a few spoonfuls without any appetite. His thoughts were far removed from us all . . . My brother-in-law Galeazzo was sitting to his right and kept his usual superior and aloof attitude that bothered my mother so much. He was wearing a beautiful light gray suit with an immaculate white handkerchief flowing out of his breast pocket . . . His hair was carefully slicked back . . . Once in a while he even managed to make us smile . . . Edda sat next to me in silence, trying to eat something, anything. But by now her only interest was in saving her husband's life."

There had been a clearing of the air of sorts because of Edda's attempt to act as go-between for Mussolini and Ciano immediately after the Duce's return from Rastenburg. But in the end, everything remained unchanged. Galeazzo said he acted in good faith and was well intentioned when he took Grandi's side; he wanted to force the King to come out in the open and had not intended to cause the fall of the Duce. Ciano said he would take whatever job Mussolini would give him in the new Republican government, and should this not be possible, he would join the new air force. Edda clashed with the maneuvers of the Fascist extremists determined to put Ciano on trial for treason and then have him shot, and tried to stand up to the hatred displayed by the Führer and his entourage.

Even Joseph Goebbels was well aware of her intrigues: "Edda Mussolini has successfully reversed the opinion her father had originally formed of Ciano. Immediately following Mussolini's arrival at Munich she had a long meeting with him that ended in a reconciliation between the Duce and Ciano, who is now back in his father-in-law's good graces. This means that the poison mushroom is once again growing in the middle of the Italian Fascist Republican Party." The reconciliation was only supposition on Goebbels' part, because the Duce knew by now that Ciano's fate was sealed. At that Sunday dinner table, Mussolini suddenly got up and, with a tired gesture, waved good-bye to everyone. Vittorio Mussolini: "Once he had left, Edda and Galeazzo also left to return to their villa at Almaschausen, where the Germans had put them . . . Only my mother was left in the large dining room. I shall always remember her eyes at that moment; they were staring far away, without any tears."

On September 24, the first Republican government was formed. Mussolini had succeeded in halting the intrigues by Roberto Farinacci, who demanded an appointment to the ministry of internal affairs. But the position was given to a lawyer from Pisa, Guido Buffarini-Guidi, the former undersecretary, who was friendly with both Mussolini's wife Rachele and his mistress, Claretta Petacci. As undersecretary for foreign affairs he named Count Serafino Mazzolini, who was to have become Italian high commissioner in Egypt. After these decisions, Mussolini immediately returned to Romagna, something he had wanted to do since the evening of July 25. He arrived by plane at Forlí on September 23. The German plans to "protect the Duce" were now operational. Waiting for him at the airport were his two German "keepers," Rahn and Wolff. And to make sure that everyone clearly understood that this would be a Mussolini with limited freedom, the Führer had placed the Duce under the protection of a unit of the SS Leibstandrte Adolf Hitler, his personal bodyguard regiment.

The inaugural cabinet meeting of the Fascist Republican government was held on September 27 for the first time at the Rocca delle Caminate, the Duce's private residence. Mussolini explained the plans he had discussed with Hitler, including the constitutional assembly and the special courts passing judgment on the traitors. He could feel the oppressive German presence in every one of his moves, and was followed or spied upon everywhere by the German police or a military official. This prompted him that evening, to write a long letter to Hitler, wherein, among other things, he said:

"As you know the Italian Fascist government held its first meeting and announced its program, making an excellent impression. The personality of Marshal Graziani gives the government its stamp of approval . . . If we wish to rebuild the country, the new government I have formed must be able to have enough autonomy to govern, enabling it to give the right orders to the civilian administration. The Republican government that I have the honor of leading has only one objective: to ensure that Italy can once again actively participate in the war. But to reach this goal, it is essential that

German military authorities limit themselves to military tasks and allow Italian civilian authorities to properly administer the country. If these conditions are not met, Italian public opinion, and world opinion, will conclude that this government is unable to function, and the government itself will become a laughingstock and fall into chaos. I am certain, Führer, that you understand the importance of the points I have made and the seriousness of the problems that I must face and whose solution is a matter of concern not only for Italy but for Germany as well."

Hitler did not answer this anguished "appeal" and, in fact, clearly showed during the next nineteen months that he was unwilling to consider the Italian situation from Mussolini's point of view. The Führer's answer to all such appeals was that everything would be settled after the war ended in victory. Therefore, as Mussolini had intuitively understood, the government born at Rocca delle Caminate desperately tried to function during the entire period of the Repubblica Sociale Italiana (RSI) but was beset by inefficiency, confusion, and ridicule. Mussolini's government did have a useful function in maintaining the token presence of a rump Italian state and making sure that the population had somewhat tolerable living conditions, and at times in preventing excesses by occupying troops. The RSI was able to hold the value of the Italian lira and maintain the productivity of industry and agriculture at tolerable levels despite relentless Allied bombing. The Italian people were convinced that, in the final analysis, the war was now definitely lost.

After having written his letter to Hitler, the Duce took a long seventeen-day vacation. During this time, Rome was finally ruled out as the capital of the RSI because the Germans were about to declare it an "open city" at the Vatican's request. The decision was made to place the government at Salò, a pretty resort town on Lake Garda, where Mussolini arrived on October 8. The Duce and his family were accommodated at Villa Feltrinelli, while his offices in the neighboring town of Gargnano were at Villa delle Orsoline where he would spend most of his time far from his wife. At Gardone, another small town nearby, Claretta Petacci had moved into Villa Fiordaliso—with German approval.

The relations with Berlin were the responsibility of Filippo Anfuso, one of the few diplomats who joined the RSI following Mussolini's appeal. Anfuso, a dreamy cynic, was unable to refuse the call coming from the sinking Duce, who begged for support and understanding. He reacted from his post at Budapest by sending a telling cable to Mussolini: "Duce, I am with you until death." Anfuso remembered: "During the evening of September 13 a German voice called me from Berlin." It was Baron Alexander Dörnberg, chief of protocol of the foreign ministry, who told Anfuso that a journalist friend wanted to say hello: "As I asked myself which journalist would pick Dörnberg to reach me, a deep unmistakably Italian voice said: "Anfuso, I received your cable, that's what I expected of you . . . " Anfuso made his decision to throw away a brilliant diplomatic career at Budapest. It was a reaction to the sarcasm he felt coming from the German and Hungarian officials in the Hungarian capital when the Italian surrender was made public. Anfuso confided to the author just a few days before he died:

"It is impossible to understand, if one has not physically experienced it, what it means to be alone on a stage facing an audience that only wants to cover you with insults. Here is the Italian, the eternal traitor, Caporetto, the mandolin players, macaroni, and so on. I had also experienced the signs of being double-crossed in the worst way. To attribute every mistake to Mussolini was for me an act of cowardice and opportunism. There undoubtedly were responsibilities all around, within the Crown, the Palazzo Venezia, the generals, the Fascist leadership, big industry, and even local Fascist leaders. Then that ambiguous phrase, 'The war goes on,' that ended with the King fleeing from Pescara—all this bothered me very much. One day, History will judge whether people like me, who decided to defend the Italians who had remained under German control after September 8, deserve to be condemned or thanked. As the British say, and they are always quoted when it suits everyone: 'My country, right or wrong.'" This was the Anfuso who followed Mussolini as he attempted to give credibility to the RSI and was named to the unenviable position of Italian ambassador to Berlin.

After the first cabinet meeting of the new Mussolini government, Hitler sent the Duce the following cable: "I received with joy and satisfaction your message regarding the formation of the Italian Fascist government. I am honored to inform you that the German Reich hereby recognizes the government you have formed and is ready, as your loyal comrade and ally, to continue the war side by side with your government until its victorious conclusion." As he arrived in Berlin, Anfuso told one of his assistants: "We must not say it, but the war is lost. It is so far lost that there are only a few of us left. But because it is lost, we can't abandon Mussolini and the Italian people."

He went to work, presenting his credentials to Hitler on November 13, a full month after his arrival in the German capital. "Hitler told me: "You have done well to remain faithful to Mussolini. To serve the Duce is a great honor for a man and any Italian." The Führer carelessly dropped the letter from the head of the new Italian Social Republic on the table. He never did approve of the term "social." The new regime was referred more realistically as "the north," that included the strange mixture of political agitators surrounding Mussolini at that time. There was also a bizarre contrast with the monarchist south that had some negative racial and moral connotations.*

After being able, by chance, to meet Hitler in person, since the Führer now rarely left the Wolf's Lair, Anfuso attempted to discuss four issues which, unknown to him at that time, would remain unresolved during his entire period as ambassador: the question of Alto Adige and Trentino; Trieste, and the Venezia-Giulia region; the new Italian army; the fate of the Italian prisoners in German camps. Hitler had no special bias regarding the two territorial questions, but he did repeat what he had told Mussolini. He had not made any final determination regarding the two regions; they were Italian and would stay that way until the war ended in victory. He

---

* The Italian north vs. south rivalry is what is meant.

added a sentence regarding Italy's rights in the Mediterranean. As for the army, Hitler was opposed to any special favors at hard labor camps for the "prisoners who followed Badoglio."

Upon arriving at Villa Feltrinelli, Mussolini immediately declared his aversion for the location the Germans had selected: "I hate lakes. They are a stupid compromise between rivers and the ocean." Following the agreement reached at Rastenburg, he had to respect two deadlines: the foundation and organization of the Fascist Republican Party and the punishment of the July 25 traitors. Until he fulfilled these two obligations, he would be unable to make contact with Hitler, who became suddenly unavailable, thanks to the various bureaucratic filters he hid behind. The Duce pretended not to understand that the Führer was testing his resolve and responding to pressures coming from Nazi hard-liners and the German high command, two groups opposed to Italy's return as a full Axis partner.

In the meantime, there were many problems still unresolved. One morning a report from Anfuso regarding the lack of resolution to the problem of Italian prisoners annoyed the Duce, who angrily told his secretary, Giovanni Dolfin: "It's useless for these people to call us allies! Why don't they drop the mask and say that we are a country and a people under occupation . . . " Dolfin replied: "Why not try to meet with Hitler in private without the usual entourage? Maybe that way you can find the solutions to the problems that divide us?" Mussolini replied: "Such a meeting would not resolve anything, because Hitler is paying attention to events much bigger than our problems right now. Immediately after my return to Italy, I wrote him a letter, which Graziani brought to him, explaining all these points. I followed up with a very explicit cable . . . asking for his help to save the city of Zara . . . I have received no answer to date . . . many promises . . . just promises coming from Rahn . . . "

In this atmosphere, on November 14, in a room of the Castelvecchio of Verona, took place the first meeting of the national assembly of the Fascist Republican Party. It was an acrimonious gathering that, predictably, featured every one of the most extreme, angry, and despicable people in northern Italy. After reading a message from the Duce and hearing a speech by Fascist party secretary, Alessandro Pavolini, the Fascists, who had debated the prerequisites for the true Fascist militant, approved an eighteen-point document, the manifesto of the Fascist Republican Party.

The program described the new Fascist philosophy in the light of recent events. It announced a new assembly that was to draft a constitution for the new Fascist Republican State, whose leader would be democratically elected. The social policies of corporate economics had a more left-leaning slant. Not all Fascists agreed with this revolutionary switch to the left by Mussolini, who wanted to return to his socialist origins. The question of race was also included, and singled out the Jews as belonging to an "enemy nationality," the same position as Nazi Germany. The motion that did get a unanimous vote was the one relating to the organization of special courts, and that demanded justice be done to punish the traitors to the ideal and "the criminals who had dishonored the country." The most vigorous applause went to the speakers who demanded the firing squad for Ciano and his accomplices.

Ciano, who had been in Verona since October 19, was following the proceedings of the congress of Castelvecchio from cell number 27 at the Scalzi prison. He was waiting for his trial as well as that of all the members of the Grand Council who had voted in favor of the Grandi Agenda. Besides Ciano, only five of the nineteen accused had been arrested: Giovanni Marinelli, Emilio De Bono, Tullio Cianetti, Luciano Gottardi, and Carlo Pareschi. The thirteen others had succeeded in escaping arrest and were in hiding. Much has been written about the legitimacy of the Verona court. Everyone agreed that it was, in fact, a revolutionary attempt by the Fascist regime to purge the more moderate wing of the Fascist party and create a new, more extreme and "pure" Fascist regime. Mussolini agreed with this view as he told Fascist Justice Minister Pesenti, who had many reservations regarding the entire case: "You only see the legal aspects of this trial. You see it from the magistrate's point of view. I must look at it from the political point of view. Reasons of state overwhelm any other consideration. Now we must go to the bitter end." The Fascism of Salò had found its Robespierre in Pavolini, who indeed went to the bitter end. Only Cianetti was able to save his life because of a letter he sent to the Duce on the morning of July 25, after the Grand Council meeting, to withdraw his vote. Ciano and his four unfortunate companions were shot on the morning of January 11, 1944, at the firing range just outside the Porta Catena gate in Verona.

In death, Ciano achieved the consensus that had eluded him in life. Mussolini was at his worst during the entire tragedy. By sacrificing so cruelly the life of his own son-in-law, he thought he would create an image of himself as the great dictator who shows no pity for his opponents. This turned out to be useless and out of character, since deep down, Mussolini was, among other things, quite an emotional and shy man. Furthermore, he had never been a bloodthirsty tyrant, like Hitler.

Worried, after the fact, that his popularity might suffer because he would be accused of sending five of his own men to the firing squad, he created a tragic charade of the pardon requests which had been withheld from him, begging ignorance. It was a flimsy excuse, of course, because everyone knew all Mussolini had to do to stop the execution was to get on the telephone. But he made sure that the firing squad had done its evil deeds before he called anyone. Those calls were only to take punitive action against Pavolini and his henchmen, who had stalled the pardon requests for the five victims, but, predictably, no action was ever taken.

Once the "Ciano case" was closed, Mussolini was certain there would be no obstacle to his renewed dialogue with Hitler. He assumed he was by now out of his "quarantine" period. But real problems surfaced with the inconsolable and angry widow of Galeazzo Ciano, Mussolini's daughter, Edda, who, just before crossing the border into Switzerland, had written two letters, one to her father and the other to Hitler. To the Duce, she wrote: "I waited until the very end, hoping you'd show some honesty and a bit of human feeling, but since I see you doing nothing, I shall know how to strike." To the Führer, she reserved the epithets of liar and traitor as she reminded him: "Twice you misled me with assurances you did not keep. Enough! Think of the blood that has been spilled and show some justice and compassion." But her last minute attempt came to nothing, even though the Germans were worried about her threat to wash the dirty Axis linen in public by publishing her husband's famous *Diaries*.

Mussolini, who favored Edda because she resembled him the most, did not know how to react. He found a priest who was friendly with his daughter from her days in Milan, Don Giusto Pancino. He asked the priest to bring Edda back to Italy since she was under Allied protection in Switzerland. Upon his return, Father Pancino told Mussolini that his daughter refused to forgive her father. At the Villa Orsoline, more problems arose. Dolfin told the Duce that he must break his isolation and demand an urgent meeting with Hitler. The Duce replied: "It's not possible right now. The insulting letter my daughter wrote has thrown cold water on our relationship. I do not have direct contact with the Führer, and the problems we discuss are not the most serious ones that separate us."

Mussolini then turned to politics. On February 12, during the sixth meeting of the cabinet, he presented the "socialization" decree. It was to be a formula to regulate the relationship between workers and owners in industry. To his German doctor, Zachariae, who asked for an explanation of the revolutionary law, Mussolini replied: "I came to politics as a socialist, and that's how I intend to depart."

At home, he sometimes expressed his frustration to his sister Edvige: "By now I am just a secondary figure compared to Hitler. I was defeated and saved by a strong ally who now has given me a hand. The Germans are against my socialization policies: the German generals are excluding as many factories as they can from the new law." In the military field, things were going better. Since October 13, 1943, Graziani had succeeded in seeing Hitler at Rastenburg. In the room where he had been received, the Italian marshal had to endure alone a tough interrogation by other members of the German high command. Graziani wrote: "The top echelon of the OKW all came into the room, and I was there alone, like a beggar. I carried a letter from Mussolini, in which he asked that Rome be defended . . . The two German marshals in Italy, Guderian and Rommel, were at odds on this point. Guderian favored defending the city, Rommel was for a defensive line crossing Italy from La Spezia to Rimini to cover the Po Valley. Hitler agreed with Mussolini on this issue, and so it was not a subject for discussion. The Duce also requested the means to rebuild the Italian army. "I asked that volunteers be taken from the newly set up prison camps to create a certain number of divisions . . . Hitler and his high command considered those men too demoralized to be of any use." Graziani was not allowed to visit the prison camps to evaluate the situation from the morale point of view. The Germans expected only the officers to be recruited from the camps, but the troops would have to be recruited in Italy. The classes of 1924 and 1925 were called up. The recruits were concentrated at Vercelli, and the young men were then sent to Germany, where four divisions were being trained: the San Marco at Grafenwöhr, the Monterosa at Münsingen, the Italia at Henberg, and the Littorio at Senne Lager. Each division had a strength of about 15,000 to 20,000 men and would be in training for six months. Italian and German plans called for four more divisions to be trained right after the first four.

Six months after the last meeting with Hitler, Mussolini angrily told Rahn that this was no way to govern or administer the RSI. All his requests were ignored. "I absolutely must speak with the Führer." Rahn immediately warned his superiors that the Duce was ready to explode. He wanted to see Hitler at all costs. After finally agreeing with the Duce's request, Rahn underlined the importance of "helping the desire of the Italians to assert their independence, even giving some kind of satisfaction to the Duce that would quiet his depressive anxieties." Finally, from Rastenburg came the long-awaited confirmation: Hitler was ready to meet with Mussolini. The summit would take place in April at the quiet castle of Klessheim. Rahn replied that two days of discussion with the Führer would be sufficient for the Duce to illustrate the RSI's situation with respect to the most urgent political and military problems. Mussolini's only timid request was to be able to have his meals alone, given the doctor's prescriptions. The Duce also wished to visit the camps where the new Italian divisions were being trained. Hitler agreed and set the dates for April 22 and 23, 1944.

Mussolini's special train left Milan on April 21. The Duce was going on an official visit to Germany for the first time as head of the RSI for a meeting with the Führer. With him went Graziani, Mazzolini, his son Vittorio, and the two German "counselors," Rahn and Wolff, and Colonel Dollmann. Anfuso was to meet them at Salzburg. As usual, early in the evening, Mussolini shut the door to his compartment and kept it closed until dawn, when the convoy was already in Germany.

XVII

Final Meeting at Salzburg Castle

Klessheim: April 22-23, 1944

Mussolini reached Salzburg on the morning of April 22, 1944, for his next-to-last meeting with Hitler. He was given the usual apartment at Klessheim Castle. This conference, while not producing significant results, was much better organized than the others. The Führer had Ribbentrop, Keitel, Rahn, and Wolff with him. With the Duce were: Mazzolini, Graziani, Anfuso, and General Morera, the new military attaché in Berlin. The meeting took place in the grand ballroom of the ancient manor. Mussolini began speaking by describing the state of confusion he had found in Italy when he returned in September. He had prepared his presentation in German and was able to hold everyone's attention.

He then discussed the situation of the internment camps in Germany: "to secure a promise that his compatriots will be treated with some degree of humanity." Regarding the so-called "operational zones" (such as Alto Adige and Trieste) as the Germans called them, the Duce pointed out that the decisions of the German commanders did not always correspond to operational requirements. His Republic had not achieved much popularity because the authorities had to work around many difficulties created by the German authorities themselves. This made it impossible to fulfill the requests for soldiers and workers set forth by Minister Fritz Saukel, Marshal Göring, and Field Marshal Kesselring. Saukel wanted one million workers, Göring asked for two hundred thousand men for his antiaircraft batteries, and Kesselring needed sixty thousand auxiliary personnel for the support services of the Wehrmacht.

Mussolini asked Graziani to address military matters, with another laundry list of grievances regarding the lack of cooperation by German military authorities. The marshal complained about the antipartisan warfare in which many of his troops were engaged. The morning session ended with Mussolini retiring to his room and the others sitting down for lunch. Anfuso commented:

"Göring and Himmler were close by but never showed up at the castle. Klessheim was the opposite of Rastenburg: a stately castle, with its resplendent eighteenth-century decor of the court of the Margrave, it also overflowed with the Nazi military pomp of the Führung. Mussolini and Hitler theatrically went up and down the staircases, pausing to meet under high mirrors and tapestries. It would be the last time I would witness such scenes—that were interrupted at times by air raid sirens. Mussolini had prepared some notes regarding the problems of his new State, describing them as contingent problems caused by the suspicious attitude of the Germans toward the new RSI . . . While he spoke, Hitler was chewing on tiny pills. Graziani, sitting near the Führer, took notes and sometimes asked loud questions that drew Hitler's attention. The Germans were somewhat cold and distant; someone mentioned that he found "der Duze" had changed and it was obvious they were trying to bridge the gap between the Mussolini they had known and what he had become. Their respect for him had vanished because the "Duze" had, in their eyes, fallen from his pedestal as a dictator. They compared the simple, clear images of the Mussolini of 1937 at the Maifield in Berlin with the person now before them and saw a drastic change, when, in fact, their own perceptions had changed."

That afternoon, Hitler held a separate military conference. The second summit meeting with Mussolini began only after 5:00 p.m. The Führer proceeded immediately to break down point by point whatever had been stated earlier that morning by the Duce and Graziani, starting with the general situation of the war, which was now close to "being five years old." Hitler was cautious as to the course of the war. He did not minimize the increasing difficulties and proceeded to heap much of the blame on his allies, Italy and Hungary. The crises in these countries had forced Germany to take harsh measures, diverting large and vitally important forces from the front. However, the conflict would be resolved in the west with Germany victorious "because no coalition has endured more than five years in any war." Therefore it was necessary to resist at all costs until the unnatural marriage between Bolshevism and the Democracies would break up. Finally, Hitler announced a renewed submarine struggle in the Atlantic and new jet fighter aircraft faster than any American plane. Regarding the historical collapse of any coalition after five years, it appears that Hitler had been studying every precedent in the past, "especially the end of the coalition that eventually ensured the triumph of Frederick II of Prussia."

At dinner an exhausted Mussolini went back to his apartment since his appointed doctor and guardian Zachariae required that he rest as much as possible. Mussolini said he much preferred reading "the poetry of Goethe, which has the greatest calming effect." The next morning, April 23, Hitler rejected all accusations that the pro-Badoglio Italian soldiers were being mistreated by the Germans. He related an episode of "sedition" which had taken place at Linz, fomented by Italians who were certainly "Communists who have the protection of the Italian Fascist embassy in Berlin. They do not deserve anything and whatever you do for them, Duce, believe me, will only bring you disappointments."

Anfuso: "He went on this way, decrying the collapse of Fascism. 'But what was this Fascism if it just melted like the snow?' asked Hitler, who criticized himself when he stated: 'For years I guaranteed to my generals that Fascism was the most secure alliance for the German people. I never listened to my own suspicions toward the monarchy. Because of your requests, Duce, I never did anything to thwart your work on behalf of the King. I must confess that we Germans never did understand your attitude on this issue." I had never seen Hitler so brutal and true to his own legend. He recounted the history of the Badoglio conspiracy and asked the Germans present if such a thing could happen in Germany."

One of the reasons for friction between Salò and Berlin was the decree regarding the "socialization of businesses," which had produced a thick correspondence between Mussolini, Economy Minister Angelo Tarchi, Rahn, and Ribbentrop. Two months before, on the eve of the decree, Rahn had cabled Ribbentrop:

"The Italian government's plan to rebuild the economy is the Duce's personal project and has created widespread uneasiness in German military circles, especially those working with General Hans Leyers, who controls Italian armaments plants, and the experts within his office who are probably being influenced by Italian businessmen. I receive continuous requests to put an end to this Italian project and in particular the enactment of the laws and regulations. Since I know the Duce has discussed the project and reached an agreement with the Führer and the foreign minister, I am reluctant to follow up on the requests I have received. During my meetings with the Duce, I repeated to him the need to proceed much more cautiously and to reach an agreement with German authorities before making important decisions. I found a friendly but uncompromising resistance during this conversation. The Duce says that the attitude of the Italian leaders of industry, the majority of whom are secretly favorable to the British, has been responsible for the poor results of Italian armaments production. Mussolini's project has met with the same resistance as the 1906 nationalization of the railroads when it was proposed. His next objective is to nationalize electric power."

Mussolini also told the German ambassador: "This new system will give the Italian worker a feeling of participation in the welfare of his factory. Up to now this has been impossible due to the opposition of the big industrialists . . . " A confused Rahn requested precise instructions directly from Hitler: "Must we firmly oppose the Duce's projects, or should we allow him to carry out his experiment under our guidance and control?" Rahn received his answer via Ribbentrop on February 14: "The Führer has no interest in the Duce's socio-economic measures. Mussolini discussed this with him, and he feels that in this area Mussolini can act as he sees fit . . . We Germans must get over the habit of thinking that we are the doctors of Europe." But after German and Italian industrialists, the Swiss, who also had many interests in Italian industries in northern areas, explained to Minister Tarchi that the RSI projects would hasten the exit of Swiss investments from Italy. Labor unions also noted that the workers would reject "anything at all coming from Fascism." In the final analysis, the whole operation was a net loss to Mussolini, internally and internationally.

Hitler also addressed the subject of the recruitment of soldiers and workers by the German authorities a subject that had drawn protests from Mussolini. He declared that "I had to take emergency measures to place Italian troops in camps because they were not trustworthy. This was a burden for the German people, who demanded that the Italians be put to work." He also compared the excellent results of the French workers in Germany to the mediocre results of the Italians. He was well aware of the bitter medicine he was about to give the Duce and inquired about Mussolini's health; Dr. Morell was able to reassure the Führer on that subject. On the staircase of the castle, Hitler saw the Duce's son, Vittorio: "When Hitler saw me he smiled and shook my hand, saying: 'How is the young Mussolini?' I thanked him, thinking this would be the end of the conversation, but he then said: 'I'm pleased that Professor Morell has examined the Duce and found that he has almost completely recovered. Now it's necessary to continue the cure and follow Dr. Zachariae's prescriptions. I'm counting on your affectionate cooperation.' I reassured him and thanked him again as he said: 'Always stay near him.'

Regarding the proposed army of the RSI with German weapons and equipment, Hitler said that German industry was going through a difficult moment, and, in any case, the Wehrmacht had the right of precedence. He repeated again and again that the "Italians were not to be trusted," which obviously made Mussolini extremely angry. Even though one-third of the Italian troops in the camps had volunteered for the new army, it would only be the same old group of clever fellows trying to improve their position and their food rations. However, given the Duce's insistence, he would do what he could to allow the youngest Italians with the best fighting spirit to become the nucleus of the new Italian army, as was being done with the four Italian divisions now being trained in the Reich.

Hitler gave no ground on the subject of the "operational zones." These were essential to the security of the German army in Italy: "We cannot allow any kind of crisis to erupt behind the lines. However, the cancellation of these measures will depend upon the strengthening of the Fascist regime, and this will depend on the Duce. It is, therefore, essential that he stay in good health." Hitler had a strange way of being interested in Mussolini's welfare after denying him all his requests. Mussolini was now only the shadow of his former self. His wife had to call a tailor to Lake Garda to take in the clothes that kept sagging on an ever-thinning body.

The final meeting to work out a compromise between the Duce's demands and Hitler's decisions took place during the afternoon of April 23. Both dictators attempted to help each other and exchanged broad smiles for the benefit of those in attendance, who had been shocked by the three previous rounds of discussions. The agreement was intended to support German interests. The Duce agreed that the Italian troops would remain in German camps while he continued his requests for improvements. He also agreed to the extended training of the new Italian army in Germany because it was the most efficient and economical method. Finally, he agreed that the soldiers to be set free would be those who could be counted on, as the Führer suggested. Mussolini gave in to satisfy the demands coming from Saukel and Göring, and he confirmed that he would call the class of 1914 for the work service and the classes of 1916 and 1917 for Göring. Twenty battalions were to be used for civilian purposes.

Hitler was very pleased with the agreement they had reached and kept heaping praise on Mussolini: "Duce I am with you! You'll have a free hand in Italy. Whatever you may need will be given to you within the limits of what is possible. Always talk with Rahn, who will then refer back to me." As to the German divisions defending Rome at the time, Hitler said: "They are young, Duce, still boys, who have been fighting since September down there in the mud and the quagmire, for your Italy. I am pleased to know that they will soon have their Italian comrades fighting at their side who have been trained in Germany and that you are about to inspect. Together they will bring this war to its victorious conclusion."

The next morning Vittorio asked his father about his conversations with Hitler after telling him of his own short encounter. Mussolini replied:

"It's true. Ever since I stopped the milk diet, my ulcers are better. I really feel good. Dr. Zachariae is the one responsible, with those colored pills he forces me to take. Hitler is worried. The Russians are at the gates. We talked about the importance of time and space in politics and strategy in Russia. Hitler is convinced that had he not attacked in the summer of 1941, Stalin would have done so in the fall. He admitted that the policy of collaboration with France has been a vast strategic mistake. Fortunately, we Italians did not participate in *that* episode. But this is no time for recrimination; it appears that the secret weapons are now ready to be deployed. They are supposed to turn the situation around in our favor. I sensed much tension between the Nazi leaders and the generals. When things go wrong, the whole world is the same."

Eugen Dollmann has his version of the Klessheim meeting: "The conversations and their results were just as bad as the foul air that blew over the meetings and through the pleasant rooms of the castle. The sad theme of the deportations of Italian workers to Germany dominated the talks. It was uncomfortable watching the former dictator making weak attempts to obtain an improvement in the conditions of the concentration and work camps where his countrymen were being held." That evening, exceptionally, Hitler and Mussolini had dinner alone together. Anfuso recorded: "When they parted, the Duce confided to me that the Führer's declarations regarding the end of the war seemed wildly optimistic to him."

While Mussolini and Hitler were having, unbeknownst to either of them, their "last supper" together, the members of the entourage were drafting the usual communiqué. The document said:

"The Duce and the Führer have met on April 22 and 23. During the meetings, which took place in the spirit of the old friendship that exists between the Duce and the Führer, the discussions concentrated on political, military, and economic issues of interest to both countries and their common objectives. The Duce informed the Führer of the decision of the Italian Fascist government, as the only representative of the Italian people, to further intensify its participation in the war with the allies of the Tripartite Pact. This decision is confirmed once again by the warmest recognition of the Duce's war effort, which is fully supported by the government of the Reich."

The next morning, April 24, a column of cars left Salzburg, heading north toward Bavaria. Mussolini was in the third car, on his way to inspect the San Marco division, then being trained in the Grafenwöhr military camp. The visit to the marines of the San Marco division (which included 600 officers and 14,000 troops) was uplifting for Mussolini after two full days with Hitler. Vittorio remembered: "My father felt in much higher spirits after visiting the San Marco division. The oppressive atmosphere we lived in, in northern Italy, was swept away for all those who were present. Most of all, for Mussolini, who was greeted with wild enthusiasm by the soldiers. The popularity he still enjoyed with the Italian people of every class was still very high." (This charisma, however, would not prevent massive desertions, over twenty-five percent, from the ranks, once this unit returned to Italy that summer.) A grand review of the troops on parade took place. The division under the command of General Princivalle, who would later be replaced by General Farina, was reviewed by an energetic Mussolini, who gave each battalion the new Republican flag. Then he made a fiery speech: "Beyond the Garigliano River there are not only at bivouac the cynical British, but Americans, French, Poles, Indians, South Africans, Canadians, Australians, New Zealanders, Moroccans, Senegalese, Negroes, and Bolsheviks. You will have the joy of shooting at this mixture of bastard mercenary races who respect nothing and no one in occupied Italy." Ambassador Rahn, who remained at Mussolini's side, was impressed by the Grafenwöhr camp's enthusiasm at the Duce's presence.

Dollmann's comments were more cautious: "The parade of the San Marco was typical of troops marching in front of kings, emperors, and dictators. The tanned faces of the men did not betray any of the horrible suffering they endured in the German POW camps. On the contrary, one had to admire the effects of rigorous Prussian discipline on their bodies. Everything would have gone smoothly if fate had not decided to issue a warning. As the Duce left the camp, accompanied by Keitel, with the knowledge of having at least one division under his control, he felt himself reborn. Out of the thin fir trees suddenly appeared a large unit of the San Marco that had not taken part in the parade. Wading through swamps and water, they managed to reach and surround the Duce's car, cutting off the roadway with a barrier of nervous and agitated human bodies. They saw the man whom they long ago saluted as young boys in uniforms, screaming in unison 'Duce! Duce!' The founder of Fascism now expected to hear something similar under the trees and the pale sun of the German spring, but the hundreds of voices yelled 'Italy! Italy!' . . . Not a single one yelled 'Duce!'"

Anfuso also remembered: "Among the soldiers of the San Marco that day, he found himself again and told us so. He even forgot the terrible meetings at Klessheim, which had yielded very little but had convinced me that the entire enterprise was much more difficult than I had imagined. Various Nazi groups had succeeded in confusing the notions of our political existence, which since the Greek campaign had become progressively negative. In spite of the fact that I was aware of these feelings, even after Klessheim I continued to recommend in Italy and in Germany new meetings between the Duce and the Führer. The meeting at Klessheim had not been successful, but I found that the only useful instrument which could possibly improve the conditions of the minority that had decided to fight was only in the formal agreement between those two men . . ."

Once the Duce returned to Villa Feltrinelli, everyone agreed that the trip to Germany had lifted his morale enormously. The faithful Mazzolini wrote in his diary: "He found renewed faith in himself and in the future of the fatherland." His aides and his family did not know that the excitement they could see in his eyes was not so much because of his visit to Grafenwöhr, but rather because he was preparing a journalistic coup: the publication in the *Corriere della Sera* of a series of articles which would be published as a book entitled: *Storia di un anno—Il tempo del bastone e della carota* (*The Fall of Mussolini - His own story*). At the end of May 1944, the editor-in-chief of the daily newspaper, Ermanno Amicucci, was informed that an "anonymous" journalist would be contributing a series of articles on one of the most dramatic periods of Italy's history: October 1942 to July 1943.

On Saturday, June 24, 1944, the first installment was published under the title "From El Alamein to Mareth (or The Defeat of the Axis in North Africa)." Publication continued until July 18. On August 9 the identity of the author was revealed when the installments were bound into a single volume and 900,000 copies were printed with the Duce's name. In the introduction, Mussolini wrote: "In response to an overwhelming demand, the series of articles published in the *Corriere della Sera* in June and July is assembled here in one volume. There is a need to explain the facts and the events which took place during the most tragic months of Italy's history. We wanted to give a factual account that will be completed in due course, but never altered because everything that is mentioned here is true—it all actually took place. The moral of the story can be gleaned from the details of the story itself and its fateful consequences. Italy is today nailed on the cross, but on the horizon you can see the dawn of its Resurrection." But this magic moment, this return to his origins as an influential journalist, lasted only an instant, because on June 4, the Germans had evacuated the Italian capital to spare it from the horrors of war, leaving it open to immediate Allied occupation. After Rome, the Allies occupied Siena on

July 3, and on July 19 they were in Leghorn, on the western coast, and Ancona, on the Adriatic.

Mussolini took the loss of Rome as a personal affront. The first news coming from the city was such a crushing psychological blow that Dr. Zachariae, who observed the resulting debilitating physical effects (the aggressive ulcer problem, for one), was extremely worried. Mussolini had been told that a few hours after Kesselring's last units had left, the event was being celebrated in the Piazza Venezia. A Fascist journalist wrote: "At dawn on June 5 the girls who like to flirt were surrounding the monstrous Sherman tanks of the Americans, in search of romantic encounters and Camel cigarettes. They have just finished whispering 'auf wiedersehn' and were already tenderly practicing saying 'hello darling.'" All those who were near Mussolini at the time agree that he was unable to accept that "his beautiful Rome had fallen so low. Without any other weapon but his typewriter, he began writing some bitter commentaries and philosophical essays."

From his syndicated newspaper column, "Republican Correspondence," he launched an appeal, similar to that of Garibaldi's, to all Italians: "Rome or Death." He chronicled Italy's misfortune: "July 25, September 8, June 4. These are the stations of the cross of our country: the revolting trap perpetrated against a regime that had given Italy dignity and power, the shameful capitulation and the flight of the cowardly King and the treacherous marshal, the invasion of the capital by the hordes of Australians, Canadians, New Zealanders, Senegalese, and Americans. Three dates, three events that have upset the life and the destiny of our country. The news of Rome being occupied by the new barbarians wounds our honor as soldiers to the core . . . " Most of the themes used in these articles were to be the core of much of post-war right-wing Italian politics, especially concerning the neo-Fascist party.

While the Duce was mourning the loss of Rome, the Führer also had his own losses to count. Allied troops landed on the beaches of Normandy on June 6 and finally opened a second front in Europe. For the Axis, the third and final act had begun. The changed situation prompted Marshal Kesselring to recommend the transfer of the Italian divisions to northern Italy (i.e., to Liguria and Piedmont). Graziani approved the idea and requested that the soldiers who had not had any leave in years be given a short leave now. But if they were allowed to go, in all probability most of them would never return. Then again, desertions could also be expected even if no leave were granted. It was decided that before bringing the troops back to Italy, Mussolini would inspect them, using all his prestige to convince the men to accept new sacrifices. A real propaganda tour. It was also a very good reason to make a pilgrimage to the oracle at Rastenburg. The initiative was approved by Rahn and Hitler. On the morning of July 15, Mussolini left his retreat on Lake Garda and went to Mattarello di Trento, where a special German train was waiting for him. The Duce was welcomed by the chief of protocol of the Wilhelmstrasse, Baron Dörnberg. The first visit was to the Alpine division "Monterosa," under the command of General Mario Carloni. The day before, Hitler had left Berchtesgaden to return to Rastenburg.

Mussolini was accompanied by his son Vittorio, Graziani, Mazzolini, Rahn, Dollmann, and Anfuso, who noted: "The divisions were spread out at the four corners of Germany, which forced us to travel around the Reich, leaving the train once at Chemnitz on Dörnberg's orders because he feared some big Allied bombers over Dresden ... Mussolini resented these stops, and the Germans complained to me that the Duce's obstinacy would get them into trouble with Hitler. Keitel even said, 'Thank God there are only four divisions.' At every stop there was a bulletin on the air war situation and sometimes a request from Hitler on the progress of the trip. Enemy planes were everywhere . . . Dörnberg was under orders from Hitler that Mussolini should never be at risk. We arrived at Münsingen on July 16, where the Monterosa division was being trained and witnessed scenes of enthusiastic fanaticism, similar to those of the San Marco during the previous trip, which both amazed and embarrassed the Germans."

In speaking to the Alpine troops of the Monterosa (about 19,000 men and some 650 officers), Mussolini said: "You are the first large unit to go back to see the sky and the sunshine of the motherland betrayed, divided, and tormented by the enemy. You are therefore the master columns of the temple, the rock of the reconstruction of the Italian army. As you go back to Italy, do not be worried to find on the opposing side other Italians who may be naïve or treacherous . . . " The next day, after another rail trip, the Duce reached Henberg, near Ebingen, where the "Italia" division made up of bersaglieri, about 14,000 men in all, was encamped. The encounter between the former corporal and his old unit took the form of a dialogue. Mussolini said to the troops, "Hello, comrades!" They responded "Hello, Duce!" He then said: "For over a century you have been the symbol of the Italian army—not just for the Italian people but also for every other nation . . . For me and for you today there is only one Italy: the RSI." Then he visited the Littorio division at Senne Lager, near Heidelberg.

During a pause the Duce asked for permission to visit the convent of the Benedictines at Beuron. Dollmann recalled: "Mussolini stopped in front of each painting and compared the Beuron school to that of Fra Angelico, and just when everyone thought he had finished, he walked solemnly toward the library. An old and half-blind monk came up to him to show him a manuscript. 'Oh, how happy I am to speak the language of Dante,' said the old man. He went on to tell his life story: he had lived in Rome for decades under Pope Leo XIII, worked in the Vatican archives, and had participated in the Lateran Pact. 'My most cherished memory, Your Excellency,' said the monk, 'is the Concordat, and I wish to offer you a copy of the text decorated by our friars.' Mussolini, visibly moved by the generous offer, humbly accepted the gift."

On the morning of July 20, at the conclusion of the long inspection tour, Mussolini boarded the train that, via Halle, would take him to Rastenburg. The itinerary placed the arrival at the Wolfsschanze at 3:00 p.m. The train was suddenly ordered to stop in the middle of the forest just one hour away from its final destination. Dörnberg was nervous but unable to explain the delay, saying that these were orders coming directly from Rastenburg. The passengers were ordered to close the windows and not walk through the corridors. The nervousness of the diplomat and the scenario being enacted led Dollmann to believe that something big had happened. The train remained there until 3:00 p.m., then began moving again.

Mussolini was not alarmed at the delay because at a previous stop, caused by the fear of a bombing attack, the Germans had pleasantly surprised him with an "improvised" meeting with a peasant family. Dollmann witnessed the episode: "Out of the small house belonging to the forest guard came the guard's mother and her grandchildren, boys and girls. One carried a plate full of raspberries, another a plate with a cake, and the third had small plates and utensils. The children bowed to the bald foreigner who looked at them with his big eyes, and they recited a few verses: "Lieber Duce; Tritt hier ein; Was wir haben es ist dein; Sollst uns Hochwilkommen sein" (Enter, dear Duce. What we have is yours. May you be welcome). The foreigner thanked them and patted their heads, and everyone sat down at a round table in front of the small house in the forest. It looked like a fairy tale. The Duce ate freshly picked raspberries for the first time in his life. A bottle of mediocre sparkling wine appeared, and he lifted his glass to thank the old woman. On the banks of Lake Garda he had learned German customs . . . The children produced a large album, where the great man signed his name. Then everyone went back aboard the train while the woman had the children sing the old song: "I had a comrade once . . . "

As Mussolini's train went deeper into the Prussian forest, he was unaware that a plane had left Berlin-Rangsdorf at 7:00 a.m. and had flown over his train that morning. Two passengers on the plane were to become part of history: Colonel Count Claus Schenk von Stauffenberg and his assistant, Lieutenant Werner von Haeften. Their plane landed at Rastenburg at 10:00 a.m. They were carrying two bombs in their bags, each one meant for Adolf Hitler.

XVIII

July 20, 1944: Farewell Tea at the Wolf's Lair

Rastenburg: July 20, 1944

A few minutes past four in the afternoon on July 20, 1944, Mussolini's train pulled into the station of the Wolf's Lair, whose conventional name was Görlitz. The Duce was at the window with Marshal Dollmann at his side. Adolf Hitler was on the platform ready to greet him. Behind the Führer were Ribbentrop, Himmler, Bormann, Keitel, Göring, and Dönitz. The air was damp with fog and rain, and the trees waved gently in the wind. Despite the humidity, Hitler was wearing his black coat; his right arm was in a sling. His face was red, his hair appeared burnt, and his ears were protected by cotton balls. Mussolini approached the Führer with a look of utter astonishment at the sight.

Hitler went up to the Duce and with a slow intensity said: *"Duze, man hat eben eine Höllenmaschine über mich losgeissen"* (Duce, they have just thrown an infernal machine at me).

As Anfuso recounted: "Just one look at the Führer's face would have been enough to convince us that they had indeed hit him with an bomb, but the term he used led Mussolini to believe that Hitler was talking about a political machination, which would have been more typical of his usual phraseology." In response to Mussolini's puzzled look, the Führer pointed to his own head with his left hand. In a few minutes, aboard the Reich Chancellor's powerful car, they reached the compound. Hitler continued what he had started to say at the railroad stop: "Duce, just a few moments ago, I was given the greatest sign of my good fortune." Only four hours earlier, Nazism had just lived through its very own "July 25" attempt, which was to be much more tragic than the Italian one, with many more victims, dead and wounded. A huge bomb, placed by Stauffenberg at 12:42 p.m. had destroyed the hut where Hitler was meeting with twenty-four other German officers and staff.

The thirty-six-year-old Colonel Stauffenberg was the point man of a vast military conspiracy that included over twenty "red striped" members of the German high command——field marshals, generals, and other high ranking officers. Ever since the Sudeten crisis of 1938, that would end with the Munich agreement Chamberlain had accepted, the conspirators had been planning to free Germany from Hitler's dictatorship. The motivations of the group were contained in the political testament left by the leader and organizer of the conspiracy, General Henning von Tresckow: "The assassination of Hitler must be attempted at any cost; even if we were to fail . . . we must demonstrate to the world and to future generations that the men of the German resistance dared to take the fateful step at the risk of their own lives." The coup had been planned at least eleven times prior to the July 20 bomb. The last two times had been on July 11 at Berchtesgaden and July 15 at Rastenburg, both by Stauffenberg. The July 11 plan was canceled because Göring and Himmler were not present because they too had to be eliminated; on July 15 it went nowhere because of a change in Hitler's schedule that day. Stauffenberg decided to go ahead on July 20 in any case. He was close to a nervous breakdown because he had already failed twice before. Shortly after 10:00 a.m. he arrived at

Rastenburg and met briefly with Keitel to receive last-minute instructions regarding the conference with Hitler, which he was attending as chief of staff of the home army.

There were some unpleasant surprises in store for Stauffenberg. After presenting his plan to Keitel on the creation of the divisions of People's Grenadiers, who were to replenish the losses of the armies fighting on the eastern front, the field marshal said: "This morning's program has changed. The meeting will begin at 12:30 p.m., a half hour ahead of time, so you will have to limit yourself strictly to the most urgent problems." Hiding his disappointment, Stauffenberg asked: "Will there be enough time for my presentation?" . . . "I think so," answered Keitel, "but unfortunately we have had to change the agenda because we expect an important visit. Early in the afternoon, the Führer is expecting a guest with whom he wishes to spend the rest of the afternoon." "May I know who this person is?" asked Stauffenberg. Keitel replied: "Yes, I can tell you. It's Mussolini."

It was already noon, and Stauffenberg, with military efficiency, had planned the beginning of the Walküre operation—the code name of the military coup—for 1:00 p.m., to coincide exactly with the scheduled opening of Hitler's military conference. Stauffenberg and the other conspirators in Berlin, Paris, and Brussels had set their watches to Rastenburg time. But Mussolini's arrival changed the schedule one half hour ahead of the planned time. This was not to be the only modification: as Stauffenberg was leaving, Keitel told him, "Come with me, we must go quickly, there is also another change. The meeting is not in the underground bunker but in the Gästebarake (the guest house)."

The switch had been motivated perhaps by the intense humid heat or the by need to speed things up. It made a considerable difference in the plans of the conspirators because the power of the blast would decrease significantly if it detonated in a wooden hut with glass windows rather than the concrete underground chamber the Führer used as an air raid shelter. Besides, the heavy-set Keitel was now walking next to Stauffenberg, making it impossible to secretly break the acid capsule that would activate the trigger of the bomb he was carrying in his briefcase. Saying that he had forgotten his cap, Stauffenberg turned back and, fearful and anxious, was able to break the capsule. The bomb was now armed. He then entered the conference room of the hut, where he saw three open windows. He quickly left the room saying he had to make an urgent phone call to Berlin. Before he left, Stauffenberg had placed his briefcase with the bomb under the map table the Führer was using. The blast went off at 12:42 p.m., just as Stauffenberg had successfully passed through the gates. He flew back to Berlin in the same Heinkel that had taken him to East Prussia that morning.

Everyone's first reaction was that an enemy plane had bombed the hut, but the truth was quickly discovered. Of the twenty-four persons at the conference, one stenographer died instantly, while three others, two generals and a colonel, were near death. The rest, including Hitler himself (whose clothes were torn to shreds), were all more or less seriously wounded. The Führer was burned on his right arm and leg, and his hair was on fire. His eardrums were damaged, and he had lost his hearing. Keitel was the luckiest and the first to help Hitler and congratulate him at having escaped death. Hitler would never fully uncover the details of the conspiracy. He told an astounded Mussolini, who for a brief moment considered leaving Rastenburg immediately, the details of the dramatic events.

Arriving at the Wolf's Lair, Hitler was joined by Himmler while the Duce walked with Göring and other officials behind them. Himmler then concluded his excited discussion with Hitler and immediately took off for Berlin with the mission of wiping out all the traitors. Once again, Hitler turned to Mussolini. Anfuso recalled: "The Führer wanted the Duce to see the hut where the bomb had gone off. In the center of the room was a fairly wide crater. The main beams were broken off, the windows themselves and the contents of the hut and its furniture had been blown outside, into the surrounding field. Hitler pointed out that had the blast occurred in the usual bunker, no one would have survived . . . " Hitler was continuously on the phone with Goebbels in Berlin. In fact, only when news had come from the capital back to Rastenburg did it become clear that the bomb was the signal for a putsch, rather than an isolated attempt. The colonel's responsibility became apparent after a sergeant remembered the phone call Stauffenberg made to the war ministry in Berlin right after the blast.

Hitler was proud at having escaped with his life and told Mussolini: "I was here, near this table. The bomb exploded at my feet. Look at my uniform. Look at my burns. When I think of all this, it's obvious that nothing can happen to me now! It is my destiny to continue on my path and complete my mission. It will not be the first time that I have miraculously eluded death. What happened here was the most extreme attempt on my life. Having been spared death in such extraordinary circumstances, I am now convinced more than ever that the great cause I am serving will survive all the present dangers and that all will end well." Mussolini replied: "You are right, the Almighty has extended his protective hand over you. After the miracle that took place in this room today, it is inconceivable that our cause could fail."

Hitler finally sat down on a box, and Mussolini took a chair. The Duce was uncertain as to what he should do. He had prepared some notes on the issues he wanted to discuss, in particular, the Italian divisions that were trained and now ready to be sent back to Italy's southern front, as well as the problem of the poor treatment of Italian soldiers still held in concentration camps in Germany. But he did not know how to begin, with so many excited people screaming and gesticulating as they entered and left the room. Anfuso: "Mussolini looked at me as if to ask whether we should remain at all. Fortunately Hitler, perhaps thinking this would be the best way of getting us out of there, suggested that we discuss the points of our agenda. Mussolini then explained the Italian situation in an abbreviated version as he saw the face Hitler was making . . . "

The Duce first spoke of the fall of Rome and its disastrous impact on morale. The increase in desertions from the ranks of the RSI army and the dramatic drop in volunteers were only the first symptoms. He then insisted that an "elastic defense" would be inapplicable to Italy, since a break in the defensive line in the Apennine Mountains would provoke the collapse of the RSI government.

After thanking the Führer for training the Italian divisions in Germany, he requested the two units that were ready, the Monte Rosa and San Marco, now be sent back to Italy at once. Mussolini also asked for an immediate answer from German authorities regarding their plans for the Italian military prisoners. The Duce handed the Führer the memorandum he had written on the train, in which all open issues were restated, and in particular the express desire of the Fascist government to participate in the defense of the country, the improvement of the relationship with German authorities in Italy, and the request of a pardon for four Italian naval officers, who had just been condemned to death by a military court in France.

Hitler, now convinced that his destiny was assured because of his miraculous escape that afternoon, not only accepted most of what Mussolini requested but was even more generous than expected. He was sure that he would win the war, and while he complained of shortages in supplies, both of food and weapons, he said that the secret weapons, now pounding London and other enemy targets since June, would prove decisive. He was certain of this because he was about to fire new, even deadlier, missiles against the British and to effect this plan he needed more workers for industrial plants. Therefore the Duce's requests would be accepted, and he said: "I think that we can change the status of the Italian prisoners into free workers beginning today, and this will no doubt have a positive effect in Italy."

Hitler decided to release the other two units, Littorio and Italia, as well in order to form a larger army under Graziani's command (to be called "Liguria") which would be reinforced by German units. Hitler was making these decisions against the recommendations of the German high command that wanted to transfer the Italian units into the war on the eastern front to cover some of its own losses. There were also antiaircraft requests made by Göring for the defense of armament factories, and these would be supported by other units. The strategy in Italy would be coordinated with Kesselring, who was ordered to fight delaying actions to allow more troops to arrive from Germany. Finally, Hitler agreed to pardon the four Italian officers who had been condemned to death. All this was much more than Mussolini expected, as he told his son: "I got what I wanted and more . . . Today Hitler couldn't deny me anything. I also received the promise that all the Italians in prison camps after September 8, the "Badoglio officers" and others, will be treated as free workers. He told me that Germany can't increase rations, but it will try to make improvements. The divisions will also be transferred to Italy much faster. Hitler gave Graziani and me this news with great enthusiasm." Vittorio saw that his father, in talking about his conversation with Hitler, was grinning: "I figured what that ironic and slightly teasing smile meant: like all the Italians in the group, Mussolini had suddenly been freed of the accusation of treason, the continuous German complaints about the events in Italy before and after July 25 and September 8. Traitors were no longer only Italians. True, there had been no surrender and no collapse of the Nazi party, but some consolation was derived from the situation."

Back at the Villa Orsoline during the entire summer of 1944, Mussolini kept talking with personal satisfaction of his luck at having witnessed the "Nazi July 25." Everyone who approached the Duce at the time would hear him say: "We are no longer alone as far as treason goes!" At Rastenburg, things fell into place, while in Berlin, the first arrests and executions were taking place. Himmler was immediately named commander of the home army, the very center of the failed putsch. Before going to Berlin, he told Hitler: "My Führer, let me take care of this."

At 5:30 p.m., tea was served. The table was set for a party. Dollmann recalled: "The young soldiers serving were as blond and as blue-eyed as ever." There were plenty of biscuits, sweets, and tarts. The Führer was silent after having spoken with the Duce. New guests arrived in the room. Except for Goebbels and Himmler, who were in or on their way to Berlin, the entire Nazi constellation was present. Then began a scene that frightened Mussolini and his group. Suddenly all the Führer's aides and Nazi leaders began accusing each other, shouting threats, with each one trying to show how much more faithful and important their services were to the cause. Göring had descended like a firestorm on Rastenburg from his own nearby HQ. Ribbentrop, who was also close by at Schloss Steinort, was also present. Dönitz had just arrived by plane from Berlin.

Göring began: "My Führer, now we know why our heroic armies were falling back in the east. They have been stabbed in the back by the generals. My invincible "Göring" division will bring the traitors to justice."

Dönitz: "My Führer, my men want you to know only one thing; they will fight to full victory or death. Now that these generals have been swept aside, the fortress England will fall."

Bormann: "My Führer, the awful attempt on your life has brought the entire nation tightly together. Now the sabotage by the generals or the middle class will be impossible. The party will go back energetically to its duty and fulfill it with renewed enthusiasm."

Ribbentrop: "My Führer, from now on, this spells the end for the traitors. Going forward, everything will be different. My diplomats in the Balkans will see to it that we have the upper hand. My colleague Mazzolini has just told me earlier that we must be extremely vigilant in that area due to the political situation."

Bormann was interpreting his colleagues' thoughts and forecasting correctly what was about to take place. But at 3:00 p.m. Hitler, once the Duce's train had been allowed to proceed, told one of his secretaries, Christa Schröder: "I must meet with the Duce. What would the world press say if I didn't hold this meeting?" For the first time, everyone saw Mussolini drink some cognac, as if to celebrate the priceless scene he was witnessing.

Then Hitler spoke: "Never before have I felt the strength of Providence to be with me. The miracle of these last few hours has reinforced my conviction that I am called to accomplish even greater tasks and that I should guide the German people to the greatest victory in their history. But I want to destroy and crush the criminals who have attempted today to oppose Providence and me. As traitors to my own people, they deserve a shameful death, and they shall have it. This hour shall see punished anyone who participated and their families as well if they knew anything whatsoever about it. The nest of vipers trying to stop the ascent of my Germany will be exterminated once and for all!"

The Führer's words did not succeed in quieting the arguments. Göring was being bitterly attacked by Dönitz. The fat Reich marshal was berating Ribbentrop, to whom he attributed all the foreign policy mistakes of the Wilhelmstrasse. At dusk, Hitler calmed down. The news from Berlin was that order had been reestablished in the capital and that the plot had been foiled. The calm made an impression on Vittorio Mussolini: "Führer, allow me to congratulate you at having escaped such treachery."

"He looked at me as if noticing my existence for the first time, even though I had been sitting next to him for more than an hour. Then he said: 'Ach so, the young Muzzolini. Thank you. Providence did not want Germany to lose its leader at such a decisive moment. Nothing can stop our victory now. We must double our fighting spirit with the energy of desperation. A people willing to resist, like the Germans, deserves the greatest destiny.' Hitler then sipped his tea and ate a few biscuits."

By now Mussolini had been at Rastenburg for three hours. To the Duce, it felt like thirty years, with all that he had seen and heard. His presence had allowed the Führer to ease the tension at the Wolf's Lair after the attempt on his life, as a last service the Duce performed for his friend. On April 24, 1945, some nine months later, Hitler, under siege in his Berlin bunker, was to send Mussolini his final message:

"The struggle for existence and nonexistence has reached its climax. With huge masses of men and equipment, Bolshevism and Judaism are engaged on German soil with all their destructive forces to plunge the continent into chaos. However, in its spirit of complete disregard for death, the German people and all the others who share the same feelings, will seek vengeance, however hard the struggle, and with their unparalleled heroism, they will change the course of the war at this historic moment when the future of Europe is being decided for centuries to come." Mussolini did not answer this message. He had neither the time nor the inclination. He was already in Milan to begin his own race toward death. In the meantime, the soldiers of the US Sixty-ninth Infantry regiment were linking up with the Fifty-eighth Soviet Guards division at Torgau on the Elbe River. It was 4:40 p.m. on April 25, 1945.

Some ten days before came the final news that had convinced Hitler about the benevolent signs of Providence: President Roosevelt had died at Warm Springs, Georgia, on April 12. But Hitler would never know the decision of British voters who three months later would vote Winston Churchill out of office. He could never have imagined that some sixteen years later his implacable adversary, Joseph Stalin, would be expelled from the mausoleum on the Red Square, as he was no longer deemed to deserve the spot next to Lenin. Nor could he have foreseen the collapse of the USSR and the sweeping changes to come out of those events

At Rastenburg at 7:00 p.m. on July 20, 1944, ended the seventeenth and final meeting between Hitler and Mussolini. It lasted only three hours, but it was certainly the most dramatic of all. Ten years had passed almost to the day since their first encounter at Venice on June 14, 1934. During those ten years not only the geopolitical map of the world had been profoundly changed but also the lives of people, nations, religions, and races had been radically and brutally affected forever.

Hitler accompanied his guest to the station at Görlitz, always deferential and polite to the end. Before Mussolini got into the train, the two shook hands at length, and Hitler, visibly emotional, said: "Duce, I consider you to be Germany's and my own best friend. The German people will be eternally grateful to you. Whatever may happen, Germany and Italy will live on for a more glorious tomorrow."

Chronology

July 29, 1883	Benito Mussolini, born in Predappio, near Forlì.
April 20, 1889	Adolf Hitler, born in Braunau, Austria.
1900-1914	Mussolini joins the Italian Socialist party and becomes editor of the party newspaper, *Avanti!*
1906-1913	Hitler's years in Vienna.
August 1914	Hitler in Munich joins a Bavarian regiment.
1914-1918	Hitler participates in World War I.
November 15, 1914	Mussolini breaks with the Socialist party; is founder and editor of *Il Popolo d'Italia* in Milan.
1915	Mussolini calls for war against Germany and Austria.
1916-1917	Mussolini fights at the front.
1918	Hitler is gassed and temporarily blinded at the end of the war.
1919	Mussolini creates the "Fasci di Combattimento" in the Piazza Sansepolcro in Milan.
1918-1920	Hitler remains in the German army as a speaker and propagandist in Munich.
1919	Hitler joins the National Socialist Workers Party, the NSDAP.
October 28, 1922	The King of Italy asks Mussolini to form a government after the "March on Rome."
1922-1923	Initial contacts between Hitler and Mussolini, now Head of the Italian government.
1923-1925	Failure of the beer hall "putsch" in Munich; Hitler sentenced to prison at Landsberg; while incarcerated he dictates *Mein Kampf.*
1924	Mussolini implicated in the murder of Socialist Deputy Giacomo Matteotti.
1925-1932	Mussolini consolidates his power and crushes the opposition.
1925-1930	Hitler rebuilds the Nazi party and seeks to meet Mussolini, but is rebuffed.

1929	Wall Street Crash, the Great Depression spreads to Europe.
1932	Hitler receives 13 million votes in the presidential election, von Hindenburg is reelected President. There are 6 million unemployed in Germany.
1932	Achille Starace becomes secretary of the PNF (the Fascist Party).
January 30, 1933	Hitler named Chancellor of Germany.
August 1933	Galeazzo Ciano named to head Mussolini's press office.
March 31, 1933	Nazi Party declaration on the Jews; worldwide boycott of Germany.
October 1933	Germany leaves the League of Nations.
June 14, 1934	Hitler and Mussolini meet in Venice for the first time.
June 30, 1934	Hitler purges the SA: Röhm, Strasser, and many others are executed during the "Night of the Long Knives."
July 25, 1934	Nazi "coup" attempt fails in Austria; Dollfuss is murdered; Mussolini pledges to defend Austrian independence.
1935-1936	Mussolini declares war on Ethiopia; the League of Nations votes sanctions against Italy.
1935	Nazi Germany enacts the Nuremberg racial laws.
June 10, 1936	Galeazzo Ciano becomes Italian Foreign Minister.
July 1936-1939	Civil War breaks out in Spain; Mussolini sends troops and Hitler commits the Luftwaffe in support of Franco.
September 1937	Mussolini visits Germany.
March 12, 1938	The *Anschluss* of Austria is not opposed by Italy.
May 3, 1938	Hitler visits Italy.
July 15, 1938	Italian state-sponsored anti-Semitism begins.
September 29, 1938	Munich Conference, mediated by Mussolini, leads to the dismemberment of Czechoslovakia.

March 15, 1939	Hitler enters Prague and proclaims a German protectorate over the Czech State.
March 1939	Great Britain and France extend guarantees to Poland.
April 9, 1939	Italy occupies and annexes Albania.
May 22, 1939	Ciano and Ribbentrop sign the military alliance between Germany and Italy, known as the Pact of Steel.
August 23, 1939	Ribbentrop signs the Non-Aggression pact between Germany and the USSR in Moscow.
September 1, 1939	Germany attacks Poland; World War II begins.
September 3, 1939	France and Great Britain declare war on Germany, Italy remains neutral.
March 9, 1940	Germany invades Denmark and Norway.
March 18, 1940	Mussolini meets Hitler at the Brenner Pass, commits to war once Germany attacks in the west.
May 10, 1940	Germany begins its offensive into the Netherlands, Belgium and Luxembourg.
May-June, 1940	Battle of France, Dunkirk; French army is defeated.
June 10, 1940	Italy declares war on France and Great Britain.
June 18, 1940	Hitler meets Mussolini in Munich to set terms for the armistice with France. Pétain becomes head of the Vichy government.
October 4, 1940	Mussolini and Hitler meet at the Brenner Pass to discuss the possible entry of Spain into the war.
October 28, 1940	Hitler meets with Mussolini in Florence, while Italy attacks Greece.
January 19, 1941	Mussolini travels to Berchestgaden to meet with Hitler regarding the disasters facing the Italian army in Greece and Libya.
May 12, 1941	Rudolf Hess flies to Scotland and bails out of his fighter plane.
June 2, 1941	Hitler and Mussolini meet at the Brenner Pass.
June 22, 1941	Ribbentrop announces the German attack on the USSR with the participation of Hungary and Romania.

July 1941	Italy commits an expeditionary force to Russia.
August 25, 1941	Hitler and Mussolini meet at Rastenburg and tour the Russian front.
April 29, 1942	Mussolini meets Hitler at Klessheim near Salzburg regarding military operations in Egypt and Russia; the Malta invasion plan is discussed.
October 23, 1942	Battle of El Alamein ends in defeat for Rommel now in full retreat.
November 1942	Battle of Stalingrad begins.
November 11, 1942	Allied forces land in Morocco and Algeria; German forces occupy Tunisia.
April 7, 1943	Mussolini and Hitler meet at Klessheim after the defeat at Stalingrad and before the final battle in Tunisia.
July 19, 1943	Hitler requests an emergency meeting following the Allied invasion of Sicily. The meeting is held at Feltre, near Treviso.
July 25, 1943	Mussolini is voted down by a majority of the Fascist Grand Council and is arrested by the King. Badoglio is Prime Minister.
September 8, 1943	Badoglio signs an armistice with the Allies.
September 12, 1943	Mussolini is liberated by German paratroopers led by Otto Skorzeny, while German troops occupy northern Italy.
September 14, 1943	Mussolini meets Hitler at Rastenburg, agrees to set up the Fascist Republican regime.
January 1944	Ciano and other Fascist leaders are executed by the Republican Fascists at Verona.
April 22, 1944	Mussolini and Hitler meet at Klessheim.
July 20, 1944	Final meeting between Hitler and Mussolini at Rastenburg on the same day von Stauffenburg places a bomb that fails to kill Hitler.
April 28, 1945	Mussolini and Claretta Petacci are executed and their bodies, along with that of Achille Starace, are hanged upside down in public in Milan.
April 30, 1945	Hitler and Eva Braun commit suicide in the bunker under the Chancellery in Berlin.

Bibliography

In addition to the works and persons we have consulted, and referenced within the text itself, the following is a partial list of related books and articles used in writing this book. Since the quantity of publications concerning the Second World War has by now reached gigantic proportions, we have made a selection of the sources we have used.

Books

Acerbo, Giacomo, *Fra due plotoni di esecuzione*, Cappelli, Bologna 1968

Alexandrov, Victor, *L'orso e la balena*, Bompiani, Milan 1959

Alfieri, Dino, *Due dittatori di fronte*, Rizzoli, Milan 1948

Amè, Cesare, *Guerra segreta in Italia*, Casini, Rome 1954

Amicucci, Ermanno, *I 600 giorni di Mussolini*, Faro, Rome 1948

Anfuso, Filippo, *Da Palazzo Venezia al Lago di Garda*, Cappelli, Bologna 1957

Arena, Nino, *Assalto dal cielo*, Mursia , Milan 1975

Aron, Robert, *La Francia di Vichy*, Rizzoli, Milan 1972

Attanasio, Sandro, *Sicilia senza Italia*, Mursia, Milan 1976

Auty, Phyllis, *Tito*, Mursia, Milan 1972

Badoglio, Pietro, *L'Italia nella seconda guerra mondiale*, Rizzoli, Milan 1946

Balabanoff, Angelica, *Il traditore*, Napoleone, Rome 1973

Ball, Adrian, *L'ultimo giorno del vecchio mondo*, Garzanti, Milan 1964

Bandini, Franco, *Tecnica della sconfitta*, Sugar, Milan 1963

Bandini, Franco, *Claretta*, Longanesi, Milan 1969

Bartoli, Domenico, *La fine della monarchia*, Mondadori, Milan 1947

Bastianini, Giuseppe, *Uomini, fatti, cose*, Vitagliano, Milan 1959

Battisti, Vacante, *Alto Adige*, Cappelli, Bologna 1961

Bedeschi, Giulio, *Centomila gavette di ghiaccio*, Mursia, Milan 1963

Bekker, Cajus, *Storia della Marina del Terzo Reich*, Longanesi, Milan 1974

Bellomo, Nicola, *Memoriale*, Mursia, Milan 1978

Berezhkov, Valentin, *In missione diplomatica da Hitler*, Cei, Milan 1965

Bernotti, Romeo, *Cinquant'anni nella Marina Militare*, Mursia, Milan 1971

Bertoldi, Silvio, *La guerra parallela*, Mondadori, Milan 1966

Bertoldi, Silvio, *Vittorio Emanuele III*, UTET, Torino 1970

Bertoldi, Silvio, *Mussolini tale e quale*, Longanesi, Milan 1973

Bianchi, Gianfranco, *25 luglio, crollo di un regime*, Mursia, Milan 1963

Bianchi, Pietro, *Mussolini pro e contro*, Mondadori, Milan 1972

Bocca, Giorgio, *La repubblica di Mussolini*, Laterza, Bari 1977

Boldt, Gerhard, *Ero con Hitler*, Longanesi, Milan 1967

Bolla, Nino, *La battaglia di Catania*, Erp, Rome 1961

Bolton, Glorney, *Pétain*, Longanesi, Milan 1958

Bonacina, Giorgio, *Obiettivo Italia*, Mursia, Milan 1972

Bonacina, Giorgio, *Comando Bombardieri*, Longanesi, Milan 1975

Bongiovanni, Alberto, *La fine dell'Impero*, Mursia, Milan 1974

Boschesi, Palmiro, *Come scoppiò la seconda guerra mondiale*,
    Mondadori, Milan 1974

Bottai, Giuseppe, *Vent'anni e un giorno*, Garzanti, Milan 1949

Bragadin, Marc'Antonio, *Il dramma della Marina italiana*,
    Mondadori, Milan 1968

Brown, Anthony Cave, *Una cortina di bugie*, Mondadori, Milan 1976

Bryant, Arthur, *Tempo di guerra*, Longanesi, Milan 1966

Buffarini Guidi, Glauco, *La vera verità*, Sugar, Milan 1970

Cabiati, Aldo, *Cronistoria di questa guerra*, dall'Oglio, Milan 1942

Caccia Dominioni, P., *Alamein 1933-1962*, Longanesi, Milan 1966

Calic, Edouard, *Himmler e il suo impero*, Feltrinelli, Milan 1971

Carboni, Giacomo, *Memorie segrete 1935-1948*, Parenti, Firenze 1955

Carboni, Giacomo, *La verità di un generale distratto*, Beta, Rome 1966

Carloni, Mario, *La campagna di Russia*, Longanesi, Milan 1956

Cartier, Raymond, *La seconda guerra mondiale*, Mondadori, Milan 1977

Castellano, Giuseppe, *La guerra continua*, Rizzoli, Milan 1963

Caudana, Mino, *Il figlio del fabbro*, Cen, Rome 1960

Cavallero, Carlo, *Il dramma del maresciallo Cavallero*, Mondadori,
    Milan 1952

Cerruti, Elisabetta, *Visti da vicino*, Garzanti, Milan 1951

Cersosimo, Vincenzo, *Storia del processo di Verona*, Garzanti, Milan 1949

Cervi, Mario, *Storia della guerra di Grecia*, Sugar, Milan 1966

Churchill, Winston S., *La seconda guerra mondiale*, Mondadori,
    Milan 1952

Ciano, Edda, *La mia testimonianza*, Rusconi, Milan 1975

Ciano, Galeazzo, *Diario 1937-1938*, Cappelli, Bologna 1948

Ciano, Galeazzo, *Diario 1939-1943*, Rizzoli, Milan 1950

Cione, Edmondo, *Storia della repubblica sociale*, Cenacolo, Caserta 1948

Colacicchi, Paolo, *L'ultimo fronte in Africa*, Mursia, Milan 1977

Collier, Richard, *Duce! Duce!*, Mursia, Milan 1971

Clark, Alan, *Operazione Barbarossa*, Garzanti, Milan 1967

Corradi, Egisto, *La ritirata di Russia*, Longanesi, Milan 1965

Crespi, Benito, *La battaglia di Natale*, Longanesi, Milan 1965

Cross, Colin, *Adolf Hitler*, Mursia, Milan 1977

D'Aroma, Nino, *Vent'anni insieme*, Cappelli, Bologna 1957

D'Aroma, Nino, *Mussolini segreto*, Cappelli, Bologna 1958

D'Aroma, Nino, *Hitler: rapporto a Mussolini*, Cen, Rome 1974

Davanzo, Giuseppe, *Ali e poltrone*, Ciarrapico, Rome 1976

Davis, Melton S., *Chi difende Roma?*, Rizzoli, Milan 1973

De Begnac, Yvon, *Palazzo Venezia*, La Rocca, Rome 1951

De Biase, Carlo, *L'aquila d'oro*, Il Borghese, Milan 1969

De Felice, Renzo, *Storia degli ebrei italiani sotto il fascismo*,
    Einaudi, Turin 1961

De Felice, Renzo, *Il problema dell'Alto Adige*, Il Mulino, Bologna 1973

De Felice, Renzo, *Mussolini, il duce*, Einaudi, Turin 1981

Del Boca, Angelo, *La guerra d'Abissinia*, Feltrinelli, Milan 1978

De Risio, Carlo, *Navi di ferro, teste di legno*, Ciarrapico, Rome 1976

Dollmann, Eugenio, *Roma nazista*, Longanesi, Milan 1949

Donosti, Mario (Mario Luciolli), *Mussolini e l'Europa*,
    Leonardo, Rome 1945

Dorso, Guido, *Mussolini alla conquista del potere*, Mondadori, Milan 1963

Dupuis, Dobrillo, *Forzate il blocco*, Musria, Milan 1975

Dupuy, Ernest, *Seconda guerra mondiale*, Longanesi, Milan 1975

Eisenhower, Dwight D., *Crociata in Europa*, Mondadori, Milan 1949

Faldella, Emilio, *Lo sbarco e la difesa della Sicilia*, L'Aniene, Rome 1956

Faldella, Emilio, *Due guerre mondiali*, Sei, Turin 1974

Federici, Federico, *La Francia di Vichy*, Gentile, Milan 1946

Federzoni, Luigi, *Italia di ieri per la storia di domani*, Mondadori, Milan 1967

Fest, Joachim, *Hitler, una carriera*, Rizzoli, Milan 1978

Fiore, Ilario, *La campagna d'Italia*, Canesi, Rome 1965

Foley, Charles, *Teste calde*, Longanesi, Milan 1973

François-Poncet, André, *Ricordi di un ambasciatore a Berlino*,
    Rizzoli, Milan 1947

Gallo, Max, *Vita di Mussolini*, Laterza, Bari 1967

Galland, Adolf, *Il primo e l'ultimo*, Longanesi, Milan 1972

Gayda, Virgilio, *Che cosa vuole l'Italia?*, Il Giornale d'Italia, Rome 1940

Ghetti, Walter, *Storia della Marina italiana nella seconda guerra mondiale*, DeVecchi, Milan 1968

Gigli, Guido, *La seconda guerra mondiale*, Laterza, Bari 1964

Gilas, Milovan, *Conversazioni con Stalin*, Feltrinelli, Milan 1962

Giovannini, Alberto, *8 settembre 1943*, Ciarrapico, Rome 1973

Goebbels, Josef, *The Goebbels Diaries 1939-1945*, Doubleday 1948

Graziani, Rodolfo, *Ho difeso la patria*, Garzanti, Milan 1948

Guariglia, Raffaele, *Ricordi 1922-1946*, Esi, Naples 1950

Guerri, Giordano Bruno, *Galeazzo Ciano*, Bompiani, Milan 1979

Gun, Nerin, *Eva Braun*, Longanesi, Milan 1970

Hamilton, James Douglas, *Il folle volo di Hess*, Palazzi, Milan 1973

Hitler, Adolf, *Mein Kampf*, Bompiani, Milan 1938

Höhne, Heinz, *La vera storia dell'orchestra rossa*, Garzanti, Milan 1972

Iachino, Angelo, *Tramonto di una grande Marina*, Mondadori, Milan 1959

Infield, Glenn, *Adolf Hitler e Eva Braun*, Corno, Milan 1979

Jacobsen, H. A., *Battaglie decisive della seconda guerra mondiale*, Baldini e Castoldi, Milan 1966

Katz, Robert, *Sabato nero*, Rizzoli, Milan 1973

Kemski, Lorrain N., *La notte dei lunghi coltelli*, Longanesi, Milan 1965

Kirkpatrick, Sir Ivone, *Mussolini*, dall'Oglio, Milan 1981

Kurzman, Dan, *Obiettivo Roma*, dall'Oglio, Milan 1977

Lacouture, Jean, *De Gaulle*, Longanesi, Milan 1971

Langer, Walter, *Psicanalisi di Hitler*, Garzanti, Milan 1975

Langer, William, *La sfida all'isolazionismo*, Macchia, Rome 1954

Launay, Jacques de, *Ore decisive della storia*, Casini, Rome 1967

Leto, Guido, *OVRA*, Cappelli, Bologna 1951

Licheri, Sebastiano, *L'arma aerea italiana nella seconda guerra mondiale*, Mursia, Milan 1976

Liddell Hart, B. H., *Storia militare della seconda guerra mondiale*, Mondadori, Milan 1970

Lualdi, Aldo, *Nudi alla meta*, Longanesi, Milan 1969

Lualdi, Maner, *Italiani per aria*, Longanesi, Milan 1968

Luciolli, Mario, *Palazzo Chigi anni roventi*, Rusconi, Milan 1976

Ludecke, Kurt, *I Knew Hitler*, Scribner's, New York, 1937

Ludwig, Emil, *Colloqui con Mussolini*, Mondadori, Milan 1965

Mayda, G., *Come ci hanno visti*, Della Volpe, Milan 1965

Manvell, Roger and Fraenkel, Heinrich, *Göring*, Longanesi, Milan 1964

Manvell, Roger and Fraenkel, *Il complotto di luglio*, Longanesi, Milan 1966

Manvell, Roger and Fraenkel, *Heinrich Himmler*, Longanesi, Milan 1966

Manvell, Roger and Fraenkel, *Canaris*, Longanesi, Milan 1971

Marchesi, Luigi, *Come siamo arrivati a Brindisi*, Bompiani, Milan 1969

Marcon, Tullio, *Augusta 1940-1943*, Mendola, Augusta 1976

Martinelli, Franco, *Hitler dietro le quinte*, De Vecchi, Milan 1967

Maser, Werner, *Hitler segreto*, Garzanti, Milan 1974

Maurois, André, *Storia degli Stati Uniti*, Mondadori, Milan 1957

Messe, Giovanni, *La mia armata in Tunisia*, Rizzoli, Milan 1960

Monelli, Paolo, *Mussolini piccolo borghese*, Garzanti, Milan 1950

Monelli, Paolo, *Roma 1943*, Longanesi, Milan 1963

Montagna, Renzo, *Mussolini e il processo di Verona*, Omnia, Milan 1949

Montanelli, Indro, *L'Italia in camicia nera*, Rizzoli, Milan 1976

Montanelli, Indro, *L'Italia dell'asse*, Rizzoli, Milan 1981

Mosley, Leonard, *Il tempo a prestito*, Longanesi, Milan 1972

Mosley, Leonard, *Hermann Göring*, Sperling & Kupfer, Milan 1977

Musco, Ettore, *La verità sull'8 settembre*, Garzanti, Milan 1976

Mussolini, Benito, *La dottrina del fascismo*, Treccani, Rome 1934

Mussolini, Benito, *Parlo con Bruno*, Fpe, Milan 1966

Mussolini, Benito, *Storia di un anno*, Mondadori, Milan 1944

Mussolini, Vittorio, *Vita con mio padre*, Mondadori, Milan 1957

Mussolini, Vittorio, *Mussolini e gli uomini del suo tempo*,
   Ciarrapico, Rome 1977

Navarra, Quinto, *Memorie del cameriere di Mussolini*, Longanesi,
   Milan 1972

Orano, Paolo, *Mussolini da vicino*, Pinciana, Rome 1941

Padoan, Gino, *Polonia ora X*, Capitol, Bologna 1977

Pack, S. W. C., *Night Action Off Cape Matapan*, London

Pagliano, Franco, *Aviatori italiani*, Longanesi, Milan 1964

Pansa, Giampaolo, *L'esercito di Salò*, Mondadori, Milan 1970

Papagos, Alessandro, *La Grecia in guerra*, Garzanti, Milan 1950

Pavolini, Paolo, *La caduta del fascismo*, Fratelli Fabbri, Milan 1973

Petacco, Arrigo, *Le battaglie navali nel Mediterraneo*, Mondadori,
   Milan 1976

Pignatelli, Luigi, *La guerra dei sette mesi*, Longanesi, Milan 1972

Picker, Henry, *Conversazioni di Hitler a tavola*, Longanesi, Milan 1952

Pini, Giorgio, *Itinerario tragico 1943-1945*, Omnia, Milan 1950

Pini, G. and Susmel, D., *Mussolini: l'uomo e l'opera*, La Fenice,
   Florence 1958

Pisanò, Giorgio, *Mussolini e gli ebrei*, Fpe, Milan 1967

Piscitelli Taeggi, O., *Diario di un combattenet nell'AS*, Longanesi, Milan 1972

Plehwe, F. K., *Il patto d'acciaio*, Longanesi, Milan 1970

Pricolo, Francesco, *La Regia aeronautica nella seconda guerra mondiale*, Longanesi, Milan 1971

Quaroni, Pietro, *Valigia diplomatica*, Garzanti, Milan 1956

Richelmy, Carlo, *Cinque Re*, Casini, Rome 1952

Ridomi, Cristano, *La fine dell'ambasciata a Berlino*, Longanesi, Milan 1972

Rocco, Rocco, *La razione di ferro*, Longanesi, Milan 1972

Rothberg, Abraham, *La seconda guerra mondiale*, dall'Oglio, Milan 1969

Roux, Georges, *Benito Mussolini*, Lessona, Rome 1967

Ruland, Bernd, *Wernher von Braun*, Mondadori, Milan 1970

Rzhevskaia, Elena, *Berlino, Aprile 1945*, Milan

Shepperd, G.A., *La campagna d'Italia 1943-1945*, Garzanti, Milan 1970

Shub, David, *Lenin*, Longanesi, Milan 1972

Smith, Peter, *L'ultimo convoglio per Malta 1942*, Longanesi, Milan 1972

Spampananto, Bruno, *Contromemoriale*, Cen, Rome 1974

Speer, Albert, *Memorie del Terzo Reich*, Mondadori, Milan 1971

Speer, Albert, *Diari segreti di Spandau*, Mondadori, Milan 1976

Starhemberg, Ernst, *Memorie*, Volpe, Roma 1980

Strasser, Otto, *Hitler segreto*, Donatello de Luigi, Rome 1944

Susmel, Duilio, *Vita sbagliata di Galeazzo Ciano*, Palazzi, Milan 1962

Susmel, Duilio, *Corrispondenza inedita*, Il Borghese, Milan 1972

Terzi, Ottobono, *Varvàrovka alzo zero*, Longanesi, Milan 1974

Tolloy, Giusto, *Con l'Armata italiana in Russia*, De Silva, Turin 1947

Toscano, Mario, *Dal 25 luglio all'8 settembre*, Le Monnier, Florence 1966

Trionfera, Renzo, *Valzer di marescialli*, Editoriale Nuova, Milan 1979

Trizzino, Antonino, *Settembre nero*, Longanesi, Milan 1956

Trizzino, Antonino, *Mussolini ultimo*, Bietti, Milan 1968

Vailati, Vanna, *Badoglio risponde*, Rizzoli, Milan 1958

Valle, Giuseppe, *Pace e guerra nei cieli*, Volpe, Rome 1966

Venturi, Alfredo, *Garibaldi in parlamento*, Longanesi, Milan 1973

Vergani, Orio, *Ciano una lunga confessione*, Longanesi, Milan 1974

Wheeler-Bennett, J., *Il patto di Monaco*, Feltrinelli, Milan 1968

Winterbotham, F., *Ultra secret*, Mursia, Milan 1976

Young, Desmond, *Rommel*, Longanesi, Milan 1951

Zangrandi, Ruggero, *1943—25 luglio-8 settembre*, Feltrinelli, Milan 1964

Zullino, Pietro, *Il 25 luglio*, Mondadori, Milan 1973

Documents

Il giorno che uccisero Dollfuss - SS Report edited by C. Fruttero and F. Lucentini
    Mondadori, Milan 1967

L'Alto Adige fra le due guerre, ICS Rome, 1961

I generali di Hitler, edited by I. Montanelli, De Agostini, Novara 1973

La campagna di Russia, various authors in Storia Illustrata,
    Mondadori, Milan 1975

Dossiers della seconda guerra mondiale, Various Authors,
    Casini, Rome 1968

Roosevelt pro e contro, edited by R. Margotta, Mondadori, Milan 1972

Roosevelt-Stalin War Correspondence, Schwarz, Milan 1962

Bollettini di guerra del Comando Supremo 1940-1943,
    Ufficio Storico dello Stato Maggiore Esercito, Rome 1973

Le Medaglie d'Oro al valor militare, edited by MOVM Group of Italy,
    Rome 1973

Il "chi è" della seconda guerra mondiale by B. P. Boschesi, Storia Illustrata,
    Mondadori, Milan 1975

Le azioni navali in Mediterraneo 10 giugno 1940-8 settembre 1943, Ufficio Storico
    della Marina Militare, Rome 1970

L'oganizzazione della Marina durante il conflitto, Ufficio Storico della Marina
    Militare, Rome 1972

L'Aeronautica italiana nella seconda guerra mondiale, edited by General
    G. Santoro, Esse, Milan-Rome 1957

La battaglia d'Inghilterra, edited by G. Mayda, Mondadori, Milan 1974

Le armi segrete del Terzo Reich by David Irving, edited by C. Fruttero and
    F. Lucentini, Mondadori, Milan 1968

Additional bibliography
for the English-language edition and the
publisher's foreword:

Arendt, Hannah, *The Origins of Totalitarianism*, Harcourt, NY 1958

Cospito, N. and Neulen H.W., *Salò-Berlino: L'Alleanza Difficile*, Mursia,
    Milan 1992

Deakin, F. W., *The Brutal Friendship*, Harper NY 1962

De Felice, Renzo, *Mussolini*, 8 volumes, Einaudi, Turin 1999

Kahn, David, *Hitler's Spies*, Macmillan NY 1975

Kershaw, Ian, *Hitler 1889-1936, Hubris*, W. W. Norton, NY 1999

Kershaw, Ian, *Hitler 1936-1945,* Nemesis, W. W. Norton, NY 2000

Lupo, Salvatore, *Il Fascismo,* Donzelli Rome 2000

Mack Smith, Denis, *Mussolini: A Biography,* Knopf, NY 1982

Minerbi, Sergio, *Eichmann. Diario del processo,* Luni, Milan 2000

Mosse, George L., *The Fascist Revolution,* H. Fertig, NY 1999

Phillips, William, *Ventures in Diplomacy,* Beacon Hill, Boston 1952

Schellenberg, W., *The Labyrinth,* Harper, NY 1956

Sherwood, Robert, *Roosevelt and Hopkins,* Harper NY 1948-1950

Sudoplatov, P., *Special Tasks,* Little, Brown, Boston 1994

Wiskemann, Elizabeth, *The Rome-Berlin Axis,* Oxford, 1949

Acknowledgments:

The Publisher wishes to extend special thanks to Robert
Stewart, Editorial Director; Roland Winter; Jay Wynshaw;
Charles Miller; Josh Beatman; and Tony De Santoli.

Illustrations:

Cover photo by Culver, New York. All the photographs in
this edition are from the author's collection or from the
ADS collection, Rome, Italy.

INDEX